FROM CHRIST TO CONFUCIUS

ALBERT MONSHAN WU

From Christ to Confucius

GERMAN MISSIONARIES, CHINESE
CHRISTIANS, AND THE GLOBALIZATION
OF CHRISTIANITY, 1860–1950

Yale UNIVERSITY PRESS

NEW HAVEN AND LONDON

Yale University Press books may be purchased in quantity for educational, business, or
promotional use. For information, please e-mail sales.press@yale.edu (U.S. office) or
sales@yaleup.co.uk (U.K. office).

Set in Scala and Scala Sans type by IDS Infotech Ltd., Chandigarh, India.
Printed in the United States of America.

Library of Congress Control Number: 2016936804
ISBN 978–0–300–21707–0 (hardcover: alk. paper)

A catalogue record for this book is available from the British Library.

This paper meets the requirements of ANSI/NISO Z39.48–1992 (Permanence of Paper).

10 9 8 7 6 5 4 3 2 1

To my beloved parents,
吳茂昆 *(Maw-Kuen Wu) and* 唐慧晴 *(Huichin Tang),*
whose unconditional love
propelled every word

CONTENTS

ABBREVIATIONS

BMS	Berlin Missionary Society
CCP	Chinese Communist Party
NCC	National Christian Council
SVD	Society of the Divine Word (Societas Verbi Divini)
YMCA	Young Men's Christian Association

Perceptions of Failure

IN 1902 GEORG STENZ, a German Catholic missionary from the Society of the Divine Word (Societas Verbi Divini, SVD), met with the seventy-sixth direct descendent of Confucius and the Holy Duke of Yen, Kong Lingyi. It had taken Stenz years to set up this meeting. He regarded Kong—the heir to Confucius's legacy—as a human capsule of Chinese culture, its living embodiment.

The meeting left Stenz underwhelmed. "Kong did not impress me," he later wrote. "He knew almost nothing of the situation and learning of Europe. He was also extremely corpulent and lived a thoroughly Chinese existence."[1]

Nor did Stenz's criticisms end there. He sarcastically referred to Confucius as "his holiness," ridiculing the deference that ordinary Chinese paid their sage. He called Qufu, Confucius's hometown, a "Chinese Mecca, the bulwark of all pagans."[2] Beyond Confucianism, Stenz excoriated the myriad religious rituals that he saw around him. For him, the temples and pagodas that dotted the Chinese rural landscape reflected a decadent, depraved, and fallen culture. As he watched pious Chinese burn incense and paper money to the gods, he lamented, "How many millions are wasted each year!"[3]

Stenz was not alone in condemning Chinese religiosity. In the SVD's monthly periodical, *Little Messenger of the Sacred Heart*

(*Kleiner Herz-Jesu-Bote*), Stenz's fellow SVD missionaries dismissed Chinese religions as "superstition," calling the Chinese pagodas and temples "houses of the devil." They referred to the Chinese who worshipped at temples as "servants of the devil." The SVD apostolic vicar Johann Baptist von Anzer dubbed Yanzhou, the seat of his vicariate, the "bulwark of the devil." The SVD's writings were meant to be both descriptive and cautionary. These rival religious practices, with Confucianism at its head, prevented the spread of Christianity in China. As forces of evil, traditional Chinese religions needed to be overcome or, even better, destroyed.[4]

By 1935, however, the SVD had changed its tune. The same periodical that had denounced Confucianism now revered it. If just thirty years before, Qufu was the "bulwark of the devil," now it was the "greatest Confucian sanctuary in all of China, the hometown of the Sage" (*Weisen*). A sarcastic tone no longer accompanied references to Confucius. When the Chinese Nationalist government decreed it would celebrate Confucius's birthday as a national holiday, one missionary praised the news, proclaiming, "As the star of Confucius rises, so he will point further to Jesus Christ."[5]

The SVD was not an exception: other missionary organizations also dramatically altered their relationship to Confucianism and, more broadly, traditional Chinese culture. In the same year that Stenz met Kong Lingyi, Carl Johannes Voskamp, an influential missionary in the Protestant Berlin Missionary Society (BMS), published an anti-Confucian tract, *Confucius and China Today*. Like Stenz, Voskamp included an account of a visit to Qufu. Masses of Chinese worshippers, he wrote, with their "eyes fixated on the shadow of Confucius," held slabs pronouncing his greatness and "prostrated themselves" before Confucius's tombstone. He denigrated Confucian rituals as unthinking, the worshippers as brainwashed. The tract, along with a series of others books and materials, established Voskamp as one of the most outspoken opponents of Confucianism in his day.[6]

After the First World War, Voskamp would never again publish anti-Confucian work. He expressed respect for Confucius as a person, listing him as one of the "Great Ancient Sages." Had China followed the actual ideals and teachings of Confucius, Voskamp argued, "It would not be mired in its modern problems." Like his Catholic counterparts, Voskamp wrote about Confucianism in a completely different manner by the 1920s.[7]

The radical transformation of the SVD and the BMS—from outspoken anti-Confucians to Confucian proponents—constitutes the central inquiry of this book. Why did German Catholic and Protestant missionaries argue in 1900 that Christianity's success depended on Confucianism's demise, and how, by the 1930s, did they come to view the fates of Christianity and Confucianism as inseparable? What are the broader implications of these changes?

The astonishing shifts the BMS and SVD underwent offer us insight into processes of cross-cultural contact and exchange. Throughout the nineteenth century, European and American missionaries went abroad convinced of the transforming power of their message. Many held, at first, an antagonistic attitude toward the local cultures that they confronted. But often it was the missionaries themselves who emerged from the encounter converted. They developed more nuanced views of local religions and cultures, reformed their methods of evangelization, and in some instances abandoned their former beliefs. In this book, I focus on how German missionaries—as well as European missionaries more broadly—and Chinese Christians simultaneously shaped, and were shaped by, their encounter with each other.

German missionaries traveled to China as part of a broader global expansion of Christianity during the nineteenth and twentieth centuries. Transported by steamships and railroads, European and American missionaries exported their religion to every corner of the globe. Along with their religion, they brought Western institutions—often secular—with them. They attempted to establish alternatives to the local schools, medical institutions, and religious organizations that they encountered. Besides appearing as preachers, they assumed various roles as teachers, doctors, theologians, geologists, botanists, and anthropologists. If we accept Yuri Slezkine's definition of modernity as "everyone becoming urban, mobile, literate, articulate, intellectually intricate, physically fastidious, and occupationally flexible," missionaries embodied and galvanized all of those trends.[8] In this book I probe the story of how European missionaries globalized Christianity in the nineteenth and twentieth centuries and by extension laid the foundations for the modern global religious landscape. In short, I examine how Christian missionaries helped forge the modern world.

Yet Christianity's global spread was not only generative, it was also destructive. In the nineteenth century, many missionaries sought to supplant local religions and customs with Christianity. In turn, local actors equated Christianity with Western imperialism, viewing both as forces seeking to uproot and destroy traditional culture. Anti-Christian hostility and violence erupted throughout the world—in China, in Africa, in South and Southeast Asia. These outbursts of anti-Christian and anti-imperial sentiment swayed not just Christianity's opponents, but converts to Christianity as well: indigenous Christians argued that churches should be independent of European control, as a way to disassociate Christianity from Western imperial ambitions.

Confronted with the prospect of the collapse of their entire enterprise, missionaries began to take criticisms of Christianity seriously. Some believed that by making Christianity devoid of European "color," it could expand further and gain more adherents in these foreign lands. As a result, missionaries transferred to indigenous clergy the religious control and authority that they once wielded. Other missionaries sought cultural solutions, hoping to find a way to synthesize Christianity with local tradition. But not all missionaries accepted such a synthesis. Some denounced the "syncretism" between Christianity and local religions, dismissing it as a watered-down version of Christianity. Fearing "impure" belief, these missionaries refused to relinquish power over their congregations.

The question facing missionaries—whether and how to make Christianity "indigenous"—dates back to the earliest foundations of Christianity. At Antioch, Peter and Paul debated whether converted Gentiles should observe Mosaic law. Peter believed that converts ought to be circumcised and follow Jewish dietary restrictions. Paul resoundingly rejected Peter's reliance on exterior rituals as markers of faith. More broadly, the debate centered on the convert's relationship to missionaries. Should the convert adopt the culture that missionaries brought with them, or should missionaries adapt Christianity to the local forms that they encountered?[9]

As the influential mission historian Andrew Walls has shown, two broad principles, both rooted within the Gospels but often working at cross-purposes, emerged: the "indigenizing principle" and the "pilgrim principle." The indigenizing principle assumes that God created and celebrates the diversity and plurality of world cultures. Potential Christians cannot—and should not—be asked to forgo the culture, place, and social relations of their birthplaces. The indigenizing principle demands that missionaries translate Christianity into a local context and make the church indigenous to the culture that it encounters. Holding the indigenizing principle in check is the pilgrim principle. This principle assumes that Christian converts must transcend the society in which they are born, since Jesus's gospel opposes almost all secular values. With the pilgrim principle as their guiding light, missionaries expect new Christians to convert not only to Christianity, but also to a new social and political culture: Christian converts are expected to leave their cultural values behind.[10]

The "indigenous question" became particularly urgent for missionaries in the nineteenth and twentieth centuries, and it energized widespread discussion and debate. As Protestant and Catholic missionaries marched to the ends of the world, they were forced to reflect upon how to engage with cultures and religions different from their own. Missionaries argued about "best practices" at international conferences, in journals, and in their individual congregations. They struggled to make a religion with universal claims adopt particular forms; they questioned how a global religion should assume local guise.

Two conflicting impulses undergirded these debates. Throughout the nineteenth and twentieth centuries, missionaries oscillated between moments of self-assured outward projection and intense inward self-reflection. On the one hand, nineteenth-century missionaries were filled with confidence, certain in the world-historical role they had to play. Some called it arrogance. Charlotte Brontë described the missionary St. John Rivers in *Jane Eyre* in these terms: "Firm, faithful, and devoted, full of energy, and zeal, and truth, he labors for his race; he clears their painful way to improvement; he hews down like a giant the prejudices of creed and caste that encumber it." At the same time, missionaries fretted that their missions had failed. The realities in the field often fell far short of their own lofty rhetoric. They expressed dismay over paltry conversion numbers and despair over the violent anti-Christian movements that their work engendered.

In this book I explore the consequences of the missionary sense of failure. How did the experience of failure influence thoughts about mission work? What happened when parts of the missionaries' worldview and theological outlook became partially untenable? Did they cling more fervently to their faith, or did they abandon it? Did they modify their beliefs and think about Christianity differently?

WHY CHINA?

Almost no part of the world has gone untouched by Christian missionaries, so why focus, as I do in this book, on China? Partly, I followed the interests of my missionary subjects. Ever since Marco Polo's travels to China in the thirteenth century, Europeans have been fascinated by that vast country. To European observers, its powerful civilization, shrouded in mystery and glamor, possessed complex systems of belief that rivaled Christianity. Tales of the Middle Kingdom enthralled European missionaries, and from the Jesuits in the seventeenth century to the Protestants in the nineteenth, they poured resources into China, with the hopes of gaining a foothold in the empire.

Furthermore, I am interested in how the Chinese encounter with Christian missionaries sheds light on key themes in the history of modern China, such as the relationship between the Chinese state and religious minorities, the place of religion in modern Chinese society, and the contact between China and the West. Indeed, the interactions between Christian missionaries, the Chinese state, and Chinese society intersect with key moments in modern Chinese history, from the Qing dynasty to the present. Qing rulers of the sixteenth and seventeenth centuries viewed the Jesuits as curiosities, useful in introducing the empire to Western commodities and ideas, but not a civilizational alternative. To the Qing, Christianity seemed a religion that could supplement Chinese civilization, not supplant it. Still, the missionaries repeatedly met resistance. In 1724, angered by Vatican pronouncements in the Chinese Rites Controversy, the Qing outlawed Christian missionary work throughout the empire.

By the nineteenth and twentieth centuries, when Western imperialism forced China to reopen its doors to Christianity, Protestant and Catholic missionaries flooded into China, dreaming to bring millions to salvation. Buoyed by Western expansion, Protestant and Catholic missionaries led an offensive on traditional Chinese society. They were involved in, as Ryan Dunch notes, "the introduction of Western medicine; campaigns against footbinding (in the name of the 'natural' foot), opium consumption, and 'superstition'; the adoption of rationalist, graduated, and (in theory) universal education; individual choice in marriage; demands for political representation."[11] They introduced the Chinese to Western legal concepts and new geological and scientific techniques. And for the most part, the missionaries relished their perceived intellectual, cultural, and political superiority. Almost all American and European missionaries, Catholic and Protestant alike, portrayed traditional Chinese culture—which they termed, largely incorrectly, as "Confucianism"—in a negative light, and they explicitly sought to destroy Confucianism and replace it with Christianity. Confucianism, they believed, was the primary stumbling block to the spread of Christianity in China. By the late nineteenth century, Christianity—made possible by Western imperialism—presented an unprecedented political, intellectual, and social challenge to Chinese culture and civilization.[12]

The missionary assault on Chinese culture produced a violent backlash. Anti-Christian violence erupted throughout the late nineteenth century, finding its most ferocious expression in the Boxer Uprising of 1900. The shocking carnage—a conservative estimate counts approximately one hundred thousand deaths—braced missionaries to face the facts: the Chinese had rejected the Christian message.[13] Global comparisons further worsened missionary anxieties. Missionaries in China read reports of the rapid spread of Christianity throughout Africa and agonized over the lack of similar conversion rates. Christianity's survival, they began to recognize, depended on its becoming "indigenous."

Missionaries after 1900 agreed that they needed to foster a Chinese Christian church independent of Western power structures. But little consensus emerged about how a Chinese church should look. Protestant missionaries replicated in China the denominational battles that raged in Europe and the United States. Catholics disagreed about how quickly they should turn over power to the Chinese, as well as the practical steps to establish a Chinese episcopacy. Even after the Boxer Uprising, missionaries refused to relinquish control of their power to the Chinese. They justified their reluctance by citing the "spiritual immaturity" of Chinese Christians, who, missionaries alleged, were not prepared to assume power without Western guidance and leadership.

Then came the onslaught of the First World War, which dealt a devastating blow to the supply of financial and personnel support to European missionary societies. In the 1920s, desperate for money and staff to continue basic operations, European missionary societies were forced to incorporate non-Europeans into their ranks. Chinese church independence was no longer an abstract future, but an urgent reality.

Missionaries not only began to relinquish power, they renounced their previous criticisms of Chinese culture. Once the enemy, Confucianism became an ally after the First World War. During the 1920s Christian missions came under severe attack from secular critics both in the West and in China, especially from Communists. Missionaries believed that in order for Christianity to retain its relevance in the face of new global ideologies such as Fascism and Communism, it needed to adapt itself to local concerns and cultures. Hoping to find more allies in China, missionaries sought to make Christianity more "Chinese."

Chinese Christians themselves spearheaded efforts to find common ground between Christianity and traditional Chinese culture. Among them was a new generation of Chinese Christian intellectuals who had received their training in the West. Criticizing European missionary practices and ideas, they sought to interpret Christianity as compatible with traditional Chinese culture. Their attempt to find a synthesis between Christianity and Confucianism—between the West and East—provoked resistance from several sides. Some European and American missionaries considered synthesis a dilution of Christianity. Traditional Confucian scholars deemed Christians as traitors to traditional Chinese culture. Secular Chinese intellectuals, who were rapidly consolidating political power and seeking to rid the nation of all religious influence, attacked their thinking as regressive. Furthermore, from the escalation of the Sino-Japanese War in the early 1930s to the Communist expulsion of foreign missionaries in 1951, Chinese Christians fought to defend and uphold their cultural syntheses as they witnessed the collapse of the world around them. Political instability convinced Chinese Christians of the importance of their work: they believed that the fate of the nation, and Christianity more broadly, hinged on their finding a bridge between Confucianism and Christianity.[14]

By the 1960s, scholars of China deemed the work of Chinese Christians a failure. Historians read the history of Christianity in China in the light of the overarching question that dominated Cold War–era studies of China—why had Communism succeeded in 1949? This framework views Chinese Christians, while brave in their attempt to synthesize

Christianity and Confucianism, as having failed to offer a compelling alternative to Communism. The collaboration between Chinese Christians and Western missionaries could not stem the advance of Communism.[15]

In the past thirty years, however, historians of Christianity in China have reassessed the narrative of "success" and "failure" regarding the missionary enterprise. With the loosening of restrictions on religion in China during the 1980s, journalists and other China-watchers began reporting that a religious revival was gripping the Chinese religious landscape. By 1996, scholar Daniel Bays was estimating that there were some thirty million Chinese Christians, almost ten times the number of Christians thought to be in China in 1949. The Pew Research Center estimated in 2010 that about fifty-eight million Protestants and nine million Catholics lived in China, more than double the numbers of twenty years earlier. These reports surprised scholars who thought that whatever religious institutions existed had been decimated during the Cultural Revolution.[16]

Recent works have thus cast the study of mission work in China in a new light. Some scholars argue that even though missionaries may have failed to transform China into a Christian nation, they introduced elements of what the missionaries had all along assumed would be a by-product of their goal: China's modernization.[17] Drawing on these works, I assume that Christianity was much more "successful" than the scholarship of the 1960s and 1970s portrayed it. But I am less interested in assessing whether Christianity "succeeded" or "failed" in China. Rather, I am interested in why Christian missionaries themselves viewed their mission as unsuccessful and the revisions they made to their work because of such perceived failure. Their self-reflection and self-criticism led to more sustained dialogue with Chinese Christians about how they should evangelize in China. In short, I argue in this book that the missionary encounter with China catalyzed new ways of Christian thinking.

WHY THE GERMANS?

Of all the various missionary nationals who worked in China, why study the Germans? For one reason, the history of German missionaries in China has been largely overlooked in scholarly literature: the dominant narratives of Christianity in China have been shaped by studies of American, British, and French missionaries. Statistics explain the scholarly neglect. American and British Protestant missionaries outnumbered

Germans, and the number of German Catholic missionaries ranked below their French and Belgian counterparts. The traditional Anglophone scholarly narrative has portrayed the German missionary enterprise as insignificant, particularly after the First World War decimated the missionaries' work in China.[18]

But numbers are not the only way to measure significance. Although German missionaries were numerically small, they were a remarkably active presence in the global missionary community during the nineteenth and twentieth centuries. They were dynamic participants at conferences and other gatherings where missionaries engaged in discussion and debate about the future of missionary work. And because of the towering influence of German theology throughout the nineteenth century, the international missionary community took German theologians seriously. Within both Protestant and Catholic spheres, German missionary ideas often defined the grounds for the debate.

On the other hand, in a field where success was measured by how many converts missionaries won, how many church buildings they built, and how much territory the missions covered, numbers did matter. The Germans were constantly measuring themselves against their competition, and they used statistics as a barometer of their success. They were always aware that they were numerically outnumbered and outmatched by their American, British, and French counterparts.

Driven by competitiveness, the German missionary enterprise engaged in continual self-reflection. Ever since German missionaries entered China, a feeling of failure suffused their writings, as they bemoaned the disadvantageous position they were in compared with their missionary counterparts. As "late-comers" in both the missionary and the imperial games, they chafed at the dominance that American, British, and French missionaries exerted in China.

Their feelings of being encircled intensified after the First World War. Stripped of their extraterritorial rights and imperial possessions in China after the war while British, American, and French missionaries were allowed to keep theirs, Germans were forced to reassess their approach to missionary work there. Germans claimed that because of their wartime experiences, they now had a special "spiritual bond" with the Chinese and were better equipped to facilitate dialogue with traditional Chinese culture. I argue that spurred by their experience with failure, Germans began to rethink the relationship between Christianity, Confucianism, and traditional Chinese culture. Ultimately, German missionaries did learn from their failure—they began to treat the Chinese as equals.

I am drawn to German missionaries precisely for the reason that engendered previous scholarly neglect: that is, the German self-perception of marginality. I am interested in probing these feelings of insignificance and alienation, which I argue were generative. They inspired German missionaries to modify their missionary tactics, find new allies, and reconsider the relationship between Christianity and traditional Chinese culture.

An examination of the Germans, I argue, helps us better understand the entire Western missionary enterprise in China. Because of the disproportionate influence that Germans held in cultural and intellectual circles, I also argue that their self-perceived marginality was largely misplaced. In fact, the changes that German missionaries underwent reverberated throughout the international missionary community. The type of rethinking in which the German missionaries engaged—retracting their criticism of Confucianism, for example—places them at the center of the most urgent debates regarding the place of Christianity in China.

German missionaries helped shape not only the trajectory of modern China, but also of modern Germany. In 1968, John King Fairbank wrote that the American missionary was the "invisible man of American history."[19] So, too, in German history—missionaries and missionary leaders on the home front have long been neglected in German histories of the nineteenth and twentieth centuries. When missionaries have entered the broader narratives of modern German history, they have, like their American and British counterparts, mostly appeared as willing cultural imperialists and lackeys of the German Empire. In these narratives, an enlightened few—liberal missionaries such as Richard Wilhelm or trailblazers like Karl Gützlaff—have been credited with challenging the triumphalist, essentialist, and racist assumptions of their time, but they are seen as voices crying in the wilderness.[20]

Drawing on recent revisions of the relationship between mission and empire, I argue that German missionaries were also complex figures who wielded broad influence at the German provincial and national levels in ways unconnected to geopolitics and imperialism. Through their journals and letters, German missionaries often shaped the public imagery of foreign lands. These journals and letters provided the only point of contact that broad segments of the German population had with foreign lands, civilizations, and ideas. *Missionswissenschaft,* or missiology, was considered a serious realm of theological study, and missionaries occupied important academic positions long before Germany developed significant imperial ambitions. The Protestant and Catholic mission societies at the heart of this book lived through the end of two empires—Bismarck's and Hitler's—and a republic. By comparing these mission societies and investigating the broader changes in the German missionary enterprise over more than a century, I show that the missionaries' allegiances were never a mere reflection of the state and the society to which they belonged. Likewise, the Germany that these missionaries inhabited was sometimes far from the nationalist, imperialist, and militaristic Germany portrayed in much of our state-centered literature. This book joins the growing recognition in modern German historiography that the state and its representatives are not always the most significant agents, and certainly not of cultural change.[21]

It is true, as the previous historiography emphasizes, that nationalism undergirded and permeated missionary action. Throughout the nineteenth century, German missionaries adopted racialized views of the Chinese. They often attributed China's geopolitical and cultural stagnation to Chinese racial defects. Consciously or unconsciously, they perpetuated ideas of European racial superiority. The transnational actors in this story remained at heart nationalists, certain of their own German intellectual and spiritual heritage and of its capacity to convert the world.

But, as I argue in this book, German missionaries also held surprisingly nonhierarchical views toward cultural differences. At the height of German imperial expansion, missionaries argued that Chinese converts need not become "European." Christianization, they asserted, should not be synonymous with "Europeanization." More, missionaries expressed equal abhorrence toward Europeans whom they considered enemies of Christianity—such as merchants who sold opium in China and atheists who challenged Christian doctrines—as they did toward their Chinese opponents. Missionary notions of race also underwent decisive change. At the same time Germany witnessed the rise of virulently racist politics in the 1930s, missionaries wrote and preached passionately that Chinese Christians were their equal.

A cynic might argue that the about-face of German missionaries was driven primarily by geopolitical resentment and alarm over the spread of global Communism. Certainly my book tells a story of German missionaries driven by the appearance of new enemies on the global stage. The rise of Communism and Fascism in the 1920s made Confucianism an obsolete foe. Yet as I also show in this book, German missionaries sincerely grappled with the contradictions of their own beliefs. Driven by more than just politics, Protestant and Catholic missionaries tailored and altered Christian rituals to a Chinese audience. They began to ordain more Chinese clergy, in order to prepare the Chinese to lead the missionary work independently. Publicizing their efforts to their German audience, missionary reports adopted pro-Confucian tones that would have seemed repulsive to missionaries only a generation earlier. Slowly, missionaries began to renounce their conviction regarding the superiority of Eurocentric forms of Christianity. By studying how Germans came to think of, and represent, Confucianism differently, we can map the contours of Germany's transnational history and investigate how international and national thinking changed, coexisted, and conflicted with one another.[22]

THE GLOBALIZATION OF CHRISTIANITY AND ITS DISCONTENTS

The renunciation of Christianity's Eurocentrism belongs not just to the history of Germany or China but tells a story of Christianity's globalization. As early as 1949, the historian Kenneth Scott Latourette noted a process of transformation that was occurring in global Christianity. Latourette argued that Christianity, long associated with the West, was becoming a truly "universal" religion. Rid of imperial baggage, Christianity would spread in parts of the world that had previously rejected the religion on anti-imperial grounds. Here, Latourette proved a prophet. During the second half of the twentieth century, Christianity advanced rapidly throughout the "Global South"—a moniker for Latin America, Africa, and Southeast Asia.[23]

Latourette did not find any drawbacks with the potentially rapid spread of Christianity. A believer in the restorative and unifying message of the Christian gospel, he expressed confidence in Christianity's ability to heal the divisions and conflicts of the world. Latourette believed that Christianity could be simultaneously flexible and rigid: it was open enough to encourage a diversity of Christian expression, while at the same time it was dogmatic enough to join a fragmented Christian community through common piety.[24]

Much of the recent scholarship in the study of "world Christianity" or "global Christianity" has shared Latourette's optimism in Christianity's ability to embrace diversity. Scholars such as Lamin Sanneh and Joel Carpenter extol Christianity's transformation into a global faith, arguing that the religion "is more vigorous and vibrant in the global South than among the world's richer and more powerful regions." Studying the globalization of Christianity, these scholars argue, reminds us that Christianity was always a malleable, global religion and that the Western European dominance of global Christendom constituted only a brief moment in the broader historical trajectory of Christianity. In Sanneh and Carpenter's vision, Christianity trends toward the inclusive.[25]

In this book I question the optimism that Latourette and subsequent scholars have had in Christianity's unifying power. I seek to show how the process of globalization created a fragmented church, racked with divisions, rather than the unified and coherent one that Latourette envisioned. The idea of the "indigenous church" itself was vague and contested: Western missionaries disagreed about how to actually *make* an indigenous Christian church. Liberal Christian visions clashed with conservative ones; denominational and confessional cleavages that divided Europe were exported to China.

Nor did Chinese Christians passively accept the Western ideas that missionaries proposed for building a Chinese church. Rather, they selectively appropriated the version of the indigenous church they wanted to advance their own political agendas. Throughout the 1920s, Communists fought with Christians over the place of religion in the public sphere. Yet liberal Chinese Christians and Communists also shared much common ground: for instance, they were united in their opposition to Western imperialism, and both groups wanted to minimize the influence of Western missionaries in China. Thus, after 1949, it was not that far a leap for Chinese Christian intellectuals to reject their former Western Christian mentors. Here, Latourette's prediction was wrong: the Chinese church's independence did not forge global unity. Rather, it exacerbated the rifts between Western and Chinese Christianity. These schisms are still operative today.[26]

The missionaries of the 1920s unintentionally contributed to another schism within the global Christian community: the divergence between an increasingly secular Europe, which by the twenty-first century has largely abandoned its Christian faith, and other parts of the globe where Christianity has gained fervent followers. Writing in 1962, Latourette predicted that Christianity in Europe would decline, but he did not see this as a trend to be mourned. Instead he celebrated the possibility of Christianity's spread throughout the rest of the world.[27]

And indeed, Latourette's vision of the advance of Christianity world-wide at the expense of Christianity in Europe has come to pass. Church attendance in the Global South has already far surpassed that in Europe. The 2010 Pew Forum report on global Christianity found that of the 2.18 billion Christians worldwide, more than 60 percent (1.3 billion) come from the Global South, while around 39 percent live in the Global North (Europe and North America). This is a stunning reversal of statistics from a century ago. In 1910, more than 93 percent of Christians lived in the Global North, with about two-thirds (66.3 percent) of the world's Christian population being European. Now only about one-quarter (26 percent) of the entire Christian population lives in Europe.[28]

Scholars since Latourette have located the crucial moment of Europe's secularization in the postwar period, especially the 1960s. In an *ad limina* address to Brazilian bishops in 2009, Pope Benedict XVI described the secularization within the Catholic Church as a by-product of the Second Vatican Council, which led to a process of "self-secularization," when "people stopped speaking of certain fundamental truths of faith, such as sin, grace, theological life and the last things. They were unconsciously caught up in the self-secularization of many ecclesial communities."[29]

For Benedict, the motors of secularization came from within the church itself. As he tells it, church members, spurred by Vatican II, gave up on basic tenets of Christianity. Scholars of European religious history tend to agree, dating Europe's moment of religious change and secularization to the 1960s.[30] While I agree that secularization in Europe intensified in the early 1960s, I locate the seeds of these shifts in the 1920s. During the two decades after the First World War, I argue, missionaries had already laid the groundwork for Europe's future secu-larization. By presenting religions and cultures that they had once seen as antagonistic in a positive light, and suggesting that Christianity needed to find a synthesis with other religions to survive in Europe, missionaries sowed the seeds for Christians in the 1960s to reject Christianity's exclusive salvationist claims. It was through the work of missionaries in the 1920s and 1930s that it became possible for a young Joseph Ratzinger, who later became Pope Benedict XVI, to write in 1964, "We are no longer ready, no longer willing, to think that eternal corruption should be inflicted on people in Asia, in Africa, or wherever it may be, merely on account of their not having 'Catholic' marked in their passport."[31]

Much of the literature that focuses on the postwar era attributes secularization to mainline ecumenical Protestantism. In this narrative, the softening of the missionary impulse is associated with the advance of religious liberalism. Christian missionaries embraced other cultures and religions because they were moved by liberal trends in Christianity, such as a historical-critical reading of the Bible, and within the U.S. context, the rise of the Social Gospel.[32]

In this book, however, I examine shifts in thinking among conservative German missionaries. By focusing on conservatives, another narrative, running counter to that of the triumph of liberal Christianity, emerges. Conservative German missionaries, I argue, adopted openness to the world and to other cultures not because they were persuaded by the liberal challenge to accept religious diversity. Even though on the surface conservatives welcomed pluralism and devolved institutional authority just as liberals did, they articulated a different version of indigenization, often drawing upon Pietist and conservative Catholic traditions. They formulated new approaches to missionary work to serve as possible bulwarks against both the forces of secularization and the advance of "liberal-modernist" Christianity.

The need to reconsider the purpose and nature of missionary work grew especially urgent for German missionaries during the decades after the First World War, as they nervously eyed the spread of liberal Christian values worldwide. They noticed the numerical success of their liberal American and British counterparts, understanding that their own work desperately needed reform. Propelled by a sense of failure, they began a process of "self-secularization." They softened their critiques of other religions; they gave up previously cherished beliefs; and they embraced indigenization. More simply, they acknowledged that Eurocentric versions of Christianity were not the sole form of Christian truth.

Whereas Pope Benedict referred to self-secularization pejoratively, viewing it as a willing retreat from church orthodoxy, I argue that missionary self-secularization arose from a sincere engagement with the world. Missionaries traveled abroad with the highest aspirations: they hoped to transform the world. But the actual missionary encounter, particularly in China, was humbling and humiliating. Put simply, German missionaries went abroad hoping to make the globe more Christian and returned home vitally changed: in belief, in method, in fundamental assumptions about Christianity. The missionary encounter, I argue, catalyzed a revolution in thinking among European Christians about the nature of Christianity itself.

CHAPTER ONE

The Missionary Impulse

IN 1834, THE GERMAN Protestant missionary Karl Gützlaff published his *Journal of Three Voyages Along the Coast of China*. It recorded his time as an interpreter on the British East India Company's ship *Lord Amherst*, which set sail in 1832 on a secret mission to expand trade routes along the South China coast. He worked as a translator mainly to pay for his passage: Gützlaff had bigger dreams, of converting the Chinese. "I am convinced that individual Christians," he wrote, hoping to encourage his readers to care more about China, "could accomplish more for the benefit of China, than the greatest statesmen." Gützlaff's book was a massive hit. Within a decade, it was translated into a half-dozen European languages, and it was republished in three editions by 1840.[1]

In the final chapter of the book, Gützlaff presented a history of Christianity in China, at once contemptuous and well informed. While he admired his predecessors for their resourcefulness and courage in traveling to China in spite of geopolitical and technological challenges, he disparaged the form of Christianity they preached. The Nestorians, who entered China during the Tang dynasty, practiced what he called a "cold-hearted orthodoxy." Their mission failed in China because "their ignorance prevented them from proclaiming the whole gospel; they mistook a mere acceptance of their creed for living faith." They had introduced a "corrupted Christian church," diluted by "pagan rites."[2]

Gützlaff criticized the Jesuits on similar grounds. Like the Nestorians, the Jesuits had encouraged too much "syncretism" between Christianity and Chinese cultural norms. Gützlaff attacked the Jesuit policy of accommodation. The Jesuit missionary Matteo Ricci, he wrote, had "introduced the lax rule of permitting Chinese converts to retain some superstitious rites in honor of Confucius." Permitting Chinese to "indulge" in their cultural traditions, Gützlaff continued, was "the source of innumerable evils," ending in "the annihilation of very many missions." The Jesuits, Gützlaff concluded, did not preach "the pure Gospel." As a result, Chinese intellectuals believed mistakenly that Confucian and Christian rituals could coexist.[3]

For Gützlaff, the arrival of Protestant missionaries like Robert Morrison and the London Missionary Society in 1807 portended a new era of Christianity in China. "At the present time it appears probable that our great Lord and King will shortly open the door to China," Gützlaff buoyantly proclaimed. The Chinese would now finally hear the true gospel. Likewise, China presented European Protestantism with an untapped, enormous mission field: a Protestant China meant a surge for global Protestant demographics. All China needed, Gützlaff believed, was more Protestant missionaries; in due course, China would be a Christian country.

Gützlaff had good reason to feel optimistic. The nineteenth century saw a surge in European and American interest in missionary work, as thousands of young men and women traveled abroad to convert the "heathens" and "infidels" to Christianity. What motivated such intense enthusiasm? In this chapter I examine the European missionary revival of the nineteenth century and how two of the most influential German missionary organizations in China, the Lutheran BMS and the Catholic SVD, were forged in an age of rapid global Christian expansion. Yet, at the same time, distinctly local and national political concerns shaped the outlook of both societies, reflecting the interplay between global and local forces that undergirded missionary work in the nineteenth century.

THE JESUIT PRECEDENT

Nineteenth-century missionaries knew that they were indebted to their early modern predecessors; even a reflexively anti-Catholic Protestant like Gützlaff expressed a begrudging admiration for the Jesuits, admitting that he could learn from their experience in China. "Amidst so great a variety of character," Gützlaff wrote of the Jesuits, "were men of great talents, fervent zeal, and exemplary patience, together with many stupid, bigoted, and worldly-minded laborers."[4] Of course, for Catholic missionaries of the nineteenth century, Jesuits were already a source of inspiration and guidance. They served as models both to emulate and to avoid.

Founded by St. Ignatius of Loyola in 1534, the Society of Jesus spread across the globe in the wake of the Protestant Reformation, during a period of serious challenges to the Catholic Church. Jesuits fashioned themselves after the ministry of Paul and the Apostles, bringing the gospel to China, India, Japan, and the Americas. They were ambitious and expansive in their notions of evangelization: Jesuit missionaries translated the Bible into native languages, attempting to make the Christian message more relevant to the communities that they faced.[5]

The encounter with the Chinese was particularly formative for the society. Led by pioneers such as Matteo Ricci, Jesuits entered China during the years 1582–1583, gaining permission to reside in the southern province of Guangdong. After early, unsuccessful experiences with gaining converts, Ricci formulated the policy of "accommodation." He proposed that the Jesuits accept traditional Chinese rituals and beliefs, concentrate their resources on urban areas, and focus on the elite. Ricci's strategy enjoyed success, winning converts among Chinese officials, such as Xu Guangqi, a high-ranking minister in the imperial court.[6]

Yet the Jesuits did not uniformly apply their strategy of accommodation throughout their missions. With the Hurons, Iroquois, and Algonquins in North America, French Jesuits insisted that the converts abandon their customs and adopt European ones.[7] China, Andrew Walls argues, was an outlier. The Jesuit formulation of missionary practice, Walls writes, was "a new development, one born out of frustrated colonialism. . . . It was perhaps the first learning experience that European Christianity received from its contact with the non-Western World."[8]

And of course, the Jesuits were not the only Catholics interested in missions. In 1622, the Vatican established the Sacred Congregation of the Propagation of the Faith (Sacra Congregatio de Propaganda Fide, or Propaganda Fide) to organize and oversee the global mission field. The Propaganda Fide understood itself as possessing an explicit mandate to regain lost ground ceded to Protestants. As Peter Guilday notes, the Propaganda viewed its mission as reconquering "by spiritual arms, by prayers and good works, by preaching and catechising, the countries that had been lost to the Church in the débâcle of the sixteenth century."⁹

Other than battling the Protestants, the Vatican also sought to wrest control of missions from Portuguese and Spanish imperial interests. In the case of China, Macau—a Portuguese settlement that became a diocese in 1577—served as a central hub for missionaries before they traveled inland, and the Jesuits entered China through Portuguese patronage. To bypass Portuguese imperial control, in the 1630s the Vatican ordered the creation of new missionary territories (apostolic vicariates) that came under the leadership of titular bishops, or apostolic vicars. The newly formed Propaganda Fide held the authority to appoint the apostolic vicars, who reported directly to the pope. The first apostolic vicar to travel to China was François Pallu, a member of the Mission Étrangères de Paris. He was entrusted with the task of bringing the various missionary societies in the field under the Vatican's control. But Pallu's attempts to centralize power were met with strong and vigorous resistance. Increasingly, Jesuit interests collided with those of the Propaganda Fide.¹⁰

The Jesuit monopoly of the field also eroded when mendicant orders—the Franciscans, Dominicans, and Augustinians—began sending missionaries to China in the 1630s. The various missionary societies clashed over the thorny issue of how to approach traditional Chinese culture. The mendicant orders criticized the Jesuits for fixating on the Chinese elite and instead emphasized an evangelical mission that concentrated on the rural poor. Rejecting Jesuit accommodation with traditional Chinese customs and rituals, the mendicants argued that Chinese ancestor worship ceremonies were not civic functions, but religious ones.

Despite these differences over how to approach Chinese civilization, all missionaries agreed about the practical problems that they faced: China was a vast country with an enormous population. The missionaries knew that they would never have enough European missionaries to cover the entire country. In order to meet the demand for more workers, starting in 1659 the Propaganda Fide authorized missionaries to ordain Chinese diocesan priests. In instructions addressed to Pallu and the Mission Étrangères, the Propaganda sided with the Jesuits, ordering them: "Do not act with zeal, do not put forward any arguments to convince these peoples to change their rites, their customs or their usages, except if they are evidently contrary to the religion and morality. What would be more absurd than to bring France, Spain, Italy or any other European country to the Chinese? Do not bring to them our countries, but instead bring to them the Faith."[11]

The Propaganda's instructions sparked even more ferocious debate over the question of Chinese rites. Missionaries from China sent hundreds of letters to the Vatican pleading their case. In 1704, the Vatican published a decree that rejected the Jesuit accommodationist position. Chinese Christians were not allowed to participate in traditional Chinese rites or community festivals. But the Vatican overestimated its power. In the end, the arbiter of the Jesuits' fate was not the church in Europe, but the Qing emperor Kangxi. He viewed the Vatican position as European hubris. In 1706 Kangxi banished from China missionaries who rejected the accommodationist mode. Only those who followed Ricci's model, he decreed, could stay. Kangxi's son, Emperor Yongzheng, went one step further, declaring Christianity a heterodox, forbidden religion and expelling all Christian missionaries from China.[12]

The ban on Christianity resulted in a complete disruption of Chinese Catholic life. As R. G. Tiedemann writes, many Chinese Catholics "often went for years without an opportunity for confession or instruction."[13] Filling this priestly vacuum were Chinese male and female lay leaders, who now became the lynchpin of the church in China and assumed responsibility for the religious life of the community. Even though lay leaders could not administer the sacraments—perform weddings, conduct masses, hear confessions, and dispense last rites—they took charge of religious education and led worship services.

As a result, Chinese converts made Christian rituals their own. Eugenio Menegon has shown that after the official ban on Christianity, Chinese Christians in Fujian Province in South China hid European missionaries and helped them evade arrest. Imperial suppression also forced European missionaries to elevate Chinese to positions of influence: in the 1730s, Dominicans decided to admit Chinese into the order. The novices received fellowships issued by the Spanish governor-general of the Philippines to study in Manila. Some were trained at the Collegio de' Cinesi (College for the Chinese) in Naples, an institution designed to train priests from China and the Ottoman Empire. Similar developments in indigenous Christianity emerged in the northern provinces of China as well. Catholics in Shanxi, for example, incorporated

Buddhist practices, such as chanting, singing, praying, and fasting, into their daily rituals.[14]

By the mid-1700s, as Menegon argues, Christianity "had become a local religion." "For converts," he writes, "to be local and Christian in China meant creating a new religious identity, both Chinese *and* Catholic, local and yet universalistic in aspiration."[15] In select villages in northern and southern China, Catholic religious identity grafted itself onto kinship networks and lineage societies. Christian churches became the center of village life, Catholicism an inheritance. Even though in 1810 only thirty foreign missionaries remained in China, Catholicism had implanted itself within the country. As Ernest Young notes, "Chinese Catholicism, when it was reshaped in the nineteenth century, already had endured hard times and had old roots in the country."[16]

THE PIETISTS

And what of the Protestants? As Jesuits confidently marched across the globe, the Protestant world of the seventeenth century was suffused with, in W. R. Ward's words, "low morale."[17] In the aftermath of the Reformation, Protestants thought primarily about survival. They sought to solidify gains that they had made in Europe, rather than to expand. Factional and denominational disagreements further distracted Protestants from looking outward to foreign lands.

By the late seventeenth century, the Protestant world experienced a revival, driven by a movement loosely referred to as the Awakening.[18] The Awakened, also called Pietists, were rooted primarily in Germanic central Europe. They sought to challenge the structures and practices of the established Lutheran and Reformed churches. Pietism found an early articulation in the writings of Philipp Jakob Spener (1635–1705), who began his career as a pastor in Frankfurt. He blamed the orthodox Lutheran and Reformed churches for the pervading spiritual malaise. Spener did not focus his ire on just church leaders and elites: ordinary congregants were also complicit in the calcification of spiritual energy. What Protestants needed was a new spirit: all individuals had to go through a constant state of conversion, a continual "new birth." Incubating the revivalist spirit was the *collegia pietatis,* or in Ward's translation, "class-meetings." In these gatherings, the community of the faithful preached, taught, and admonished one another. All social classes and both sexes were welcome. Spener hoped to use the *collegia pietatis* as a way to put Luther's ideal of the "Priesthood of all believers" into practice.[19]

As Spener and his followers ruffled feathers, particularly among orthodox Lutheran clergy, powerful elites rose to protect and sponsor them. The elector of Brandenburg-Prussia appointed Spener to a senior church position in Berlin in 1691, seeking to establish a nondenominational state church that united the Reformed and Lutheran populations in his realm. Meanwhile, Spener's close confidant August Hermann Francke gained a position at the University of Halle. Francke's commitment and enthusiasm for the cause transformed the university into a Pietist center, and Pietism soon gained a widespread influence throughout the continent.[20]

By the early eighteenth century, the Awakened began sending missionaries abroad. The king of Denmark, Frederick IV (1671–1730), financed German-speaking Pietist missionaries to work in the Danish colony of Tranquebar. The pan-European character of Protestant missionary networks, which Herbert Lüthy has called the "Protestant International," was also on display in the London-based Anglican Society for Promoting Christian Knowledge, founded in 1698. The society's missionaries in India were all Pietists, ordained Lutheran, and endorsed by Francke and other Pietists in Halle.[21]

Francke's missionary reports, published in his journal the *Hallesche Berichte*, inspired the imagination of many pious youth across Europe. In particular, it captivated the young Count Nikolaus von Zinzendorf (1700–1760). In the 1720s, Zinzendorf offered land on his estate in Herrnhut as shelter for Protestant refugees from Catholic Moravia. Herrnhut gained a reputation as a site for religious freedom and experimentation and soon attracted a broad spectrum of German followers. Eager to build a utopian community, they espoused a simple lifestyle, an individual relationship with God, and communal worship. Zinzendorf called his community the Unitas Fratrum (often referred to as the Moravian Brotherhood or the Herrnhutian Mission). Their lives revolved around Bible study, music, and education. Radically egalitarian, they refused to elevate ordained members above others.[22]

The followers in Herrnhut also brimmed with missionary zeal. Beginning in 1732, the Herrnhutian Mission sent missionaries abroad, fervently yearning to bring salvation to non-Christian lands. When

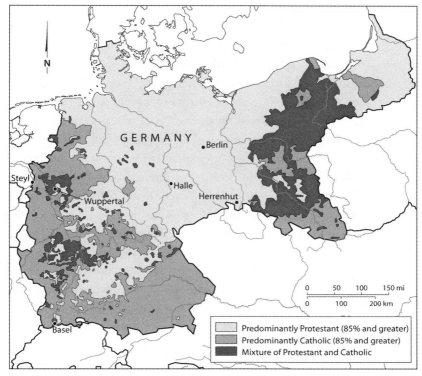

MAP 1 Confessional map of the German Empire in 1890. (Data from "Verteilung der Konfessionen im Deutschen Reich. Stand 1. Dezember 1890," Meyers Konversations-Lexicon, 4. Band. Chemillé bis Dingelstedt. 5. Aufl. Leipzig 1894, after 872.) Map drawn by Bill Nelson.

Zinzendorf died in 1760, communities based on the Herrnhut model had been established in the Danish and British West Indies, Greenland, South Africa, and North America. Their influence spread throughout Europe as well, gaining special traction in Britain and influencing the early English evangelical movement.[23]

Through Zinzendorf's efforts, Herrnhut and Halle formed the "the twin poles of Pietism" (map 1).[24] Like the Jesuits, the Pietists were beneficiaries of an increasingly interconnected early modern world. Vibrant transatlantic passages facilitated the movement and correspondence of ideas and people. Protestants were further buoyed by the successful imperial expansions of the Dutch and English, who, like the Spanish and Portuguese before them, enabled Catholic missionary work in their colonies.[25]

In the Pietist worldview, Christian faith had to be self-generated, rather than foisted upon the populace. A person became Christian through personal choice, not political, social, or territorial inheritance. Above all, the individual had to cultivate his or her relationship with God. Missionaries worked toward the goal of individual conversion, hoping to bring spiritual transformation and eternal salvation to the "heathens." Conversion began, they believed, with an intimate encounter with biblical truth. Missionaries were convinced of the transforming power of the gospel of Christ. Only through the personal encounter with this gospel could the "heathen lands" be saved and the enemies of the gospel vanquished. Like the Jesuits, Pietists focused their efforts on translating the Bible. They sought a broad coverage with their translations: they translated the Bible into the various vernacular languages in Europe, as well as in the missionary fields overseas. As Jonathan Sheehan argues, Pietist translations of the Bible belonged to a broader campaign to combat the "forces of impiety" and transcend "the confines of doctrine and dogma that [had] so shackled the spirit of Lutheranism." To carry out this form of warfare, Pietists printed astonishing amounts of scripture; by the late eighteenth century, the Halle presses had produced more than a million New Testaments and close to two million Bibles.[26]

PROTESTANT ENTHUSIASM IN THE LONG NINETEENTH CENTURY

At the same time, new "forces of impiety" appeared on the horizon, threatening to dismantle the foundations of Western Christendom. Mounting the political assault were European states: enlightened monarchs attempted to curtail the autonomy of their ecclesiastical rivals. Protestant and Catholic monarchs prohibited bishops from organizing and in some instances seized church lands for the purposes of public education and welfare. Alongside these political assaults on the Catholic Church emerged the intellectual critique of traditional organized religion, offered most trenchantly by Enlightenment *philosophes*.[27]

Bearing the brunt of these secular attacks were the Jesuits. Often finding themselves on the opposite side of colonial politics, the Jesuits provoked ire within the Spanish and Portuguese empires. Beginning in the 1750s, Catholic monarchs throughout Europe expelled Jesuits from their realms and pressured the Vatican to disband the society. They got their wish in 1773, when Pope Clement XIV suppressed the order, devastating the global network of universities and colleges that Jesuits had built.[28]

But the most violent form of de-Christianization found its expression during the French Revolution. Revolutionaries confiscated church property, eliminated ecclesiastical privileges, forced clergy to take an oath of obedience to the Civil Constitution, and executed those who refused to take the oath. The Concordat that Napoleon and Pius VII signed signaled a truce between the Vatican and the French government, but another catastrophe struck in 1803, when the majority of ecclesiastical territories of the Holy Roman Empire were annexed by surrounding secular principalities, putting more than half of German Catholics under Protestant rule. Even though Napoleon reinstated three of the largest missionary organizations and put them under the control of the French state, he disbanded the Propaganda Fide. By the early nineteenth century, the Catholic missionary enterprise was in shambles, with no papal bureaucracy to coordinate and direct the effort.[29]

Assaults on the church prompted a fervent Christian response. A period of intense religious revivalism swept through North America and continental Europe in the late eighteenth and early nineteenth centuries. The era from 1790 to 1830 was variously called the Second Great Awakening in North America, the *Erweckungsbewegung* within the German-speaking world, and *le Réveil* among Francophones.[30] The Catholic world was similarly touched by such revivalism, albeit slightly later than the Protestants. As Christopher Clark writes, European Catholicism in the early to the mid-nineteenth century saw "a proliferation and elaboration of popular devotions, church buildings, religious foundations and associations, and confessionally motivated newspapers and journals."[31]

Epitomizing this broader Christian renewal was the founding of new missionary organizations. Britain emerged as the center of Protestant evangelical fervor. Diarmaid MacCulloch estimates that by 1830, around 60 percent of British Protestants engaged in some form of evangelical activity.[32] The expansion of the British Empire led to an explosion of knowledge and access to the religions and cultures of the non-Christian world. The most influential organizations among this new crop of missionary societies were the Baptist Missionary Society in 1792, the interdenominational London Missionary Society in 1795, and the Church Missionary Society in 1799. As Andrew Porter writes, the appearance of these mission societies in such close succession "was no mere coincidence."[33]

The transatlantic networks formed by the Pietist revival a century before had served as an incubator for cross-denominational cooperation, and the missionary societies drew upon these channels of communication to disseminate reports and ideas. The British missionary societies worked closely together and debated with one another about theology and how to reorganize their societies. Starting in 1810, Americans joined this broader evangelical revival and increased their presence abroad with the creation of the American Board of Commissioners for Foreign Missions.[34]

Missionary enthusiasm spread throughout the European continent as well: the Netherlands Missionary Society was formed in 1797, the Basel Missionary Society in 1815, the BMS in 1824, and the Rhenish Missionary Society in 1828. Differences emerged between the German missionary societies and their Anglo-American counterparts. In both Britain and the United States, missionary societies that had begun as interdenominational became increasingly governed by individual denominations. By the early 1820s, Baptists, Methodists, Episcopalians, and Presbyterians all had founded their own missionary organs. In contrast, German missionary societies organized along regional lines and remained interdenominational: both Lutheran and Reformed missionaries joined the Basel Missionary Society, the Rhenish Missionary Society, and the BMS.[35]

German missionary societies all had roots in the conservative German Christendom Society (Deutsche Christentumsgesellschaft). Founded in 1780 by Johann August Urlsperger, a Lutheran pastor, the society advanced a critique of the Enlightenment and rational theology. It sought to unify the German-speaking lands through a revival of Pietistic teachings. In the early 1800s, the society became a vociferous critic of the Napoleonic conquests of the German lands, and its members mounted a literary campaign and built a densely connected network of German evangelistic societies through print.[36]

Influenced by the German Christendom Society, the founders of the first wave of German Protestant missionary societies espoused an anti-revolutionary position. Theologically, the societies saw themselves as forming a bulwark against both the "the soul of odious Rationalism" (*der Seelen verhassten Rationalismus*) and the "enthusiasms of Romanticism" (*Schwärmereien der Romantik*). Ludwig von Rohden, a missionary inspector for the Rhenish Missionary Society, expressed this anti-Enlightenment stance when he wrote in 1857 that the society was formed "in a barren and stormy time, when faith had died everywhere and love had grown cold, when the revolutionary storms coming from France were filling our German fatherland with poisonous vapors. Rigid death prevailed in the Protestant church of Germany."[37] A similar account can be found in the internal histories of the BMS: Julius Richter, an influential member of the Berlin missionary leadership, wrote that the BMS was founded to counterbalance the "long spiritual winter of the Enlightenment and an Age of Rationalism."[38]

Missionary leaders believed that traditional church structures had failed to prevent the rise of secular challenges. Many who claimed to be Pietists, missionary leaders argued, had lost their original evangelical fervor and had become ensnared by the institutions of the established church. German missionaries saw themselves as the inheritors of the Pietism of Spener, Francke, and Zinzendorf, and they invoked the original Pietist ideas as "spiritual sustenance."[39] Only new forms of religious community, infused with a Pietist spirit, could stem the further advance of their opponents. For von Rohden, missionary societies of the early nineteenth century marked the "first appearance on German soil of a free Christian association that would reach its hands across all barriers of churches, confessions, and parish boundaries to pursue a common goal without mediation by the hired clergy and the church authorities." The founders of these voluntary societies envisioned their organizations as spiritual enclaves, protecting the pious individual from an encroaching secular world. The believers, von Rohden claimed, "joined for regular prayer, a conscientious observance of Sunday, the maintenance of household devotion, and strict discipline and self-examination."[40] Whereas the traditional church parish drew upon believers who were tied to a fixed location, the neo-Pietist vision of the voluntary association—rooted in individual conversion, spirituality, and piety—sought to foster broader regional and international networks.

Industrialization accelerated the creation of these new associational networks. Leslie Page Moch has shown that from 1750 until 1815, much of northwestern Europe saw a steady increase in population due to rural industrialization. "The countryside was alive with movement," Moch writes, "as men and women found work in booming industrial villages and small towns that could retain and support increased numbers."[41] The city of Barmen, the base of the Rhenish Missionary Society, is an example of a provincial town that morphed into a major industrial center. In 1750, its old textile industry supported a population of 3,790. By 1809, its population had increased almost fourfold. The trend continued unabated into the twentieth century. By 1910 Barmen had become a major manufacturer of textiles, with a population of 169,214. Much of the population growth was a result of migration: by the second half of the eighteenth century, about 40 percent of the population of Barmen were migrants, who had fewer rights and were socially ostracized by the locals.[42]

Missionary societies and other voluntary religious organizations acted as forces of integration, offering peripatetic individuals a spiritual home.[43] Many missionaries began their careers not as theologians or pastors, but rather as provincial artisans. Karl Gützlaff (1803–1851), the influential German Protestant missionary who arrived in China in 1830, apprenticed as a saddler before entering Johannes Jänicke's seminary in Berlin. Another famous German Protestant missionary to China, Ernst Faber, was the son of a blacksmith and worked in Saxony, Silesia, and Berlin before joining the Rhenish Missionary Society.[44]

Missionary organizations were filled primarily with young men; the average Berlin missionary entered the society before he turned twenty. Upon entrance, each missionary had to write a personal testimony. The archives brim with such testimonies; in account after account individuals stress that religious community gave them a sense of purpose and meaning. "The Spirit of God worked mightily on my soul," wrote Carl Johannes Voskamp of his experience in communal Bible study. "My time in Bible study helped me to let go of my own desires." The missionaries believed that they had found their life's calling: to fulfill Jesus's Great Commission of going forth to spread the gospel.[45]

Other than nurturing a sense of belonging, the missionary life also offered the promise of adventure, the chance to travel overseas, and the possibility for upward mobility. As Andrew Walls notes, "The typical missionary long remained, as he had been in the first generation, a man of humble background and modest attainments."[46] Educational training equipped the men with a potential career as an ordained minister—a position otherwise unattainable to an artisan trained in a special craft. For these provincial youth, the missionary society liberated them from the narrow confines of their backgrounds, integrating them into a broader global community.

Such integration was not just international, but intranational: within the missionary society different social classes worked together. Nowhere was this more evident than in the BMS. Its founding members, religiously Awakened noblemen, had been inspired by Johannes Jänicke, a pastor at the Bethlehem Church in Berlin. Jänicke had close ties with the Moravians and in 1800 founded the first German-speaking missionary school, which served as the training ground for many of the most influential early German missionaries, including Karl Gützlaff. Jänicke's work attracted the attention of Prussian elites, all of whom were committed to anti-Napoleonic action through a strengthening of Prussia's moral and Pietistic values. When the BMS was founded in 1824, its governing board was filled with Prussian officials and state administrators, while missionaries came from more modest social backgrounds. For the most part, the missionary society was able to foster, as Jon Miller writes, "class collaboration for the sake of religion."[47]

From its inception the BMS enjoyed a special relationship with the elites of the Prussian state. Such connections gave it a certain amount of influence; the conservative counsels of Friedrich Wilhelm IV, for example, granted it postal concessions and donated money to the organization. The board was also filled with famous Berlin pastors, who were invited by board members to join the committee because of their "upstanding moral character." The BMS director was typically an accomplished Lutheran pastor or theologian who had ties to Prussian nobility.[48]

Despite these personal ties to the Prussian elite, the BMS received little money from the state. Missionary leaders had to seek other sources of funding. Revival meetings provided one such avenue. Following the lead of the Basel Missionary Society, the BMS began to organize mission festivals where missionaries who had returned from abroad played the part of the itinerant preacher, gave a sermon, reported on their experiences in the field, and exhorted the audience to support missionary work. Pastors also read aloud testimonies and accounts from the field. For the majority of the audience, the tales they heard at mission festivals comprised their sole encounter with foreign lands.

The festivals proved wildly successful and soon spread throughout the Continent. After 1838, for example, the Rhenish Missionary Society held an annual Wuppertal Festival Week (Wuppertaler Festwoche) in August, replete with sermons, gatherings under the night sky, evening prayers, and concerts. The festival attracted an audience of thousands who pilgrimaged from all over the German lands. Festivals became so popular that missionaries replicated them in Africa and Asia.[49]

Print also helped mobilize popular support. By the early 1800s, printing costs were cheaper: the British and Foreign Bible Society alone printed more than forty-six million complete Bibles. Through their own journals and publications, missionary societies generated a wealth of stories, publicizing their activities and informing the public of their work abroad. In Britain, more than three hundred missionary periodicals were founded in the nineteenth century, and hundreds more appeared throughout North America and Europe. At the 1860 Liverpool conference for Protestant missions, one missionary boasted that more than two hundred thousand Protestant missionary periodicals existed.[50]

In the German lands, missionary periodicals were also popular. In 1832, for example, the *Missionary Register* of the Church Missionary Society reported that the journal of the Rhenish Missionary Society had a circulation of 12,706 subscribers and claimed, "There are many towns and villages in Germany where this Religious Gazette is more read than any Political Journal."[51] The Rhenish used the profits from these publications to invest in infrastructure for missionary houses and other projects. The BMS also produced a range of publications. Besides monthly and annual missionary reports, it put out children's literature, popular tracts, and other short pamphlets that digested the society's strongest material about its successes abroad.[52]

Missionary organizations further relied on an extensive ecosystem of auxiliary institutions (*Hülfsvereine*) to funnel support, financial and otherwise. Located in the hinterlands, these auxiliary societies circulated the mission's reading materials, organized festivals, and hosted church services—all for the purpose of raising funds for the missionary societies. In 1854, the Berlin Missionary Association for China, an organization created to raise money for the China missions, listed twenty-eight auxiliary societies that supported its work. By 1866, the BMS boasted 259 *Hülfsvereine*. Local auxiliary organizations also provided a crucial resource to the missionary society: talent. They identified pious young men enthusiastic for missionary work and encouraged them to become missionaries.[53]

With no empire to which they could turn, German missionaries drew upon an international network of support. Evangelical, interdenominational, and international, the early-nineteenth-century Protestant missionary societies worked in conjunction with one another. The first Berlin missionaries sent to Africa and China traveled on British ships. Funds from London, Copenhagen, and Stockholm helped defray the costs of book printing and language training. Gützlaff's career exemplifies the international nature of the early-nineteenth-century missionary world. Early in his career, Gützlaff received training from the Dutch Missionary Society, and he thought he was destined for a life of missionary work in the East Indies. When the Dutch sent him for further studies with the London Missionary Society, he came in contact with Robert Morrison's extensive Chinese-English collection, which in turn sparked his interest in China.[54]

Once they were in the field, missionaries employed various strategies to convert indigenous populations to Christianity. They devoted their resources to building institutions that could help foster the inner spiritual lives of the "heathens." German Pietists believed that foreign nations could be converted only through "individual conversion" (*Einzelbekehrung*), one soul at a time. They emphasized the necessity of church building as the primary path toward eternal salvation, and missionaries spent a good amount of time building churches and engaging in street evangelism. Pietist missionaries prized the narratives of emotional individual conversion, but they also focused on educating the indigenous populations they encountered. They printed Christian tracts and pamphlets in indigenous languages, taught basic literacy, and supplied the converted with free elementary education and medical care. Through these various avenues of work, missionaries believed, foreign lands could one day be converted to Christianity.[55]

THE CATHOLIC REVIVAL

A similar faith in missionary work galvanized popular Catholicism in the nineteenth century. The revolutionary assault on the ecclesiastical structures of the *ancien régime* served as an act of creative destruction, clearing the path for a new religious landscape to flourish after the Napoleonic wars. Like Protestantism, the Catholic world after 1815 saw a dramatic growth of new voluntary devotional associations. Pious Catholics joined religious orders and founded religious houses. In France, the revolution sparked mass devotions toward the Sacred Heart, which became emblematic of antirevolutionary Catholic piety. The most spectacular public acts of devotion came in the form of pilgrimages throughout Europe. Half a million pilgrims traveled to Trier in 1844 to see the shroud of Jesus, while tales of Marian apparitions drew hundreds of thousands Catholic faithful to Lourdes and Marpingen in the 1860s and 1870s.[56]

Yet the French Revolution's successful assault on the foundations of the Catholic Church meant that Protestant missionary societies had almost a two-decade head start on their Catholic counterparts. Still reeling from confiscations and the destruction of church property, Catholic missionary societies required several decades to reorganize their missionary efforts. Most Catholic missionary societies appeared on the scene in the 1820s, while many Protestant missionary societies had swung into action a decade earlier.

Unlike Protestants, Catholics could rely on a central organ to coordinate efforts among different religious orders—the Vatican. And in Pius VII (1742–1823), they had a pope who recognized the importance of rebuilding the church's influence through missionary work. He restored the Jesuits in 1814, reinstituted the Propaganda Fide in 1817, and chartered several new missionary organizations. Other than worrying about overseas missions, the church also directed its concern toward Europe. Older missionary orders, such as the Redemptorists and Franciscans, spread across Europe, hoping to win back lost souls. The restored Bourbon monarch, Louis XVIII, issued a royal ordinance in 1816 that created a domestic mission society, the Society of the Priests of Mercy (Société des Prêtres de la Miséricorde), known as the Missions of France.[57]

In 1831, Gregory XVI, previously the prefect of the Propaganda Fide, became pope and devoted more resources to expanding missionary networks. The Vatican formed five new missionary societies in the following decade that sent missionaries to Syria, Peru, the South Pacific, China, West Africa, and Madagascar. Between 1800 and 1914, twenty-nine missionary orders and congregations were formed in Europe.[58]

Like their Protestant counterparts, Catholic missionaries throughout Europe organized large, public mission festivals—involving sermons, processions, bonfires, and the raising of giant crosses—with the goal of re-Christianizing individuals lost to the revolution. In order to support these efforts, Catholic auxiliary missionary associations spread throughout Europe. Between 1818 and 1921, more than 246 missionary associations emerged to help raise funds for overseas missions.[59]

The most successful of these newly formed associations was the French Oeuvre de la Propagation de la Foi (the Society for the Propagation of the Faith). Founded in 1822, the organization consisted primarily of lay faithful. Learning from their Protestant competitors, the leaders of the Oeuvre created innovative ways to secure funds for the society. Just as the Protestants relied on small donations from local congregations, the Oeuvre also, as J. P. Daughton has shown, "adopted entrepreneurial schemes to draw small donations from the broadest spectrum of society."[60] It instituted a weekly subscription for a small sum, promising that the donations propelled missionaries globally. In 1825 it started publishing its monthly journal, the *Annales de la Propagation de la Foi*. It was a hit. By 1845, the Oeuvre was collecting more than two million francs a year, and its success helped to catapult the French to dominate global Catholic missions. Ernest Young estimates that of all contributions to Catholic mission work from 1822 to 1872, an astonishing two-thirds came from the French.[61]

The *Annales* was only one journal among many that appeared in the early to the middle part of the nineteenth century. As Christopher Clark has shown, the explosion and rapid diffusion of Catholic print culture during that time helped contribute to the broader movement of "ultramontanism," which fortified the authority of Rome.[62] While some voluntary organizations asserted their independence, the majority of the revivalist organizations expressed devotion to papal initiatives. Closely attuned to these broader developments, the Vatican furthered the spread of Marian devotions and the cult of the Sacred Heart. Furthermore, new techniques for mass marketing, including souvenirs, newsletters, and other ingenious marketing ploys, widened the Vatican's influence.[63] A positive feedback loop emerged: revivalism bolstered the pope's authority, and the papacy in turn consolidated its ecclesiastical control by encouraging the establishment of new missionary societies.

The German SVD was one of the societies created in this ultramontane milieu. Its founder, Arnold Janssen (1837–1909), was among the thousands of Catholics in the nineteenth century inspired by the image of the Sacred Heart. The second of eleven children, Janssen came from a farming family. His parents were devout Catholics: they subscribed annu-ally to the *Annales* and "read the letters from the missionaries with warmth and enthusiasm." Janssen was a gifted student and studied theology at Münster. Ordained in 1861, he then taught at a secondary school in the Rhineland. In 1866, he joined a devotional prayer group, the Apostleship of Prayer, which had been formed by French Jesuits in 1844 and spread into the German lands during the 1860s. The group hoped to renew personal spirituality, exhorting its members to meditate upon the Sacred Heart during their prayers. Janssen became an active participant in the association's activities and promoted its beliefs in the Rhine region.[64]

Bismarck's *Kulturkampf,* which began in 1871, radicalized Janssen.[65] In 1873, he left teaching to become an activist. Founding a monthly peri-odical, the *Little Messenger of the Sacred Heart (Kleiner Herz-Jesu-Bote)*, he sought to strengthen the piety of Catholic readers besieged by German anti-Catholicism. A chance encounter with the apostolic prefect of Hong Kong drew Janssen's attention to the monetary needs of overseas missionary work. Hoping to raise support for the missions, Janssen began reporting on missionary work abroad.[66]

The *Little Messenger* presented the conversion of the foreign heathen as inextricably linked with the plight of Christianity in Europe. Stories of missionary work in East Asia appeared alongside tales of Catholic suffering at the hands of political persecution under the *Kulturkampf.* The April 1874 issue of the *Little Messenger,* for example, begins with a report of Archbishop of Cologne Paul Melcher's imprisonment under the *Kulturkampf* before turning to reports of the Chinese state persecuting European missionaries. Missionaries pushed their readers to link the challenges that Catholics experienced in Europe with the plight of Christianity globally. Christians in China suffered persecution similar to that of Christians in Germany; they faced the same "forces of Satan."[67]

Besides exhorting their readers to think globally, the editors of the SVD's journals also pushed them to think historically. Reports of missionary deaths proliferated in the journal, explicitly equating mission-aries' sacrifices with martyrdom in the apostolic church. Missionary editors depicted the oppression that Christian missionaries faced as a recurring battle between Christianity and the secular state, dating back to the Roman Empire. Like the early church martyrs, the missionaries had lost their lives to implant Christianity in foreign lands that did not know the gospel. So as to not overwhelm their readers with fear, the journal's editors explicitly stated that they wrote for their audience in a "child-like and devotional tone," as a way to articulate clear methods for how ordinary Germans could contribute to the missionary effort, both through their prayers and through their donations. And the journal successfully appealed to a broad readership. Within six months, it had turned a profit.[68]

Janssen wanted to direct his money to missionary organizations, yet he failed to find any German priests to fund. *Kulturkampf* legislation had suspended the training of Catholic missionaries in Germany; the 1872 anti-Jesuit law expelled the Jesuits from Germany; and the Congregations Law of 1875 banned religious orders and eliminated state support to Catholic churches.[69] Janssen wanted to create a seminary that would train new missionaries and offer a safe haven for German priests. He purchased land in Steyl, in the Netherlands, as the recent imprisonment of one of his major benefactors, Bishop Johannes Bernard Brinkmann, had convinced him that Germany had become too hostile for the venture. To display his dedication to the Sacred Heart, Janssen consecrated the grounds on June 16, 1875, the two-hundredth anniversary of the appearance of the Sacred Heart to Margaret Mary Alacoque.[70]

Despite Janssen's optimism, his missionary society began in a state of disarray. His funds could not cover the cost of furniture in the missionary house, and Janssen's idiosyncratic personal spirituality clashed with some of his new recruits, all newly ordained priests.[71] Nonetheless, the society grew. Janssen began to accept secondary school students and seminarians to offer them further training. Within four years, he had recruited sixty students, and by 1886, he had two hundred.

Like their Protestant competitors, the priests who joined the order came from provincial backgrounds. The first two SVD missionaries sent to China, Johann Baptist von Anzer and Josef Freinademetz, were both the sons of farmers. Even though the missionaries all spoke German, the society was from its inception an international organization: Anzer came from Bavaria, Freinademetz from Tyrol, and other priests hailed from Luxembourg and Holland. In 1879, Anzer and Freinademetz set sail for China (map 2). With the *Kulturkampf* waning in Germany, the SVD also now had established its first presence in China. The potential for the gospel's advance throughout the globe seemed bright.[72]

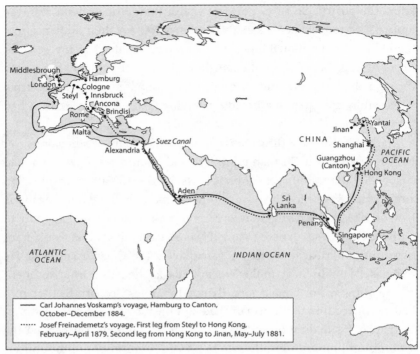

MAP 2 The voyages of Carl Johannes Voskamp and Josef Freinademetz to China. Map
drawn by Bill Nelson.

CONCLUSIONS: A GLOBAL BATTLE FOR LOST SOULS

"And alas, what of our present time!" lamented the first issue of the
Annales. "Impiety has marshaled the strongest efforts that it has ever
made against the Church. It slanders, it proscribes, it slaughters; the
temples and altars have fallen under its blows. The sacred ministers and
virgins, though they have escaped the sword of the executioner, are scat-
tered like dust throughout the world."[73]

Such lamentation was a common sentiment in nineteenth-century
Protestant and Catholic missionary journals. Forged in a new devotional
culture that emerged after the French Revolution, missionary societies
framed the rise of irreligion and secularism as the central problem facing
the universal church. Missionaries conceived of their work as a way to
battle these various forces; spiritual revival could further serve as a
bulwark against the advance of anti-Christian sentiment. Through their

pamphlets, journals, festivals, and evangelization, missionary societies sought to stoke the flames of revivalism in the nineteenth century.

A central component of nineteenth-century European revivalist thinking was its international character. By the late nineteenth century, the battle for lost souls had acquired global dimensions. The heathen soul in China was just as damned as the socialist in Europe. While the forces of irreligion and secularism might have scored temporary victories in Europe, the missionaries argued that they could gain new ground by going abroad. To justify its decision to send missionaries to China—that "great country of Jesus's hopes and pain"—the SVD offered a number: 555 million people.[74] Even converting a fraction of the Chinese population could balance the books, reversing the losses that Christendom had sustained in Europe.

Other than expanding the spatial imaginations of their readers, missionary publications also sought to inspire their historical imaginations. The pages of the Catholic missionary journals abounded with veneration of the missionary martyrs who had sacrificed themselves for the spread of Catholicism in the early modern era. Protestants lionized their Pietist predecessors, distributing pamphlets glorifying Spener, Francke, and Zinzendorf. By linking themselves to historical acts of heroic piety, missionaries placed themselves within a long lineage of anti-Christian persecution. The first issue of the *Annales* ridiculed contemporary attacks on the church: "the impious [of our time] think that they represent something new and even more forceful than the anti-Christian forces of the time of Diocletian."[75] Instead, the writers in the missionary journals reminded their readers that their battle with anti-Christian forces had endured since the days of the early church. Pointing to heroic stories of martyrdom, missionary journals sought to reassure their readers of Christianity's eventual triumph. The church had survived and thrived despite worse challenges in the past—most certainly it would withstand contemporary secular gnats.

Optimism, much of it warranted, characterized the nineteenth-century missionary movement. In a time of unprecedented Western imperial expansion, missionaries now had the ability to access remote areas previously thought unreachable. The missionary theorist Gustav Warneck proclaimed that "the nineteenth century is a missionary century," and in 1900 the American missionary John Mott would boldly predict that the modern missionary movement could bring about the "evangelization of the world in this generation."[76]

Yet—in China, at least—such optimism would not last. Soon after entering the country, missionaries became disenchanted with their approach, frustrated with the slow speed of their expansion, and openly acknowledged their methods as failures.

CHAPTER TWO

Responding to Failure

THE YEARS FROM 1811 to 1813 were catastrophic for the North China plains. Droughts and floods meant famine everywhere. Officials traveling through the area described scenes of horror and desolation: villagers scavenging for grass roots and tree bark, towns abandoned by families seeking food. Social values disintegrated. Looters ransacked villages; parents sold their children.[1]

Members of a secret society called the *Bagua jiao* (Eight Trigrams), a loose coalition of religious sectarians who claimed to know the exact date of the world's end, saw the devastation as proof of the impending apocalypse. They believed that the last days of their historical age—in traditional Buddhist thought, the *kalpa*—were nigh, and the mounting signs of worldly cataclysm only further reinforced their belief. It was prophesied that a messianic savior—typically, the Maitreya Buddha—would come to restore the world and save the faithful.[2]

In 1813, the Eight Trigrams coordinated a massive uprising of more than one hundred thousand people across northern China. Carrying knives and wearing their signature white sashes, about seventy-five of these men entered the Forbidden City in Beijing, hoping to start an insurrection in the capital. But Qing palace guards quickly apprehended them, and within three months, the Qing state crushed the broader rebellion. About forty thousand people surrendered; another seventy thousand died.[3]

The crushing of the Trigrams did not quell millenarian fervor. Rather, discontent toward the Qing was a widespread phenomenon throughout China. In the south, the Heaven and Earth Society (Tiandihui, also known as the Chinese Triads), originating in Fujian Province, spread along the coasts and farther inland, gaining traction among the Hakka populations of Guangdong. Scholars such as Frederic Wakeman have attributed the proliferation of such secret societies to the strength and vitality of Chinese society in the early nineteenth century. A vibrant market economy and the development of new regional commercial networks, Wakeman notes, "detached the bandit from the peasant village."[4] The introduction of foreign trade, especially the smuggling of opium, stimulated a growth in secret society membership. Urban laborers, dockworkers, and other transport workers joined such groups in ports like Guangzhou, also known as Canton, with a bustling foreign presence. Throughout China, popular religious sects and secret societies mobilized nonelite Chinese, offering them a space for voicing their political and social frustrations. It is no coincidence that these groups flourished in areas where the Qing imperial apparatus was weak or nonexistent.[5]

In China, just as in Europe, voluntary religious associations increasingly challenged state authority in the early nineteenth century. The Qing government did not categorically suppress such popular religious expression. Rather, it adopted a laissez-faire attitude toward religious associations that it considered orthodox and outlawed religious groups that it felt were a threat, labeling them as heterodox and "immoral."[6]

Christianity was among the religions the Qing deemed heterodox. To Qing authorities, Christian belief, like the cosmology of the Eight Trigrams, threatened the legitimacy of the state; in both, a messianic figure promised to offer a more just form of power. The central deity of the Eight Trigram sect was an Eternal Mother who weeps for her lost children, beckoning them to return to the Pure Land. The similarities to the Christian worship of Mary seemed suspiciously self-evident.[7]

To Qing authorities, heterodox religious sects not only professed dangerous ideas, they "looked" the same: they carried out subversive practices. Christianity and secret societies alike relied on charismatic itinerant preachers and teachers who formed reading clubs and created smaller units of community. The communities were organized around texts: Christians circulated Bibles, Chinese Triads passed along oath books.[8] Like the secret societies, Christianity had esoteric initiation rites. Catholics baptized with water, and the Chinese Triads initiated their members through a blood covenant of drinking liquor mixed with animal and/or human blood. (And of course, the invocation of blood plays a central part in Christian liturgy.)[9]

Equally threatening, Christianity, like other heterodox religions, seemed to draw from similar social groups, especially among the marginalized and dispossessed. It had not always been so: many early converts were Confucian elites. The Jesuits had successfully instituted a policy of accommodation, and the scientific practices that the Jesuits brought with them had intrigued high-level officials at the Qing court. After the 1724 edict banning Christianity in China, however, Confucian officials could no longer outwardly support the religion. By the early nineteenth century, then, Christianity drew from the social strata that the Qing state had abandoned. Like the Chinese Triads, Catholicism made claims about heaven and earth and offered a cosmological alternative to the hierarchical structures of orthodox Confucian belief. The narratives of conversion and the rituals of initiation offered the dispossessed a new identity and a group to shelter them from an unforgiving and chaotic world. For Chinese Catholics and Chinese Triads alike, religion promised salvation from a Confucian world order that had abandoned them.[10]

Immediately after the Eight Trigrams uprising, the Qing Empire accused Chinese Christians and European missionaries of participating in the insurrection. In 1815, approximately eight hundred Christians were arrested in Chengdu. Among the arrested was the French bishop Gabriel Taurin Dufresse, who engaged in illegal missionary activity in Sichuan. He was beheaded, and his head was displayed on the Chengdu city gates. In 1816, Shanxi Catholics were accused of aiding a White Lotus rebellion and forced to abandon Christianity. Those who refused were exiled.[11]

Undeterred by these injunctions, and excited at the prospect of martyrdom, Catholic missionaries smuggled themselves into the interior of China, often with grave consequences. The French Lazarist Jean-Gabriel Perboyre disguised himself as Chinese and met with Christians in the night. One of his catechumens reported him to the local officials, and after a four-month trial in 1840, he was executed in Wuchang.[12]

But one crucial difference between Christianity and the secret societies soon became apparent: increasingly, Chinese Christians could depend on foreign assistance. Starting in the nineteenth century, Western missionaries, undeterred by the injunctions against Christianity, increased their presence in China. In 1807, Robert Morrison, a missionary for the London Missionary Society, arrived in Guangzhou, establishing Protestantism's first contact with China.[13] Catholics also began to send more workers. In the decades between 1810 and 1840, five missionary groups committed personnel to China: the Spanish Dominicans, the Paris Foreign Mission Society (Société des Missions Étrangères de Paris), the Italian Franciscans (sent by the Propaganda Fide), the French Lazarists, and the reestablished Jesuits.[14]

For both Catholics and Protestants, the work in the first half of the nineteenth century grew slowly, limited by Chinese restrictions on both Christianity and the presence of foreigners. Missionaries found common cause with merchants, who wanted to open China to the free flow of goods and trade. Missionary and merchant alike advocated the use of European imperial power to compel China to open its borders. Favoring military intervention in China, Gützlaff wrote in the 1830s, "when an opponent supports his argument with physical force, [the Chinese] can be crouching, gentle, and even kind."[15]

Gützlaff and others hoping for a more active European intervention in China got their wish during the First Opium War, fought between 1839 and 1842 and ending in a resounding British victory. The Treaty of Nanjing established five treaty ports at Guangzhou, Shanghai, Fuzhou, Xiamen, and Ningbo where missionaries were allowed to enter and proselytize. Subsequent edicts in 1844 and 1846 granted more toleration for Christian missionary work, but missionary movement remained restricted to the Treaty Ports.[16]

Gützlaff had been a key player for the British during the First Opium War, recruiting Chinese spies and offering the British strategic advice. He assumed multiple guises as both statesman and missionary: during the treaty negotiations in Nanjing, where he interpreted on the side of the British, he distributed New Testaments to Chinese officials. After the war, he sensed opportunity and traveled through Europe, trying to drum up financial support and attract new personnel for the missions in China. His tours sparked a "China fever" in the German lands during the late 1840s and early 1850s. The Prussian king and queen gave him a personal audience, and major newspapers throughout Europe advertised his travels. Hundreds of support societies formed in the wake of his European tour, including the Berlin Missionary Association, which raised funds for the missions in China.[17]

Gützlaff exhorted Germans to support missionary activity in China, noting that German missionary societies lagged behind their English and American counterparts. Persuaded, the Basel and Rhenish missionary societies decided to send missionaries to China, even though they had previously focused their work solely on Africa. In 1847, four missionaries—Rudolf Lechler and the Swedish Theodor Hamberg of the Basel Missionary Society and Ferdinand Genähr and Heinrich Köster of the Rhenish Missionary Society—arrived in Guangzhou.[18]

Even with an increase in missionary presence, the Europeans knew that they could not convert the Chinese by themselves. The number of missionaries sent to China was minuscule compared with the vastness of the country. Gützlaff argued that Christianity in China needed to rely on indigenous clergy, rather than on foreign missionaries. For China to ever become Christian, it needed to be converted by the Chinese, so he founded the Chinese Union, an organization that drew heavily upon indigenous Chinese Christians. European funds soon flowed to the Chinese Union. The model attracted attention: the Rhenish Missionary Society, for example based its early organizational structure in China on Gützlaff's Chinese Union.[19]

Yet Gützlaff and the Chinese Union immediately faced a problem: how could they ascertain the sincerity of a new convert's faith? As Jessie Lutz has written, missionaries were distressed by the permeable boundaries between the "proliferating heterodox groups," such as the Christians, Triads, and other religious sects.[20] Chinese Christians expelled from their churches often found themselves unable to integrate back into their original communities, as they were now branded with the taint of collaborating with foreigners. Secret and heterodox societies like the Triads offered them a new home. Similarly, former heterodox rebels joined Christian churches as a way to garner extraterritorial protection.

Ascertaining sincere belief of recent converts was one problem, but an even thornier issue lay with the question of Chinese leadership. The missionary community was split over how rapidly it should develop independent Chinese clergy. Inspired by Moravian ideals of radical equality, Gützlaff allowed the Chinese to operate with a good deal of autonomy.

Opponents repudiated his laissez-faire methods, claiming that many of Gützlaff's trusted Chinese assistants were in reality "unscrupulous characters" who "spent their expense money on opium."[21] Gützlaff's opponents swayed missionary leaders in Europe, who began to withdraw support to the Chinese Union, leading to its dissolution shortly after Gützlaff's death. Its failure served as a cautionary tale. Critics claimed that missionaries like Gützlaff had become overconfident in the spiritual readiness of Chinese Christianity and turned over the reins to the Chinese too quickly. The Chinese still needed European oversight.

The problems and questions that Gützlaff's Chinese Union raised were paltry compared with the cataclysmic events that followed. In 1850, uprisings broke out in Guangxi Province. Led by the charismatic Hong Xiuquan, who believed he was the brother of Jesus, the rebels called themselves the Society of God Worshippers. They aimed to create the Kingdom of Heavenly Peace, or the Taiping Tianguo, and launched a decade-long assault on the Qing government. The historian Stephen Platt has called the Taiping Rebellion "not only the most destructive war of the nineteenth century, but likely the bloodiest civil war of all time." When the dust had settled, somewhere between ten and twenty million people had died.[22]

The Protestant missionary establishment's involvement with the Taipings left many Westerners deeply embarrassed. Few in the missionary establishment could claim to have remained uninvolved. Even Gützlaff, who died in 1851 before the Taiping uprising had escalated, was indirectly linked to the Taipings: the Bible that introduced Hong to Christianity had been partly translated by him. Furthermore, Gützlaff had encouraged and financially supported Rev. Issachar Jacox Roberts, who later joined the Taiping rebels in propagating their gospel. Roberts was not their only Western supporter; many missionaries initially supported the Taipings, glimpsing within their movement the potential for a revolutionary advance of Christianity in China. But as the insurrection grew in size and scope, Roberts and other missionaries soon realized that a "wide gap" stood between the Taiping beliefs and the Christianity that the missionaries considered orthodox.[23]

Despite their humiliation during the Taiping Rebellion, Western missionaries soon found a new opportunity to increase their presence in China. Dissatisfied with the gains they had received from the First Opium War treaties, the British found a pretext to declare war when Qing officials arrested crewmembers aboard a British-registered ship that they suspected of engaging in smuggling and piracy.[24] The same year, a French missionary, Auguste Chapdelaine, was executed for illegally entering Guangxi Province. Citing these incidents, the French also declared war on the Qing. Faced with internal and external threats, the Chinese were unable to withstand the attacks of the French and the British. The treaties of the Second Opium War, signed in Tianjin in 1858 and Beijing in 1860, opened China further to Christianity. It allowed Chinese Christians the right to practice their faith, and Catholic and Protestant missionaries could now preach and spread the gospel in the Chinese interior, as long as they obtained special passports. The new treaties laid the foundation for the creation of the French Religious Protectorate. The French claimed that their passports now offered better protections and access to the Chinese interior. After the 1860s, all Catholic missionaries applied for French passports, identifying themselves as "French" regardless of their country of origin. As Ernest Young writes, "For the non-French, the anomaly was said to be worth it for the extra efficacy that went with the document and for the implied promise of official French backup when needed."[25]

Now with access to inland China, European missionaries flooded into the country. Between 1860 and 1899, the number of foreign Catholic missionary priests quadrupled from two hundred to about nine hundred, and the number of Protestant missionaries increased almost twentyfold, from about one hundred Protestant missionaries in 1860 to two thousand by the end of the nineteenth century. In terms of conversions, missionaries counted around seven hundred thousand Chinese Catholics in 1899, while Protestants reported more than one hundred thousand.[26]

The rapid growth of Christianity after 1860 spawned a widespread backlash among the Chinese. Christianity posed myriad political, social, and ideological challenges to the power structures of the Chinese elite, and Confucian intellectuals fought back. Local gentry and officials incited violence and printed anti-Christian tracts that soon proliferated throughout the country.[27] Rumors that Catholic sisters kidnapped and sacrificed Chinese children abounded among popular and elite circles, and many Chinese feared the specter of the foreign religion. The most spectacular case of anti-Christian violence, known as the Tianjin Massacre, occurred in 1870 when an angry Chinese crowd killed twenty-one foreigners. Conflicts that involved Christianity—not only foreign missionaries were targeted, but

Chinese Christians as well—were widely referred to as *jiao'an* (missionary cases). Such cases increased each year from 1860 to 1899; the scholar Chen Yinkun offers a conservative estimate of almost sixteen *jiao'an* a year.[28]

Violence against Christianity appeared not just in China, but also across the world. As Diarmaid MacCulloch notes, between the 1850s and 1870s Western imperialist expansion had engendered fierce and varied responses. From missionaries who were killed in the Sepoy Rebellion in India to the Xhosa in South Africa who slaughtered their own cattle to the *ee ja nai ka* carnivals in Japan during which participants danced in support of a threatened and waning Tokugawa regime, indigenous populations protested, and in some cases, violently resisted Western expansion into their territories. Linking Christian expansion with imperialist encroachment, indigenous resistance movements often targeted and attacked missionaries and converts.[29]

The most spectacular assaults on Christianity garnered attention in the European media: reports of violence against missionaries spread in the Catholic, Protestant, and also secular journalistic organs. Such attacks did not dampen missionary optimism, however. Instead, Catholic and Protestant missionaries celebrated the martyrdom of their colleagues, believing that their sacrifices were necessary to pave a path for Christianity's eventual global triumph.[30]

Still, the widespread anti-Christian violence proved effective in one sense: it provoked reflection within missionary circles. Mission leaders concluded—more publicly than before—that foreign rejection of Christianity was the fault of the missionaries themselves. Between the 1860s and 1870s, Protestant and Catholic mission leaders examined critically their missionary practices and strategies and instituted wide-ranging reforms. Missionaries revamped the institutional makeup of their societies and altered their tactics.

INSTITUTIONAL REFORM

The worldwide anti-Christian violence stimulated responses that were global in scope. Throughout the late nineteenth century, Protestant and Catholic missionaries gathered at respective international missionary conferences to take stock of the state of missionary work. They never held conferences together. Rather, each used its conferences to formulate strategies to gain a competitive edge over its confessional rival. But Protestants and Catholics did agree on a basic idea: intraconfessional disunity—disagreements between individual Protestant denominations and Catholic religious orders—had contributed to Christianity's failures. Only through regular discussion and coordination could their form of Christianity gain further ground abroad.

Within the Catholic world, special sessions concurrent with the First Vatican Council in 1869 and 1870 were dedicated to missionary issues. British and American Protestant missionary societies began meeting in New York and London in 1854. Subsequent conferences were held in Liverpool in 1860 and in London in 1878. The largest general missionary conference was held in 1888 in London: 1,579 missionaries from 139 societies throughout Britain and continental Europe attended.[31] Large international conferences continued into the early twentieth century, with the Ecumenical Missionary Conference in New York in 1900 and the World Missionary Conference at Edinburgh in 1910.

Regional conferences abounded. Starting in 1866, Friedrich Fabri founded the Continental Missionary Conference in Bremen, which delegates from France, Holland, Denmark, Sweden, Norway, and all of the German missionary societies attended.[32] German Protestants further organized provincial missionary conferences in Saxon-Anhalt, Brandenburg, Braunschweig, Silesia, Bavaria, Pomerania, and Thuringia. Britain also witnessed a spate of missionary congresses. In the 1890s alone, British missionary societies organized meetings in 1892, 1895, 1899, and 1898. The conference reports had a broad circulation among the fascinated British public.[33]

Conferences took place not just in Europe, but in the field as well. In Shanghai, Protestant missionaries held conferences for all American and European missionary societies in China in 1877, 1890, and 1907. They held regional meetings more frequently. For example, Protestant missionaries in Shandong met every five years.[34] Similarly, Catholic missionaries met at regional assemblies since the Synod of Sichuan in 1803, the first time that Chinese and European priests convened in one place. In 1880, Pope Leo XIII and the Propaganda Fide divided China into five missionary regions, and missionaries were expected to attend the regional synodal meetings.[35]

Missionaries had numerous venues—at the regional, national, and international levels—to reflect upon their progress. Most were unsparing.

The editors of the London Missionary Conference Report of 1888 wrote that there was "no desire on the part of any [of the missionaries at the assembly] to conceal failures where these had taken place." The mission-aries acknowledged, as the editors wrote, that "the limited number of conversions up to the present time" had disappointed them.[36] Missionary work was harder than they had expected.

How did missionaries explain the foreign rejection of Christianity? Christ's gospel remained the key to salvation, and most missionaries did not seek to alter their message doctrinally. Instead, many blamed the slow rate of conversion on missionary conduct. Missionary leaders acknowl-edged that the work was difficult and put a tremendous amount of strain on the laborers in the field—they were far from home, in an unfamiliar land, and often faced a hostile audience. But precisely because the stakes were so high, missionary leaders argued that the missionaries should exhibit almost perfect behavior when abroad. Reports of unscrupulous missionary behavior—short tempers, physical abuse of indigenous clergy, missionaries returning to their compounds at odd hours—disturbed leaders in Europe. In 1858, one missionary leader commented, "We need humble, quiet, and persevering men, with some natural apti-tude to acquire a foreign language, and above all, men of yielding tempers, who live near to God, and are willing to labor under the most trying and perplexing discouragements." Up until that point, he noted, missionary societies had failed to attract the best talent, and in the future, they needed to find better workers.[37]

More importantly, European leaders feared that missionaries would lose their zeal for Christianity once they encountered difficulties abroad. It was essential that the Europeans maintain their enthusiasm for the gospel, lest they fail to set a good Christian example for the newly converted. At the 1877 Shanghai conference, one American Protestant exhorted the others: "Much must depend on ourselves . . . we ourselves must seek the baptism of fire and be filled with the Spirit. We cannot reasonably expect [the converts] to rise above ourselves. Some of us seem to wonder that the Chinese Christians are so slow to rise to a high standard of Christian excel-lence, though perhaps conscious of a terrible void in our own spiritual life. Let us be what we wish them to be, and they will spontaneously catch the inspiration; for there is something contagious about the life of God as fully realized and powerfully expressed in the life of man."[38] Many missionary leaders were aware that their workers in the field did not set good examples of Christian piety and devotion for Chinese Christians, and they blamed missionaries for failing to serve as good examples.

At conferences they proposed regulations on how missionaries should behave, particularly with regard to treating converts. As early as the 1803 synod in Sichuan, the Catholic missionary bishops issued a series of guidelines regulating missionary conduct. Missionaries were charged to treat their converts with "love and patience." They faced severe "ecclesiastical punishment" if they doled out corporal punishment, "even a slap to the face." Male missionaries having private conversations with women, other than during confession, was strictly forbidden. The regulations emphasized that missionaries honor their oath of poverty—"they have to live frugally, and wear clean and decent clothes." They were also discouraged from showing preferential treatment to the rich.[39]

Missionary leaders did not blame just missionaries; they faulted their own lack of leadership as well. They acknowledged that they had not prepared missionaries to deal with the challenges from abroad. Missionary training was haphazard and improvisatory. Missionaries sent to China received little language training in Europe, learning most of their Chinese upon arrival in the country. When they arrived in the field, they found understaffed mission stations, leading many to feel that the missionary societies at home had abandoned them. Other than the physical danger of entering areas that were hostile to Christianity, tropical and parasitical diseases were widespread. Missionary leaders were conscious that they had not established any infrastructure to deal with individual medical problems.[40]

Psychic burdens were just as destructive as physical ones. Emotional breakdowns were common, as missionaries suffered from loneliness and homesickness. Commenting on the difficult lives that Catholic missionaries led, the Jesuit Bertram Wolferstan remarked: "These poor men submit to many privations and dangers for the cause they have espoused. . . . European customs, habits, and luxuries, are all abandoned from the moment they put their feet on the shores of China; parents, friends, home, in many instances are heard of no more; before them lies a land of strangers, cold and unconcerned about the religion for which they have sacrificed everything; and they know that their graves will be far away from the land of their birth and the home of their early years."[41]

Because of the physical and psychological stresses that missionaries had to endure, high attrition rates were common. The scholar Jessie Lutz estimates that among Protestant missionaries, well over half of the men and close to the two-thirds of the women spent less than ten years in China, either dying in the field or returning to Europe because of illness.[42]

Faced with the loss of such numbers in the field, missionary societies sought to reform their practices. They held conferences that addressed how to deal with health problems ranging from common tropical illness—typhus and dysentery, for instance—to more rare diseases. They also established medical missions that created temporary hospitals to attract converts but also provide care for missionaries and their families. Some societies, like the BMS, sought to minimize the incidence of disease by building larger missionary compounds in areas with more temperate climates. Because of this greater attention to missionaries' health and well-being, attrition started to decline during the 1890s.[43]

Missionary leaders in Europe also sought to regulate missionary actions in the field. Ever since the seventeenth century the Propaganda Fide had tried to assert its authority over the various Catholic missionary societies. At the 1803 synod in Sichuan, the apostolic vicar of Sichuan, Gabriel Taurin Dufresse, mandated that missionaries write annual reports to their superiors. The reports were then collected, a summary was written, and the reports were circulated to other missionaries in the field, as a way for missionaries to learn from one another and keep informed about missionary advances elsewhere. Yet individual missionary societies, such as the Jesuits, resented the Propaganda Fide's desire to micromanage and resisted the Vatican's attempts to institute controls over their work. Depending on the missionary society, relationships between the Vatican and the missionaries in the field remained fraught throughout the nineteenth century.[44]

Similarly, Protestant missionary leaders in Europe wanted to subject their missionary subordinates to more institutional supervision. Fearing individual missionaries who "went rogue," missionary societies began to demand more institutional methods of control starting in the 1860s. The BMS was a fairly typical case of an organization that instituted a more stringent internal hierarchy. During the first few decades of the society's existence, Berliner missionaries operated independently of the home leadership. In fact, the leaders in Berlin encouraged missionary autonomy. Citing Pietist egalitarian principles, the board of directors believed that as fellow brothers, missionaries should be granted the freedom to act on their own initiative abroad. Yet the home board came to disdain missionary independence in the field. Reports of "unruly" missionary behavior shocked the German home office. One missionary leader reported, with horror, that a missionary in the field was caught returning home at "irregular hours," and the home office viewed with disdain the frequent personal clashes and rivalries among individual missionaries.[45]

The BMS leaders achieved the goal of centralizing power by establishing new bureaucratic controls. In 1866, they implemented a new Missionary Constitution (*Missionsordnung*), which reshaped the society's institutional hierarchy. The main architect behind the *Missionsordnung* was Hermann Wangemann. His political and social consciousness forged by the 1848 revolutions, Wangemann was known for possessing authoritarian tendencies.[46]

Wangemann's *Missionsordnung* established a clear chain of command, starting with the director at the top. The language of the constitution designated the director as a paternal figure, a "fatherly and spiritual advisor," who oversaw his "children"—the missionaries in the field. Wangemann conceived of the director as an active presence in missionary life. To gain a clear view of work in the field, the director was now required to travel abroad and inspect missionary progress personally. Wangemann himself journeyed twice to Berlin mission stations in Africa, and he published reports that circulated among supporters of his society.[47]

Besides strengthening the power of the director, the *Missionsordnung* also created a new group of regional mission inspectors, who were expected to act as intermediaries between the missionaries in the field and the home board as well as directly supervise the individual missionaries in the field. Before appealing to the home board with any problems they encountered, missionaries had to first consult with their supervising missionary inspector. Inspectors read and summarized individual missionary reports, made quarterly examinations of the conditions of missionary stations, and communicated with the leadership board at home about concerns that arose in the field.[48]

The *Missionsordnung* also defined individual missionary responsibilities more clearly. The missionary leadership now tasked individuals with giving a regular accounting of their activities to the home leadership. An important aspect of the missionary's daily responsibility was to keep a journal, write reports, and fill out statistical tables. In particular, missionary leaders were fixated upon documenting their "wins" and "losses." The BMS published many missionary reports in monthly and annual newsletters. Newsletters, including complete tables of the statistics, were then circulated to the local auxiliary societies, providing another layer of accountability. At first, missionaries in the field resisted these new tasks, but as a new generation was trained, resistance waned.[49]

In the field, missionaries wore multiple hats. Their primary function was to preside over church services, administer the church sacraments, and preach the gospel. But the *Missionsordnung* also listed other occupations that missionaries were expected to master, including "explorer, itinerant preacher, linguist, writer, doctor, nurse, arbitrator."[50] In particular, missionaries had to build schools and teach in them. Especially after the Shanghai Missionary Conference in 1877, missionaries in China recognized that they needed to devote effort to more educational work. The Berlin missionaries were no exception. When they initiated their mission work in Guangdong in 1882, they immediately took over schools and educational work that the Berlin Missionary Association for China had started fifty years earlier.[51]

To prepare missionaries for such a dizzying array of duties, the BMS broadened the training that individuals received. In total, Berlin missionaries spent eight years in training before ordination. Educated as generalists, they were expected to acquire knowledge in a wide range of subjects, including English, theology, and musical training. They also studied secular subjects—geography, world history, and natural sciences—and received training in industrial labor. In their fifth or sixth year, the candidates took an oral exam, requiring them to preach and offer exegeses of a range of biblical texts. After finishing their exams, they spent six months as interns in hospitals or universities. Once they received their missionary posting, they spent another year and a half studying local dialects and languages. To be officially ordained, they were required to pass a final oral and written exam, administered in the local languages that the missionary was required to know.[52]

As part of the attempt to require more stringent qualifications for ordination, language study became a more central part of missionary training. The lack of language instruction was widely known across European missionary circles. As early as the 1860s, societies had pushed for more rigorous language instruction. While official institutions of Chinese language study had existed since the first chair of Chinese literature was founded at the Collège de France in 1814, most missionaries to China were either autodidacts or received private language lessons from others who had traveled there.[53] One missionary in India, C. B. Leupolt, lamented that he had been too old to learn Hindi when he arrived in the country and suggested that all missionaries arrive there before the age of twenty-five. He wrote: "Every missionary committee should make a law, as inflexible as the laws of the Medes and Persians ever were, that no missionary going to a new sphere of labor should have anything to do with English for a year and a half, even though he be appointed a teacher to one of the English colleges. He should be requested to spend his first year and a half entirely in studying the language of the new scene of his efforts; and if he does not acquire the language in that year and a half, he will never learn it at all."[54]

Yet language instruction remained haphazard. The field of European Sinology was still in its infancy, and it took time to establish language institutes. Even by the 1880s, missionaries had few formal institutes where they could enroll to receive language training. The SVD Catholic missionaries Josef Freinademetz and Johann Baptist von Anzer, for instance, studied Chinese for only a week before leaving for China in 1879. Their training was informal; they received private lessons from a missionary who had recently returned to the Netherlands. Similarly, the Berlin missionary Carl Johannes Voskamp learned Chinese in part from private tutors on the ship during his voyage to China in 1884 (see map 2). He found the tones especially hard to master. Trying to say the sentence "Jacob was very rich," Voskamp felt chagrined when his teachers informed him that instead he had said, "Jacob had a large bump on his face."[55]

AN INDIGENOUS CLERGY?

Other than lackluster missionary training, European missionaries pointed to another reason for Christianity's slow growth: the paucity of indigenous clergy. Questions of "native clergy" and how to train more of them were passionately debated at missionary conferences and persisted through the nineteenth century. As early as 1803, at the synod in Sichuan,

Catholic bishops raised the issue of establishing a Chinese clerical hierarchy. It remained a central concern at the 1851 conference in Shanghai
and later at regional conferences in 1880.[56] Among Protestants, Gützlaff's
Chinese Union had presented a template for the future of an independent
Chinese clergy in China. His controversial precedent provoked vigorous
discussion on the "indigenous question" among the Protestant missionary
community in China. At the General Conference for Protestant
Missionaries in Shanghai in 1877, six different sessions were devoted to
the subject of local clergy—by far the most widely addressed topic at the
conference. Similarly, questions related to indigenization and indigenous
clergy dominated the agenda at the 1890 Protestant General Conference
in Shanghai.[57]

A broad consensus emerged around the question of indigenous
clergy: all missionaries, Protestant and Catholic, agreed that the development of more non-European priests and pastors was crucial for
Christianity's prospects in China. The Franciscan apostolic vicar of Hubei,
Eustachio Vito Modesto Zanoli, wrote, "the future of the mission in China
depends wholly upon the development of a large number of native
clergy."[58] The advantages of Chinese clergy were self-evident. For one, the
existence of more Chinese pastors and priests could quell anti-Christian
sentiment, blunting accusations that Christianity was a force of imperialism. Other missionaries supported a more rapid development of indigenous clergy for strategic and practical reasons: countries like China and
India were too big for European missionaries to tackle alone. Missionaries
knew that they needed to rely on local help.

But they disagreed on how to put these ideas into practice. What
should an indigenous church look like? How would the missionaries
know when to turn over control to indigenous clergy? The missionary
administrators Henry Venn, a member of the British Church Missionary
Society, and Rufus Anderson, from the American Board of Commissioners
for Foreign Missions, became two of the most influential leaders to offer a
vision for the future of the indigenous church. In articles published
throughout the 1860s, they suggested three criteria for ascertaining
whether an indigenous church was "mature" enough for independence.
First, indigenous congregations had to be "self-supporting": indigenous
clergy needed to achieve financial independence from the Western
missionaries. Second, churches needed to be "self-governing," that is,

leadership should come from indigenous clerical leaders. Finally, churches had to be "self-propagating," meaning that indigenous converts would no longer just passively listen to or receive the gospel but would become missionaries themselves and in turn spawn new congregations. Venn and Anderson's "Three-Self formula"—self-supporting, self-governing, and self-propagating—became a popular mantra that missionaries invoked to measure the progress of individual congregations and missions as a whole.[59]

Yet Venn and Anderson's proposal for establishing a "Three-Self" church was only one idea among many, and missionaries clashed at the various conferences over how they envisioned indigenous church growth. Some missionaries followed Gützlaff's model and wanted faster independence for indigenous churches, but others argued for a more cautious, gradual approach. They believed that indigenous converts were not ready—or spiritually "mature" enough—for independent church governance. Both sides invoked the Three-Self formula to support their own arguments.

Clerical education was a constant concern. Few could agree on how to train indigenous clergy, and missionaries quarreled over the methods and the content of indigenous clerical education. At the 1851 conference for Catholic missionary bishops in Shanghai, the Vatican and the apostolic vicars in China argued over the seminary curriculum for Chinese priests. The Vatican, wanting a more rapid development of priests, requested a shorter formation period for older men and widowers who had found their calling late in life. But the bishops rejected this idea, arguing that less educated priests "possessed no prestige in China." Further debate arose over whether missionary leaders should send talented Chinese catechists to Rome and whether they should be allowed to study at secular Chinese schools. The missionary bishops rejected both proposals: they thought that the Chinese catechists, still young in the faith, needed to be insulated from the temptations of the secular world. The young converts, the bishops believed, were particularly susceptible to a range of "European vices" in Rome. Advising caution, they suggested to the Vatican that it could afford to take a longer time to develop indigenous clergy. Quality over quantity was the gist of their message.[60]

Protestants also understood the tension between the need for more clergy and the "quality" of faith. Evangelism was labor intensive.

Missionaries needed not just pastors, but street evangelists, teachers in missionary schools, and Bible peddlers. The easiest, and most common, way to recruit more workers in the field was to pay Chinese assistants for their work. Yet such monetary compensation was controversial. Paid employment might, it was feared, create insincere faith—hence the epithet "rice Christians"—and a dependence on Western funds. "A church that is held together by no stronger bond than a mutual dependence upon foreign silver may reasonably be expected to speedily disintegrate, and become defunct, when once the flow of the silver stream is checked," one missionary argued.[61] Others defended the system of payment, suggesting that it was a necessary evil.

In reality, paying Chinese workers was more cost-effective. One missionary calculated that the amount of money it took to train and send one foreign missionary equaled the payment of more than a dozen Chinese assistants, who could do the same work of distributing tracts and preaching in rural areas. Employing Chinese assistants also had extra benefits: compared with the foreign missionary, who had to adjust to and learn a new landscape, the Chinese were familiar with the customs and the locales of their own country.[62]

Discussions of compensation pointed to another deep-seated problem: relations between the foreign missionaries and their indigenous "helpers." The unequal power relations between the missionaries and their Chinese laborers made some missionaries uncomfortable. They acknowledged the potential for abuse of position. "We should be careful," one missionary cautioned at the 1877 Protestant missionary conference in Shanghai, "not to force our own views on the Chinese, but state clearly and calmly the reasons for them." He argued for a more equal and open relationship between the missionaries and the Chinese. Any decisions that the church made in relation to Chinese customs—such as bans on opium use or footbinding—must coalesce with "the convictions of the native church."[63]

A small number of missionaries went even further, arguing that Western missionaries should take traditional Chinese culture and Confucianism seriously. Missionary-scholars like James Legge and Young J. Allen began to engage earnestly with Confucian ideas. Both had begun their careers as evangelists, but they gradually turned toward a more sustained literary engagement with Chinese tradition. Legge became the preeminent translator of the Confucian classics into English and was appointed the first professor of Chinese studies at Oxford University in 1876. Toward the end of his life, he began to argue for the compatibility between Christian and Confucian ideas and shocked the missionary field when he insisted that Christianity be placed within a broader comparative context.[64]

Most missionaries, however, recoiled at Legge's liberal approach to missionary work—pejoratively referring to it as "Leggism"—and refused to concede that Christianity could learn from Confucianism. They rejected proposals to reform the missionary society on the basis of an egalitarian standing between missionaries and their indigenous assistants, insisting that Europeans commanded moral and spiritual authority over indigenous clergy and converts. At the conference for missionary bishops in China held concurrently with the First Vatican Council, the apostolic vicars asserted that Chinese priests needed to remain under the control and direction of European priests.[65] Protestant missionaries shared similar sentiments. At the international missionary conference held in Liverpool in 1860, one British Protestant missionary justified the subordinate position of the Chinese thus: "The superiority of the European over the native arises from many considerations. It arises partly from his being a European; also from his energy of character, his superior knowledge; and especially from his being, as a missionary, the source whence knowledge of the doctrine and life of Christianity, the new religion which has displaced the old, is to be derived."[66]

Such comments reveal some of the underlying assumptions that operated among missionary circles. The scholar W. R. Hogg argues that a "Kiplingesque," "patronizing attitude" characterized Protestant missionary gatherings. Most missionaries believed that they were tasked with a "white man's burden" to civilize the natives. The majority of Western missionaries in the nineteenth century pushed for the "Europeanization" of the cultures they encountered, calling for their destruction. As vibrant as their vision of indigenous churches may have been, the missionaries assumed they would continue to dictate the church's future development. Even Venn and Anderson assumed the superiority of the West in their formulation of the Three-Self church.[67]

Such condescension to other cultures was generated partly by racial chauvinism. Racial stereotypes regarding the Chinese suffused nineteenth-century missionary writings. As the literary scholar Lydia Liu has noted, "avarice, cowardice and callousness are staple categories of a long-standing missionary discourse about Chinese character that need not surprise the reader."[68] The archbishop of Turin, Cardinal Gaetano Alimonda (1818–1891), represented many in the missionary community when he wrote in a summary of the 1880 synodal reports: "The Chinese priests are like the people amongst whom they were born. They are fickle, lazy, ambitious, vain, cunning, hypocrites, liars, ungrateful, extremely greedy for money, easily rebellious and with regard to chastity extremely weak."[69]

Immersed in these racial discourses, missionaries doubted the veracity of Chinese Christian faith. They invented ways to measure the integrity of Chinese Christian belief and eliminate "rice Christians." They instituted controls over everyday practices, enforcing regimens that they believed would root out inauthenticity. They decided what food converts ate; they monitored bodily hygiene; and they regulated books converts read. As the scholar of Chinese religion Eric Reinders has noted, Christian missionaries throughout the nineteenth and early twentieth centuries forced Christian converts to eat meat, attacking vegetarianism as a marker of Buddhism. "The constant doubts about the sincerity of would-be converts," Reinders argues, "generated a whole hermeneutics of suspicion applied to Chinese converts by Western missionaries." Missionaries feared that new converts would quickly revert to their previous ways: without a broader Christian culture to insulate them, Chinese Christians were subjected to a constant barrage of threats and temptations from the traditional Chinese culture that surrounded them.[70]

To strengthen the faith of converts, missionary societies established regulations specifically addressing the behavior of new believers. In 1886, the SVD missionary Josef Freinademetz issued the order's *Guidelines for Catechists* (*Chuanjiao yaogui*), modeled on the regulations for missionaries from the 1803 synod in Sichuan. The *Guidelines* reveal the SVD's outlook toward its Chinese Christian assistants. In the document, the Europeans are designated as moral and spiritual superiors: they are the "shepherds" who possess a duty to save the lost Chinese. However, Europeans could not "purify" all Chinese; they needed Chinese who could "courageously cooperate" with the Europeans in their work.[71]

The *Guidelines* also reflect the SVD fear of insincere conversion. Freinademetz exhorted the Chinese catechists not to focus on their worldly, "base" desires. To tame these impulses, the SVD missionaries demanded bodily discipline—the *Guidelines* restricted both the clothing and the diet of the Chinese workers. The male catechist was prohibited from wearing "flashy clothes. Instead, he should wear simple, yet clean clothes. His diet should be frugal, not opulent nor extravagant. He should only drink spirits in moderation." The rules were more restrictive for women: female evangelists should wear only "demure" colors, either "navy blue or black, and never clothes made of silk, satin, or batiste." The regulations continued: "From head to toe, she should dress respectably and modestly. In Church she should conceal her face with a veil."[72]

Even though the rules were oppressive, they were also meant to protect the Chinese Christians from possible harassment or abuse. Freinademetz warned Chinese catechists that they should stay away from "bad people." Women were instructed to take a companion with them when they visited priests. Freinademetz also stipulated that women were permitted to meet with priests only at church. Those younger than thirty were required to work in a group. Coming from a society that observed a strict separation of the sexes, the *Guidelines* followed suit: they did not subvert social convention.

Yet in crucial instances, the rules were also emancipatory, empowering women to carry out the same tasks as men. The *Guidelines* authorized Chinese Virgins, an order of Catholic women who took a vow of celibacy and dedicated their lives to the church and mission work, to perform emergency baptisms in the case of serious illness. It allowed the women to teach the faith in the same capacities as male catechists. The missionaries recognized that the Chinese Virgins had played a crucial part in Christianity's survival in China, and they needed to rely on their work for Christianity's future growth.[73]

The *Guidelines* illuminate one of the central tensions that undergirded the missionary approach to the indigenous church. To satisfy their European audience, missionaries wanted a rapid growth of Christian conversion; a stunning statistical report could generate funding. But they also wanted to ensure that their converts possessed a sound understanding of Christian doctrine. They feared a repeat of the Taiping Rebellion, which they saw as evidence of the dangers of "weak" faith: the Taiping rebels had caused widespread death and destruction while claiming to be Christian. And so the debate continued throughout the nineteenth century: do we want faster growth or more "high quality" conversions? Few had solutions to ensure them both.

NATIONAL RIVALRIES

Other than debates surrounding the indigenous clergy, another controversial matter dominated missionary conferences: international cooperation. Recognizing the fractured nature of the missionary field, missionaries at the conferences sought to form unified policies. Yet, despite the explicit goal of forming a united front, national rivalries divided both Protestant and Catholic international meetings.

Among Catholics, imperial conflicts persisted between the Propaganda Fide and individual missionary societies, which possessed divergent national and imperial interests. In 1838, Pope Gregory XVI reorganized the missionary administration in China, hoping to centralize the various missionary areas under the control of the Propaganda Fide. But the entrenched interests were difficult to overcome, and the missionary landscape remained fragmented. As Ernest Young writes, "The divisions were not superficial but rather reflected radical contrasts in kind and serious factional infighting."[74] At the Shanghai conference of 1851, for example, the Catholic apostolic vicars, mostly French, argued for more autonomy from the Propaganda. Despite the Vatican's strong desire to centralize control, most religious orders and missionary societies worked as independent actors in the field. In many cases, missionary orders chose their own apostolic vicars; the Vatican's approval in those instances was merely a formality.[75]

Instead, another force emerged on the horizon, seeking to represent the voices of Catholic missionaries and Chinese converts: the French Religious Protectorate. The Sino-French Treaty of Tianjin of 1858 assured religious toleration for the Chinese throughout the empire, legalizing Christian missionary evangelization and granting missionaries the right to purchase and rent property in the country. For the ensuing decades, all Catholic missionaries who entered China applied for and received French passports. The French imperial presence and protection for Christian missionaries and converts raised tensions with local Chinese authorities. The Protectorate also exacerbated tensions with the Vatican, which yearned to speak for all Catholic missionaries. The Vatican saw the rise of the French Protectorate as a return to the Portuguese *padroado* system, which they had sought for so long to dismantle.[76]

In the Protestant missionary world, the dominance of the British Empire—and English-speaking missionaries in general—raised similar fears. Protestant missionary conferences, like their Catholic counterparts, were also divided by national rivalries, despite the rhetoric of promoting unity and cooperation. As W. R. Hogg notes, Anglo-American missionaries "assumed that everything important happening in missions was British or American in origin," and "there was almost complete failure to regard Continental missions as of any consequence."[77]

The Germans were particularly sensitive to these slights. William R. Hutchison writes that at the German Continental Missions Conference held in Bremen in 1866, German Protestant missionary leaders exhibited "a growing consciousness and concern about Anglo-American missionary methods and presuppositions."[78] After German unification in 1871, these concerns grew into an outright attack on American missionary methods. During the 1840s, German missionaries like Karl Gützlaff had to rely on British help. By the late nineteenth century, however, Germany's imperial reach expanded into Africa and Asia, and German missionaries believed they no longer needed their British competitors.

Within the German missionary establishment, the most vocal critic of Anglo-American missionary work was the missionary theologian Gustav Warneck. Warneck established his reputation in the 1870s as one of the leading theorists of global missions, devoting his energies to transforming the study of missions into an academic discipline. He viewed American and British missionaries with distaste; he thought of them as theologically juvenile and politically opportunist, describing them as "whimsical," "self-righteous," and "romantic will o' the wisps . . . more likely to confuse than to enlighten."[79]

The Anglo-Americans, on the other hand, dismissed Warneck as a crank. As William Hutchison has noted, American missionary leaders such as John Mott ignored Warneck's criticisms, seeing Warneck as "a somewhat isolated problem in public relations, not as the voice of a broad constituency or serious ideological alternative."[80] Snubs by the Anglo-American leaders further fueled the German sense of beleaguerment within international missionary circles.

To better coordinate a unified national direction for missionary work, German missionary leaders founded a nationwide federation, the German Protestant Missionary Committee (Deutscher Evangelischer

Missionsausschuß), in 1885. Warneck served as the committee's first chairman. Fourteen missionary societies—all of which brandished Pietist credentials—joined the committee, which was responsible for organizing annual mission conferences and forming unified policies for future missions work.[81]

The dominant personality behind the Missionsausschuß was Friedrich Fabri, director of the Rhenish Missionary Society. Fabri had made his mark on the question of colonies in 1879 when he published an influential political pamphlet, *Does Germany Need Colonies? (Bedarf Deutschland der Colonien?)*. In it, Fabri argued for the necessity of German commercial and colonial expansion. He further believed that missionaries had an essential part to play in spreading German civilization abroad. Under Fabri's direction, the Missionsausschuß staked out a pro-state outlook: its bylines stated explicitly that it would cooperate with the Reich and "provide to the Colonial Office all the information required by it on missionary issues." Fabri conceived of the Missionsausschuß as a way to better represent German missionary interests to the Reich. With a unified voice, German missionaries could better lobby imperial authorities to advance their interests.[82]

Yet members of the Missionsausschuß tried to temper Fabri's enthusiasm for European imperialism. Warneck, in particular, was openly critical of all colonial policies that he deemed harmful to the spread of Christianity abroad. The opium trade, he denounced, was "the evil odor in which the whole English nation has brought itself, [and] forms till this day a frightful counterweight against all the efforts of individuals to benefit the Chinese people." He disdained British colonialism in India, which contributed to high levels of "religious indifference," as well as "gross materialism and haughty socialism."[83]

At times, Warneck and others in the Missionsausschuß were critical of the actions of the German Empire. As Jeremy Best argues, "German Protestant missionaries, though socially and politically conservative, rebuked efforts to appropriate their evangelical and other activities in Germany's overseas colonies for empire-building purposes."[84] In the *Allgemeine Missions-Zeitschrift*, a journal that Warneck edited, missionaries criticized nationalist fervor as an impediment to their work abroad. They encouraged Germans to collaborate with other Protestant nations. The Missionsausschuß also used its political connections to challenge

German imperial policies that it thought hampered the progress of overseas missions. It tried, for example, to exempt missionaries from military service. Members of the Missionsausschuß protested the deportation of criminals to colonies, as well as German sponsorship of the alcohol trade in Africa.[85]

Not just the Germans found themselves in an awkward position with regards to the policies of European imperialism. During the late nineteenth century, British and American missionaries became increasingly vocal opponents of the opium trade, criticizing merchants and state officials who endorsed the business. British and American missionaries drew upon their extensive international network of missionary journals, conferences, and associational groups to mount a moral "crusade" against the opium trade in China. As Kathleen Lodwick writes, "More than any other group at the turn of the twentieth century, the Protestant missionaries in China truly understood the nature of opium addiction and had the courage to pursue their campaign against the drug until they finally convinced others of the correctness of their position."[86] In short, Protestant missionaries in the late nineteenth century represented some of the most critical voices of European empire.

Catholic missionaries similarly had to wrestle with a complicated relationship with the state. Juggling multiple loyalties, missionary societies like the SVD had to prove to the German Empire that they were willing subjects, while also showing their allegiance to the worldwide directives of the Vatican and the Propaganda Fide. The case of German Catholics was particularly fraught, given the anti-Catholic laws promulgated by Bismarck during the *Kulturkampf*. Even though German Catholics resisted Bismarck's laws at home, they trumpeted their nationalist loyalties when it came to German colonialism abroad. As Horst Gründer has noted, even within the Catholic Center Party, "a fundamental rejection of German colonial politics never existed."[87] The missionaries accepted support from the German imperial authorities when it benefited the society's expansion. In return, Catholic missionaries advanced the cultural and political aims of the German Empire.

In China, the friction between these allegiances came to a head when the Qing, the Vatican, the French Religious Protectorate, and the German Empire clashed in the late nineteenth century. For years, both the Qing Empire and the Vatican had wanted to curtail the French

Protectorate's influence in China, and both had attempted to circumvent the Protectorate by establishing direct diplomatic relations. The Qing and the Vatican had come close to an agreement in 1886, but the French Republic sent an ultimatum, threatening retaliation on Catholics in France. Feeling the pressure, Pope Leo XIII broke off talks with China. Nonetheless, they still hoped to find a solution to undercut French influence in China.[88]

Around the same time, the German Empire also expressed greater interest in using Catholic missionaries to carve out a sphere of influence in China. Up until that point, the government in Berlin had cared little for the well-being of the Catholic missionaries in China. During the Sino-French War of 1884–1885, the German government had adopted a neutral position, informing the missionaries that the empire would not extend assistance to them even if they needed it. Instead, they should turn to the Russians in times of need. However, the Sino-French treaty of 1885, which extended French dominance in the region, persuaded the German ambassador in China, Max von Brandt, to take a more proactive diplomatic stance. In 1888, following the lead of the Italians, Brandt petitioned the Qing to allow Germany to issue passports to all Germans, and the Chinese agreed. Now Brandt had to persuade the Catholic missionaries to accept German protection, which signaled a real disruption in the French Religious Protectorate's dominance. In 1888, Brandt courted the German SVD bishop Johann Baptist von Anzer, trying to sell him on the idea of choosing the German Protectorate over the French.[89]

Anzer felt torn. Being German did not mean, in any way, automatic loyalty. But he was certainly no fan of the French Protectorate. When he and Freinademetz had applied for travel passports from the French in 1882, the French had obstructed and delayed the authorization of the passes.[90] After Anzer arrived in China, for years he had expressed his dissatisfaction to the Chinese government over French inefficiency. But he also distrusted the German Empire's sudden expression of interest. Anzer understood that, for Brandt and the Foreign Office, his missionaries were pawns in an imperial game; if he refused the German proposal, he feared that the German authorities would retaliate by cutting off the SVD's access to German colonial holdings in Africa. Anzer also understood there was no proof that the Germans would be more effective in providing the missionaries with security than the French. Furthermore, the German agreement excluded Chinese Christians from legal protection, while the French Protectorate extended to Chinese converts. Last, he feared severing ties with the French and jeopardizing relations with the dominant Catholic power in the region. In a letter to the SVD superior general Janssen, Anzer wrote, "I sit between two envoys (the German and French) who love me and treat me both excellently, and we cannot afford to spoil relations with either."[91]

Conflicted, Anzer tried to deflect responsibility for the decision onto the Vatican. Harassing the prefect of the Propaganda Fide, Cardinal Giovanni Simeoni, through multiple telegrams and letters, he asked for guidance. But the Vatican also wanted to remain neutral. Simeoni and the pope pushed the decision back toward Anzer, ordering him to choose.[92]

After more waffling and attempts to extract more promises from Brandt, Anzer chose in favor of the German Protectorate in 1890. Ever the political operative, he tried to persuade the French that both the Germans and the Vatican had made the final call. In a letter to the French minister to China, Victor-Gabriel Lemaire, Anzer wrote, "Your Excellency knows very well that during my long stay in China, I have worked on behalf of the French Religion Protectorate, and in the past two years have resisted the repeated attempts to detach me from France."[93]

In the end, Anzer got his wish: he assuaged both the Germans and the French. Convinced by Anzer's letters, the French ambassador to the Vatican, Edouard Lefebvre de Béhaine, did not hold Anzer personally responsible and assumed that he ultimately had acceded to German pressure.[94] Meanwhile, in a trip to Germany in 1890, Anzer was celebrated by the German Empire for his "patriotic feat" of carving out a German Protectorate from the French. He earned private audiences with Kaiser Wilhelm II and King Albert of Saxony and received a Prussian decoration.[95] Politically savvy, Anzer manipulated the various national and international conflicts for his own agenda. Among other agreements, he made Brandt promise to offer physical protection to not only German missionaries, but also Chinese converts.

Besides an example of Anzer's personal deftness, the case of the German Protectorate also demonstrates the complicated positions that German Catholics negotiated in the late nineteenth century. For German Catholics like Anzer, loyalties were transient: at times they pronounced their commitment to the aims of the German Empire, and at other times they opposed them. Without a strong Vatican to protect German missionaries on the ground, German Catholics recognized the French as possibly the most effective agent for protecting Catholic interests in China. The *Kulturkampf* made German Catholics distrustful of the government in Berlin, and the German Empire's economic interests in Africa diminished its credibility. When the German government later repealed its promise to protect only German missionaries and not their converts, Anzer protested and sought to return to the French Protectorate.[96]

CONCLUSIONS: A GLOBAL HERMENEUTICS OF SUSPICION

Seeking to explain the slow growth of Christianity in China in the late nineteenth century, Chinese Protestant leaders in the 1920s pointed to the divided missionary landscape as the main culprit. They argued that in the last decades of the nineteenth century, national rivalries intensified as Western imperial ambitions in China grew. Even though missionaries called for a united Christian front in China, divergent national interests led them to work against each other. There is some truth to the claim of a missionary field fractured by nationalism. Catholic and Protestant missionaries often engaged in rivalries fueled by nationalist sentiment. Missionaries debated theology and trumpeted the superiority of their own national approaches. German Protestants called their American counterparts "naïve," while German Catholics wondered whether they should subvert the French Protectorate. But nationalism also did not always translate into conflict between missionaries. Catholic and Protestant missionary circles were abuzz with international dialogue. At conferences held around the world, missionaries from various nations discussed strategies, coordinated future plans, and sought to pool resources.

Naturally, such contact also fostered disagreement. Little consensus existed among missionaries on the question of evangelization methods. While most agreed that Christian conversions abroad were growing at too slow a pace, few could agree on a solution. Some, like Gützlaff, wanted to turn over control to local converts immediately. Others were wary of the rapid devolution of missionary power, remaining unconvinced that Chinese or African Christians were ready for independence from missionary control. Witnessing the rise of anti-Christian violence in the mid-nineteenth century, many missionaries held a deep suspicion toward native converts, and they introduced a series of checks and controls meant to ascertain the sincerity of faith.

Yet, I argue, missionaries and missionary theologians cast their "hermeneutics of suspicion" on non-Europeans and Europeans alike. Missionaries criticized secular Europeans with equal, if not more, venom as the "heathen" Chinese. The Chinese, they allowed, could not be blamed for inheriting two millennia of Confucian teaching. But the Western merchants and government officials who supported the opium trade were "un-Christian." No simple lackeys of empire, missionaries advanced trenchant criticisms of foreign encroachment in China. European opium dealers and state officials who tended to only national interests committed a far graver sin: they betrayed their Christian roots.

Gustav Warneck, for example, believed that the problem of "Christian overculture" in Europe was more pernicious than the lack of faith abroad. Warneck wrote that missionaries faced a "twofold cultural contest," which he defined as "a struggle against the heathenish unculture, and a struggle against the Christian overculture—and we suspect the latter is the more difficult." For Warneck, Christianity in Europe had become calcified, and Europeans needed to reexperience the transforming power of the Christian gospel. "Christian overculture," Warneck argued, meant that secular Europeans had forgotten the radically egalitarian message in the Bible. Instead, Westerners carried their racial chauvinism abroad, failing to treat non-Europeans as "equal-born human beings."[97]

Even missionaries, Warneck argued, had fallen into the trap of equating Christianity with Western civilization. Having been raised in the West, missionaries had presumed the superiority of their cultural forms. Too many missionaries assumed that spreading the gospel meant replicating European schools, hospitals, "social order, and a certain correctness of morals and manners." They wanted to mold converts into replicas of European piety. "And just so we must recognize," Warneck intoned, "the identification of Christianization and civilization as an evil for the mission of the present day." He continued, "We need among the missionaries men of the originality and large-heartedness of a Paul, who, with their personal life of faith firmly rooted in the central truths of the Gospel, shall know how to distinguish with Christian tact the essence of Christianity from those adjuncts which have grown with it among us through our cultural development, but yet not essential to it, and who shall understand to strike out original ways among people and circumstances entirely different from ours."[98] Warneck exhorted missionaries to be constantly vigilant: they had to be careful that they did not mistake their assumptions of cultural superiority for the message of the gospel. It was up to Christian missionaries, Warneck concluded, to "atone for" and "neutralize" the pernicious influences that Western civilization had brought to the non-West.[99]

Warneck's self-critical pronouncements reflect the contradictory nature of the nineteenth-century missionary enterprise. On the one hand, nineteenth-century missionary writings brimmed with triumph and optimism about European culture. Even a self-critical missionary like Warneck was convinced of the cultural and racial superiority of the West; he called Western civilization a "higher culture" in comparison to the uncivilized "natives." Plentiful statements of European racial and cultural superiority accompanied missionary pronouncements, which evinced a confidence that they were saving their converts from the clutches of a savage civilization.[100]

But missionary assertions of European superiority were also tempered by cultural self-critique. Partly, missionaries were responding to the widespread anti-Christian movements that swept throughout the world during the second half of the nineteenth century and revealed the possible limitations of their gospel. These violent outbursts—coupled with disappointing numbers of conversions—spurred missionaries to confront themselves. Even during the height of European imperial conquest in the nineteenth century, missionaries were reflecting on their own failures.

Scholars of the nineteenth-century missionary movement have seen the missionary belief in their own cultural superiority as a reflection of imperial arrogance.[101] Yet when the missionary responses to failure are examined, the global missionary scene suddenly looks more dialogic, more open, and more receptive to change than the previous historiography allows. Failure, in this respect, was generative: it bound the missionary movement together, laying the seeds for future ecumenical cooperation. It also helped to form new ways of thinking, new academic disciplines, and new channels of interdenominational communication.

The experience with failure also pushed missionaries to start thinking more deeply about their relationship to other religions and cultures. Jeffrey Cox has referred to "the 'double-vision' of missionary rhetoric," where missionaries "simultaneously defamed and praised" other religions and cultures.[102] In China, despite a general attitude of suspicion toward Confucianism and traditional Chinese culture, missionaries began to reorganize their institutional hierarchies and create more opportunities for Chinese Christian leadership.

CHAPTER THREE

Missionary Optimism

IN 1898, THREE VISIONS of modernity competed for China's future. The first came in the form of European colonialism. A treaty in March established a German leasehold (*Schutzgebiet*), making it the first European colony on China's mainland. The duration of the treaty was set to last ninety-nine years. The German navy sent troops to the village of Qingdao, situated around Jiaozhou Bay in Shandong, with the goal of transforming it into a European metropolis; the Germans built sewers, piers, wide streets, churches, and colonial palaces. The German action sparked an era of "New Imperialism" in China. Soon the Russians, the British, and the French all followed suit, hoping to expand their spheres of influence beyond the coasts and farther inland. For European imperialists, China could be awoken from its slumber, its potential unlocked, if it became more "Western."[1]

A second vision of modernity came from Chinese intellectuals, who hoped to transform the Qing Empire into a modern nation-state. Still reeling from the defeat in the Sino-Japanese War of 1895, Chinese intellectuals saw the German occupation as the last straw in China's humiliating nineteenth century. In the summer of 1898, the young Guangxu emperor, with the help of intellectuals like Kang Youwei and Liang Qichao, attempted to enact a series of reforms. As Peter Zarrow writes, "The reform movement engaged in a creative appropriation, based on limited knowledge of the West, of several notions that were seen as compatible with Chinese culture: the nation-state, mass citizenship, a constitutional monarchy and representative government (local self-government and national parliaments), and commercial development."[2] Kang and Liang, along with other reform-minded intellectuals, believed that China's political future depended on the fusion of what they deemed as useful Western ideas with Chinese ones. Other aspects of Western culture—essential Christian doctrines, for example—were rejected as incompatible with Chinese culture. The actual reform itself was a failure: it lasted only one hundred days before reactionary forces reasserted control, putting the emperor under house arrest while forcing Kang and Liang into exile. But the movement's effect on China's broader political culture was wide-ranging, as powerful alternatives to state orthodoxy had penetrated, even briefly, the highest echelons of political power: China could become "modern" by integrating Western ideas with traditional Confucian ideas and institutions.

But the most dramatic and unlikely vision of modernity was offered in the fall of 1898 by large bands of discontented religious sectarians, whose actions would trigger unprecedented transformations in the Chinese political and religious landscape. They called themselves the Boxers United in Righteousness (Yihe quan) and they thought that foreigners had angered the gods. The Boxers believed that they were spirit soldiers, entrusted with a divine mission of driving out foreigners. Drawing upon traditional religious practices, they were convinced that their rituals could render them invulnerable to Western weapons. They began to attack Christians in the name of protecting the Qing dynasty. For the Boxers, Chinese strength could be revitalized only by exorcising the foreign element from its midst.[3]

German missionary activity, particularly that of the Catholic SVD in Shandong, had helped to set in motion the dramatic events of 1898. Resentment toward the SVD had been building for years. Locals had grown tired of missionaries meddling in local lawsuits. Allegations of missionary crimes further escalated discontent toward the foreigners; for instance, oral histories collected later accused the missionary Georg Stenz of raping more than ten women.[4] In November 1897, about thirty men from a gang known as the Big Sword Society (Dadaohui) raided the SVD's mission station at Zhangjiazhuang in Juye County, just northeast of the city of Jining. During the attack, the band killed two SVD missionaries, Richard Henle and Franz Nies, and wounded Stenz. The incident gave Kaiser Wilhelm II, who had long had ambitions to expand Germany's naval presence in East Asia, pretext to act. Within days of the murders, German marines entered Jiaozhou Bay.

German colonial officers wanted to use missionaries for their project of building colonial modernity in China. A month before German and Chinese authorities had even signed the official lease treaty, the naval office invited the Berlin missionaries to help administer the new German-Chinese school in the leasehold and authorized them to build a missionary residence in Qingdao. The Berliners leaped at the opportunity. One mission inspector, who had argued that North China was too important a field "to leave alone to the Catholics," prompted the director to send north two of the most experienced workers in the society, Carl Johannes Voskamp and August Kollecker. The Berlin missionaries traveling to Qingdao wanted to ensure that Protestantism occupied a prominent place in the colonial space there.[5]

The Germans were not the only ones convinced of the public utility of religious belief; Chinese reformers argued that a renewed Confucianism could reorient a rudderless China. Kang Youwei, for example, hoped to establish a state-sanctioned national "Confucian church." An avid reader of Western missionary publications in Chinese, Kang took seriously the missionary idea that religion functioned as an integral element in state building. As Ya-pei Kuo notes: "Kang did not conceal the fact that his idea of a national religion was based on a foreign model. He made frequent references to Christianity and candidly acknowledged the Western source of his inspiration."[6] He was convinced that Confucianism offered superior moral and ethical teachings to those of Christianity, and the establishment of a Confucian church could revive China's flagging spirit. For Kang, the state could mobilize the religious spirit among the Chinese people for its own purposes.

The Boxers advanced yet another religious solution for China's salvation. Joseph Esherick has called the movement "an instance of mass shamanism" in response to the myriad social and ecological disasters that plagued Shandong during the 1890s.[7] Heavy downpours throughout the summer of 1898 caused the Yellow River to flood. More than thirty-four counties were affected in North China. Millions had to abandon their homes. Missionaries called the flood "MORE APPALLING AND DISASTROUS than any within living memory," and Western travelers reported areas in the countryside where the river was indistinguishable from fields. During the winter of 1898, a new set of problems plagued the region: drought. These natural catastrophes led directly to the rise of the Boxers. Idle farmers participated in the public rituals, setting up altars and performing prayers for rain. Through the Boxers' operatic dances, spirit possessions, and trances, Boxer allegiance spread quickly among the young, dispossessed, and marginal. These religious performances served as a balm that soothed a discontented populace, but also as a rallying cry for its mobilization.[8]

The Boxers spread rapidly throughout northern China. By the summer of 1900, they had surrounded the foreign legations in Beijing and began burning churches. Approximately 250 foreigners died, including a secretary of the Japanese legation and the German plenipotentiary Klemens von Ketteler. After fifty-six days, an international coalition of eight nations marched into Beijing, breaking the siege. The foreign troops brutally quashed the uprising.[9]

How did the defeat of the Boxers affect German missionary ideas? Did it push missionaries to rethink their antagonism toward Confucianism, and more broadly, traditional Chinese society, which had served to exacerbate the tensions with local Chinese society in the first place? In this chapter, I examine how, despite the cataclysm that the Boxer Uprising presented to the Chinese religious landscape, the defeat of the Boxers did not alter missionary ideology. Missionaries continued to profess their antagonism toward their Confucian enemies even after the Boxer defeat.

However, missionaries did alter their methods and practices. After the Boxer Uprising, the everyday interactions between missionaries and Chinese Christians began to change. Emboldened by a rapidly evolving cultural, political, and social context, Chinese Christians pushed for more responsibility in their congregations. And missionaries listened: they began to reorganize the institutional hierarchies of their churches and altered the approaches to their work. While missionary thinking about Chinese culture remained largely unaltered after the Boxer cataclysm, missionary practices slowly began to change. In order to trace these lines of continuity and discontinuity, I first examine the entrance of the BMS and the SVD into China, almost two decades before the Boxer unrest began.

THE EARLY YEARS OF THE SVD AND THE BMS

As late arrivers to China, both the SVD and BMS felt they had to catch up with their competitors, who all had decades of a head start on them when they entered China in the late 1870s. They faced another uphill battle: China was rife with xenophobic sentiment. In turn, the missionaries lacked the desire to ingratiate themselves. The SVD, in particular, was known for its brash and confrontational tactics. Johann Baptist von Anzer, one of the first two SVD missionaries sent to China, was not a man of understatement. Within three days of arriving in the village of Poli, in southern Shandong in January 1882, Anzer organized a two-week festival celebrating the Virgin Mary. Poli was one of the only villages with a preestablished Christian presence in the SVD's region of southern Shandong, and Anzer intended to use the festival to mobilize the Chinese Catholics who lived in the village and attract the attention of non-Christian villagers. As he preached in "imperfect" Chinese, local literati beseeched their fellow villagers to "ignore the European devil! He is only here to deceive us!"[10]

The hostility did not subside. During the SVD's early years, its missionaries confronted constant resistance from antimissionary and xenophobic forces. A few months after his arrival, Anzer was almost beaten to death by an angry mob. Anti-Christian tracts—labeling Christianity a "hateful sect of the devil" and calling for the expulsion of the "foreign devils"—permeated the countryside. Missionaries worried about the safety of their Chinese catechumens. "Anger against Christians knows no bounds," Anzer reported in 1883. "Our catechumens are constantly ridiculed and slandered, threatened with eviction from their homes, their homes are damaged, their religious books torn apart, and their bodies bloodied."[11]

Meanwhile, in the south, the Protestant BMS fared no better. BMS missionaries encountered similar instances of resistance when they established missionary stations in the southern province of Guangdong in 1883. Antiforeign organizations such as the Triads, as well as other unaffiliated robbers and bandits, frequently stormed missionary property. The Protestants were also convinced that the local Confucian bureaucracy sought to prevent missionary expansion. When the BMS tried to purchase the house of a Chinese merchant in Huizhou, Guangdong, as a base for its missionary work there, the local prefecture vehemently protested the sale, arguing that Christian chapels should not be allowed in such a central position in the city. The German missionaries noted that an atmosphere hostile to Christianity had penetrated all levels of society.[12]

The SVD and BMS, of course, were not the only missionary societies that encountered active resistance. Throughout the late nineteenth century, anti-Christian sentiment spread across China due to the rising number of *jiao'an*, referring to disputes between non-Christians and Christians. These "missionary cases" were often resolved only through threats of or, in some cases, active foreign intervention. Already burning with resentment toward the unequal treaties and the humiliation of China on the global stage, local literati further incited anti-Christian sentiment. Not all of the anti-Christian violence that followed was motivated purely by xenophobia. The harassment that Christians experienced reflected age-old feuds, as opportunistic locals settled old scores in the name of patriotism.[13]

SVD missionaries intervened in *jiao'an*, often confronting local officials. The SVD missionary Josef Freinademetz reported one particularly dramatic instance that occurred in May 1889 in Cao County, located in the southwestern part of Shandong, which was filled with bandits and home to the Big Sword Society. A village of about ten families had recently converted to Christianity. The head of the village, a man named Xu, had further engaged in active evangelization throughout the county. News of the village's conversion and Xu's activities caused alarm in neighboring areas. Soon, accusations of Xu's evangelism reached the ears of the county magistrate, who subsequently brought him in for questioning. According to Freinademetz's reports, during the interrogation the "local mandarin" accused Xu of "welcoming the European devil into the village" and "spreading a bad religion." He commanded Xu to stop meeting with the foreigners and cease evangelizing. Xu refused and was subsequently sentenced to six hundred lashes, leaving him "unable to sit, lie down, or stand." He was then thrown in prison.[14]

Upon hearing news of the detention, Freinademetz rushed to the court to demand Xu's release. The official showed Freinademetz a paper signed by twenty-seven other village heads in the region denouncing Xu and accusing him of harboring members of an evil sect. Freinademetz soon realized that the magistrate had never heard of Christianity and did not know that Xu was a Christian; he had just assumed that Xu had participated in an evil sect. Freinademetz invoked the Tianjin Treaty of 1858 that protected Christians and gave missionaries extraterritorial rights.

The magistrate released Xu, and Freinademetz offered to accompany him home.[15]

Their troubles did not end there, however. Freinademetz returned to the inn where he was staying, but he soon found it surrounded by a "horde of young fellows, armed with bludgeons," who burst into the inn. They brought Freinademetz out into the courtyard and beat him. Freinademetz thought that it was "the last hour of my life." In his report, he wrote that he began to preach: "Even though you have treated me so inhumanely, and I do not know where such anger against me comes from, I feel not even the slightest resentment toward you in my heart. If you came to know the religion that I preach, you would show the same amount of enthusiasm for it as you have against it." Freinademetz claimed that he continued to preach for the next fifteen minutes, "bound prostrate on the ground, about the glories of Christianity." His preaching calmed the angry crowd, and they let him go.[16]

Freinademetz's retelling of the event, which was subsequently dramatized in the SVD's missionary journals, represents the general attitude that SVD missionaries held toward local Confucian officials and anti-Christian violence. They attributed Chinese hostility toward Christianity directly to the actions and, more perfidiously, inaction of Confucian officials. Missionaries from both the SVD and the BMS repeatedly lambasted local Confucian gentry for turning a blind eye and failing to uphold the imperial edicts that protected Chinese Christians and foreign missionaries from harm.[17]

Even further, missionaries accused Confucian officials of fanning the flames of anti-Christian and xenophobic sentiment. Local bureaucrats, one SVD missionary wrote, feeling threatened by the spread of Christianity through the region, had come under the influence of the "Prince of Darkness," who had "aroused an all-encompassing and violent storm" to stem the tide of the young church in China. The missionary invoked the devil's sin of arrogance as infecting the Chinese literati: "Just as Lucifer's first rebellion was the sin of pride, so he has used a proud class of scholars who refuse to yield to the gentle yoke of those with a childish, simple faith." Spurred by these dark forces, most Confucian scholars, the missionary claimed, had "sworn in pagodas in front of their idols, to resist the Christian doctrine to the death." The SVD missionaries believed that they were engaged in a cosmic battle with the devil, and the

Confucian bureaucrats were a manifestation of the evil that sought to destroy Christianity.[18]

While the BMS in the south was not as active in intervening in *jiao'an* as the SVD, it shared a similar critique of local Confucian officials. Like the Catholics, the German Protestants attributed the escalation of anti-Christian sentiment to the enduring vestiges of the Confucian order, which contributed to the rejection of Christianity. The missionary inspector Friedrich Leuschner wrote: "It is well known that the Chinese are the oldest cultured civilization in the world. . . . When our predecessors were still wrapped in bearskin and wandered through the humid forests of our country, they were already wearing fine silk clothing as they do now." Armed with this ancient culture, "the Chinese think that they know everything well. And as their nature is filled with self-conceit, they reject what we Europeans have to offer them out of pride." His colleague Carl Johannes Voskamp expressed a similar sentiment when he wrote, "the xenophobia of the Chinese is a result of their worldview, a combination of their religion and their patriotism. In the eyes of the Chinese, China is the Middle Kingdom, the center of the world."[19]

In response to their perceptions of Chinese arrogance, SVD and BMS missionaries showed mutual intolerance toward Confucianism and, more broadly, traditional Chinese culture. They were not alone in their condemnation of Chinese traditions. As the scholar George Steinmetz argues, the late nineteenth century witnessed a period of heightened "Sinophobia," which depicted the Chinese in increasingly racialized terms as a way to demote China from the ranks of advanced civilizations. Whereas China had once loomed far ahead of Europe, now European culture had surpassed that of the Chinese. Reports from the SVD and BMS supported these views. The SVD missionary Georg Stenz wrote that China was now stuck "in an earlier stage of civilization," as opposed to the modern and dynamic West. Similarly, the BMS missionary Leuschner wrote: "Now, the Occident possesses a higher culture. We have separated ourselves from the Chinese, just as a grown man has from a child." China now depended on Western, and more importantly, Christian guidance to enter a more modern age. Leuschner argued that "Christianity can demonstrate to them the foolishness and brutishness of their culture."[20]

The BMS and SVD explained the stagnation of Chinese civilization partly in cultural and racial terms. Stenz, for example, portrayed the

Chinese as pathological liars, suspicious, materialistic, unthankful, and lazy. "One can not find much good in the Chinese," he concluded. The BMS, on the other hand, advanced more positive diagnoses of the "essential Chinese character." Voskamp praised the Chinese as possessing "many talents, high intelligence, and a strong will to learn." But overall, BMS reports presented China as having succumbed to a degenerate culture. Missionaries focused their reports on practices such as footbinding, opium smoking, gambling, and polygamy. "Immoral behavior," missionaries argued, had led to the decline of a once powerful civilization.[21]

To the missionaries, religion, and by extension Christianity, was yet an even more important factor that contributed to the divergence between European and Chinese civilization. Missionaries such as Voskamp argued that like Europe, China had a long history of wars, rebellions, and dynastic change. Both Europe and China were once mired in the muck of paganism and barbarism. But Christianity had arrived, serving to unify the fragmented European tribes into one common culture. The Christian church had developed organized institutions, serving to counter the threats of oppressive secular states. China needed the organization, hierarchy, and unifying spirit of these religious institutions, as opposed to inchoate, messy, and disorganized local rituals. What the Chinese needed, missionaries believed, was to recognize the inferiority of their "superstitious" traditions and abandon them for a more modern faith like Christianity.[22]

For the SVD and the BMS, the primary forces preventing China's advance were spiritual. China's traditional religious culture, missionaries believed, impeded the country's development. German Protestant and Catholic missionaries saw themselves as warriors for God, charged with the task of destroying the "power of Satan in China," which oppressed and held the Chinese in a state of darkness and despair. For both missionary societies, Christianity was a revolutionary, earth-shattering ideology. Conversion to Christianity, the missionaries believed, was the only solution for Chinese liberation and could elevate the country from its premodern, oppressive state into the modern world.[23]

RAPID EXPANSION AND EDUCATION
Armed with conviction, both missionary societies sought to expand their operations rapidly. They were buoyed by financial support from their respective home boards. In 1883, the BMS employed one missionary and

MAP 3 Major missionary stations of the Berlin Missionary Society (BMS) in southern China, 1905. Map drawn by Bill Nelson.

had a yearly budget for its mission work in China of seventeen thousand marks. Within approximately two decades, the society had increased the budget for the China missions almost tenfold, employed ten mission-aries, and had five new major stations (map 3).[24] Similarly, the SVD backed its mission in China with institutional and financial support. In its first three years of existence, the mission society sent eight new

MAP 4 Major missionary stations of the Society of the Divine Word (SVD) in Shandong, 1905. Map drawn by Bill Nelson.

European missionaries to central and southern Shandong. The work grew even more quickly than the Protestants' in the south: by 1884, the missionaries had built 104 new stations throughout the region and reported more than nineteen hundred catechumens. Seeing these numbers, the Propaganda Fide elevated the SVD's region of southern Shandong to the status of an apostolic vicariate, installing Anzer as its first bishop (map 4).[25]

The SVD's strategy for expansion evolved through time. At first, Anzer had his sights set on the densely populated cities of Caozhou, Yanzhou, Yizhou, and Jining. However, encroachment into urban areas inspired vehement resistance from local officials. Anzer's intentions to establish a footing in the city of Yanzhou also alarmed the French, who had agreed to refrain from missionary activity in the area out of respect for the Confucian and Mencian temples in Qufu. The Germans abandoned their plans for targeting cities and went to work first in poor, rural areas, with the hope of eventually making their way into urban centers.[26]

Similar to the SVD, the BMS founded stations first in rural areas. The strategy was also not its initial choice and stemmed from the society's latecomer status. Another German-speaking organization, the Basel Missionary Society, had been in Guangdong since 1847 and had already established a solid presence in several cities. Drawing upon the Pearl River as its guide, the BMS traveled to regions in Guangdong not yet covered by the Basel missionaries. After establishing headquarters in the city of Guangzhou, the Berlin missionaries traveled east along the river, building three major stations close to the city of Huizhou in 1885. They then moved north, settling in the northeastern corner of Guangdong, in Nanxiong, in 1893. Within little more than a decade, they had created missionary stations in the central part of the province.[27]

In the midst of this growth in southern China, the BMS also began work in northern China in 1898, when the German navy invited BMS missionaries to work in the new Jiaozhou Bay leasehold (map 5). They focused their attention first on Qingdao, hoping to establish a presence in the new colonial space. In 1901, after the Boxer unrest had been quelled, they expanded farther into the province, to the county seat of Jimo, located northeast of Jiaozhou. In 1898, German soldiers had occupied the city and raided its Confucian temple as a way to avenge the death of the two German missionaries killed by the Big Sword Society. In the process, they damaged a statue of Confucius, raising the ire of Chinese intellectuals, including Kang Youwei. The action paved the way for the BMS's later entrance into the city. Unlike in southern China, where the BMS operated independently of the German state, in northern China, the BMS directly benefited from German imperial power.[28]

To maintain a rapid pace of expansion, Protestant and Catholic missionaries knew that they had to employ more Chinese to work for the missions. Training European missionaries was costly, and Chinese labor was cheap. Yet the missionaries were reluctant to put in power rural Chinese converts, whom they criticized as being illiterate and having a poor grasp of the fundamental doctrines of the gospel. If empowered to evangelize, missionaries feared, the converts could spread heterodoxy, as Hong Xiuquan had with the Taipings. Nonetheless, the missionaries

MAP 5 Major missionary stations of the Berlin Missionary Society (BMS) in northern China, 1905. Map drawn by Bill Nelson.

agreed that they needed to establish an infrastructure that could train local priests and pastors to be theologically sound. Among the first tasks of both societies was to create an educational ladder that selected talented Chinese youth for the eventual goal of ordination.

The SVD and BMS missionary schools became the first encounter that Chinese children in rural Guangdong and Shandong had with formal education, let alone foreigners and Christianity. Elementary schools offered free schooling; in contrast, Chinese schools required payment, making them inaccessible to the rural poor. Missionary schools were more egalitarian than Chinese ones: traditional Chinese schools did not accept girls, while missionary schools did. The schools were popular. By

1908, more than nine hundred students attended the elementary schools of the BMS, while the SVD boasted more than two thousand students.[29]

The Berlin missionaries taught a mixture of both Chinese and Western ideas, offering secular as well as religious training. The missionaries adapted, for example, the *Three Character Classic (Sanzijing)*, a classic primer that taught children Chinese characters and basic Confucian ideas, by swapping Confucian doctrines in it with Christian ones. The primary focus of the curriculum was religious: the children learned biblical history, sang church songs, and "shared stories about Heathen conversion."[30] Religious instruction was supplemented with basic courses in reading, writing, and arithmetic. Students were also exposed to classic Chinese texts. For their Chinese instruction, missionaries employed non-Christian Chinese to teach in their schools; BMS missionaries boasted that they hired "heathens and Christians alike."[31]

For the majority of the students, education ended at the elementary level—students entered at the age of five or six and graduated when they were twelve or thirteen. The missionaries selected talented boys and sent them to continue their education at the middle school located in Lukeng. They were selective: in 1908, only forty-four students enrolled in the middle school, about 5 percent of the total student population. At the middle school, students continued basic studies in all subjects, and they learned an additional trade or craft so that they could earn some income on the side.[32]

Students with potential for future employment in the BMS were then chosen for the Preacher's Seminary (*Predigerseminar*). By 1905, the BMS had established two seminaries: one in the south in Guangzhou and the other in Jimo, in the north. The curriculum for the Berliner Preacher's Seminary was rigorous, designed to prepare the Chinese for independent ministry. Naturally, students received a heavy dose of theology and were required to take classes in scriptural interpretation, homiletics, and biblical history. But they were also exposed to secular subjects, including the natural sciences, history, and geography. Even though the seminary offered instruction in English and German, missionaries complained that very few of their Chinese students ever became proficient in German. The missionaries themselves were partly to blame: hoping to make the Chinese Christians proficient in their preaching, catechism classes were conducted in Mandarin, Hakka, and Cantonese.[33]

To graduate from seminary, candidates had to pass a series of oral and written examinations, administered at the BMS's annual synodal gathering in Guangzhou. They were tested in theology, liturgy, church history, and homiletics. For their final examination, students were required to preach a sermon in front of all the German missionaries at the synod. The missionaries then transcribed, translated, and graded the exams and delivered the results back to Germany, where a board of missionary inspectors verified the results. Upon approval, the Chinese Christian received his ordination papers, earning him the title of vicar, or assistant pastor (*Vikar* in German; *Fumushi* in Chinese). Ordination signaled the final stop in a long and rigorous process. For Chinese Christians who entered the missionary society when they were children, the process took sixteen years, comparable to what a pastor in Germany had to undergo to achieve ordination.[34]

Like the BMS, the SVD established a clear system for educational progress. Contact began at the preparatory school, which admitted students from ages nine to twelve and lasted for three years. Above all, the preparatory school stressed religious teaching, but the students also received basic training in Chinese, mathematics, and music. In 1897, Bishop Anzer entered into negotiations with Chinese authorities to administer a secular Chinese school. At first, missionaries like Josef Freinademetz objected to the idea, arguing that the missionary society should focus its resources on evangelizing and inculcating religious piety. After the Boxer Uprising, hoping to make further inroads into elite circles, Bishop Anzer decided to accept the invitation of running several secular schools.[35]

Like the BMS, the SVD used its preparatory school as a way to identify future clergy. SVD missionaries encouraged pious students in the school to continue studying at the SVD's minor seminary, where training lasted for eight years. Along with continuing their studies in Chinese, students also learned Latin, with the eventual goal of learning how to read the works of Caesar and Cicero. Like the BMS students, they were also introduced to secular subjects, including history and the natural sciences.[36]

Talented students advanced to the major seminary in Jining for further training in philosophy and theology. There, students were exposed to a curriculum based on a classical Western model of theological training. Catechists observed a strict schedule. They arose daily at 4:30 in the morning and headed to Mass. Afterwards, they recited from the *Treasury of Meditation (Moxiang baojian)*, a compendium of contemplative prayers.[37] Breakfast was at 7 a.m. Studies began after breakfast and went until noon, with a short break in between. More hours of study followed lunch and communal prayer, until dinner at 7 p.m. Students were expected to be in bed by 9:00. They ate simply. One SVD missionary reported: "The students' main course is normally unsalted rice porridge. Salted vegetables and sorghum bread are also served. Meat is only served five times a year: at Christmas, Easter, Pentecost, Assumption, and Chinese New Year."[38]

After graduating from the major seminary, the candidate underwent a two-year probationary period, during which he was tested to see whether he could withstand the hardships of the priestly life. Afterwards, he had to undergo yet another four years of theological training, where he took a long list of theological classes, including dogmatics, apologetics, ethics, biblical exegesis, church history, liturgy, and canon law. If the candidate passed all of his courses, he was ordained at the end of his eighth semester and assumed his post two months later.[39]

Such stringent training reflects the high expectations that the SVD and BMS placed on their Chinese clergy. Knowing that converts faced an environment hostile to Christianity, missionaries wanted their Chinese leaders to be impeccably trained so that they could counter challenges to Christianity, whether from skeptical neighbors or high-powered literati.

Yet the strict requirements also suggest missionary distrust. They not only prepared converts to combat external opposition—those who wanted to rid China of Christianity—but to destroy the enemy lurking within. For at any moment, the missionaries suspected, Chinese might "relapse" and fall back into the superstitions of their youth. Rigorous training worked as an axe at the root of a tree: it struck at any lingering remnants from life before conversion. There was always a part of the convert's soul that could not be reached, that threatened to revert to its old ways.

A NEW DAY

Soon, missionaries had overwhelming proof of the grave danger that Chinese Christians faced. By early 1900, the Boxer movement had matured and continued to attract new followers at a rapid pace. Boxers marched through the Shandong countryside, setting fire to churches and killing Christians. During the unrest, they killed thousands of Chinese

Christians and hundreds of foreign missionaries. The case that garnered the most international attention erupted during the Taiyuan Massacre in July 1900, when forty-five foreigners, including women and children, were reported killed. Reports of the widespread violence only further convinced missionaries of Chinese society's incompatibility with Christianity, as well as the constant danger that Christians faced.[40]

The international community mobilized quickly. After a failed initial expedition in June 1900, in August a coalition of about eighteen thousand international soldiers, mostly Japanese, marched on Beijing and broke the Boxer siege. The ensuing foreign occupation "desacralized" the Qing Empire's authority, as diplomats posed for photographs on the imperial throne and marched freely throughout the Forbidden City, which had previously been shrouded in mystery.[41]

The humiliation of the Qing did not end there. After the siege of Beijing was lifted, the international forces began to wage a "pacification campaign" against villages with suspected Boxer presence. The Germans played a significant part in these retaliatory expeditions: seventeen thousand of the sixty-four thousand foreign troops were Germans. In one particularly brutal act, German and British forces shelled a county twenty-five kilometers south of Beijing suspected of harboring Boxers, razing it to the ground. In total, the international troops burned twenty-six villages between Tianjin and Baoding. To add insult to injury, Western powers also imposed hefty reparations on the Qing government, which it was to pay in full by the end of thirty-nine years.[42]

Western missionaries interpreted the defeat of the Boxers as a caesura, believing it marked a new era for Christianity in China. Prominent American missionaries such as W. A. P. Martin and Arthur Smith saw the bloodshed as laying the foundation for China's Christianization. The elimination of the Boxer threat offered China an opportunity to resurrect itself and embrace, in James Hevia's words, a "Christianized modernization."[43]

For missionaries, the crushing of the Boxers signaled the beginning of a new era for Christianity in China. "In 1900 the Chinese Boxers drank deep of Christian blood, but once more this blood of the martyrs became the 'seed of new Christians,' " proclaimed the SVD missionary Georg Stenz.[44] Finally, Stenz believed, the Chinese could now dismantle the shackles chaining them to their religious past. With superstitious beliefs and traditional religious practice discredited, Christianity could fill the spiritual vacuum left on the Chinese religious landscape. The graves of dead Christians were grounds upon which to erect its church.

Many reform-minded Chinese intellectuals agreed with the missionary critique of Chinese society. As Vincent Goossaert and David Palmer have shown, like their missionary counterparts, Chinese activists were convinced by the distinction between "religion" and "superstition." Drawing upon nineteenth-century missionary rhetoric, they defined religion as a "strong, moralizing, and unifying force behind the Western nation-states." After the uprising, antisuperstition reformers, inspired by ideals that Kang Youwei and Liang Qichao had proposed but failed to enact in 1898, launched a campaign seeking to eliminate from society what they believed to be backward elements. Throughout China, reformers confiscated temple properties and converted them into schools. They suppressed religious festivals and gatherings. Despite the outright attack on sacred spaces, intellectuals claimed that they espoused a "proreligious" and "antisuperstition" stance. They sought to redefine "religion" to suit their own political projects.[45]

Encouraged, missionaries saw the antisuperstition campaign as a sign of a growing alliance with the Chinese intelligentsia. They reported back to the home board that Chinese intellectuals—once their most belligerent opponents—now engaged in the same project of modernizing the country by attacking China's traditional religious culture. In turn, Western missionary societies poured resources and personnel into China, inaugurating a "Golden Age" for missionary work in China. Missionary societies—especially British and American ones—received floods of applications, as the news of tragic martyrdom inspired enthusiasm. By 1907, forty-four new Catholic missionary societies operated in China. In 1900, 886 Catholic priests worked there; by 1930, that number had almost tripled to 2,068. The growth on the Protestant side was even more impressive: in 1905, approximately 3,500 Protestant missionaries worked in China; within a decade, that number had grown to 5,500.[46]

Their efforts bore fruit, as the number of converts grew rapidly. Chinese Protestants numbered around 100,000 in 1900, almost tripled by 1915 to 270,000, and by the early 1920s had grown to around 500,000. A large number of converts received education from missionary schools: by 1915, Protestant missionaries counted more than 170,000 students enrolled in their schools. The most brilliant among them traveled abroad, mainly to the United States or Britain. A new generation of Chinese Christian leaders emerged from these experiences, and they viewed Western missionaries not as adversaries, but rather as partners in the construction of a Chinese church. Meanwhile, Catholic conversions grew at a slower, but nonetheless steady pace, and the total number of reported Chinese Catholics far outnumbered Protestants.[47]

As part of this broader enthusiasm for missions, the BMS and SVD also experienced rapid growth in their work. By 1905, the Berlin missions had created 12 major stations and 112 smaller stations. It employed twenty European missionaries and had baptized more than eight thousand Chinese Christians. In the same year, the SVD counted forty-four European priests and more than thirty thousand baptized Chinese. They oversaw 15 major churches and 118 smaller chapels.[48]

Among these Chinese Christians, the majority of the converts were men. When missionaries reported the number of conversions in their yearly and quarterly reports, the number of women was a third of the number of men. In 1908, for example, the BMS reported that there were 1,096 baptized female members of its congregations in all of southern China, compared with 4,955 baptized men. The number of converts in Africa did not have such a discrepancy. In the same year in the Cape Colony, where the BMS had one of its oldest and largest missionary presences, female converts outnumbered male, 1,842 to 1,476; and in the British colony of Natal, the number of female converts was almost twice the number of male converts, 1,393 to 743.[49] Pui-lan Kwok has argued that the slow adoption of Christianity among Chinese women can be attributed to social and cultural obstacles. In China, Kwok writes, "decent women were not supposed to appear in public, let alone worship together with men in a church." As a result, "Rich and upper class families would not allow their female family members to join a foreign religion." For many women, publicly joining a church was a major social taboo.[50]

Recognizing the unequal number of conversions between men and women, the BMS began to send women into the field. Ever since 1850, the missionary society had maintained loose ties with the Berlin Ladies Association for China (Berliner Frauen-Verein für China), an independent organization that established a foundling home in Hong Kong in 1854.[51] In 1882, the BMS decided to take over the association, changing its name to the Berlin Women's Missionary Society for China (Berliner

Frauen-Missionsverein für China). The missionary society was now also responsible for training and educating missionary sisters, and soon it sent their first, Käthe Schöniger, to China. With a staff now dedicated to educating women and girls, the BMS hoped to balance the gender inequality that it saw in its statistics.[52]

Like the BMS, the SVD also began recruiting and sending women to China. One missionary argued, "In China, the male and female sexes have been separated by walls that are thousands of years old," and he appealed to the missionary board to assign nuns to work there.[53] In 1905, SVD superior general Arnold Janssen sent missionary sisters from the religious congregation of the Servants of the Holy Spirit to China. Janssen, along with Maria Helena Stollenwerk, founded the congregation in 1889 and had assigned sisters to Argentina in 1897. By 1902, the Holy Spirit sisters had a presence in New Guinea, the United States, and Brazil. The first three Holy Spirit sisters arrived in China in October 1905. Within five years, thirty-seven missionary sisters moved to Shandong, helping to run the hospital and orphanage that the SVD had established.[54]

By the first decade of the twentieth century, all signs pointed to a bright future for the SVD's and BMS's missionary work in China. The vanquishing of the Boxers had persuaded missionaries that traditional Chinese religious culture was lying on its deathbed. Funding from Europe had increased, which enabled them to expand their work among groups previously thought inaccessible, such as women. Even Chinese intellectuals seemed to have adopted missionary beliefs about the need for religious reform. A new day had dawned; Christianity, missionaries believed, was poised for a breakthrough in China.

THE SVD AND ITS HERMENEUTICS OF SUSPICION

Yet the signs of a flourishing mission did not lead to better fortunes for Chinese clergy working in the missionary societies. By 1900, the SVD had ordained only eleven Chinese priests, who worked alongside forty-three European missionaries. From its own seminary, the SVD had graduated only six priests.[55] The BMS also had a poor showing. In 1905, only seven Chinese Christians had reached the position of *Vikar*. All Chinese *Vikare* were assistant pastors—none ran a congregation independent of missionary supervision. In contrast, the BMS's congregations in Africa had ordained indigenous pastors and made them independent as early as the 1860s.[56]

But the number of ordinations did increase. After the Boxer Uprising, the SVD reversed a previous policy of selecting only "old Christians," that is, children who came from multigenerational Catholic families. They began to ordain first-generation converts—in their terms "new Christians." Their first "new" priest was Petrus Chang (Zhang Zhiyi), who had grown up in the SVD's orphanage after being abandoned as an infant. SVD superiors lauded Chang for his perseverance; he had overcome not only his tragic childhood, they said, but also transcended "many generations of old pagan blood."[57]

Still, Chang remained an outlier, and for the most part, the SVD missionaries expressed doubts about their "new" converts. Many of them, they feared, still did not grasp basic theological concepts. In 1905, when Josef Freinademetz traveled to Shanxian to inspect parishes, he lamented the "immense ignorance" of the new believers. They did not know "who the crucified was, why we wanted to baptize, and what the purpose of confession was." He had "many grievances" against his Chinese converts, who continued to engage in "superstition."[58]

Surrounded by what it believed to be evidence of Chinese spiritual immaturity, the SVD refused to admit Chinese priests as full members into the mission society.[59] Freinademetz had first broached the question of Chinese membership in the SVD in 1894. He had wanted to allow his personal secretary, Josef Xia, to enter the order. Xia had served the missions faithfully and was instrumental in establishing the SVD's presence in Shandong. But old age and failing health made evangelization in rural areas more difficult for him. Entrance into the order would guarantee Xia a stable retirement. Freinademetz thought that the society owed Xia.

Freinademetz's request sparked a contentious debate within the society. Most of the missionaries in the field recoiled at the thought of admitting Chinese priests to the order. Freinademetz lamented: "Overall, our men are completely unenthused about the Chinese priests joining the order. Even if relationships with the Chinese improved, I cannot see much of a working relationship. Based on the current situation, there is not much that we can do." Although Superior General Janssen was prepared to admit non-Europeans into the order, Xia did not excite him as a prospect. Having received a letter, written in halting German, directly from Xia, Janssen wondered whether Xia had good enough German to interact with the other members of the society. Ultimately, he denied

Freinademetz's request, writing, "The time for admitting Chinese into the mission society is not yet ripe."[60]

Ten years later, in 1904, Freinademetz raised the issue with Janssen again because Xia had applied to join the order once more. Xia was still rejected. Janssen reiterated his belief that Chinese priests were not ready for entry into the society. After his second rejection, Xia left the SVD and joined the Trappists in Beijing. Upon his departure, Freinademetz remarked, "I very much regret losing this Father from our service."[61]

The SVD's reluctance to ordain more Chinese clergy belonged to a broader suspicion of Chinese readiness for church leadership. As historian Ernest Young has shown, a systemic suspicion toward Chinese priests existed among European missionaries. In 1901, the Vincentian bishop of Zhili and Beijing, Alphonse Favier, wrote a long memorandum arguing that Catholic mission societies had across the board failed to encourage more local Chinese clergy. While Favier believed that Chinese clergy should remain subordinate to European missionaries, he nonetheless argued that many parishes were ready to be handed over to Chinese priests. Delay could not be justified.[62]

CHINESE CATHOLIC BACKLASH

Backlash ensued. The persistent disdain European missionaries held toward their Chinese converts generated a response from Chinese Catholics, who became increasingly vocal during the early 1900s. Led by the prominent intellectuals Ma Xiangbo (1840–1939) and Ying Lianzhi (1867–1926), Chinese Catholics criticized Western missionary methods as paternalistic and overly dismissive of Chinese culture. Ma, a Jesuit who had studied in France, was frustrated with the way that Europeans belittled Chinese priests. Having left the priesthood because of arguments with his Jesuit superiors, Ma became an outspoken critic of European dominance in the Chinese church. He found an ally in Ying, a lay Catholic who created and edited the influential newspaper Dagongbao (published under the name L'Impartial). Ying used his newspaper to highlight and criticize oppressive missionary practices and attitudes.[63]

Nonetheless, Catholics like Ma and Ying did agree with the missionary diagnosis of China's political woes: spiritual void was the root of China's national crisis. China needed religion. Without it, Chinese modern development would remain rudderless. Even if the Chinese gained the technology and instruments of the West, they did not have the spiritual or moral means to employ them correctly. But Ma and Ying argued that the majority of Chinese could never accept Christianity as long as it continued to oppose Chinese ideas and customs. They sought to find common ground between Catholicism and traditional Chinese culture and dreamed of building Chinese Catholic institutions that could transform Chinese morality and strengthen the country.

That institution, for Ying, was *Dagongbao,* which he founded in Tianjin in 1902. Tianjin had been the city most heavily affected by the Boxer Uprising and the subsequent reconstruction efforts by the Western powers in the uprising's aftermath.[64] Ying had witnessed the destruction wreaked by both the Boxers and the foreign troops. His blood boiled when he saw foreign soldiers occupy the Temple of Heaven in Tianjin, and he lambasted the foreigners for "desecrating the sacred space." But Ying placed most of the blame for the destruction on the "moral decay and stupidity of the Chinese people." Like Liang Qichao and other Chinese reformers, Ying believed fervently in the printed word's ability to transform society. The *Dagongbao* would "enlighten the people," lifting China from a state of moral and intellectual decay.[65]

Ma and Ying also wanted to create Catholic universities to educate a new generation of Chinese converts. In 1903, with the funding and partnership of French Jesuits, Ma established Aurora University (Zhendan Daxue) in Shanghai. He developed a curriculum that combined the best of the Jesuit humanist tradition with a rigorous training in the Chinese classics.[66] But in 1905, Ma had a falling-out with the Jesuits in charge of Aurora, who wanted to base the university curriculum on the French model and feared that Ma helped to harbor anti-Manchu revolutionaries. Frustrated, Ma left Aurora and founded a new university, Fudan, backed by Shanghai merchants and intellectuals.

Beyond their cultural and educational work, Ma and Ying also became political activists. In their writings, published in the *Dagongbao* and other popular Catholic journals, such as the *Revue Catholique* (*Shengjiao Zazhi*), Ma and Ying argued for the reform of the empire into a constitutional monarchy. A "strong" nation, they believed, possessed a constitution that guaranteed the freedom of religious expression and belief and would protect Chinese Catholics. They exhorted Catholics to become more politically aware and active. Ma's and Ying's writings served as models for Chinese Catholic nationalism: they demonstrated to Chinese Catholics that the task of "saving the nation" (*zhiguo*) did not clash with their religious faith.[67]

Early-twentieth-century Catholic Chinese intellectuals shared a common obsession with their secular Chinese counterparts: how could religion help modernize China? For Ma and Ying, China needed a new Catholicism, a hybridized civic religion rooted in both the traditions of Catholicism and classical Confucian learning. If the Boxers had demonstrated the destructive power of "superstition," the unrest also reflected the religious energy of the Chinese populace. Western missionaries, Ma and Ying asserted, could tap into Chinese religious potential and reorient it toward constructive purposes. But in order to harness Chinese religious strength, missionaries needed first to abandon their contempt for Chinese spirituality. They had to trust the Chinese and allow them to inhabit new positions of church leadership and direction. Without such reforms, Ma and Ying believed, missionary work was destined to fail in China.

THE BMS AND THE *GEHILFEN* CONFERENCES

Like Catholics, Protestants became increasingly concerned with the question of Chinese leadership after the Boxer Uprising. Protestant missionaries in China came under international pressure that urged them to speed up the process of ceding control to indigenous clergy. Facing budget deficits, board leaders in Germany pressed missionaries in the field to shoulder more of the financial burden. International comparisons further weighed on them: the leadership in Berlin complained that the number of indigenous ordinations in China lagged far behind the numbers reported from Africa. When Arthur Brown, the general secretary of the Presbyterian Board of Foreign Missions, visited East Asia in 1909, he found far fewer Chinese ordinations than those reported from Japan and Korea. He concluded that missionaries in China should dedicate more time and energy to increasing the number of indigenous clergy. The Berliners understood Brown's report as a direct criticism of their work and felt embarrassed that they did not have higher numbers to boast to the international community.[68]

To encourage a more rapid development of indigenous clergy in China, in 1905 the Berliners organized a conference that gathered all

Chinese assistants (*Gehilfen*) working for the mission society. The *Gehilfen* conferences (*Gehilfenkonferenzen;* they became an annual event) signaled the first time that the BMS initiated a formal conversation about the future of indigenous clergy. They were also attempts to address the power imbalances between missionary and convert. All parties were involved in this dialogue: the missionary leadership in Berlin, the missionaries in China, and the Chinese employed by the society. The conferences gave Chinese assistants the opportunity to express the daily frustrations they encountered, such as low attendance rates in their congregations and difficult congregants. The Chinese proposed ideas for how to improve the work and what steps could be taken to achieve eventual financial independence from the Europeans. Beyond addressing immediate practical concerns, Chinese assistants also had the opportunity to present a range of issues that Christians in China faced more generally, including the relationship of Christianity to other Chinese religions, Christianity's place within the contemporary political environment, and the limitations of missionary methods.[69]

Still, the missionaries controlled every facet of the proceedings. The conferences may have opened up a new channel of communication, but they did not treat the Chinese as equals. For instance, missionaries chose the topics the Chinese would present. More, the Berliners turned the conferences into pedagogical sessions, demanding that the Chinese demonstrate orthodox belief. The Chinese preached on biblical passages that the missionaries selected and received grades on their sermons: "good," "satisfactory," "mediocre," "insufficient," and "completely inadequate."[70]

Missionaries left the 1905 *Gehilfen* conference pessimistic, convinced that the Chinese were unprepared for independence. One missionary concluded that the "spiritual state" of the Chinese was just like that of a "child," and that the Chinese congregations were still too "weak" for true independence.[71] The missionary inspector Gabriel Sauberzweig-Schmidt, who had overseen the establishment of independent congregations in Africa, agreed. Comparing the spiritual state of China to that of Africa, Sauberzweig-Schmidt wrote that it was much easier to convert the "primitive people" (*Naturvolk*) of Africa. Because the Chinese were a "civilized people" (*Kulturvolk*) who possessed an ancient and proud history, they believed that they had no need for Christian faith. Arrogance prevented the Chinese from developing a "true Christian character." The Chinese

BMS staff remained "immature and sheep-like," unprepared for more ecclesiastical responsibility.[72]

The missionaries hoped that the annual conferences would eradicate such spiritual immaturity.[73] The conferences served as moments to reinforce orthodox belief, as well as to ascertain whether heterodox belief existed in their congregations. In the 1909 *Gehilfen* conference, for example, one Chinese assistant gave a presentation on the question, "How far has atheism spread among Chinese assistants, catechists, and congregants?"[74] Shocked by the title, the missionary leadership in Germany responded: "We are horrified that the question . . . is even broached at this conference! We have never even heard anyone talk of 'atheist Christians,' not to mention 'atheist *Gehilfen*.' If we discover that such atheists do exist, then they must be driven out of our congregations."[75] The missionaries also attempted to eliminate what they believed to be immoral behavior from their congregations, expelling assistants for opium use, sexual indiscretions, gambling, and other behavior that the missionary society considered taboo.

Faced with disciplinary actions, some Chinese Christians protested. As records of the *Gehilfen* conferences indicate, the Chinese often felt that the missionaries meted out unjust punishments. Missionaries, the Chinese complained, adjudicated on situations shaped by complicated backstories and other factors that they did not fully comprehend. The punishment that missionaries delivered often did not fit the crime and revealed complete disregard for the broader context surrounding the misdeed.

Urged on by the Chinese converts, the BMS instituted a system of appeals, allowing Chinese Christians to explain their circumstances or ask for forgiveness. In 1903, for instance, a Chinese assistant Ma was dismissed from the ministry because he was found selling opium. After his expulsion from the society, Ma fell into "the most bitter financial distress," returned to the BMS, "fell on his knees," and begged the missionary leaders to reinstate him. After the missionaries ascertained that Ma had stopped dealing opium, they allowed him to return to the society. Ma's case reveals the unequal power relationships between the missionary and Chinese Christian, and how Chinese Christian assistants desperately relied on the missionary society for their livelihoods.[76]

Some cases involved more complicated conflicts between members of the congregation. The *Vikar* Jin ("Tschin" in the German spelling), who had been involved with the BMS since it first settled in Guangdong in 1882, was accused of raping a member of his congregation with the last name Fan. According to Fan's husband's testimony, "Jin came naked in the unlocked room of Mrs. Fan and forced her to engage in sexual intercourse." This was not Jin's first case of sexual misconduct: he had four charges pending. Ren, another Chinese *Vikar,* attributed Jin's bad behavior to alcohol. Jin, he claimed, "loved wine more than was allowed."[77]

The missionaries were split on how to handle the case. One missionary, Emil Gramatte, vouched for Jin's character, arguing that Jin had a good reputation and was well loved by his congregation. The accusations against Jin were not based in fact but motivated by "personal animosities. Ren and Jin have been rivals for a long time." Gramatte cautioned his supervisors: "We must be extraordinarily careful; we should not rashly expel a man who has had thirty-seven years of service."[78] But wary of the bad publicity that the case had already generated, the missionary leaders in Germany decided to expel Jin from the missions.

Missionaries often disagreed over disciplinary actions, as missionaries themselves could be unsure of where to draw the line between traditional practices that they should condemn and those they should allow. Debates erupted over how to handle Chinese who continued traditional Chinese practices such as polygamy or those who worshipped at ancestral altars. One *Vikar,* for example, was betrothed to a woman when he was a child, but he took a second wife as an adult without ending his first marriage. He was devout: he tithed regularly and devoted his energies to work. The missionaries examining the case asked, "Shouldn't we keep such a man in our service?"[79] They decided to let him stay. In other cases, however, missionaries forbade their assistants from participating in public ancestral worship and prohibited poor families from selling their children—one missionary condemned the practice as no better than "auctioning their children as slaves to heathens."[80] Missionaries adjudicated these issues on a case-by-case basis. Personal biases often softened religious ideology; encounters with individual Christians blurred the lines that missionaries sought to draw in the sand.

While the records of the *Gehilfen* conferences highlight moments of conflict between German missionaries and Chinese Christians, they also reveal instances of cooperation and genuine negotiation. The missionaries took the objections of their Chinese assistants seriously. Above all, they listened to Chinese Christian complaints about how European missionaries violated Chinese social norms and taboos. In 1910, missionaries wanted to decorate the altar with crucifixes, candles, and European pictures presenting the "naked" image of Christ. The Chinese assistants asked the missionaries to remove the decorations. A painting of a half-naked Jesus, they argued, "is an aesthetic taboo among the Chinese." The Chinese insisted that such paintings created a distance between the congregation and people in the community. The crucifix and portrait also confused non-Christian Chinese, making them think that the BMS was "half-Catholic." After hearing the arguments of the assistants, the missionaries deferred to them and removed the devotional objects. On certain issues, missionaries were happy and willing to compromise with the Chinese.[81]

The missionaries also carefully considered the financial requests of their Chinese helpers. At the 1911 *Gehilfen* conference, the Chinese Christians collectively bargained for a pension fund, asking the BMS to provide financial support for older assistants who had devoted their lives to the society's work. Superintendent Friedrich Wilhelm Leuschner and other missionaries supported the request. Since the BMS assistants earned less than other Chinese working for American missionary societies, the missionaries agreed that a pension fund could help the BMS attract more workers and reward loyalty. In Germany, the BMS leaders unanimously approved of the fund.[82]

Buoyed by their success, the Chinese Christians negotiated for a salary increase the following year. A petition signed by all assistants in Guangdong explained that they needed higher wages because of uncontrollable inflation. Years of bad harvests, civil unrest, and rebellions had led to skyrocketing prices for rice, vegetables, oil, and meat. The missionaries at the conference relayed their requests to the leadership. In May 1912, the committee acquiesced to the Chinese demands, offering a monthly raise of two dollars, slightly more than the Chinese had requested.[83]

THE CHINESE REVOLUTION OF 1911

Soon, another political upheaval forced missionaries to reassess their relationship to Chinese Christian leaders. In October 1911, the Wuchang Uprising, led by Chinese nationalists against the Qing Empire, began. Revolution soon spread through China. By the first of January 1912 Sun Yatsen announced the formation of the Republic of China in Nanjing, and a month later Emperor Puyi resigned, ending the Qing dynasty. In March, Sun Yatsen's revolutionary party, the Zhongguo Tongmenghui, became an open political party, the Chinese Nationalist Party, or Guomindang.[84] The party, seeking educated members, actively recruited from Chinese Christian circles. An exodus ensued. Many of the BMS Chinese Christians, excited about the prospect of building a new nation and lured by higher pay, left the mission society and took the newly instituted governmental exams. The BMS lost many Chinese members whom they had educated since childhood.[85]

Missionary attitudes toward the Chinese Revolution, and politicians who stood behind it, were divided. The Berliner Voskamp lauded Sun Yatsen as "a Protestant" who represented a new era for Chinese religious freedom. When Sun visited Qingdao, Voskamp took his students to one of Sun's speeches.[86] But not all BMS missionaries shared Voskamp's sympathies. The missionary Oswald Töpper criticized Sun, calling him an idealist with "fantastical ideas." He questioned the sincerity of Sun's Christian faith, pointing out that Sun had two wives. Töpper warned that nobody knew Sun's true identity: "To a Christian he is a Christian, to a heathen a heathen. With the Germans he is German, with the English or Americans, he is American or English."[87]

Many Western missionaries backed the revolution, seeing it as the breakthrough that Christianity needed to gain a more solid foothold in China. Even for Voskamp, who was a monarchist and certainly no fan of revolutionary upheavals, the end of the Qing signaled that the time was ripe for China to sever its ties with Confucianism. Voskamp wrote: "During times of Revolution, it has been revealed how rotten the Chinese national character has become through the long years of injustice, tyranny, and the shameful oppression of all human rights. The Chinese lack a spirit of liberated courage, and instead the Chinese spirit is dominated by slavish fear. That the Holy Spirit, that wonderful artist, will build his church on such material and in such conditions is something unprecedented and worthy of praise."[88] Another BMS missionary triumphantly declared that the new Republic could destroy "Confucian orthodoxies" that assumed "only the Emperor and his officers are worthy of representing heaven and earth."[89]

Not all German missionaries wanted Confucianism to be eliminated. "All those with a passing interest in China's well being should hope that

Confucianism remain a force in the country," the liberal Protestant Richard Wilhelm argued. For Wilhelm, Confucianism could act as a stabilizing force, and its "culture of humanity" (*Menschheitskultur*) offered many positive attributes to Chinese society as a whole. Wilhelm saw Confucianism as a source of moral, political, and spiritual stability in turbulent times rather than a competing religion that needed to be destroyed. Drawing upon the ideas of Kang Youwei, Wilhelm insisted that Confucianism could be renewed to address China's modern needs.[90]

On the other hand, the Catholic SVD was unequivocally critical of the Chinese revolutionaries. The traumatic memory of the two martyred SVD priests under the Boxers was still fresh, and missionaries feared that revolution signaled another period of chaos and disorder. With a power vacuum at the center, the new political scene meant little protection for Christianity. Catholic missionaries distrusted the revolutionaries, who seemed antagonistic to Christianity. The SVD bishop Augustin Henninghaus observed that "modern disbelief" (*moderner Unglaubens*) permeated the revolutionary ranks. Henninghaus also lacked faith in democracy. He scoffed at the idea that contentious issues now had to be discussed and decided by "a new age of the parliamentary system, freedom of the press, and within individual state legislatures and representative governments." With such widespread anti-Christian sentiment in China, there was no guarantee for religious toleration in the new China.[91]

Henninghaus's statements proved prophetic: the question of religious freedom became one of the most hotly debated—and unresolved—issues in the early Republic. Political and intellectual rivals clashed. Confucians such as Kang Youwei wanted to create a Confucian state church, aiming to revitalize Confucius's ideas for a modern age. Chinese Christians such as Ma Xiangbo and Ying Lianzhi advanced their visions for a Chinese Christianity that could strengthen the nation. Atheists like Chen Duxiu wanted to rid China of religious belief altogether. All agreed that the place of religion in China was an important issue, but few subscribed to the same solutions.

The president of the Republic, Yuan Shikai, supported Kang Youwei's position and mobilized traditional Confucian rites to legitimize his power. In June 1913, he issued orders to restore the national worship of Confucius. In August, members of the Confucian Religion Association (Kongjiao Hui), headed by Kang Youwei, proposed clauses in the constitution that made Confucianism the "national religion" of the Republic of China. Yuan supported these proposals and started to rededicate old imperial temples in Confucian rituals. In response, a United Petition League of All Religions formed, criticizing Yuan's moves as an encroachment on religious freedom. In 1914, it became clear that Yuan never had been interested in parliamentary rule. He dissolved the parliament and proclaimed himself the emperor of the Chinese Empire the next year. His empire did not last long, however: he died in 1916.[92]

Missionaries were unsure of how to assess Yuan and his attempts to grab power. Conflicting opinions of Yuan emerged in German missionary circles. One BMS missionary wrote that even though Yuan was "an energetic man," he was a "man of two souls" who could not be trusted. Another admired Yuan, calling him "clever" and "a man of action, who knew very well what China needed to become a modern state." Yet other missionaries were fatigued by the political infighting and refused to pronounce their sympathies. Bishop Henninghaus commented, "in terms of politics in China, we are completely indifferent, and just hope for the best."[93]

In the end, how did the 1911 revolution change the SVD and the BMS? In reality, not much—the German missionaries maintained their antagonistic position toward traditional Chinese society. Nor did they reform the hierarchical organization of their congregations. Chinese Christians did not gain substantially more power from their European missionaries, despite a period of nationalist fervor. The revolution further deepened the missionary hermeneutics of suspicion toward Chinese Christianity: missionaries witnessed Chinese Christians, many of whom they had trained and educated, abandon the church to join the new government. In a murky, unstable political situation, the missionaries did not know whom to trust.

CONCLUSIONS: UNABATED SUSPICIONS

From the time German missionaries entered China in the 1880s until the 1910s, a continuous distrust of Chinese Christian spirituality characterized German missionary practice. This disdainful attitude had real implications for Chinese Christians. The SVD refused Chinese priests entry into the mission society and rarely allowed Chinese priests to run their own mission stations. In annual reports, missionaries designated Chinese priests as "assistants." The BMS used similar language, and assistant pastor remained the highest rank that Chinese could achieve. Even though African congregations had become independent by the early 1900s, no Chinese pastors ran a congregation without European supervision. Missionaries kept the number of official ordinations low. Missionary leaders from both the SVD and the BMS justified their actions by pointing to the infancy of the congregations and the absence of "mature" Christians to whom they could entrust the work.[94]

Of course, not all missionaries shared such mistrust of Chinese Christianity. A few, like Josef Freinademetz, argued for Chinese inclusion. But most missionaries disagreed. "The native priest, apart from some honorable exceptions, is not equal to the European in efficiency, intelligence, administrative ability, reliability," said one SVD missionary, reflecting the dominant sentiment toward Chinese clergy. "Giving these mission churches too much independence too soon is not desirable in their own interest."[95]

Yet, the place of Chinese Christians did start to change during the first decade of the twentieth century. Even though the missionaries held financial power, they knew that the Chinese possessed valuable skills and knowledge of local customs and taboos. More importantly, they provided the scarcest commodity of all: willing labor. During the first decade of the twentieth century, the BMS and SVD reported dramatic growth in their missionary congregations, part of a "Golden Age" for Christianity in China. The Germans recognized that they had to hold on to any dependable workers they could find to maintain their rate of expansion. Hoping to foster theologically orthodox Chinese Christians, both the BMS and the SVD concentrated many of their resources on creating an educational structure that could locate and funnel local talent into their ministries.

And slowly, missionaries began to engage more with Chinese Christian demands. Catholic missionaries read the writings of prominent Chinese Catholics like Ma Xiangbo and Ying Lianzhi. Within the BMS, missionaries created new channels of communication between the missionary leadership in Berlin and the Chinese Christians in the field. Annual *Gehilfen* conferences permitted Chinese Christians to speak. When Chinese assistants requested better working wages and a pension, missionaries agreed. The Berliners also established an appeals process, allowing Chinese to voice their displeasure over punitive measures. In practical terms, the relationship between the missionary leadership and the Chinese Christian did begin to change during the first decade of the twentieth century. Missionaries began the process of engaging the Chinese in more dialogue and discussion over the future of Christianity in China.

Ideologically, however, both missionary societies had not altered their stance toward traditional Chinese culture and Confucianism. Both held on to their conviction that their vision for a Christianized China remained the best solution for the country's political future. Although the Boxer Uprising had been a traumatic experience for European and Chinese alike, it had not brought about major shifts in missionary attitudes toward China. In fact, both the Boxer Uprising and the Chinese Revolution of 1911 only further confirmed that traditional Chinese and Confucian values needed to be discarded and replaced. Missionaries still believed that Christianity was a modern, progressive force that could transform the backwardness of traditional Chinese society, and they evaluated potential political allies in China on the basis of their willingness to become Western. Many missionaries, for example, embraced Sun Yatsen because of his Westernized attitudes and customs.

When German missionaries surveyed the Chinese religious scene after 1911, they felt confident in the future. Of the three dominant visions for the modernization of China, Christianity seemed the most viable. Traditional Chinese religion—in their definition, "superstition"—had been trampled when international troops defeated the Boxers. Similarly, the old Confucian order had been overturned with the dissolution of the Qing Empire. With it, the Chinese reformist view of synthesizing Confucianism with Western ideas also was in peril. The chaos that surfaced during parliamentary debates only confirmed to missionaries the fragmentation within the Chinese intellectual sphere. Where, then, could Chinese intellectuals, and the Chinese people in general, turn? With Confucianism and traditional Chinese religion no longer legitimate competitors, missionaries believed that only Christianity could fill that ideological vacuum. Just as history had shown how Christianity had united fractured barbarian tribes in Europe after the fall of the Roman Empire, missionaries believed that the Christian faithful could unite China. They were optimistic that Christianity could become the foundation for the new Chinese nation.

Although missionary practice began to evolve during the first two decades of the twentieth century, for the most part missionaries continued to hold traditional Chinese culture in disdain. They continued to define Christianity as modern, forward, and progressive, diametrically opposed to the backwardness and stagnation of Chinese ideas. Anti-Confucian attitudes proved tenacious, intact after more than a century of Christianity's being in China. It took another cataclysmic political event—the First World War—to change them.

CHAPTER FOUR

A Fractured Landscape

ON AUGUST 15, 1914, two weeks after war was declared in Europe, Japan issued an ultimatum to Germany, demanding that the Germans withdraw their warships and relinquish control of Qingdao. They were given eight days to respond. The day the ultimatum expired was a Sunday; Protestant and Catholic services in Qingdao "attracted enormous crowds." The governor of Qingdao, Alfred Meyer-Waldeck, made an appearance at both services. By the end of the day, he had issued the German response: "If the enemy wants Qingdao, he must come and take it."[1]

The military preparedness of the Germans could barely match their bravado. The rag-tag group of reservists that they called up was no match for the professional Japanese forces intent on claiming the area. The Germans had four thousand soldiers who relied on outdated weaponry; the Japanese deployed some sixty thousand men armed with artillery and airplanes. By September 2 Japanese troops had landed on the northern part of the Shandong peninsula. A little less than two weeks later, they had reached the borders of the German leasehold.[2]

On October 26, Japanese troops positioned their artillery around Qingdao and proceeded to rain fire down on the city. The study of the Berlin missionary Carl Johannes Voskamp was an instant casualty. Voskamp had been an avid collector of Chinese paintings, and a blast demolished his collection. "Everything was destroyed, as if wiped out by a giant hand! In such times, it is better that one loses all feelings and sentiments for material goods," Voskamp lamented.³

Soon, Voskamp experienced a far more tragic loss. On the night of November 4, he received a telephone call asking him to hurry to the military hospital. Upon arrival, he found his son Gerhard "deathly pale, with sunken cheeks and a look of death in his eyes." Gerhard, who had been conscripted into the infantry, had been shot through the back. The bullet had punctured his internal organs. Upon sight of his father, Gerhard, barely conscious, asked: "Is that you, Papa? I seem to have been properly injured."⁴ He died that night, only three days before the Germans surrendered Qingdao. Gerhard was one of the 199 Germans who perished during the siege.⁵

Voskamp was inconsolable; Gerhard had been his favorite son. Born in Qingdao and fluent in Chinese, Gerhard had worked for a prominent German company before the war and was expanding its business into the province of Sichuan. Gerhard's cosmopolitanism—his comfort in both China and the West—had been a source of both pride and unease for Voskamp. "Gerhard has always been my joy and delight, but also a source of constant worry," he wrote in his diary. "I was unsure of whether [he] could resist all the temptations that the Far East offered."⁶

Voskamp emerged from the war a man transformed. The war humbled him. Rabidly anti-Catholic before the war, Voskamp had worked with a young priest from the SVD at the military hospital. The priest made a positive impression on Voskamp. "He had an agreeable openness and a considerable theological education," Voskamp remarked. In a moment of communion between the two, he wondered aloud, "Why has no German Catholic ever been chosen as a Pope?" Thinking that he had crossed a line, Voskamp apologized. The priest laughed and responded: "We often express the same questions within the mission society. But the Italian clique will never let a German through. Germans and heretics are synonymous in Italy."⁷

Reflecting on Germany's defeat in the war, Voskamp wrote, "Truly, God has consumed our people in a fire, so that we atone for our sins and turn to him." He continued, "These painful experiences have given us new perspectives on Germany's relationship to the other peoples [*Völkern*] of the world."⁸ But what were these new perspectives that German missionaries gained from the First World War? And how did they affect their approach in China?

In this chapter, I focus on how the First World War transformed German missionary work in China. I show how these changes occurred amidst an outburst of anti-Christian Chinese nationalism that forced the entire missionary community to reconsider its relationship to Chinese Christianity. As a result, German missionaries were pushed to seek new political alliances and rearticulate their approach to international cooperation in China. By examining how German missionaries reacted in a new geopolitical landscape, I show how the war brought to the fore the persistent conflict that they had faced since the nineteenth century: the tension between the nationalist and international dimensions of missionary work. The war further fractured a missionary landscape already facing unease.

"RUINS OF DESTROYED WORK, OF DASHED HOPES"

The First World War ended Germany's imperial ambitions in East Asia. China reclaimed Germany's colonial possessions, and the Allied Powers confiscated German property and businesses in the British and French Concessions. After the war, Germans no longer enjoyed extraterritorial rights, which the victorious powers continued to exercise. German Protestant and Catholic missionaries were expelled from Allied colonies in Africa and India. Under pressure from the Allied Powers, the Chinese government began the process of repatriating German missionaries from Shandong in 1919. Friedrich Wilhelm Mohr, a government translator who lived in Qingdao, wrote that Germans faced "ruins of destroyed work, of dashed hopes for the future."[9]

The BMS confronted the ruin that Mohr evoked: the war decimated its work in North China. The mission in Qingdao had depended heavily on patronage from the German colonial government. Japanese occupation ended such protection. Three of the missionaries spent the war in Japanese prisoner of war camps. After the war, only two missionaries remained in Qingdao. No longer able to afford to pay the salaries of Chinese preachers, evangelists, and teachers, the society let many of them go.[10]

In 1922, Siegfried Knak, the newly appointed director of the BMS, visited China to inspect the conditions of its mission stations.[11] Realizing that the society did not have the resources to maintain the work in northern China, Knak decided to abandon it and focus the society's resources in the south. He approached the United Lutheran Church of

America, offering it the opportunity to acquire the BMS's missionary properties in the north. The American Lutherans agreed, and in February 1925, the BMS sold its northern missionary stations to the Americans. Voskamp chose to stay in the north, becoming an employee of the National Lutheran Council of Baltimore. Knak, in a letter to his old friend, intended perhaps as consolation, wrote: "Despite the new American leadership, do not forget that you are, and always will be, a German. The blood that your beloved son shed for the Fatherland will bind you to our people ever more tightly and strongly."[12]

Besides dealing a blow to the BMS's operations, the First World War fractured relationships between Germans and the rest of the international Protestant missionary community, particularly Anglo-American missionary leaders. The disagreement centered around Article 438 of the Versailles Treaty, which turned over German missionary property in Allied territories to a trusteeship of other international missionaries. The article stated that such property could not be converted to other purposes and must retain its missionary character. The architect of the article, J. H. Oldham, an influential Scottish missionary who later became the secretary of the International Missionary Council, argued that a trusteeship would safeguard German property from Allied troops and continue the shared mission of Christian evangelization. Unlike the troops, who viewed Germans as "aliens on enemy territory," Anglo-American missionary leaders claimed that they could help Germans maintain their operations before returning the properties at a future date.[13]

German missionary leaders, Catholic and Protestant, doubted Anglo-American declarations of solidarity: the article, in their view, plainly authorized confiscation. Article 438 was "a complete destruction of German missions inside Allied controlled territories," said the influential Catholic missionary theologian Joseph Schmidlin.[14] Likewise, Karl Axenfeld, a leading member of the German Protestant missionary establishment, condemned the article as an "outrage" and "the most immoral demand ever made by any government."[15] The Germans felt betrayed by Oldham and the rest of the international missionary community, accusing them of using the war to get ahead in the race for missionary territory.

Oldham sought repeatedly to mend relations with the Germans and prove to them that he was acting in good faith. In 1921, he appealed to

German missionary leaders to join the International Missionary Council and "come back to a world which is learning more and more to think internationally—a world enormously different from the world of 1914."[16] The Germans rejected his invitation. "As long as the unholy measures of the Versailles Treaty are in force and our people in the homeland are mercilessly burdened with unbearable sufferings by our enemies," wrote the Berlin missionaries in South Africa in an official statement, "so long is it impossible for German missionaries to take part in a general missionary conference."[17]

For many Anglo-American missionary leaders, such as Frank Lenwood of the London Missionary Society, the German refusal to join the international conference was a serious affront to international cooperation. In a series of contentious letters with Friedrich Würz, the missions director of the Basel Missionary Society, Lenwood remarked: "There is still something of the feeling that Germans belong to a different type of humanity. . . . Once more I say it would have been impossible to make a greater mistake, or to do anything more hostile to the essential interests of German Missions and to their return, than that at this great Conference Germany should have refused to be represented. . . . It seems to me that the Germans have ceased to remember the possibility that they themselves may be, or have been, wrong at all."[18]

Lenwood's comments reflect an outburst of nationalist outrage, commonly felt among British and American missionaries, about German recalcitrance. The Germans, Lenwood believed, were acting as sore losers. Assuming that German missionaries had been complicit in supporting the actions of the German Empire, Lenwood and other more belligerent missionaries wanted to see displays of contrition from the Germans. Without such public apology, future international cooperation was impossible.

Other, more internationally minded missionaries, like Oldham and John Mott, lamented the regression in ecumenical cooperation. Before the First World War, encouraged by the display of cross-denominational cooperation at the 1910 World Missionary Conference in Edinburgh, many missionaries, including those associated with the BMS, expressed optimism about the possibility of a unified Western Christendom working together to spread the gospel. After the First World War, Oldham and Mott sought to recapture and rebuild international missionary solidarity.[19]

But to German Protestants, the Versailles Treaty had fractured these nascent bonds. Burning with nationalist resentment, many German Protestants refused Anglo-American overtures for future collaboration. The Germans, believing themselves victims of an unjust treaty, viewed their British and American counterparts as double agents. The German missionaries charged that while on the surface British and American missionaries seemed to work for international collaboration, in reality they did so for the sake of extending British and American national interests. Nationalist resentment, coupled with suspicion toward the dominant Anglo-American missionary groups, marked the general attitude that German missionaries held toward the international missionary society in the immediate aftermath of the First World War.

In contrast to its Protestant counterparts, the SVD's Catholic identity pushed its missionaries to seek help from an international network and foster closer collaboration with their Catholic counterparts. The SVD could rely on a major international advocate—the Vatican. Monsignor Stanislas Jarlin, the bishop of Beijing, procured a guarantee from Marshal Ferdinand Foch that Bishop Augustin Henninghaus and his missionaries could remain in China. Faced with the possibility of expulsion from China, Henninghaus sent letters and telegrams to various bishops, including the seven French bishops in China, asking them to support the German missionary presence in the country. The French, seeing an opportunity to reestablish France's Protectorate over Shandong, refused to support the Germans. Yet the SVD found allies elsewhere, in particular the Dutch Franciscan bishop of North Shandong, Ephrem Giesen. Giesen was an active advocate for German interests, and he persuaded the Dutch ambassador, Beelard van Brockland, to argue on behalf of the Germans. As one German wrote, "During the expulsion of the Germans from China in the year 1919, Bishop Giesen showed an energy and consideration which surprised us all and spared us all the pain and the humiliation of deportation."[20] SVD superior general Nicholas Blum called Giesen "a true friend in these hard times."[21]

The SVD found another important source of international support: the United States. Starting in 1895, the SVD had sent missionaries there. The work had grown rapidly, and by 1909 the SVD had opened a seminary in Techny, Illinois. In the United States, the SVD had garnered a progressive reputation, as it founded some of the earliest African

American parishes in Mississippi, and later, in 1920, one of the first seminaries that accepted African American candidates.[22] The society earned the support of Cardinal James Gibbons, an influential liaison between the Holy See and the U.S. government. On behalf of the SVD, Gibbons made a plea to the U.S. State Department protesting the Chinese government's plans to expel German missionaries from China. Gibbons's efforts succeeded, and the Americans lobbied the Chinese in support of the SVD's requests. One SVD missionary acknowledged that "we have America to thank for being able to stay and continue our work in China."[23]

In the postwar landscape, what surprised the German Catholics the most was the support they received from non-Christian Chinese. A coalition of local elites, including notable and worthy members of various organizations, literati, merchants, and government officials, had petitioned the government to allow the German missionaries to stay. Even the descendants of Confucius had signed the petition. Henninghaus was shocked by Confucian support, writing: "This is noteworthy, because for decades, the largest opposition to the establishment of missions in Yenzhoufu has come from the descendants of Confucius, who were afraid of losing the sacred hometown of Confucius to Catholic missionaries. But it has come to pass that those who twenty-two years ago were enemies now have proven to be sincere and sympathetic friends."[24] Henninghaus went on to explain that the Confucians must have noticed the continuous medical work the SVD had performed in the region and the good reputation of its hospital.

Ultimately, the international lobbying effort worked. Even though Chinese authorities expelled twelve SVD priests from Shandong in 1919, by October, the government abolished its restrictions on German missionary activity and allowed the repatriated missionaries to return to China.[25]

Despite the lifted restrictions on German missionary activity, like the BMS, the SVD faced serious concerns of personnel after the war. The SVD's headquarters in Steyl no longer had the same financial capability for training European missionaries. A debate ensued over whether to send missionaries from its U.S. seminary. Some SVD leaders believed that the China missions should retain their European character. One missionary leader wondered, "Will cooperation between American and European missionaries create problems, since worldviews and living habits are so different?"[26] Mixing American and European missionaries represented a serious roadblock to missionary efforts in China, as converts would witness a clash in culture and style. Others, like Henninghaus, argued that the SVD should rely on its American brethren. For one thing, American support increased the SVD's political cachet because, as Henninghaus noted, "The Chinese now hold the Americans in very high esteem."[27] He also argued that the SVD had a debt to pay: it had promised to send priests from its American seminary in exchange for U.S. diplomatic support. Ultimately, the SVD leadership sided with Henninghaus; they agreed to send American missionaries. In October 1919, the first three missionaries from the American Province of the SVD received their orders to enter China.

The SVD had a solution to its personnel crisis that the BMS did not have: it could internationalize. Like the Protestant BMS, the SVD faced a European landscape that was increasingly unwilling to fund missionary work in China. In a war-torn Europe, it also faced a decreasing number of candidates. But unlike the BMS, the SVD had an international network that it could rely on for replenishing its labor. The society's international character helped it to survive the immediate postwar years intact.

While the Protestants remained a predominantly national and increasingly nationalistic organization, the Catholics accelerated the process of internationalizing missionary personnel during the decade after the First World War. The SVD founded new branches across the globe, including mission seminaries in Poland, Slovakia, Gansu, Honan, England, and India. By the mid-1920s, the mission society witnessed a drastic change in its sociological and demographic makeup. The newer generation of missionaries, spanning a broad range of nationalities, worked side by side in China for the gospel under the SVD banner. What began as a nationalistic, predominantly German missionary society in the nineteenth century had now transformed into a genuinely international organization, with an increasingly diverse membership.

THE NEW CULTURE MOVEMENT AND THE FRACTURING OF CHINESE CHRISTIANITY

Of course, it was not just the German missionaries whose lives were transformed by the First World War. The Japanese occupation of German colonial holdings in Shandong during the war angered Chinese nationalists, and they were further united in their disgust over the proceedings at the Paris Peace Conferences in 1919. The main Chinese aim at the Peace

Conferences was to reclaim the occupied territories, but the Versailles Treaty handed the territory to Japan instead.[28] Outraged by the outcome in Paris, on May 4, 1919, three thousand students gathered at Tiananmen Square, urging the Chinese representatives not to sign the treaty. Throughout China, people boycotted Japanese goods. The young Mao Zedong saw the treaty resolutions as proof that the Western powers were "a bunch of robbers bent on securing territories and indemnities" even as they "cynically championed self-determination."[29]

The student leaders who organized the May Fourth demonstrations had been inspired by the heterogeneous New Culture Movement. Beginning in the mid-1910s, Chinese intellectuals sought new cultural solutions to China's spiritual crises. While many in the New Culture Movement agreed that Chinese civilization needed to be reinvigorated— through the creation of new vernacular languages, for example—few could agree on the philosophical and moral foundations for a new China. Radicals such as Chen Duxiu argued that China needed to replace traditional Confucianism with the progressive and secular values of the West, such as science, democracy, and Communism. Liberals, like Hu Shi, brought John Dewey's pragmatist philosophy to China. Conservatives yearned for a return to traditional Confucianism. Liang Shuming, for example, claimed that Confucian learning could serve as a bulwark against the onslaught of Western utilitarian thinking.[30]

Where did Chinese Christians fit into this intellectual landscape? Along with the rise of the New Culture Movement, a new generation of liberal Chinese Protestants emerged on the national scene. The majority of these leaders had been educated in missionary schools; the most brilliant had traveled abroad—mainly to the United States—on Boxer indemnity funds. Between 1910 and 1920, a cohort of Chinese Protestant intellectuals had returned from the West with diplomas from the best divinity schools. As Daniel Bays notes, these articulate, confident young men railed against "the dead hand of Confucius and tradition, a patriarchal social structure that was obsolete, and a venal and corrupt politics."[31]

Liberals such as Cheng Jingyi (1881–1939), Yu Rizhang (1882–1936), Liu Tingfang (1891–1947), Zhao Zichen (1888–1979), Wu Yaozong (1893–1979), and Wu Leichuan (1870–1944) viewed Western missionaries not as adversaries, but rather as partners with whom they could work to create a new, Chinese church. Many of them became faculty members at Yenching University, a missionary school founded in Beijing in 1916. The university helped to foster connections between the Chinese Christian leaders and the foreign faculty. New literary societies such as the Shengming she (Life Fellowship) and its journal *Shengming yuekan* (*Life Monthly*) emerged from such collaboration.[32]

The Chinese YMCA also witnessed a meteoric expansion, helping to incubate a more confident Chinese leadership. By 1920, within just twenty-five years of entering China, the YMCA could claim a presence in almost every single province, with almost fifty thousand registered members. As Jun Xing notes, between 1895 and 1919, "the Chinese YMCA had become a genuine community organization" through its diverse social work in the realms of health, education, and leisure.[33] With its focus on the Social Gospel, the YMCA presented a nonthreatening form of Christianity to Chinese nationalists who associated Christianity with nineteenth-century Western incursions on Chinese territorial sovereignty. The YMCA offered nationalist Chinese Christians a way to bridge the gap between East and West, between Christianity and Confucianism. The institution gave Chinese Christians an opportunity to draw upon the traditions of Christianity to transform and modernize the nation.

Other than the development of a liberal Chinese Protestant elite, a significant Chinese conservative Christian presence also appeared by the 1920s. Beginning in the early 1900s, revivalist groups, many adopting a Pentecostal flair, had begun to spread throughout China. Initially they had been associated with established conservative missionary organizations, such as the China Inland Mission (the largest Protestant missionary organization in China), the American Southern Baptists, and the Christian and Missionary Alliance, which helped fund the travel of itinerant evangelical preachers. By the 1920s, smaller communities, led by charismatic Chinese preachers who had been touched by the radically egalitarian Pentecostal message of the ability for all to receive God's spirit, had splintered from Western missionary groups. Preaching a message of premillennialism and criticizing established church groups, these independent Chinese church groups kept their distance from—and at times advanced a vocal critique of—the educated urban elite of the liberal Protestant establishment.[34]

After the First World War, tensions between conservative and liberal groups came to a head, and the "nineteenth-century evangelical missionary consensus," as Daniel Bays calls it, broke down. In the summer of 1920, debates erupted between "fundamentalists" and "modernists" throughout China. The conservative fundamentalists attacked the historical-critical approach that modernists took to biblical interpretation, as well as liberal advocacy of scientific ideas such as evolution. Liberals, on the other hand, saw the fundamentalists as theologically retrograde and defended the compatibility between science and religion. The argument in China portended the "fundamentalist-modernist controversy" that racked the global Protestant community throughout the 1920s.[35]

Other than dealing with internal fissures, the Chinese Christian community also had to face secular Chinese attacks on Christianity. Buoyed by Chinese nationalist fervor, a wave of anti-Christian sentiment spread throughout the country, just as it had during the nineteenth century. The critique of Christianity stemmed partly from political discontent. Prominent figures in the Chinese legation at the Paris Peace Conferences in 1919 were Christians: the leader of the delegation, Lu Zhengxiang, had converted to Roman Catholicism, and one of the main negotiators at the conference, the charismatic Wellington Koo, had studied at the missionary-operated college in Shanghai, St. John's.[36] Viewing the failure of the Chinese delegation in Paris, radicals like Mao Zedong and Chen Duxiu criticized the religion as politically impotent. Furthermore, the fact that missionaries continued to wield extraterritorial rights in China needled secular intellectuals. They considered missionary unwillingness to relinquish those privileges further proof of Western imperialist hypocrisy. Calling Christianity an arm of Western cultural imperialism, critics of Christianity hoped to eradicate it from the Chinese landscape.

Moreover, secular Chinese elites were intellectually dissatisfied with Christianity. They turned the missionary critique of traditional Chinese culture on its head: Chinese intellectuals, under the influence of Karl Marx and John Dewey, now called Christianity "superstitious," referring to it as regressive and unmodern. As Joseph Levenson has argued: "In the seventeenth century, Chinese opposed Christianity as un-traditional. In twentieth-century China, especially after the First World War, the principal anti-Christian cry was that Christianity was un-modern. In the early instance, then, Christianity was criticized for not being Confucian; this was a criticism proper to Chinese civilization. In the latter instance, Christianity was criticized for not being scientific; and this was a criticism from western civilization."[37] Just as European missionaries in the nineteenth century had sought to eradicate Chinese "superstition," now educated Chinese called for the destruction of Christianity on the grounds that Christianity itself was "superstitious."

Organized opposition to Christianity appeared in 1922, when students in Shanghai formed the Anti-Christian Student Federation to protest a conference organized by the World Student Christian Federation. The movement soon spread, and students in Beijing renamed the organization the Great Federation of Anti-Religionists. Its manifesto declared: "We swear to sweep away the poison and harm of religion on behalf of human society. . . . If there is to be a religion, mankind may just as well not exist; if there is to be a human race, religion must not subsist." Influential Chinese scholars and politicians, such as the president of Beijing University, Cai Yuanpei, the nationalists Dai Jitao and Wang Jingwei, and radicals Chen Duxiu and Li Dazhao, endorsed the group. By the early 1920s, Chinese scholars and politicians who held influential positions in Chinese higher education championed a generally antireligious stance.[38]

Chinese Protestant church leaders closely monitored the development of the national antireligious movement. But responses to the group varied, depending on the theological outlook of the church group. Conservative Chinese Christians went on the offensive, seeking to discredit the secularists. One Chinese pastor, Wang Hengxin, called the anti-Christian sentiment a "water monster" and exhorted all Christians to unite "to quell the monster's poisonous attacks, and prevent it from doing harm to the rest of society." Adopting the nineteenth-century rhetoric of missionary martyrdom, conservatives portrayed the anti-Christian movement as only the latest in a long line of secular challenges to the Christian church. They further accused secular activists of ignorance, selectively reading the history and development of Christianity. While the anti-Christians claimed to be defending "science," in fact they were not following a rigorous, "scientific" method when constructing their attacks on Christianity. It was the duty of Chinese Christians, conservatives urged, to publicly correct lies and distortions of the anti-Christian claims. By revealing their distortions, the anti-Christian groups would ultimately be defeated.[39]

On the other hand, liberal Chinese leaders expressed ambivalence toward the secular attacks. In an editorial in *Shengming yuekan,* published immediately after the anti-Christian gathering in Shanghai, the editors argued that the anti-Christian movement "holds a mirror to the state of Christianity in China. Western missionaries and Chinese Christians alike should use this opportunity to reflect on the shortcomings of the church in China. Their criticisms should encourage us to engage in the hard work of improving our churches. This is the greatest gift our secular critics have given us." Chinese Christianity, liberals argued, had to undergo a process of internal reform. It needed to be stripped of outmoded beliefs— including fundamentalist literal readings of the Bible—and instead embrace a modern, scientific approach to religion. Only then could Christianity become a positive force in transforming China.[40]

Conservatives and liberals did agree that the anti-Christian movement presented a major challenge for the future of Christianity in China. Seeing slogans throughout demonstrations calling Christians "running dogs" of Westerners and the "vanguard of imperialist capitalists," Chinese Christians across the theological spectrum recognized that most Chinese people still linked Christianity with Western imperialism. Filled with patriotic fervor, Chinese Christians had equally been disappointed with the outcomes of the Paris Peace Conferences and felt that China had gotten a bad deal at the end of the war. Liberal and conservative Chinese Christians argued that they needed to begin the process of disassociating their churches from Western Christianity. The Protestant church leader Cheng Jingyi, for example, represented many in the Chinese church community when he argued that Chinese Christians needed to persuade the Chinese that Christianity "is a universal religion and is capable of adapting itself to the needs of every land in every age." The first step in the process was for Chinese Christianity to become "independent of foreign control." Only then could it free itself from "the stigma of being a foreign institution." Chinese Christians were not immune to the inflamed nationalist rhetoric surrounding them: they wanted a church that they could call their own, unencumbered by subordination to the West.[41]

FRACTURED MISSIONARY RESPONSES

How did foreign missionaries respond to these broader challenges coming from both inside and outside the Chinese church? An independent Chinese church, after all, presaged the irrelevance of foreign missionary involvement. Reeling from the aftermath of the war, no longer confident in their historical or moral superiority, and feeling the urgency of a new approach to missionary work because of the threat of the anti-Christian movement, many missionaries agreed with Chinese criticism of Western dominance. The time had come, they argued, for a more rapid development of an independent church. Self-critical missionaries believed that Chinese Christianity had to disassociate itself from imperialist labels to survive. Writing in 1929, the missionary-turned-historian Kenneth Scott Latourette wrote in the decade after the First World War, the term "indigenous," once rarefied and divisive, "became a slogan."[42]

The Western commitment to developing an indigenous Chinese church found its most public expression at the May 1922 National Church Conference in Shanghai. Having monitored closely the anti-Christian protests that had erupted throughout the country just months before, missionaries were on edge. They knew that they lived in a different political landscape. The more than 130 denominational groups and one thousand missionaries that attended the conference agreed that a tidal shift had occurred in Chinese Christianity. Christian missionaries needed to work together to construct a new church in China. Missionary leaders announced, "The time has already arrived when Church and even Mission policies should no longer be so largely determined by the foreigner."[43]

Enthusiasm for an independent Christian church was not just rhetorical. Chinese Protestants outnumbered foreign missionaries for the first time at a Protestant conference in China. The National Christian Council (NCC) emerged from the meeting with the mandate to coordinate future discussions and debates. The council had sixty-four delegates; thirty-eight were Chinese, and Cheng Jingyi was elected chairman. The American missionary Frank Rawlinson, editor of the *Chinese Recorder,* the most influential and widely read missionary journal in China, encouraged by what he saw at the conference, triumphantly proclaimed, "For the first time in China, Christian opinion found national and united expression."[44]

Rawlinson's pronouncements masked the deep-seated theological disagreements that persisted. The NCC leadership board was composed primarily of mainline, liberal missionaries. From its inception, conservative missionary groups criticized the council for its heavy emphasis on the Social Gospel and its support of modernist theology. The U.S. Southern Baptists rejected the invitation to attend the conference in 1922, and by 1926, the China Inland Mission and the Christian and Missionary

Alliance, two of the largest members of the group, withdrew from the organization. Instead, they dedicated their efforts to building the Bible Union of China, founded in 1920 when the fundamentalist-modernist controversy first erupted.[45]

Other than theological disagreements, nationalism continued to divide Christian circles in China. From the beginning, the Germans, still sore from the fallout of the Versailles Treaty and perceived betrayal by Anglo-American missionaries, were torn over whether to accept the invitation to attend the conference in 1922. Ultimately, they decided to send four missionaries and four of their Chinese assistants to the conference. The newly appointed director, Siegfried Knak, used the conference as an opportunity to make his first official tour of China. Voskamp also attended the meeting. In contrast to Rawlinson's confidence in ecumenical cooperation, the German missionaries of the BMS expressed pessimism about the future of a united Chinese church. Rather than noticing unity, as Rawlinson had, the overwhelming impression left on the Germans was the feeling of fragmentation. Knak noted that no language unified the Chinese, let alone the foreign mission societies. The field remained fragmented by a multitude of languages and nationalist agendas.[46]

More importantly, the Germans expressed their resentment toward the dominance of American and British missionaries at the conference. Knak mocked what he called the "American peculiarities" that he saw there. He scorned the "constant, often senseless hand-clapping." He expressed disgust over the frequent "invocation of the so-called equal rights for women." The Americans were not serious theologians, Knak charged. Rather, they were more interested in political ideas like "democracy" and "progress" than the gospel.[47]

Voskamp suggested that the Americans were manipulating the conference for their own political gain. "For Anglo-American missionaries," he wrote, "the development of missionary work means an advancement of their political interests." He accused American and British missionaries of deploying insincere rhetoric when they trumpeted the indigenous church: "I believe that the practical Americans have handled the situation cleverly to stress an independent national church during a time of nationalist awakening." The Americans were not truly interested in the hard work of church building. Rather, they were intent on mobilizing the wave of Chinese nationalist sentiment to broaden their dominance in China.[48]

Even worse, the Germans lamented, the Chinese had bought what the Americans were selling; they had not detected the political machinations of the cunning Americans. Knak depicted the Chinese Christians he met at the conference as possessing a weak understanding of fundamental biblical principles. American liberal theology—which he referred to as "modernism"—had swayed the nascent faith of the Chinese Christians. Voskamp agreed, reporting, "The enthusiasm among the Chinese for [American ideas] was enormous." The Germans came away from the conference convinced that Chinese leaders were all swept up by the talk of indigenization, convinced that a new independent Chinese church could be built on democratic and liberal principles.[49]

Yet Knak did support some of the public goals of the NCC. He agreed with its chairman, Cheng Jingyi, that the time had come for the church in China to become independent from foreign influence. All missionaries in China, including the Germans, needed to work together to push forward the goal of Chinese church independence. Furthermore, Cheng had left a good impression on Knak; he was a man one could "look up to with confidence and respect." In 1923, Knak invited Cheng to give a talk in Berlin, introducing him to the public as an "excellent Christian."[50]

Publicly, the BMS expressed its support for the NCC, despite its internal criticisms of it. In a letter to Henry Hodgkin, one of the NCC secretaries, Knak wrote, "The results and fruits of the Conference in Shanghai are not alone very interesting in my opinion, but are of greatest importance for the future of the Chinese Church." Knak said further that he had already begun implementing in BMS congregations the ideas expressed at the Shanghai conference. "There were, perhaps, very few mission leaders in China, who realized the words and resolutions of Shanghai as quickly and consequentially as myself," Knak claimed. He also sought to distance the BMS from the fundamentalist Bible Union, claiming that even though he had participated in some of its Bible studies, he did not see how the organization "is quite adapted to the tasks of the Chinese Church."[51]

As time passed, the BMS's resentment toward Germany's politically disadvantageous position in China subsided. As relations with the Chinese normalized, the Germans no longer felt angered by the loss of their extraterritorial rights in China. In 1925, British missionaries debated the question of whether to retain their extraterritorial privileges, and they asked Germans to comment on their experiences. One Berlin missionary responded: "I have great pleasure in telling you that so far the loss of extraterritoriality has not been felt as a loss at all by us. On the contrary, we feel very much relieved that we no longer enjoy this 'privilege.' As the Chinese know that we no longer are a privileged class of foreigners, they show themselves more considerate than ever and we have in no way been faced with any special difficulties, nor have we been blocked when trying to buy mission property."[52] He implored the NCC and other missionary societies to follow suit and relinquish their extraterritorial rights. The loss of extraterritorial rights had in fact aided their relationship with the Chinese, rather than hindering it.

Yet the BMS remained wary of liberal American theology and the dominance of Americans in the Chinese church scene. Despite the BMS's participation in the NCC, it kept a respectful distance. Instead, it sought to build closer ties with the Chinese Lutheran missionary alliance (Zhonghua Xinyi Hui), which had been founded in 1907 but started to attract more participants after the First World War. Besides the German-speaking societies, such as the Rhenish and Basel missionary societies, Finnish, Norwegian, American, and Swedish missionary societies also joined the group. Signs now proclaimed that it was part of the Xinyi Hui. Knak and the BMS hoped to announce to their Chinese congregants their theological commitment to Lutheran principles. In a 1924 letter to Henry Hodgkin, Knak justified the decision to join the Lutheran alliance, rather than the more diverse Church of Christ in China, by explaining that he wanted to participate in a "more intimate church foundation." In a broader church union, he wrote, it was difficult to find complete theological agreement.[53]

But claims of theological orthodoxy were often ways to mask nationalistic resentment. While the Berliners criticized American liberals, they embraced fellow German liberals on patriotic grounds. Before the war, Berlin missionaries had refused to work with liberals from the Weimar Mission. Afterwards, even though the Berliners themselves faced financial difficulties, they offered the Weimar missionaries money. Voskamp, for example, agreed to work with the Weimar Mission's congregation and affiliated school. In Qingdao, national loyalties trumped theological conviction. Voskamp did not forget Knak's exhortation: he still thought of himself as a German first and foremost.[54]

The Shanghai conference of 1922 had helped to crystallize for Knak and Voskamp what China needed and how they should craft the future of their mission work. Their primary task was to stem the tide of liberal-modernistic theology that the Americans tried to inculcate in China and offer a more biblically sound form of faith. Yet the BMS also found the theology of the fundamentalist Bible Union unacceptable. Commenting on the Bible Union, Knak wrote: "we Germans educated by Lutheran scholars cannot agree to all doctrinal statements of our brethren of Calvinistic origin. In accordance with our spiritual experience the Bible is not a book, or a code of doctrinal statements, but a great Witness, a message, a sermon."[55]

Neither fundamentalist nor modernist, the German Protestants had discovered their niche. They had found the singular contribution they could make in China: they could proudly proclaim their German Lutheranism. As Martin Luther's compatriots, they could claim a direct connection to the founding principles of the Reformation. Without an empire to extend, Germans were unencumbered by the claims of imperialism. To the Chinese, Knak argued, the Germans offered both a purity of national interests and theology.[56]

NEW VATICAN INITIATIVES: *MAXIMUM ILLUD*

Similar to the Protestants, Catholics also had to deal with national fault lines magnified by the First World War. Into this fragmented political landscape entered the Vatican, and in Benedict XV Catholics had a leader who energetically reasserted the centrality of the Vatican's power. Benedict had served as a diplomat before he became pope in September 1914. Calling the war "the suicide of Europe," he believed the Vatican could fill the spiritual vacuum that the First World War had left in global Christendom. After the First World War the Vatican asserted itself through legal and diplomatic means, seeking to establish itself as a major force in global geopolitics.[57]

As part of its broader agenda to strengthen its presence in East Asia, the Vatican sought to end the French Protectorate and establish formal diplomatic relations with China. In 1918, before the war was over, Vatican and Chinese diplomats had seemed to reach an agreement. But hearing of the deal, the French intervened and mounted a smear campaign accusing the pope of favoring the Germans. The Chinese government, a French ally in the midst of war, faced a public relations crisis and broke off talks.[58]

A groundswell against the Protectorate grew among missionaries in China. In particular, two Lazarist missionaries, Antoine Cotta and Vincent Lebbé, led the charge in identifying the Protectorate as the primary reason that the Chinese viewed missionary work as imperialistic. In order to disassociate itself from imperialism, Lebbé and Cotta argued, the church needed to put Chinese Catholics and priests on an equal footing with Western missionaries. The Chinese, they argued, had been treated as subordinates for too long. The development of more Chinese clergy had a two-pronged benefit for the Holy See: Chinese priests, loyal to the Vatican, could curtail the influence of the French Protectorate in China, and they could also stem the criticisms of Chinese nationalists who claimed that Christianity was a foreign religion. Lebbé and Cotta mounted an impassioned campaign, sending long letters imploring the Vatican to treat Chinese as equals and ordain Chinese bishops.[59]

The Vatican was moved by Lebbé and Cotta's arguments, but it wanted first to see whether other missionary leaders agreed. In July 1918, the prefect of the Propaganda Fide, Willem van Rossum, sent six bishops a questionnaire, asking them to produce detailed responses to it. The SVD bishop Augustin Henninghaus was among the six chosen.[60] The questions ranged from broad inquiries about Chinese popular opinions on Catholicism to specific inquiries about Catholic education. And the questionnaire directly addressed the issue of indigenous clergy. Were the Chinese ready for positions of institutional authority?[61]

None of the bishops advocated ordaining Chinese bishops. One bishop, Jean de Vienne, called the idea "utopian," while another, Jean-Baptiste Budes de Gubriant, referred to the prospect as "impossible." Chinese priests, all six bishops concurred, had neither the education nor the experience to manage the task of governing the church. The time had not yet come to turn over the church to the Chinese.[62]

Among the six European bishops queried, Henninghaus, as Ernest Young has noted, "offered the most positive evaluation of the contributions of the Chinese clergy." Indigenous clergy could navigate the complexities of local cultures more fluidly than European missionaries ever would.[63] Yet Henninghaus also added many caveats in his praise. Overall, Chinese clergy lacked "scientific qualities." The older generation of priests, who were "unrefined in their thinking," had difficulty keeping up with the rapid changes around them. On the other hand, the younger seminarians, he reported, had a "lower level of intellect than those of other nations." Yet for Henninghaus the "inferior intellectual qualities" of the Chinese did not prevent the Chinese from being "capable and effective for the Lord." The bigger threat, for Henninghaus, was the hostile environment around them. Surrounded by Buddhists, Confucians, and Daoists, "multiple obstacles" stood in the way of true religious freedom. An unstable political situation also threatened Catholic religious life. Henninghaus thus advised a more cautious approach to transferring power to the Chinese than Lebbé and Cotta had argued in their proposals. While Henninghaus believed that eventually the Chinese church should gain independence, for the time being, the Chinese still needed European guidance.[64]

The bishops were unsuccessful in their plea for caution; the Vatican sided with Lebbé and Cotta. In November 1919 Benedict issued the papal encyclical *Maximum illud,* which John Pollard has called "a revolution in the Church's missionary policy."[65] Never before had a pope so clearly laid out a vision for the centrality of missions to global Catholicism. Asserting the universality and non-Eurocentric character of the Catholic Church, Benedict wrote: "The Catholic Church is not an intruder in any country; nor is she alien to any people. It is only right, then, that those who exercise her sacred ministry should come from every nation." Benedict wanted to erase the binary between Europe and the rest of the world; the fate of the faith in Europe was intertwined with the state of the church elsewhere.[66]

While *Maximum illud* did not specifically refer to the problem of missionary work in China, Ernest Young has convincingly shown that more than two-thirds of the encyclical was a direct comment on the situation in China.[67] The encyclical explicitly advanced Lebbé and Cotta's arguments: it stated that local clergy should not be subordinate to European missionaries, but equal to them. "For the local clergy is not to be trained merely to perform the humbler duties of the ministry, acting as the assistants of foreign priests," proclaimed the encyclical. "On the contrary, they must take up God's work as equals, so that some day they will be able to enter upon the spiritual leadership of their people." When Lebbé read *Maximum illud,* he was overjoyed: "We can truly say that the holy cause to which we have consecrated our lives, Cotta and me, is in principle *won across the board.*"[68]

In the encyclical, Benedict did make concessions to the answers from the bishops' questionnaires. He admitted that the quality of indigenous clergy was still "of an inferior kind," and the missionary "must make it his special concern to secure and train local candidates for the sacred ministry." But it must be noted that the encyclical was as critical of European missionaries as it was of the "inferior" local priest. In particular, Benedict chastised missionaries who forgot the universality of the gospel and evangelized to advance their own national and imperial interests. "It would be a tragedy," Benedict wrote, "if an apostolic man were to spend himself in attempts to increase and exalt the prestige of the native land he once left behind him. Such behavior would infect his apostolate like a plague. It would destroy in him, the representative of the Gospel, the sinews of his love for souls and it would destroy his reputation with the populace."[69] In the encyclical, Benedict called for humility on the part of the missionary superiors.

The encyclical also raised crucial issues of missionary training and behavior. The pope urged missionaries to obtain training in both "sacred and profane" knowledge. He stressed the need for better language training and promised to devote more resources to building language centers in Rome. Most importantly, Benedict emphasized that missionaries offer an example of moral and spiritual piety to their converts. "It is of the most critical importance that [the missionary] have sanctity of life," he exhorted. "For the man who preaches God must himself be a man of God. The man who urges others to despise sin must despise it himself. Preaching by example is a far more effective procedure than vocal preaching." The missionary needed to be not only "humble and obedient and chaste," reflecting Jesus's gospel, but also self-reflective about how to spread that gospel in the world.[70]

Maximum illud created ripples among bishops in China and polarized the mission field into two camps: the proindigenization "Lebbé faction" and the "French faction" that read the Vatican's actions as an attempt to undercut the French Protectorate's influence.[71] Where did the SVD fall within this polarized Catholic landscape? Its leadership questioned the Vatican's initiatives and expressed doubt at the feasibility of a quick ordination of Chinese bishops along the timeline that the Vatican hoped. SVD missionaries in China joined the French faction in criticizing Lebbé. While Henninghaus had corresponded intermittently with Lebbé during the war and publicly expressed admiration for Lebbé's "great talent," in private correspondence with his fellow SVD supervisors Henninghaus characterized Lebbé as too polarizing a figure. He lambasted Lebbé's newspaper *Yishibao* for "produc[ing] very little value for the Catholic endeavor in China."[72]

Though critical of Lebbé and doubtful of the push to ordain Chinese bishops immediately, the SVD missionaries nonetheless recognized that *Maximum illud* signaled a new era. The missionary Georg Weig wrote: "The problem of indigenous clergy is becoming ever more urgent. In our mission society as well, the ratios are shifting constantly in the favor of Chinese priests. The number of Chinese aspirants has grown. But the aversion, and above all, the private resistance by European priests (even in our own society!) has intensified the conflicts between the two groups. The admission of Chinese into mission societies, such as to the Lazarists, has so far not resulted in any rapprochement between the Chinese and European priests. We should not also hold any illusions to how much these changes will bring."[73] Like many others in the mission field, Weig recognized that the ordination of more Chinese clergy was not a panacea. Rather, the protracted power struggles between Chinese priests and European clergy would continue well into the foreseeable future.

THE 1924 CATHOLIC SYNOD IN SHANGHAI

In 1922, Benedict XV died after a bout with pneumonia. His successor, Pius XI, wanted to continue the agenda set out in *Maximum illud*. Within five months of being elected pope, Pius XI, unafraid of threats and criticism from the French, appointed Celso Costantini as the first apostolic delegate to China. When Costantini arrived in China in November 1922, the Vatican realized its goal of establishing direct diplomatic relations with China—an aim it had been working toward since the 1860s.[74]

Costantini's appointment as apostolic delegate represented a sea change in the Vatican's top brass. By the time Costantini entered China, the leaders of the Vatican hierarchy, including the two most powerful individuals in the realm of missions, Cardinal Secretary of State Pietro Gasparri and the prefect of the Propaganda Fide, Willem van Rossum, were all devoted to the *Maximum illud* goal of elevating the status of indigenous clergy. Costantini belonged to the liberal wing of the church, and a meeting with Pius XI, Gasparri, and Rossum thoroughly convinced Costantini of the importance of the Vatican's and the Propaganda's vision for Catholic missions in China. He pledged to strip the missionary enterprise of its imperialist interests and ordain more indigenous Chinese clergy.[75]

Immediately upon his arrival in China, Costantini communicated his resolve to put *Maximum illud* into practice. He formed an entirely indigenous religious order, the Discipuli Domini. And he had a new goal: he wanted the church to *look* more Chinese. He decorated the apostolic delegate's residence with Chinese ornamentation. One writer described it as "a great and beautiful building, built in a pure, elegant Chinese style." The interior of the residence was "richly adorned with rugs, Chinese paintings, elegant furniture and antique art, some with extremely high artistic value and interest."[76] In a series of articles published in various Catholic journals, Costantini argued that the Catholic missions in China needed to develop an indigenous art form that merged traditional Chinese artistic forms with European spirituality.

In May 1924, Costantini and the Vatican organized a two-week-long national synod. It was a landmark event, gathering all bishops, all superior generals of the mission orders, and all apostolic vicars and prefects in China. That these disparate groups of people and organizations agreed to attend the national synod had symbolic importance. The idea of holding a synod in China had existed since the seventeenth century but had failed to take shape until that point because of conflicting geopolitical interests. Costantini's successful invitation to the various mission orders in China not only fulfilled a long-time Vatican wish to unify the missionary effort, but also projected the Vatican's intention to centralize the Chinese mission field under its control.[77]

The national synod began on March 25, 1924. Fifty different missionary orders, including forty-four bishops, five apostolic prefects, and one apostolic administrator, arrived at the synod.[78] In his opening homily, Costantini signaled the new directions that the Vatican intended to take in China. He greeted the first two Chinese apostolic prefects, recently ordained. Costantini announced: "Among you there are *two Chinese Prelates*, recently raised to the Dignity of Prefects Apostolic; these, Venerable Brethren, are the fruit of your past labors, the grain of mustard that will grow into a large tree, and bring forth abundant fruit in the future. We all share the same unity of Faith and obey the same visible Head on earth, our Holy Father the Pope."[79]

In his homily, Costantini further declared that the opposition between traditional Chinese culture and Catholicism had to come to an end. Instead, Confucianism and other ancient Chinese thinking had been replaced by another foe: "pernicious materialism," which "had been produced by evil parties in Europe and America." Referencing the anti-Christian movement, Costantini lamented that materialist thinking had "become popular in Chinese universities." To resist the further spread of "this dirty materialism," Costantini exhorted all at the conference to "raise up the beautiful and wonderful virtues of ancient China to entirely overthrow it." It was the depravity of Western modern civilization—not the Confucian tradition—that represented the biggest threat to China.[80]

The spirit of *Maximum illud* suffused the conference proceedings. Taking its cue from the encyclical, the synod forbade European missionaries from interfering in local Chinese politics; the council fathers emphasized that all Catholic missionaries must respect Chinese secular authorities. The synod agreed that it no longer tolerated any implicit or explicit ties to Western imperialism and prohibited missionaries from aiding Western colonial ambitions. Henceforth, the buildings of missionary congregations could no longer indicate their countries of origin; instead, missionaries had to mark the entrances of mission stations with Chinese names. Missionaries were also prohibited from forcing Chinese students to learn Western languages.

Many sessions of the conference focused on the education of Chinese clergy. The council encouraged promising young Chinese students to study abroad at Catholic universities in Europe. These new initiatives, the council recognized, created the potential for new areas of conflict between the European missionaries and the indigenous clergy. Council sessions were devoted to discussing how discord could be minimized. The council leaders emerged from the discussions convinced that hierarchical authority induced harmony: if the native clergy received a strict orthodox education, they were less likely to dissent and undermine the authority of the European missionaries.[81]

However, several entrenched policies remained; the Vatican did not completely overhaul its approach to indigenous clergy. It did not overturn its position on the Rites Controversy: it continued to reject the Jesuit policy of accommodation and forbid Catholics from attending traditional Chinese rituals. The council insisted that Catholic missionaries should seek to abolish all non-Christian funeral rites through conversion. The synod denounced Chinese spiritual practices as "superstition," labeling

Buddhism, Confucianism, and Daoism as evil religions that the missionaries needed to vanquish.[82]

During the closing ceremony of the conference, Costantini further
signaled the Vatican's commitment to the indigenous church when he
consecrated the Chinese church to Our Lady Queen in China. The bishops
raised a Sinicized portrait of the Virgin Mary, the Our Lady of Donglu,
which had gained a wide circulation among Chinese Catholics in the decade
after the Boxer Uprising. During the Boxer unrest, Catholics from the
village of Donglu, in Hebei, reported apparitions of the Madonna. Villagers
credited their survival—the Boxers had repeatedly attacked the village—to
the protection of the Virgin Mary. An enterprising Lazarist missionary who
wanted to publicize the miracles commissioned Jesuits in Shanghai to
produce an image of a Chinese Virgin Mary. The artist modeled his painting
after a photograph of the Dowager Empress Cixi, depicting Jesus and Mary
in Chinese robes and Mary sitting on a Chinese throne. The figures were
also intentionally hybridized: Mary and Jesus have European visages and
wear European-style crowns, and Mary holds a scepter. The hybridity of the
image appealed to Costantini, who saw it as a perfect symbol for the future
of the Catholic Church in China. Having protected the people of Donglu,
now she was designated as the protector of the entire Chinese nation. The
synod participants all bowed down and worshipped her.[83]

Despite the synod's overt commitment to the indigenous church,
some of its decisions provoked dissension from the two Chinese prefects
in attendance. In particular, the Chinese were displeased with the council's
allotment of two new apostolic prefectures in Hubei Province. The prefectures encompassed underdeveloped, rural areas in the province, with a
small Catholic presence. The Chinese priests interpreted the assignment
as further marginalization: the council had consigned them to the "worst"
regions and left the "better," more well-developed missionary regions to
the European missionaries.[84]

In April 1926, Costantini convened another meeting, this time to
discuss the problem of rising anti-Christian movements that were
spreading throughout China. Worried about the church's future in the
country, the Catholic leadership wanted to turn a defensive position into
an offensive one. They left the meeting in agreement: they would demonstrate commitment to the indigenous church. The Vatican rapidly delivered on the promise. On October 28, 1926, the Vatican ordained its first

six Chinese bishops. The Chinese Catholic Church now could claim that it had shed its colonial and imperialist past: it had Chinese leadership and was on the path to becoming fully Chinese.[85]

The ordination of these Chinese bishops sent shockwaves throughout the Catholic world. What had previously been an agenda held by a minority within the missionary community became the central policy of the church. Costantini had proved his efficiency: within four years of his arrival, the Vatican had ordained six Chinese bishops. Within the next decade, the ordination of non-Western bishops accelerated.[86]

Not all groups celebrated the ordinations. The Jesuit priest Pascal M. d'Elia noted, "Protestants wondered aloud whether the ordination of the Chinese Bishops was but a political move of the Holy See to face the new circumstances." Protestant missionaries in China accused the church of using the ordinations as a way to give the illusion that the church was transferring control to the Chinese. In reality, they charged, European Catholic missionaries retained their authority and power over the Chinese.[87]

Even within the Catholic world, response to the ordinations was mixed. Henninghaus admitted to an SVD colleague that while he had congratulated each of the bishops individually, he felt the ordinations "could not work miracles for the evangelization of China. Instead, it is merely a product of the times and reflects the wishes of many Chinese Christians." He felt that it was "not unreasonable" that places that had "been adequately prepared" with "good old-Christian communities" should have ordained Chinese bishops. But this made him even more convinced that for the SVD missions "the time has not yet come when we can entrust our Chinese priests to independently manage our mission. The life of faith has yet to grow deep enough in our Chinese priests and parishes." The ordinations, Henninghaus wrote, were "done too quickly, even if one had waited long enough for it."[88]

Other SVD missionaries, however, were impressed by Costantini's vision and tenacity. Georg Weig remarked that only a person of Costantini's ambition and capacity could have convened the first synod of bishops in Shanghai in 1924: "Without him, there would have been no Synod. A whole host of Bishops are openly against him; they would rather work alone and continue to muddle in the old model."[89] The SVD regional director Hermann Schoppelrey credited Costantini with the smooth proceedings of the assembly. Costantini had managed a difficult situation with a gentle and steady hand. In the midst of the fractious politics involved at the synod, Costantini's temperament provided moderation. Schoppelrey was "delighted and surprised" that "allegiance toward national and religious orders took a back seat" at the conference. In particular, he was impressed by the openness at the synod: "All questions were brought before the General Assembly. Freedom of speech was granted, and the participants used that privilege. Important points were discussed extensively." Costantini was, Schoppelrey felt, an "extraordinarily adroit Master of Ceremonies."[90]

Publicly, the SVD praised Costantini's work. Following the directives of the 1924 synod, the SVD held a Pontifical High Mass for "Our Lady of China" that Christmas. Sister Ries Bonitas, who worked in Poli, described the mass as one that was "celebrated by summoning all of the glories of the church." At the mass, the "well-known Christmas songs were sung," and the sacraments were administered. Toward the end of the ceremony, the SVD missionaries replicated the ceremonial worship of the Chinese Madonna (Zhonghua Shengmu) that they had witnessed at the 1924 synod: "The Bishop and missionaries brought lit candles to the altar. They fell to their knees. A moment of solemn silence ensued, the moment so sacred that even little babies in the pews dared not to make a sound. Then the Bishop prayed together with the priests the Latin consecration rite before the Blessed Sacrament and the Chinese image of the Virgin Mary. The congregation joined in as one, repeating the prayer of consecration for Mary solemnly as if it were a sacred oath. This was followed by the famous hymn 'Mary loves,' sung in Chinese with devotion and enthusiasm."[91] The SVD, at least in its public pronouncements, had now aligned itself completely behind the Vatican's policies. It was devoted to the agenda of *Maximum illud*.

CONCLUSIONS: LINES DRAWN IN THE SAND

The SVD, like the BMS, emerged from the First World War a changed organization. Before the war, both societies considered their Chinese congregations "immature" and unready for independence. After the war, they recognized that they needed to implement more rapid indigenization. These radical shifts were catalyzed by the gravest set of challenges the missionaries faced since they had first entered China. For one, they witnessed the emergence of new Chinese opponents: secular Chinese intellectuals, empowered by the New Culture Movement, criticized

Western missionaries as agents of imperialism, and their critiques inspired a nationwide anti-Christian movement after 1922. Chinese Christians, dismayed by what they saw as a betrayal by the Western powers at the Paris Peace Conferences, joined their secular nationalist counterparts in criticizing the chauvinist tendencies of Western missionaries.

But these critiques were not new: missionaries had been forced to face anti-Christian voices ever since the nineteenth century. What made the postwar situation particularly dire was the decimation of financial support for missionary societies from Europe. The war crippled the finances of the German missionary societies, rendering them unable to train and send missionaries. The Versailles Treaty further fragmented the tenuous relationships that Western missionary countries had developed before the war. Threatened with expulsion from China, Germans turned to their American, British, and French counterparts for aid. When the Versailles Treaty nonetheless stripped the German missionaries of their holdings abroad, German animosity toward the victorious missionary countries intensified. Confronted with vociferous opponents of Christianity, dwindling finances, and bitter resentment between Western missionary groups, the entire German missionary enterprise in China faced an acute crisis.

Western missionaries recognized the fracturing of the global mission field and throughout the 1920s tried to rebuild it. Both the 1922 Protestant conference in Shanghai and the 1924 Catholic synod in Shanghai were attempts to foster reconciliation among the various national missionary efforts, as well as counter the Chinese nationalist accusation that the missionaries were nothing more than imperial lackeys.

On the surface, the conferences were a resounding success. Both Shanghai conferences represented the first time that the diverse missionary societies in China had agreed to gather in one place and articulate a "united front." Across the board, Protestants and Catholics took the criticisms of the anti-Christian movement seriously and recognized that they needed to help push forward initiatives that could create an indigenous Chinese church. Yet, although the German missionaries in China attended the conferences publicly, privately they expressed resentment at and dissatisfaction with the tone of the conferences. They felt marginalized from the proceedings and saw the efforts at pushing forward indigenization as forms of geopolitical jockeying, rather than authentic missionary work.

In the case of the Protestants, the missionary leadership in Germany fueled these national resentments. German missionary leaders and theologians railed against what they saw as the pernicious influence of "Americanism," a form of liberal-modernist secularism disguised as religion. This broader situation was mirrored in the fate of the BMS. For one, it had a more narrow geographical reach: the financial devastation of the war forced the BMS to abandon its missionary holdings in northern China. BMS missionaries also willingly isolated themselves from the broader international community, seeking to build alliances only with other German missionary organizations. The BMS thus emerged from the war as a more nationalist organization, committed to building a more expansive German missionary presence throughout the world.

In the field, German Catholics were no less nationalistic. The war had taught them bitter lessons, and they resented the dominant positions missionaries of other nations—particularly the French—held in the field. But the Vatican counteracted such nationalist divisions: it served as a crucial centripetal force after the war. The Vatican saw the fractures that the First World War had wrought, and it asserted itself as the preeminent spiritual authority within the mission field. While the SVD missionaries who worked in the field expressed resentment toward their rival nations, the SVD leadership in Europe aligned itself further with the Vatican.

In part, the SVD embraced the Vatican because of its roots as an ultramontane society: its whole existence had depended on the spiritual protection of Rome. On the other hand, the First World War had forced the SVD to become an international organization and rely on its American branch for funds. In 1928, when the missionary society transferred the generalate from Steyl to Rome, signaling its deepened ties to the Vatican and a commitment to the Vatican's internationalizing vision, the transformation of the SVD from a predominantly German mission society to an international one was complete.[92]

The BMS and the SVD survived the war having learned very different lessons. The SVD, which already had an international element to its organization before the war, became even more global in its makeup. Becoming a more international organization helped the SVD to emerge from the First World War a stronger institution, as it could rely on its American branch for both financial and political support. The BMS, on the other hand, doubled down on its nationalist ties. Feeling resentful of the dominance of Anglo-American liberal Protestants, the BMS refused to build potential alliances.

Yet, in many ways, the war had not changed everything: the seeds for postwar German missionary developments certainly existed before the First World War. The Protestant BMS's tensions with its Anglo-American missionary counterparts predated the war, as did the Catholic SVD's internationalism. The First World War served to accelerate the development of certain trajectories and foreclosed others. For Protestants, the war strengthened their national conviction and their critique of Anglo-American imperialism. For Catholics, it strengthened their ultramontanism. Both of these proclivities had existed long before the war.

The First World War foregrounded a constant tension that both missionary societies—and all missionary societies in general—had to negotiate since their founding: the overlapping claims of transnational Christianity and national strength. The global dimension of evangelization was always taken as a given—missionaries assumed that they were working to spread Christianity throughout the world. But what were the best ways to realize that goal? In the nineteenth century, missionaries cleaved to the idea of a "Christianized modernization" and often drew upon the resources of Western imperialism to help them achieve their goals. The boundaries between the goal of expanding Christianity and Western imperialism were often permeable and fluid; at times, missionaries worked in conjunction with their imperialist counterparts, at other times, against. Yet the First World War made these previously fluid lines impermeable. It forced German missionaries to declare their commitments: with no empire to turn to, they were now decisively against any form of imperial power.

The war revealed nationalism as a double-edged sword. Not only had nationalism led to conflict between the European powers, it had also unleashed the power of the Chinese people after the May Fourth Movement. The Chinese began to define missionaries as retrograde; with capable Chinese Christian leaders, many of whom had been educated in the West, the Chinese church no longer needed missionaries to run the church in China, nor serve as intermediaries with the West.

In certain ways, the catastrophic losses of the First World War freed German missionaries from having to defend themselves against Chinese nationalist attacks. With no more empire to defend, German missionaries now could claim the purity of their intentions: they were in China solely for the sake of missionary work, rather than for the advancement of German national interests. What could the Germans uniquely offer to the Chinese that other missionary nations could not? How did the Germans articulate their vision for the future of the Chinese church? The next chapter examines some of the answers that they adopted.

CHAPTER FIVE

Order Out of Chaos

IN JANUARY 1919, STREET battles broke out in Berlin between the Spartacist League, a radical Communist group, and the right-wing paramilitary group known as the Freikorps. Roads were barricaded. Using weapons they had kept from the war, the members of the Freikorps quickly suppressed the Spartacists. By the end of the skirmishes, the dead bodies of the Spartacist leaders Rosa Luxemburg and Karl Liebknecht were fished out of the river Spree. The Spartacist uprising reflected an atmosphere of revolutionary discontent. As Eric Weitz writes, in the winter of 1918 and 1919 "politics had become the stuff of life. . . . The orderly German, so frequently stereotyped and satirized, had become an unruly figure."[1] Miners, soldiers, and factory workers went on strike, as did actors, stagehands, and cleanup crews. Farmers and industrial workers alike protested for better wages.

The leaders of the BMS expressed horror at these political developments. Three days before Luxemburg and Liebknecht were killed, Siegfried Knak, then directing mission work within Germany, preached a sermon during which he warned that the German people (*Volk*) faced an unprecedented crisis. The nation, which had once bound the Germans together and given their lives meaning and purpose, had been shattered in defeat. Without a nation to believe in, many were spiritually lost. Instead, the people had put their faith in false gods—socialism, pacifism, and "cosmopolitan idealism." All these ideas, Knak warned, reflected "demonic powers of selfishness, of hatefulness, of lies, and the human propensity to take joy in crudeness and vulgarity." They could never unify the German *Volk*. Only Christianity—and moreover, Protestantism— could bind the fragmented *Volk* together. With its clear understanding of the human condition, the church could re-create the bonds of solidarity and stability that the war had sundered.[2]

Knak delivered his sermon as Germans argued over the place of Christianity in the new state. Previously, the Prussian king had held the position of supreme governor of the Evangelical Church, defining Prussia as a "Christian state." The revolutionary provisional government that came to power after November 1918 sought to sever the links between church and state. Leading the charge was the prominent parliamentarian, journalist, cofounder of the radical left Independent Social Democratic Party, and long-standing opponent to the church, Adolph Hoffmann. He became the Prussian minister of culture, leading the ministry that oversaw religious affairs. Within less than a month of occupying the office, Hoffmann had implemented an anticlerical program mandating the freedom of religious belief, outlawing religious ceremonies and prayers in schools, allowing children without a faith background to be released from religious instruction, and abolishing confessional schools. Along with Karl Liebknecht and Ernst Haeckel, Hoffmann agitated on behalf of the movement to leave the church and avoid church taxes. Hoffmann resigned in less than half a year, but his influence lasted past his short tenure: the Weimar constitution of August 1919 adopted many of the measures that Hoffmann advocated and officially demolished the elevated position Prussian church leaders once enjoyed.[3]

Naturally, Catholic and Protestant clergy felt threatened. Catholics believed that a new *Kulturkampf* was brewing. Even liberal Protestants who were sympathetic to Hoffmann's general goals of separating church and state found his tactics repugnant. The prominent theologian Martin Rade, who edited the influential liberal journal *Die Christliche Welt*, called Hoffmann a "fanatic" and his assault on the church "overzealous and ruthless." Hoffmann, Rade charged, "had alienated the Christian voters of both confessions," turning them against the young Republic.[4]

Conservative Protestants vociferously fought back. As Daniel Borg has shown, conservative Protestant church leaders saw "the new political order as the very nemesis of Evangelical beliefs and traditions."[5] They agitated against the Republic in both the press and the pulpit. In particular, the BMS inserted itself as a central player in the debates over church and state. Mobilizing its numerous print organs, the BMS printed pamphlets and tracts and used its journal to assert the centrality of the church's position in modern society. BMS missionaries actively participated in other church institutions that sought to insert themselves into public life: missionary leaders sat on the committees of various influential church institutions, such as the Prussian Evangelical Supreme Ecclesiastical Council (Evangelischer Oberkirchenrat), the Inner Mission, and associations that sought to evangelize through print.[6]

The director of the BMS, Karl Axenfeld, emerged as one of the most prominent voices defending Christianity against its secular opponents. Axenfeld became a key figure in the governing body of Prussian Protestant churches, renamed the Evangelical Church of the Old-Prussian Union (Evangelische Kirche der altpreußischen Union). In a series of meetings from 1921 to 1922, the Old-Prussian Union drafted and ratified a new church constitution. Axenfeld was one of the members of the constitution committee, and he belonged to an alliance of so-called confessionally true (*Bekenntnistreuen*) conservatives who dominated the proceedings. The conservatives used the constitution to define the Old-Prussian Union as a bulwark against the rise of secularism and socialism. Under Axenfeld's influence, the constitution adopted missionary language, compelling church leaders to take a more active stance in shaping Germany's moral and spiritual landscapes.[7]

Axenfeld believed that Germans needed to abandon their previous model of the "state church" (*Staatskirche*) and replace it with a "people's church" (*Volkskirche*). He exhorted German church leaders to recognize that Germans no longer inherited their faith. They had to act as if they were in foreign lands, surrounded by heathens: German pastors had to proclaim the gospel and build their congregations just as missionaries had abroad. Drawing on his experiences in Africa, Axenfeld wrote that Christianity had helped to "internally bind" both the Africans and Germans in their collective work. More than ever, forces of social cohesion were needed, especially in Berlin, "where no social solidarity exists, and each group only considers its own interests." In certain cases, missionary work had helped foster more vibrant spirituality in Africa than in Germany. A German *Volkskirche,* Axenfeld proclaimed, not only could break down "barriers" that had been erected in German society after the war, it could also help the Germans catch up with broader trends in global Christianity. For Axenfeld, the task of strengthening the German *Volkskirche* was intimately linked with the spread of Christianity abroad.[8]

Axenfeld's invocation of the "people's church" belonged to a broader discursive moment when calls for creating an "indigenous church" abounded in missionary circles worldwide. As we have seen, the "indigenous church" became a slogan in missionary circles in China because of the First World War's assault on the moral and spiritual claims of European superiority and the outpouring of anti-Christian Chinese nationalist sentiment. Many missionaries found in the idea of the indigenous Chinese church a panacea for the ills that plagued Christianity in China. The idea appealed across confessional lines. For Catholic and Protestant missionaries alike, the successful creation of a Chinese church promised an end to theological factionalism, Chinese allegations of Christian ties to imperialism, and a lack of personnel in the mission field.[9]

Yet, despite the overwhelming international consensus in favor of an indigenous church, the term itself was unstable and ambiguous. European, American, and Chinese actors disagreed on what the term meant and about how to construct such a church. Among other things, they argued over the pace of ordinations and the relationship between missionaries and local clergy. Shaping these divergent visions for the indigenous church was a complicated mixture of theological traditions and geopolitical rivalries, national resentment, and racial ideologies. In this chapter, I focus on how, despite the overwhelming consensus within the international realm to support an indigenizing agenda, the process of implementing the idea was filled with conflict.

Conflicts over the future of the indigenous church emerged within missionary circles. The Catholic missionaries of the SVD found the Holy See meddlesome and complained about the Vatican's unwarranted optimism about Chinese clerical ordinations. The SVD had boots on the ground, not the Vatican. The Protestant Berlin missionaries, on the other hand, interpreted the international call for indigenous participation as an attempt by the Anglo-Americans to extend their geopolitical dominance to the spiritual realm. The Anglo-Americans, German Protestants bristled, used the term "indigenization" interchangeably with the word "democratization." The Protestants advanced their own proposals for creating a Chinese church, which they argued was singularly unique and an alternative to the Anglo-American model.

Internal arguments also surfaced within missionary societies, as factions jockeyed to assert their vision for how the societies should devote their resources to developing an independent Chinese church. I show how German missionary practices in China emerged from the conflict between the desires of the missionary leaders in Europe and the realities in the field. The indigenous church that Germans developed in China reflected more than the immediate demands of local Chinese Christians. Faced with a radically changed global political landscape after the First World War, German missionaries sought to create a Chinese church that could respond to the confusing and rapidly shifting situation around them. German missionary work in China was forged as much in Germany and Europe as it was in China.

THE *VOLKSKIRCHE*

How did German missionaries define indigenization? The missionary theologian Johannes Hoekendijk notes that various definitions of the *Volkskirche* have appeared within the theological discourse since the early nineteenth century, when theologians began to inject the *Volkskirche* with romantic and proto-nationalist sentiment. By the twentieth century, the exact meaning of the term remained vague and was often confused with other broadly used terms to denote a pan-German church above the fragmented landscape of regional churches (*Landeskirche*), such as the "national church" (*Nationalkirche*) or the "racial church" (*Rassenkirche*). But in all cases, German missionaries shared a view of the *Volkskirche* as a possible solution for the global crises in which they found themselves after the war.[10]

In 1921, Siegfried Knak succeeded Axenfeld as the director of the BMS, and he carried on Axenfeld's agenda, becoming a vocal proponent for the *Volkskirche*. Knak's vision was explicitly international: the *Volkskirche* offered an antidote to what he saw as the feeble theological positions advanced by the Americans and British. Drawing on the ideas of Johann Gottfried von Herder, Knak argued that the *Volk* was as timeless and ageless as the gospel itself—it was a category that transcended nations, states, and politics. As Hoekendijk has noted, for Knak, the *Volk* was "a vehicle for history in a holy and eschatological framework."[11]

Knak saw the world as culturally diverse and pluralist at heart. Each *Volk* had its own history, its own "cultural soul" (*Kulturseele*). Missionaries ought to honor "the different characteristics of different races as a God-given reality, and help to develop these characteristics to their full potential and maturity."[12] The task of the missionary was to identify the cultural differences of each *Volk* and build a *Volkskirche* that reflected these specific cultural traits. Each nation's *Volkskirche* had to assume a different guise; as Knak argued, "The Chinese Church should not look like the African, nor the German, nor the English."[13]

How would missionaries know how to tailor their approaches to different peoples? Here, Knak drew upon the ideas of the influential missionary theologian Heinrich Frick, who relied on racial hierarchies to differentiate between three categories of peoples (*Völker*)—"cultured peoples" (*Kulturvölker*), "natural peoples" (*Naturvölker*), and those who fell in between. He labeled the Chinese a "cultured people," since they had an ancient civilization and a long history of cultural development.[14]

For Frick and Knak, missionaries and missionary societies had to adapt their strategies according to the level of civilization that they encountered. "Cultured peoples" possessed high standards of education and a strong consciousness of their own historical development. They were in theory prepared for church independence. But advanced civilizations were proud of their own culture and tended to resist overt threats to their cultural heritages. When engaging with *Kulturvölker* like the Chinese, Frick instructed, missionaries needed to refrain from methods of "Europeanization" and engage with them on their own terms. The *Naturvölker*, on the other hand, needed more active European guidance. Frick believed that Europeans had to export their civilization and customs to countries in Africa to expedite the process of church building.[15]

Pointing to the mystical idea of the *Volk* as their crucial criterion for comparison and categorization, Frick and the rest of the German missionary establishment drew upon twentieth-century racial ideas in their prescriptions for missionaries in the field. German missionary theologians justified their racial thinking by claiming that God had created a multiracial world. Originally, God had put all races on an equal footing, but sin had entered the world and rendered the races unequal. For Frick, it was up to the more advanced Christian nations of the world to help these non-Christian nations reach the same level of spiritual development.[16]

German Protestants were not alone in employing the *Volk* as a theological concept. Among Catholic theological circles, the *Volk* also gained a political meaning. German Catholic theologians after the First World War were particularly seduced by the idea of the *Volk*, which, as John Connelly writes, "grew especially dear to German Catholics who for decades were accused of loyalties divided between the Vatican and Berlin." *Völkisch* ideas "stirred the Catholic imagination by mixing religious, ethnic, political, and cultural connotations in a radically new way."[17] With ideologies surrounding the *Volk*, German Catholic theologians found a way to translate their political allegiances into theology.

Among Catholic missionaries, however, the idea of the *Volkskirche* did not gain as much traction as it did among their Protestant counterparts. Catholic missionary theologians like Josef Schmidlin (1876–1944) criticized Protestant notions of the *Volkskirche*. The fundamental problem, Schmidlin argued, was that Protestants, "with their vague concept of the Church," could understand the relationship between the missionary church and the indigenous church only in the abstract. German Protestants, Schmidlin charged, were handicapped by their tendency to fall back on a state and national framework inherited from Bismarck's Germany (*Reichsgedanke*), which hindered global cooperation.[18] In the Catholic world, the relationship between the local and the global church was clear: all parishes and missionary congregations throughout the world folded into the hierarchical structure and framework of the Catholic Church. Catholicism, and the Catholic Church, had a long history of juggling tensions between the particular church parishes and the universal church. Instead, Schmidlin exhorted Catholic missionaries to forsake national and colonial politics; they had to give up their own national interests and follow the Vatican's lead.[19]

German Protestants used the *Volkskirche* as a way to criticize American and British missionary practices. Knak attacked Anglo-American conceptions of indigenization—most prominently represented by Social Gospel variants of the Three-Self church—as checklists. Whether in China or South Africa, the items on the checklist were the same. Indifferent to local particularities, American and British missionary practices were forms of cultural imperialism.[20]

For German Protestants, the *Volkskirche* served as a convenient defense on several fronts. On the one hand, it became a useful way to condemn what they saw as American and British imperialism. Since each *Volk* was unique, German missionaries claimed that they did not—indeed they could not—replicate a German *Volkskirche* and export it throughout the world. Such a strategy was bound to fail. Local cultures would reject a one-size-fits-all approach to congregational building. Unlike the Americans, who wanted to implement Western-style democratic practices everywhere, the Germans argued that they allowed each culture to develop on its own terms and at its own pace. As a result, the *Volkskirche* became a code for criticizing American-style cultural imperialism.

On the other hand, the *Volkskirche* allowed the Germans to retain their claims of racial superiority toward the Africans and Chinese. Since Christian Germany had progressed to a more advanced stage, it was the duty of German missionaries to aid and assist the Chinese, Africans, and Indians in developing their own unique *Volkskirche*. The Germans retained their mandate of spiritual guides and superiors because they had reached a higher plateau of racial development. The invocation of the *Volkskirche* became a way for Germans to simultaneously criticize Anglo-American cultural imperialism and justify its own culturally imperialist practices.

The *Volkskirche* also reflected the German recognition that they needed to adapt their ideas to a world transformed. In the nineteenth century, they conceived of missionary work in statistical terms: "victory" in the mission field could be determined by numbers of souls converted, church buildings built, and territories acquired. With the destruction of the German Empire, the Germans knew that they had definitively lost that fight. Now, instead of competing for territory, they sought to compete on a battlefield of ideas. German Protestants believed that they could blaze a new trail through their theology.

For German Protestants, the *Volkskirche* was the idea that provided them with a competitive edge: it distinguished them from other Christians in a secularizing world. While liberal Christians made themselves more "secular" in their trumpeting of democratic and liberal ideals, the German missionaries saw the *Volkskirche* as an authentic form of Christianity, rooted in the principles of Luther's Reformation. The *Volkskirche,* German Protestants believed, was a distinctly German contribution to the international field of missionary work and could not be stolen or acquired by other countries.

CREATING A *VOLKSKIRCHE* IN CHINA

Missionary leaders sought to put their ideas of the *Volkskirche* into practice, and in 1922, Knak and the BMS leadership began the process of reforming the institutional makeup of its Chinese congregations. Knak wanted to develop a new church constitution (*Kirchenordnung*) to implant in individual Chinese congregations. "A new constitution is necessary," Knak wrote to his fellow missionaries in 1923, "because Germany is now so poor that Chinese Christians must now come to help the mission. We must present this new Church constitution to the Chinese with as much clarity as we can."[21] The eventual goal of the constitution was to create a Chinese *Volkskirche*. Debates over the church constitution, and how to use it to create a distinctly Chinese church, occupied the mission society's attention for the rest of the decade.

It was no coincidence that, at the same time that debates ensued in Germany over the Prussian church's new constitution, the BMS began to draw up a new *Kirchenordnung* for its congregations in China. Just as a new constitution could articulate new directions for the church in Germany, where Christianity was under siege, so too could a new church constitution in China help fend off anti-Christian attacks there. Christianity's opponents were found throughout the globe, and Christians needed to formulate equally international responses to stem the influence of their enemies.

Knak modeled the BMS Chinese congregations' constitution on the old-Prussian church document. The BMS Chinese constitution began with a preamble almost identical to that of the old-Prussian church. Both claimed "an inheritance of the church fathers" and offered an orthodox defense of the faith, proclaiming that they stood "on the Gospel given in the Holy Scripture of Jesus Christ, Son of the living God, who was crucified and resurrected for us, who is the Lord of the Church." Both constitutions also recognized "the continuing truth of its confessions: the Apostles' Creed and the other creeds of the Ancient church."[22]

Yet even in the preambles of both documents, striking differences emerged between the two, particularly regarding pronouncements of confessional commitment. The German constitution stated its dual confessional allegiances, referring to both Reformed and Lutheran creeds. The inclusion of both confessional creeds had been vigorously debated in the German assembly: liberal and moderate church leaders objected to the preamble's failure to provide protection for non-Lutheran or Reformed denominations. They wanted a more inclusive understanding of German Protestantism.[23] Knak and the BMS leaders construed the Chinese constitution along much narrower theological lines. It clearly stated that the BMS's Chinese congregations adhered to the principles of the "short catechism of Luther," leaving out any references to Reformed creeds.[24] The Chinese congregations presented to the BMS what it longed for in Germany: an opportunity to create "pure" Lutheran congregations.

Despite their commitment to theological orthodoxy, the constitutions in both Germany and China instituted sweeping ecclesiastical reforms. Both sought to decentralize church power, placing individual parishes at the center of the church. The constitutions granted congregants more opportunities to participate in ecclesiastical decision-making. The old-Prussian constitution instituted a system of proportional representation, so minorities could participate in a system that elected members of the General Synod. Women were given the right to vote.[25] Similarly, the BMS constitution gave Chinese parishioners more power. It also created a system of proportional representation, giving Chinese Christians the ability to vote for representatives to send to the General Synod. Chinese Christians were granted the right to sit on committees and had more avenues for shaping the agenda of the church.[26]

The Chinese constitution reflected broader shifts in missionary attitudes toward Chinese Christians. When Hermann Wangemann wrote the *Missionsordnung* in 1882, he referred to Chinese Christians as "colored" (*Farbigen*) and Chinese Christian workers, regardless of rank, as "assistants" (*Gehilfen*). Knak and the BMS leadership stripped the 1922 *Kirchenordnung* of the old language. They struck out the word "colored" and now referred to *Gehilfen* as "ordained Chinese preachers." The highest rank that Chinese Christians could now achieve was that of pastor. Previously, they could at best rise to the rank of assistant pastor (*Vikar*), which assumed subordination to a Western missionary supervisor.[27]

Despite the change in language, old habits died hard. In a 1924 letter, Knak used the word *Gehilfen* to refer to some of the Chinese working in the congregations. Admonishing Knak, Heinrich Wahl, a missionary in China, wrote, "It is inappropriate to use the word *Gehilfen* nowadays."[28]

Still, the new constitution did not radically change the power relations between Chinese clergy and German leaders. For the most part, the Chinese church constitution protected the power and authority of the Germans. Here, again, the BMS *Kirchenordnung* replicated the old-Prussian church's power structure, which, as Daniel Borg has noted, was "far from democratic."[29] Similarly, the BMS's *Kirchenordnung* preserved the authority of the missionaries on the ground. Missionaries continued to control the selection of all members to various church committees, and they supervised the committee meetings. They could veto any Chinese decision. BMS missionary leaders also closely monitored and restricted Chinese ordinations.[30]

The BMS *Kirchenordnung* further controlled the process by which individual Chinese congregations could become independent. Continuing their prewar suspicion of Chinese faith, missionary leaders stipulated that a church congregation could become independent only if it were "spiritually mature."[31] To ascertain levels of development, three categories were denoted in the church constitution. The first, an "infant congregation," had fewer than twenty members and the missionaries judged it as far from the goal of financial independence. Members of these nascent parishes were required to contribute an annual tithe used to pay for the salaries of Chinese pastors and other workers. The Germans covered other costs, such as repairing church buildings and providing necessary materials such as Bibles and hymnals. In the second category, the "advanced congregation," members were required to pay a slightly higher annual fee, and the fund contributed to the maintenance of church buildings and the construction of other auxiliary buildings. The congregation still could request subsidies from the BMS. The third category, the "independent congregation," paid fully for both maintenance and personnel fees. As before, it was the European missionaries, in consultation with the home board, and not the Chinese Christians, who determined whether the congregations were ready for independence.[32]

Through the BMS *Kirchenordnung*, Knak and the BMS missionary leadership imposed a spiritual hierarchy in their Chinese congregations that corresponded with their ideas of racial evolution. Just as the world had "cultured" and "natural" civilizations, so did the BMS's Chinese congregations have "infant" and "advanced" statuses. The constitution's categories reflected Knak's belief that Germany possessed a more advanced spirituality. Knak argued that as "children of Luther's Reformation," the Germans had already gone through the painful historical process of forming a *Volkskirche*. He believed that German Protestants possessed a mandate to help "spiritually immature" nations like China develop; China had to progress through the same stages of church development that Germany had. The BMS's *Kirchenordnung*, Knak claimed, reflected Germany's advanced spiritual status and could help to usher Chinese congregations to a more elevated spiritual state.

Once they had formulated the *Kirchenordnung*, the BMS missionaries sought to put it into practice. Signaling its new approach in China, the BMS convened its first General Synod in 1924. The synod's participants had been chosen through a careful process articulated in the church constitution. While previously Chinese Christian assistants had been relegated to the position of petitioner, voicing their concerns at the *Gehilfen* conferences, now Chinese Christians participated in the conference as equals. The Germans were outnumbered: of the forty-three representatives at the synod, only twelve were Germans. The conference was conducted in Chinese, and all expressed enthusiasm to implement the new constitution and seek Chinese church independence.[33]

Yet the new reforms caused confusion, particularly among missionaries who had just arrived in China. These new arrivals wondered how they should relate to Chinese Christian pastors: could they order the Chinese to follow their commands? Were they expected to serve as subordinates to established Chinese pastors?

To answer these questions, the BMS missionaries decided to hold an annual missionary conference that excluded Chinese pastors. The missionaries held the conference a week before the General Synod so that they could coordinate strategies before the broader meeting. At the 1924 conference, the missionary Heinrich Wahl, who had just arrived in China, observed that the new constitution had rendered the relationship between missionary and Chinese pastor "unclear." Wahl asked, "Is the [European] missionary a superior to the Chinese pastor?"[34] Another recent arrival to China, Hugo Krause, complained that the Chinese presumed equality with the Germans: "It has been tremendously difficult to work with established Chinese pastors, who feel that they can independently run a missionary station."[35] With neither experience nor clearly delineated institutional authority over the Chinese, new missionaries were puzzled by how to relate to Chinese pastors in their congregations.

Resenting challenges to their authority, several missionaries insisted that Europeans retain their superiority. One objected to the idea that the constitution instituted equality between the Chinese pastor and European missionaries. He said, "The situation is not so difficult—we are responsible to the Committee (home board), and the Chinese Pastors are responsible to us."[36] Another missionary agreed, arguing, "The missionary should be the superior to the Chinese pastor."[37]

The home board back in Germany was impatient. After reading the transcripts of the debate at the 1924 missionary conference, a missionary inspector in Berlin, Wilhelm Spiecker, wrote, "In a very short time the Chinese pastors will have complete control and leadership of the Church in their hands." Newcomers should acknowledge this eventuality. In administrative matters—writing reports, communicating with the home board, and managing finances—the missionaries clearly had to take charge. However, younger missionaries, Spiecker advised, should enter a congregation with the attitude that they could learn from those who had already spent time in the congregation. He warned, "For a German missionary, used to Prussian discipline, it is often difficult to leave the Chinese to do as they please." The new missionary should therefore endeavor not to treat Chinese leaders too harshly. Missionaries, Spiecker advised, should be flexible and more open-minded in their relations with the Chinese.[38]

The trust that missionary leaders hoped to foster between missionaries and the Chinese leadership proved difficult to cultivate. At the General Synod in 1926, missionaries complained that the BMS's congregations remained far from achieving the goals of independence outlined in the constitution. They blamed the Chinese leadership for foot-dragging. Chinese pastors and preachers, they claimed, were unenthused about the constitution's new directives and resisted implementing them.[39]

After the conference, one Chinese Christian pastor, Ling Deyuan, admitted that the Chinese did not all support the new constitution. "The understanding of the Church Constitution among us Chinese Christians is varied," Ling commented diplomatically. Some, he stated, thought it restricted Chinese autonomy and allowed the Germans to control all proceedings. Even the Chinese who liked the constitution's agenda thought that the Berliners were too ambitious and trying to institute too many reforms at once. Ling asked the Berlin leadership to adopt a more moderate approach, writing, "A more gradual implementation of the plans for independence is advisable."[40]

Impressed by Ling's sober-minded analysis, the missionary leaders gave Ling complete control over the largest missionary station in Shixing County in 1927, making him the BMS's first Chinese pastor to manage a congregation independent of missionary supervision. The missionaries declared that he had the "same rights and responsibilities as a European missionary." For the first time, a Chinese pastor had obtained the same institutional status as his missionary supervisors.[41]

But Ling was an exception—the station in Shixing remained the only independent Chinese congregation until 1936. Adoption of the constitution's instructions was slow. Some missionaries blamed this slow pace on the framing of the document itself. One missionary agreed with the Chinese critique that the church constitution had been too ambitious; it was impossible to achieve all of its proposed reforms.[42] Another missionary argued that the Chinese Christians had not adopted the church constitution because it did not organically develop from the Chinese themselves. No Chinese had been consulted during its drafting. The Chinese pastors and congregants who resisted the *Kirchenordnung* attacked it as "un-Chinese" and "outdated."[43]

Nonetheless, Knak continued to defend the constitution, insisting that it "ensures that we can better serve the true needs of Chinese Christianity." He saw the constitution as the only intellectually viable alternative to Anglo-American dominance in China. Disparaging the "blind followers of an American attempt to create a national Church," Knak believed that the BMS constitution ensured that its Chinese leadership could be vetted through a vigorous process. The constitution promised to create more orthodox Lutheran congregations. Only then could Germans prevent the domination of Anglo-American theology.[44]

Under Knak's leadership, BMS leaders maintained a cautious approach to congregational independence. By 1936, almost fifteen years after the constitution's first implementation, the BMS could count only one congregation as self-sufficient. Even in the face of such a dismal showing, Knak did not waver in his defense of the *Kirchenordnung*. He argued that the document helped to usher in "a transitional stage, preparation for the Chinese churches to become fully independent."[45]

Placed within the broader context of Chinese Protestantism in the 1920s and 1930s, the Chinese critique of the BMS constitution as "un-Chinese" makes sense. At the same time that the BMS struggled to implement its new constitution, fully independent Chinese Christian organizations emerged on the religious landscape. Previously trained and employed by Western missionary societies, Chinese Christian leaders left those societies to create church bodies with no foreign control. Many of these organizations, such as the True Jesus Church, the Church Assembly Hall, and the Jesus Family, had a charismatic founder who employed revivalist tactics to gain a wide following.

Among them, the True Jesus Church, founded by Wei Enbo in 1917, was the most successful. Educated by the London Missionary Society and touched by Pentecostal fervor, Wei repudiated the hierarchical structure of the missionary society. "Let there be no autocratic domination of meetings and prayers by any man," Wei said. "Let all take turns to preach; let all pray aloud in meetings."[46] Wei's egalitarianism gained a huge following among the rural poor—precisely the BMS's targeted demographic. By the mid-1930s, at the same time that Knak resisted Chinese congregational independence, the True Jesus Church had become the second largest Protestant church in China.[47] Compared with these radical organizations, the BMS's church constitution must have seemed woefully out of date to Chinese Christians.

STALLING TACTICS: A CHINESE SVD

How did the Catholic missionaries of the SVD respond to the dramatically altered global religious landscape? Like their Protestant counterparts, SVD missionaries saw global Christendom as having come under attack from secular opponents. The editors of the SVD journal *Steyler Missionsbote* wrote in 1921 that the Bolsheviks had unleashed a "revolution against God" and precipitated an "awful battle between the Kingdom of darkness and the Kingdom of God." Throughout the journal, missionaries exhorted their Catholic readers to renew their commitment to the faith and support of missions. The work of spreading the gospel abroad had a direct link with stemming the tides of secularism within Europe. They asked their readers to trust in the pope and other church leaders during such "cataclysmic times."[48]

One cannot understate the importance of the Vatican in the postwar landscape. As we saw in the previous chapter, the Vatican emerged from the First World War with renewed vigor, intent on asserting the vision of *Maximum illud.* Unlike Protestants, who held contradictory ideologies about the *Volkskirche* and the indigenous church, the Vatican's statements in *Maximum illud* offered a unified clarion call for the future of the global church. In particular, the Vatican urged missionaries to help develop indigenous clergy throughout the world. In Celso Costantini, they had an energetic, committed leader to execute their plans in China.

SVD missionaries knew that they had to ally themselves with the Vatican in order to survive. Publicly, the SVD aligned itself with the Vatican by reprinting *Maximum illud* and offering editorials supporting the pope's pronouncements. At the same time, in private correspondence, SVD missionaries wondered whether the Vatican was overly ambitious and doubted that China was spiritually mature enough for a bishop. They also understood the ramifications of fulfilling the Vatican's vision: it meant the eventual irrelevance of their work, the end of their decades-long presence in China.

Nonetheless, after the war the SVD began to reform its congregations along the lines set forth in *Maximum illud.* To carry out the changes, the SVD elected a new superior general, Wilhelm Gier. Having served for fourteen years as a novice master, Gier was chosen because of his long experience of institutional building.[49] He knew how to cultivate and build talent, a skill desperately needed for a missionary society that faced a shortage in personnel. Following the pope's exhortation in *Maximum illud,* Gier acknowledged that new priests were not going to come primarily from Europe, and his plan was to globalize the society. He succeeded. During his tenure from 1920 to 1932, the SVD more than doubled in size, growing from 1,783 members to 3,782.[50]

From the beginning of his tenure, Gier's global thinking was apparent. In 1921, he embarked on a three-year tour, inspecting the society's missionary work worldwide. China was only one stop on his itinerary: his travels took him to North America, the Philippines, Indonesia, New Guinea, and Japan. Gier arrived in China in August 1922 and stayed until February 1923. His arrival marked the first time an SVD superior general had ever visited the country.[51]

Gier was pleased with what he saw there. He marveled at the infrastructural networks the missionaries had built in Shandong in fewer than forty years. Particularly impressed by the number of missionary stations the society had established, he wrote: "The network of mission stations throughout the whole region is so dense that it is possible to celebrate Mass throughout the region without even packing luggage. Every seven to ten hours, one can find another Bishop's residence or a Catholic community with churches or several rooms that provide overnight lodging."[52] The superior general also praised the system of seminary education for Chinese candidates for the priesthood, approving its high quality.

Yet Gier complained that Chinese spirituality remained underdeveloped. Priests did not care much for hygiene, reflecting a lack of spiritual "maturity." The Chinese, Gier wrote, lacked "cardinal virtues, especially prudence and fortitude." He lamented, "It cannot be mistaken that our European brothers hold contempt and dislike for the indigenous priests." The Chinese priests, Gier conceded, were not all bad. Though lacking in cardinal virtues, they did possess "theological and moral virtues." In some cases, Gier remarked, the Chinese were "equal even to the best European priests." They exhibited exceptional spiritual qualities, such as "piety, docility, and zeal in pastoral care." In a global framework, the Chinese also fared quite well. Compared with Filipino clergy, Gier noted, "They adhere to the vows of chastity much better." They were no worse than the Germans in certain cases: "Public misconduct and scandals are certainly not more common than in the best dioceses in Germany." Overall, Gier was convinced that Chinese priests had the potential to develop spiritually. He concluded, "The holy Church need not be ashamed of the clergy here in Southern Shandong."[53]

Despite Gier's generally optimistic reading of the Chinese clergy's future, he resisted the Vatican's directives to ordain indigenous bishops. In the case of southern Shandong, the immediate ordination of Chinese seemed premature. There were still too many "new Christians" in the parishes and congregations, and Chinese priests in the region needed more time before they were ready to manage the region independently.

Yet Gier and the rest of the SVD leadership also wanted to signal to the Vatican that they took *Maximum illud* seriously. They devised a plan: create a Chinese SVD novitiate, which could prove to the Holy See that the missionary society was devoting more resources to training native clergy. It further demonstrated that the society had a serious intent to allow Chinese to become full members of the SVD. At the same time, the novitiate structure gave the SVD leadership the opportunity to maintain its control over the education of Chinese clergy. Gier wrote that the novitiate placed the future Chinese clergy "under the surveillance and guidance of our fellow brothers."[54] When the time came for SVD missionaries to cede responsibility of the church work to local Chinese, they could choose Chinese priests who were educated in the novitiate and therefore members of the SVD, ensuring the mission society a constant presence within the region. For the SVD, a Chinese novitiate offered a moderate and more cautious alternative to the Vatican's push for immediate ordination of Chinese bishops. Like the BMS's church constitution, the SVD's novitiate presented a transitional step toward eventual church independence. The SVD promised to transfer power to the Chinese, but it believed the Chinese needed European spiritual guidance before they could reach the stage of spiritual preparedness for independent ministry.

Gier argued that their approach of monitored, directed indigenization was the best solution to what he called the global "race problem" (*Rassenproblem*) that had surfaced after the First World War. The SVD began experimenting with using seminaries as a way to guide the process of developing indigenous clergy in 1921 when they established St. Augustine Seminary in Bay St. Louis, Mississippi, designed with the purpose of training African American candidates for the priesthood. The seminary leaders began accepting candidates in 1923.[55]

In February 1924, the SVD founded its Chinese novitiate, admitting three novices. The SVD decided to set up the house in Daijiazhuang, placing it close to the SVD's major seminary. The regional superior Hermann Schoppelrey reported that the desire of Chinese priests to enter the novitiate was deep; numerous seminarians and Chinese priests had expressed interest in joining. A jubilant Gier ordered the new master of the novitiate, Theodor Schu, "to educate and produce well-trained, evangelical men." Gier believed that if the SVD's novitiates succeeded in producing high-quality indigenous priests, they could become models for other parts of the world.[56] And indeed, the SVD began to replicate elsewhere the model it had established in the United States and China:

a year later the SVD instituted a novitiate in Brazil and enrolled four Brazilians.[57]

Schu and the other missionary leaders chose three novices for its entering class: Petrus Sun, Vitus Chang, and Johannes Fu. Gier boasted that they had picked the perfect group: all three were twenty years old and had entered the SVD's educational institutions when they were nine. They had spent the past eleven years under the "watchful eyes" of their German instructors, who had enthusiastically recommended their admittance into the novitiate.[58]

The missionaries designed the first year of the novitiate to help ease the novices into the rhythms and expectations of communal life in the missionary order. The novices wore Chinese clothes and ate Chinese food, and according to one missionary, the food was "better than what they will eat later at seminary." They cleaned their own rooms, washed dishes, and laundered clothes. The novitiate house had a small garden, which the novices were expected to maintain.[59]

By the second year, the Chinese novices embarked on a more rigorous curriculum of theological training. The curriculum mirrored what novices in Europe and the United States received, but the missionary leaders allowed that missionary instructors could slow down the pace if the Chinese were unable to keep up with the courses. The Chinese novitiates received a "strict" and "traditional training" focused on German and Latin. In addition, they were required to take courses that focused on biblical exegesis, philosophy, church history, and mission history. The novices also followed a regimented daily schedule. Gier commented that the daily schedule "pleased him" because it ensured that the novices were "always busy."[60]

The formation of the Chinese novitiate gave missionary leaders in Europe the opportunity to communicate directly with Chinese Christians. For the first time, Chinese Christians wrote letters to the home board without intervention from their missionary supervisors. In October 1925, two of the Chinese novices, Chang and Fu, wrote reports to the superior general directly. They described the tribulations their families encountered. Chang's family had to flee from floods in their village from the Yellow River. Fu wrote of how his family had not converted to Christianity, and how he often tried to explain the faith to his siblings. They asked the missionary leaders in Germany to pray for them.[61]

Moved by these accounts, the SVD leaders were convinced that they had chosen good candidates. Schoppelrey commented: "The three Chinese candidates for the SVD seem to be really good people. We should do everything in our power for their education." In February 1926, the SVD admitted the three men into the order at a solemn high mass at the cathedral in Yanzhou. The society now had its first Chinese brothers.[62]

Still, the SVD resisted the Vatican's agenda of quickening the pace of ordination of Chinese bishops. After the 1924 General Synod in Shanghai, the Propaganda Fide had developed a plan of action. It first located thriving apostolic vicariates that had a healthy number of converts. It then carved out apostolic prefectures within the vicariates and appointed the Chinese clergy as apostolic prefects. These new assignments offered Chinese clergy a test-run to administer a smaller area. Once the Chinese prefect proved his worth, the Propaganda elevated the area into an apostolic vicariate, and by extension, the Chinese prefect became a bishop.

Ever since the end of the First World War, the Propaganda Fide had its eyes set on the SVD's Qingdao vicariate. As an urban area, Qingdao exhibited signs of a thriving Catholic presence, and the Propaganda wanted to allocate a section there for Chinese clergy. In February 1925, Costantini decided to put pressure on the SVD. He sent a letter to Augustin Henninghaus, making the Propaganda's intentions for Qingdao clear. In Rome, the Propaganda continued to press the issue. Cardinal Willem van Rossum, head of the Propaganda, approached Karl Friedrich of the SVD generalate with the idea of converting areas of the Qingdao vicariate into apostolic prefectures. Rossum knew that Henninghaus was resistant to the Propaganda's plans, and he wanted Friedrich to help lobby the case for him. When Friedrich agreed to write Henninghaus, Rossum responded that Friedrich should not only write "one time," but rather "a hundred times."[63]

The meeting made a deep impression on Friedrich: he communicated to the SVD leadership in Germany that the Propaganda saw them as laggards. In order for the SVD to maintain its good standing with the Propaganda, the leadership had to "know and understand the directions and future that the Propaganda hoped to pursue." Yet Friedrich found Cardinal Rossum's insistence discomfiting. Few people in Rome, Friedrich wrote, knew the "true state of the Chinese hierarchy," nor did Rome "truly understand the views of Bishop Henninghaus." Friedrich felt that the leadership in Rome "made rash decisions, tried to create false hopes, and provoked uncomfortable decisions" among the bishops and leaders in China. Friedrich left the matter up to Henninghaus to decide.[64]

Henninghaus had indeed bristled at the suggestion of elevating Chinese priests as apostolic prefects in Qingdao. He wrote, "With regards to the question of whether any Chinese apostolic prefects would be suitable in Southern Shandong, at the moment this suggestion is impossible and out of the question." While he was supportive of the push to consecrate more Chinese priests as apostolic prefects in areas with a longer tradition of Christian conversion, Henninghaus argued that Chinese Christians in southern Shandong were not yet ready to take over the reins since they were still "new Christians." He pledged "to make it clear to the Propaganda that the Chinese are not prepared to handle the prefecture." The Propaganda, Henninghaus wrote, had been misled by the work of the Belgian Lazarists, who overstated the spiritual maturity of the Chinese and their preparedness to assume responsibility of the mission work.[65]

The Propaganda deferred to Henninghaus: in March 1925 it appointed the SVD missionary Georg Weig as the new apostolic prefect of Qingdao, not a Chinese priest. The news delighted the SVD leaders. They publicly declared that a new apostolic prefecture could only benefit the missions, even though in private they had rejected the possibility of one less than a month earlier.[66]

By 1928, Qingdao was elevated to an apostolic vicariate. The SVD had gotten its wish: it had retained control of Qingdao and could boast of another SVD man, Weig, as bishop. The SVD leaders believed that they had also successfully challenged what they saw as the Vatican's overly optimistic view of Chinese spirituality. But the SVD's triumph came at a cost. The ordination of Weig, rather than a Chinese priest, signaled to Chinese Catholics the unwillingness of the SVD to devolve power. It damaged the trust between the society and local priests in the region. The seeds for a future conflict had been planted.

CONCLUSIONS: RETAINING INSTITUTIONAL CONTROL

In the decade after the First World War, German missionaries responded seriously to the appeals within the broader international missionary community to create an indigenous church in China. Catholic and Protestant missionary societies initiated a process that they believed could eventually lead to independent Chinese congregational leadership. The

BMS implemented a new church constitution that facilitated the transfer of power to Chinese pastors; the SVD built a novitiate that made Chinese priests full members of the missionary order. Both societies began to define the hierarchical relationship between Western missionaries and Chinese Christians differently.

But the missionary leaders continued to mistrust Chinese spirituality. Even though the SVD knew that it ought to develop more indigenous clergy, it delayed the transfer of power to local Chinese Christians on the grounds that they were not yet spiritually "mature" or "ready" for the responsibilities of independent governance. They criticized the Chinese in their regions for being unprepared for more leadership responsibilities. The SVD's resistance partly stemmed from national rivalry. It saw the Vatican's initiatives as unduly swayed by the Belgian Lazarists. To the SVD, a small group of non-German missionaries had hijacked the Vatican's policies in China. The push to ordain Chinese bishops seemed disconnected from the realities faced in the field.

The BMS also viewed the intentions of other Western missionary nations with suspicion. In particular, BMS missionaries criticized the Anglo-American missionary agenda, which they believed was suffused with impure, nonevangelistic objectives. In reality, the cleavages between German missionary theologians and their Anglo-American counterparts were not so great. Even though the Germans warned about "Americanism" and the threats of American liberal modernist theology, they agreed on the broader missionary goal of developing a native, indigenous church. But the BMS's political resentment prevented it from seeing Anglo-Americans clearly. The society viewed them primarily as competitors, rather than as potential partners. The problem of creating an indigenous Chinese church was never solely a question of theology; it also adopted a patently political character.

Politically astute, German Protestant and Catholic missionaries recognized the necessity of advancing an indigenizing agenda. On the surface, the reforms that German Protestants and Catholics implemented during the 1920s moved their congregations toward independent Chinese governance. But their sense of political beleaguerment made them wary of losing further control in a compromised geopolitical position. In turn, missionary leaders created new hierarchies as a way to maintain their influence in the congregations. The BMS's new church constitution gave missionaries the power to control the path that the Chinese church took while simultaneously appearing to advocate Chinese church independence. Similarly, the SVD novitiate slowed down the speed of clerical ordination in Shandong. Even though German missionary leaders proclaimed equal respect for different races and cultures, they nonetheless advanced a veiled paternalism under the guise of working for the creation of an indigenous church.

Why did such paternalism endure? I argue that paternalist missionary attitudes were linked to the unprecedented challenges that missionaries faced after the First World War. German missionaries in particular saw enemies everywhere. In Germany, the Weimar constitution had politically severed the traditional link between church and state. The numbers of applicants and candidates for the clergy had declined rapidly. Culturally and socially, missionaries believed that they now operated in a global environment overrun by socialists and atheists, hostile to orthodox Christianity. Everywhere, it seemed, in China and Germany alike, secularists sought to undermine Christian influence. Even self-proclaimed Christians had forsaken orthodox belief and turned toward liberal-modernistic theology.

Propelled by secular attacks on Christendom, Catholic and Protestant leaders enacted reforms in China. The SVD created a Chinese novitiate, hoping to replenish its dwindling numbers in Europe with Chinese priests. If shown to be successful, the model developed in China could later be exported to other missionary realms. BMS missionaries created a Chinese church constitution that they believed offered a clear pathway toward sustainable church growth. As Christianity retreated in Europe, these new institutions, the missionaries hoped, could serve to create new Christians abroad.

More importantly, both missionary societies envisioned their work in China as creating Christians with orthodox belief. For both, "quality" of conversion was much more important than quantity. Both stressed repeatedly the desire to create "mature" Christians who were solid in the faith. With Christianity under attack in Europe, and missionaries' grasp over European Christians slowly waning, missionaries believed that congregations in China gave them an opportunity to develop the type of faith they hoped to see. They saw in their Chinese congregations an opportunity to affirm their power while it retreated elsewhere. In the Chinese novitiate, SVD missionaries monitored and vetted the faith of their novices. The Berliners believed their constitution offered a way for them to train perfect Lutherans—so perfect that, one day, the model pioneered in China would become reimported to Europe, surpassing all of its competitors. Both societies argued that if they could create orthodox Christians in China, they could certainly re-evangelize Europe one day.

Yet significant differences also existed between the German Catholic and Protestant worlds. Most notably, Catholics were accountable to the Vatican, whose stance was clear: China was ready for indigenous bishops. Vatican officials further pressured the SVD to start the process of locating suitable candidates. The SVD, with its historical identity as an ultramontane society, knew that it needed to follow the Vatican line, even if it found the policy ill advised. In the short term, the SVD's best strategy was to stall. The Chinese novitiate offered the SVD a way to delay the inevitable. German Protestant missionaries, on the other hand, had no such external authorities to hold them accountable. They employed the nebulous idea of the "people's church" as a way to legitimize the cautious approach missionaries on the ground desired. The German Protestant theory of spiritual and racial hierarchies lent credence to the idea that Germans needed to continue to steer Chinese church practice: the Germans were more spiritually advanced and had a theological mandate to shepherd the Chinese to a state of spiritual maturity. Operating in an echo chamber of theological treatises and writing, German Protestants used their theology to justify the continuing dominance over Chinese Christianity.

Examination of the institutional hierarchies of both the SVD and the BMS shows that not much had changed from the late nineteenth century. Well into the 1930s, although the number of Chinese Christian leaders had grown, German missionaries still held on to the levers of power within their church congregations. The German reluctance to devolve power rankled Chinese leaders, setting the stage for future conflicts as support for Chinese nationalism increased.

But institutional makeup does not tell the whole story. At the same time that German missionaries maintained their institutional dominance, they began to portray traditional Chinese culture in a different light. Missionary journals and writings shed their previous disdain for Confucianism. The rise of rival ideologies, in particular Communism, sparked fear. Now—in a remarkable about-face that none could have predicted fifty years previously—missionaries sought a synthesis between Confucian and Christian cultures. No cultural and intellectual transformation had been as swift and dramatic.

CHAPTER SIX

Falling in Love with Confucius

IN 1924, CARL JOHANNES VOSKAMP wrote a long manuscript titled "The Chinese Classics and the Gospel." The piece highlights sayings of Confucius that correspond with ideas pronounced by Jesus in the gospels. Voskamp further expounds on the links between Confucianism and Christianity. In his conclusion, Voskamp suggests that Confucian thinking has much to offer Germany, "where there are no more potatoes, and the poor people have to subsist solely on beets." The Germans, Voskamp argues, can turn to the odes in *The Classics of Poetry* (*Shijing*) and draw comfort from wisdom that stems from the "beginning of humanity." The Chinese classics remind us, Voskamp writes, that "heaven creates the people, it gives wisdom and the art of governing to the princes; heaven blesses the good and curses the evil. God bestows rain and fruitful seasons, filling our bodies and hearts with food and gladness."[1]

The manuscript marked a complete transformation in Voskamp's thinking. Upon his arrival in China in 1884, Voskamp established himself as a fierce critic of Confucianism. In a series of popular pamphlets and articles published before and after the Boxer Uprising in 1900, he lambasted Confucius's teachings as evil and blamed Confucius for China's political, moral, and social problems. After the First World War, however, Voskamp never published another anti-Confucian treatise.

By the 1920s, other German missionaries had changed their attitudes toward Confucianism as well. In their writings SVD missionaries, who only twenty years earlier had denigrated Confucius, began to show their readers the commonalities between Confucian and Christian thinking. They ceased to pit Confucianism against Christianity. No longer was Confucius an enemy to Christianity's advance. Instead, for Christianity to thrive in China, SVD missionaries now contended, the Chinese church had to adopt Confucianism and become "Chinese."

In their relationship to Confucianism, both the BMS and the SVD underwent a dramatic transformation from the 1880s to the 1930s. When BMS and SVD missionaries entered China in the 1880s, they were outspoken critics of Confucianism. They described traditional Chinese culture as oppressive and regressive, bound to clash with the modern West. Yet by the 1930s, they saw the fates of Christianity and Confucianism as inseparable. How, and why, did missionaries come to view traditional Chinese culture and Confucianism as something to be admired, rather than reviled? Moreover, how did missionaries come to believe that Confucianism and Christianity, previously dogged antagonists, had to be synthesized as a way to bolster Christianity's future in China?

These cultural and intellectual transformations seem even more dramatic when compared with the institutional inertia in both societies. As we saw in chapter 5, German missionaries delayed the transfer of power to Chinese Christians. Institutionally, both missionary societies in the 1930s did not look much different from how they appeared in the 1880s. Yet in both published journals and private reports, missionaries began to write about Chinese culture in more open and accepting tones. On the surface, the two missionary societies appear as completely changed.

The BMS's and SVD's repudiations of their anti-Confucian stances is the subject of this chapter. I first examine how the two societies constructed an anti-Confucian—and more broadly, Sinophobic—world-view in the early 1900s. I then focus on the 1920s and 1930s and explore how missionaries began to alter their views of traditional Chinese society.

But I examine more than just moments of rupture; I also illuminate threads of continuity. Missionaries did not completely change their attitudes about China. German missionaries remained convinced that China was a place of danger, populated with enemies of the gospel. By the 1920s and 1930s, a different set of challengers—Communism, secularism, and a renewed Buddhism—threatened Christianity's advance in China. These new ideologies, they believed, were potentially more pernicious and threatening to Christianity's future survival in China than Confucianism ever had been. Faced with these circumstances, German missionaries sought to build alliances with their old enemy Confucianism as a way to stem the spread of new ideologies.

ANTI-CONFUCIANS

In the aftermath of the Boxers, missionaries sought to explain the outburst of violence against Chinese Christians and Western missionaries. Many pointed to Confucianism. Confucian ideas, missionaries claimed, contributed to China's xenophobia, and an enduring veneration of Confucius led to a rejection of Western ideas. A typical example of prevailing anti-Confucian sentiment among missionaries was Voskamp's 1902 book *Confucius and China Today*. Reflecting on the turbulence caused by the Boxers, Voskamp blamed Confucius for the "angry anarchy" of China. Calling Confucius the "uncrowned king of China, a demigod to his people," Voskamp belittled Confucius as "having produced absolutely nothing original. For him, progress was a burden and conservatism was to be valued above all." The biggest danger, Voskamp claimed, was how Confucianism inculcated obsessive ancestor worship. Confucianism, he lamented, "chains the living to the dead. While Western ideas inspire people to hope for the future, Confucianism impels Chinese people to stare into the darkness of their past." As a result, "almost four hundred million living Chinese are slaves to the uncounted millions of the dead."[2]

However, for Voskamp, the situation in China was not hopeless. Although Confucianism had shackled the inherent goodness of Chinese people, the Chinese possessed natural spiritual values. They were kind, patient, and "commonsensical." Once China had been released from the bonds of Confucianism, Voskamp argued, "the people can be lifted and the country will be regenerated."[3] Naturally, for Voskamp, Christianity offered the remedy that China needed: Christianity could release the virtuous Chinese from two millennia of bondage to an oppressive ideology. Christianity alone could vanquish Confucianism.

The SVD missionary Rudolf Pieper agreed with Voskamp. Pieper too wrote in the wake of the Boxer Uprising, seeking to explain the chaos he had just witnessed. He excoriated the "cult of Confucius" that reigned in China. For Pieper, Confucian devotion prevented intellectuals and elites from taking Christianity seriously: "For an educated Mandarin to convert to Christianity, it is no small sacrifice for him to leave the idea of a Confucian 'holiness' behind and accept Christian sanctity. . . . The first question that the European missionary is asked by Chinese intellectuals is, 'have you read the Books of Confucius?' If one answers 'No,' then the missionary is forever regarded as an uneducated man. Even if the missionary is well trained in the arts and sciences of his European home, it accounts for nothing in the eyes of the educated Chinese elite."[4] Catholic missionaries like Pieper argued that the dogged ignorance that the gentry evinced toward Christianity helped them to facilitate anti-Christian violence in the countryside. He accused Confucian bureaucrats of encouraging robbers and bandits to terrorize Chinese Christians and vandalize church property.

Yet Pieper admitted that there were alternative ways to interpret Confucius's legacy. He recognized Confucius's historical importance. "To the educated Chinese world," Pieper wrote, "Confucius is what Jesus is for us Christians, Muhammad is for Islam, and Socrates is for the Greeks." As a pagan who lived long before the birth of Christ, Pieper wrote, Confucius could not be blamed for not knowing Christianity.[5]

Unlike Voskamp, Pieper did not find much to object to in the ideas and teachings of Confucius. Comparing Confucius to contemporary secular European philosophers, Pieper stated, "I hold Confucius, as a pagan philosopher, in much higher esteem when compared to other so-called 'Christian' philosophers, who throw Christianity overboard, put themselves in God's throne, and search for satisfaction in dirty, vile sensuality." Instead, he criticized the followers of Confucius, who had transformed his teachings into "the most formidable bulwark of the educated elite in opposition to the advance of Christianity in China."[6] Furthermore, Pieper believed that Confucianism was not the only ideology to blame for China's backwardness. Pieper, like other European missionaries, attacked the entire Chinese religious landscape; they were equally critical of other Chinese religions, such as Buddhism and Daoism.

The SVD's writings in the nineteenth century stood in direct opposition to an earlier Jesuit tradition of honoring and venerating Confucius. As Lionel Jensen has shown, the Jesuits of the sixteenth and seventeenth centuries made Confucius into a "spiritual confrère," a forerunner to Christ who "had preached an ancient gospel of monotheism now forgotten."[7] The Jesuits presented Confucius as a philosopher of world-historical importance, drawing the connections between his ideas and the West. In contrast, the SVD sought to point out the particular "Chineseness" of Confucius. Pieper wrote that Confucius was primarily the "national hero of the Chinese people, the idol of millions." SVD missionaries sought to demote Confucius's universal significance. He had no universal lessons to teach the West; he was a false prophet who had led the Chinese astray.[8]

The SVD and BMS entered China at a time when European depictions of China became increasingly Sinophobic. As George Steinmetz notes, throughout the nineteenth century, with intensifying Western imperial ambitions in China, Europeans increasingly portrayed the Chinese as "barbarians, savages, and generic 'natives.' "[9] Missionaries contributed to this Sinophobic milieu. The SVD missionary Georg Stenz, for example, wrote, "We Europeans are repulsed by the Chinese." He portrayed them as pathological liars, suspicious, materialistic, unthankful, and lazy—all common tropes in the corpus of nineteenth-century missionary writings about China.[10]

But the missionaries deployed such tropes to create a moral critique of not only the Chinese, but Europeans as well. Stenz pointed out that even though the traits of avarice, cowardice, and callousness were "staples" among the Chinese, these defects were similarly widespread in Europe. The prevalence of such behavior among Europeans was even less excusable, since "they are surrounded by Christianity and the Ten Commandments."[11] Just as Pieper referred to Confucius as a way to criticize secular Christian philosophers, Stenz alluded to Chinese spirituality to excoriate Europeans who had left the faith, or even worse, the self-professing believers who did not exhibit Christian virtues.

In the first decade after 1900, Steinmetz notes that Sinophilia "made a powerful comeback" in the broader German public.[12] Kaiser Wilhelm II had provoked a widespread backlash when, in his infamous "Hun Speech" (*Hunnenrede*), he called upon German troops to violently handle the Boxers "such that for a thousand years no Chinese will dare to look cross-eyed at a German."[13] The socialists in the *Reichstag* condemned German policy abroad, particularly the brutal actions of the Germans in their retaliatory expedition against the Boxers. More broadly, writings about China shifted in tone: intellectuals, novelists, and journalists drew upon an older discursive tradition that portrayed the Chinese as an ancient civilization, equal to Europe's.

Liberal missionaries from the Weimar Mission had been key figures in portraying traditional Chinese culture in a more positive light. Founded in 1884, the Weimar Mission positioned itself in opposition to Pietist missionary societies like the BMS. Its founders declared that the new mission society was uninterested in the traditional methods of missionary work: they had no desire to "build new churches in heathen lands."[14] Instead, they wanted to focus on "secular" forms of missions. They built schools and hospitals. Liberals also hoped to engage Confucian literati in debate and dialogue.

Spearheading the Weimar Mission's work in Qingdao was Richard Wilhelm, who rejected the view of Western superiority over China. Wilhelm directed the Qingdao German-Chinese Seminar, which educated elementary school teachers. Most radically, the seminar offered a secular Chinese curriculum and rejected overt Christian evangelization. The school administrators even refused to celebrate Christian holidays.[15] It soon gained renown, becoming one of the most highly regarded schools in German Qingdao. Secular Chinese officials and merchants sought admission for their children. In 1913, Wilhelm founded the Confucius Society as a way to encourage dialogue between what he considered the "spiritual heroes" of German and Chinese culture.[16] The circle attracted many Chinese ex-officials and scholars loyal to the Qing regime. Even though the society was not an official governmental organization, it affected colonial policy in Qingdao because of its influential political connections.

While Wilhelm and other liberal Protestant missionaries proclaimed their approach as new and radically different, in reality their method was similar to the old Jesuit method of accommodation. Their focus on elites and more secular modes of education repulsed the conservative BMS and SVD, who focused on the rural poor. Both the BMS and the SVD rejected liberal calls for a synthesis between China and the West, and they continued their vehement critiques of traditional Chinese society until the First World War. While liberals interpreted the Boxer Uprising as a moment of reaction against Western imperialistic barbarism, for conservatives, the uprising only confirmed the hold that Confucianism had over the Chinese.

The defeat of the Boxers persuaded conservative missionaries that a new day was dawning for the spread of Christian missionaries in China. The Boxer Uprising and the subsequent demise of the Qing Empire could potentially lay the foundations for the flourishing of Christianity in China. Here, finally, was a chance for China to break with its Confucian past and dismantle the shackles of Confucian ideology. The smoldering ruins and cataclysmic suffering portended a hopeful future for Christianity in China; it was only in the wake of such radical change that Christianity could find grounds upon which to erect its church.

SEEKING ALLIANCES

After the First World War, liberals like Richard Wilhelm pushed their prewar arguments even further. The war destroyed Wilhelm's confidence in Western civilization, and he called on European Christians to turn toward the East. Embrace Confucian and Daoist philosophy, he exhorted. Chinese philosophy, which focused on harmony rather than competition and conflict, Wilhelm argued, contained the "cure and salvation of modern Europe."[17] He began to translate the Chinese classic of divination, the *Yijing* or *Book of Changes,* seeing within it ancient wisdom that could guide Europe out of its cultural malaise. Wilhelm became a regular within Chinese liberal intellectual circles of the New Culture Movement, joining, in particular, several societies that sought to update Confucian thinking for the modern world. In his influential 1925 book *The Soul of China,* Wilhelm called for a "synthesis of not only two cultural spaces, but also of two humanities." Such a synthesis, he believed, could reinvigorate Christianity in the West.[18]

Wilhelm's promotion of Chinese traditional ideas garnered a wide following in Germany. As Suzanne Marchand has shown, Wilhelm's work tapped into a broader cultural moment of pessimism over Europe's future and interest in "oriental wisdom." Thinking that they could find within ancient Eastern thought means to revitalize an enervated West, a large contingent of central European intellectuals snubbed the ideas of the West, swapping Marx and Weber for Buddha and Confucius. Wilhelm's books and translations were widely read; as Marchand notes, an admiring Carl Jung "claimed that he had learned more from Wilhelm than from any other man."[19]

Conservative missionaries of the BMS recoiled at Wilhelm's radical arguments. Siegfried Knak lambasted Wilhelm. Citing Wilhelm's "very little experience in parish work," Knak called him "hardly a missionary." Because Wilhelm lacked congregational experience and actual contact with Chinese Christians, Knak wrote that Wilhelm "idealized" the Chinese, failing to recognize their "moral flaws."[20] A cultural synthesis of equals between Chinese and Western civilization was impossible. How could Wilhelm dare to consider the Chinese an equal "humanity" to the Germans, when Chinese Christianity remained in its infancy and Germany was the home of the Reformation?

Even though they rejected Wilhelm's radical cultural egalitarianism, BMS missionaries like Voskamp were nonetheless affected by broader cultural trends. An admiration for Confucianism emerged in Voskamp's publications after the war. He began to present Confucius as a Christlike figure who through his wise teachings tried to elevate the spiritual state of the Chinese people. In *The Chinese Preacher*, Voskamp referred to Confucius as one of the few "spots of sunlight in the 3,000 years of China's dark history."[21] China's modern problems were not rooted in the teachings of Confucius. Rather, Voskamp now argued, if the Chinese had actually followed and implemented Confucian doctrines throughout its history, many of its modern problems could have been avoided.

Voskamp was self-conscious of the ideological shift in his writing. He credited the Chinese for helping to bring about a rapprochment. In 1924, he reminisced that during the time of the Boxers, participants in Confucian and Buddhist ceremonies proudly waved large banners with antiforeign slogans, antagonistic to Christianity. Since then, Confucians and Buddhists had given up their xenophobic slogans. Banners that celebrated universal humanity could now be found in Confucian and Buddhist temples. In Confucian temples, Voskamp reported, one could find names of the "Great ancient sages": Christ, Confucius, Buddha, Laozi, and Muhammad. He noted, with pride, that Christ was always listed first. For Voskamp, Confucians had stopped attacking Christianity. It was now up to Christian missionaries to reach out and build alliances, for Christianity's primary ideological competitor in China was no longer Confucianism.[22]

The real rival, he wrote with alarm, was the New Culture Movement, propelled by Chinese intellectuals who considered Christianity and

Confucianism equally superstitious. In 1919, the Lecture Association (Jiangxue She), affiliated with Beijing University and organized by leading intellectuals in the New Culture Movement such as Liang Qichao and Cai Yuanpei, invited a delegation of renowned international figures to give a series of talks in China. The group included the American educator John Dewey, the German biologist Hans Driesch, the Bengali writer Rabindranath Tagore, and the British philosopher Bertrand Russell. Voskamp attended Russell's talks, where Russell proclaimed "Christianity dead, strangled. Confucianism and Buddhism, with their patriarchal constitution, could also do little to heal the world."[23] Horrified, Voskamp reported that Russell's popularity was symptomatic of a growing problem: the rise of materialist and atheist thinking throughout China. Christianity faced attacks from those who trumpeted the supremacy of scientific thinking. Reading Voskamp's report, Knak responded: "Christendom is facing a moment of grave crisis. We have now entered into a period of secularism."[24]

With the founding of the Chinese Communist Party (CCP) in 1920, the missionaries found an even more concrete enemy. Throughout the 1920s, BMS missionaries reported with increasing anxiety the rise of Communism as a political force. In 1926, Knak described South China as overrun with "Communist propaganda" and "Russian agitators filling the land with their flyers and speeches."[25] The Russians, Knak warned, had infiltrated local militia groups and the government in Guangzhou. The BMS repeatedly warned of the possibility of a Communist takeover.

The BMS missionaries conceived of the struggle against Communism in global terms. The Chinese were not alone in facing a Communist threat, but rather, as Knak wrote, their fears were "shared by Christians in East Asia, in South Africa, in Russia, and also in Germany."[26] Other leading members within the German Protestant missionary community agreed with Knak's diagnosis. The director of the Basel Mission Society, Karl Hartenstein, similarly warned of a global "anti-Christian alliance" of relativism, secularism, Bolshevism, and nationalism. A renewed missionary effort, Hartenstein believed, could stem the growth of these pernicious ideologies.[27]

German missionaries saw themselves as standing on the front lines of a global war between atheism and religion. Missionaries believed that they were part of a timeless conflict that had recurred throughout the history of global Christianity. What was different in the 1920s and 1930s,

however, was that the missionaries saw themselves as facing an unprecedented weakness in the position of European Christianity within global
geopolitics. They recognized that the First World War had delivered a
stunning blow to Christianity in Europe, as well as its ability to project its
influence to the rest of the world.

To fight this global war, BMS missionaries needed new allies. Voskamp
argued that they should turn toward Confucianism. A strategic alliance
with Confucianism could prevent the further spread of materialist and
atheist thinking in China. For Voskamp, Confucianism, like Christianity,
advanced a "heaven-centered" view of the universe, as opposed to a secular
"human-centered" perspective. Both Christianity and Confucianism could
orient the Chinese toward a transcendental worldview.[28]

More urgently, BMS missionaries claimed that Christianity and
Confucianism offered a political, moral, and social force of stability in an
increasingly chaotic and unstable world. In their doctrines, Voskamp
argued, both Christianity and Confucianism promoted the construction
of stable hierarchies by cultivating loyalty to both the family and the state.
They focused on traditional moral and social values, such as harmony and
peace between neighbors. In the nineteenth century, missionaries had
seen Confucianism's traditionalism as the source of China's backwardness. By the 1930s, however, they saw it as a potential force for China's
salvation. Faced with increasingly dangerous global forces like
Communism, Confucianism was now an ally, rather than an enemy.

Increasingly, German missionaries spoke of Confucianism not as a
rival religion that it needed to destroy, but instead as a crucial element of
China's cultural landscape that they needed to preserve. Knak, for example,
argued in 1928 that missionaries had to recognize that Confucianism
constituted a vital part of China's "spiritual heritage."[29] In their writings,
both Voskamp and Knak stressed the commonalities between Christianity
and Confucianism and sought to articulate how both could serve as a
bulwark against the onslaught of modern atheist ideologies.

Yet Knak also warned that such accommodation could go too far. He
railed against the dangers of the "relativism that dominates our epoch."[30]
Liberal missionaries like Richard Wilhelm, Knak charged, diminished the
truth of the Christian gospel when they advertised Christianity to the Chinese
as merely a variation of Confucian ethics. Such "syncretism" betrayed the
singularity of Christian salvation. Knak remained convinced that only

Christianity could liberate the Chinese; China still needed Christianity, and the presence of European missionaries, for it to be truly transformed.[31]

When cautioning against Chinese "syncretism," Knak was referring not only to radical theologians like Richard Wilhelm, but also to the rise of a new generation of Chinese liberal Protestant church leaders and theologians who called for the synthesis of Christianity and Confucianism. He had good reason to feel threatened. Throughout the 1920s, liberal Protestants dominated the Chinese church scene numerically. The Church of Christ in China, a nondenominational coalition of twelve missionary groups, was the largest Christian organization in China, boasting a membership almost four times as large as that of the Lutherans.[32]

Liberals also wielded a broad cultural and intellectual influence. They controlled significant institutions, such as the NCC, the National Christian Literature Association of China (Zhonghua Jidujiao Wenshe, or Wenshe), the Life Fellowship (Shengming she), and the YMCA in China. Liberal church leaders mobilized these institutions to spread their message and theology. Advancing their ideas in widely read journals such as the *Wenshe Monthly* and the *Zhenli Zhoukan* (*Truth and Life Weekly*), liberals dominated debates surrounding the future of the Chinese church.[33]

In the 1920s, liberal Chinese church leaders called for the development of a new Chinese theology, which would lead to the establishment of an indigenous Chinese church (*Bense jiaohui*). Influenced by the New Culture Movement and the further politicization of Chinese intellectual thought after the May Fourth Movement, *Bense* theologians agreed with their secular critics that Christianity had to disassociate itself from the West. But Christian intellectuals insisted upon the utility of Christianity as a force for modernizing the nation. In the inaugural issue of the *Truth and Life Weekly* in 1923 the editors wrote: "China's moral and political state has reached its nadir. . . . We as Christians have a heavenly mandate . . . to construct our ideal country." Christianity, they believed, still had an important part to play in China's future: it could help to stabilize the country's disintegrating moral and political landscapes.[34]

To contribute to China's renewal, *Bense* theologians argued, Chinese Christianity had to change. The Chinese church could no longer be dominated by Western personnel: it needed to develop indigenous talent. But even more importantly, Chinese clergy had to be educated differently. More than just studying Western theology, future Chinese church leaders needed to receive training in the Chinese classics. A new Chinese Christian education, the influential Chinese theologian Zhao Zichen argued, had to "synthesize all of the best elements of both Christianity and ancient Chinese learning into a new culture."[35] For Christianity to gain further ground in China, the indigenous church needed to articulate the common ideas shared by Christianity and ancient Chinese philosophy. Some theologians went even further, arguing that Western Christianity had much to learn from the Chinese spiritual tradition. Traditional Chinese culture, the *Bense* theologians argued, could transform Christianity into a more humane and less militaristic religion.[36]

The BMS missionaries viewed the pronouncement of the Chinese indigenous church movement suspiciously. Knak disparaged the leaders of the NCC, depicting them as puppets of American liberal theology. The NCC leaders, Knak argued, were mostly intellectual elites trained in the United States and had lost touch with the everyday experiences of congregational life. The argument that the Chinese intellectuals of the indigenous church advanced—to focus on a rigorous training in the Chinese classics and the development of a new indigenous theology for China—had little applicability for most of the Chinese Christian landscape. Knak argued that instead of focusing on the commonalities of Christianity and Confucianism and seeking to synthesize the two religions into a new one, the Chinese Christians needed to first recognize the supremacy of Christianity.[37]

Knak's unduly harsh criticism of the Chinese liberal leadership suggests the degree of the BMS's political isolation. Everywhere they turned, BMS missionaries saw enemies: liberal-modernistic theology embraced by the Chinese, American and British political encroachment on German territories abroad, and the advance of secular ideas and Communism globally. Yet Knak was not completely pessimistic. He remained convinced that the Germans, as the "People of the Reformation," had an antidote to the pernicious ideologies of both secularism and American liberal theology. As long as the BMS kept working, slowly and patiently, China could be transformed by German theology and missionary work.[38]

THE SVD'S CHANGING CONCEPTIONS OF SPACE

Like the BMS, the SVD also saw itself as besieged by global enemies in the late 1920s and early 1930s. The image of China as a dangerous place, filled with adversaries to the gospel, proliferated in the SVD's journals.

SVD reports were littered with descriptions of robbers and bandits who destroyed church property. There was nothing new about these attacks on Christianity: missionaries saw them as the latest incarnation of Chinese xenophobic assaults on Catholicism, which they had been forced to confront repeatedly since the beginning of their work in China.[39]

Still, the Catholics acknowledged that they faced a different type of enemy. In the nineteenth century SVD missionaries saw the enemy as an inept, recalcitrant Confucian bureaucracy. Now they described the "battle for China" as a clash between Christianity and an alliance of "Bolsheviks" and "nationalists." Adam Mayer, a missionary in Shandong, called Communism a "brother of Chinese nationalism. They have been bound together in the past ten years, knocking on the gates of the Middle Kingdom."[40] Communists and nationalists, he believed, were united in their collective hatred of religion. Together, these secular opponents advanced an antireligious, and moreover anti-Christian, sentiment. In local elementary schools, Bolsheviks and nationalists swayed students to "reject Christ." Mayer reported with dismay that Chinese schools had begun to teach Darwinism to students. Editors of the SVD journal *Steyler Missionsbote* reprinted a drawing from Chinese textbooks that taught the progression from ape to human to show the proliferation of evolutionary thinking. The caption accompanying the image ridiculed the way that the Chinese taught evolution in their schools.[41]

SVD missionaries understood that they no longer faced a local enemy, but rather a Chinese manifestation of broader global assaults on Christianity. In 1932, the SVD director of a missionary school in Henan reported that Communists, "determined not to negotiate," stormed the school, overturned tables, and destroyed books. The vandals would be familiar to his German readers, the missionary lamented, because "similar types of people exist in Germany as well."[42] In the nineteenth century, the SVD framed Chinese anti-Christian outbursts as contained problems, inflamed by local officials who felt threatened by the incursion of foreign Christianity. Now the plight of Chinese Christianity was inextricably linked to an implacable global revolutionary insurgency.

How did the German missionaries justify their presence in China in the face of these new global enemies? Some defended the work by drawing on traditional missionary tropes, situating themselves in a long tradition of missionary martyrdom. Marshaling rhetoric similar to that of the nineteenth century, one missionary wrote, "It is honorable to shed our blood for the sake of a new, free China." SVD missionaries claimed that they traveled to China for the same reasons as their nineteenth-century predecessors. The fact that China was an enormous country, in desperate need of more Christian presence and conversion, had not changed. Some of China's fundamental problems persisted: well into the 1930s, the SVD's missionary journals continued to idealize the country's poverty. The journals described missionaries as staying in China out of an enduring and pure "love of the Chinese," not for political gain.[43]

But in certain crucial aspects, the Catholic missionaries of the 1930s wrote about China in dramatically different ways from their nineteenth-century predecessors. Like the Protestant BMS, SVD missionaries came to show an increasing admiration for their old nemesis: traditional Chinese culture. In a biography of a convert, Martha, one missionary praised her "true Chinese character." She was a "clever" woman, frugal and conscientious with her money.[44] Missionaries just thirty years before used the same word "clever" (*Klugheit*) to characterize the Chinese. But in the early 1900s, "cleverness" was a character flaw—a code word for the trickery intrinsic to Chinese character. Only Christianity, they avowed, could help the Chinese overcome their cultural defects.[45] By the 1930s, Martha's "cleverness" was listed as equally important as her "frugality, and religious piety." "Clever" meant being resourceful: she could solve problems in a chaotic and dangerous economic and political situation more successfully than her peers. Her "true Chinese character" gave her the tools to be a more faithful Christian. To be "Chinese" and "Christian" were no longer fundamentally contradictory identities.

Similarly, the SVD's depictions of Confucianism also changed. The career of Bishop Augustin Henninghaus embodies the broader transformations within the society. On the eve of the First World War, Henninghaus believed that Confucianism was in the midst of revival, and he foresaw a "battle between the young, emerging Christendom in China with the new materialistic heathens and a reanimated Confucianism." Far from being destroyed by the fall of the Qing dynasty, Confucianism was being adopted by conservative scholars, bureaucrats, governors, and military men who supported the establishment of Confucianism as a state religion. Henninghaus wrote, "The heathens have shown that they are not inclined to evacuate their positions without a battle." Confucianism,

Henninghaus remarked, exhibited a remarkable resilience; he predicted that it would be a force to be reckoned with in the future.[46]

By the late 1920s, Henninghaus no longer saw Confucianism and Christianity as antagonistic entities. In 1926, he published a biography of the early SVD missionary Josef Freinademetz. The purpose of the work was largely hagiographic, as the SVD leadership wanted to encourage the Vatican to canonize Freinademetz.[47] But it was also pedagogical: Henninghaus described his own intellectual journey as a cautionary tale to future SVD missionaries. He wrote about an argument he had with Freinademetz during their first encounter, upon Henninghaus's arrival in China in 1886. Almost immediately, Freinademetz began to "sing the praises of the Chinese. He praised their good character, their strong family values, and compared them favorably with Europeans, claiming that they possessed modern morals and customs."[48]

At the time, Henninghaus thought that Freinademetz was exaggerating. "If the Chinese were really so good as Freinademetz presented," he argued, "then there was no possibility of corruption among the heathens, which is impossible." In hindsight, Henninghaus wrote that his objections stemmed from his own "cheekiness as a young man, who could hardly speak any Chinese and had no real understanding in China." After twenty more years of experience in the country, he had come to appreciate and embrace Freinademetz's position. The missionary should not exhibit hubris. It was not the missionary's place to criticize the Chinese, especially if a missionary "knows or feels so little about China."[49]

Henninghaus used Freinademetz's example to remind his fellow missionaries that a "true China missionary must have love for the Chinese." Reflecting Pope Benedict's exhortations in *Maximum illud,* Henninghaus urged missionaries "not to make the Chinese into Germans or French, but rather to make them into good Christians." Moreover, Chinese Christians should strive to remain Chinese. Against the backdrop of secular nationalism, Henninghaus argued that Christianity should not "diminish the Chinese Catholic's love for China." He now recognized that Chinese traditions, culture, and nationalism could find resonance with the gospel. The Chinese should continue to respect and learn the Confucian classics. These ideas did not conflict with the faith.[50]

The synthesis of Catholicism, Confucianism, and Chinese nationalism found its way into the *Steyler Missionsbote,* the SVD's main journalistic organ. Reports about Confucius and Confucius's descendants became overwhelmingly positive. In 1936, the missionary Rudolf Pötter boasted that he and Henninghaus were the only two Europeans invited to the wedding of the seventy-seventh direct descendent of Confucius, Kong Decheng. At the wedding, the missionaries stressed the fraternal relationship between Confucianism and Christianity. They brought a Chinese banner that proclaimed, "All on earth are brothers." Furthermore, Pötter's report about Kong was overflowing with praise. The young Prince Kong, Pötter boasted, was "decorated with the highest honors from the Nanjing Government, and stood in the inner circles of the President." Kong was planning a worldwide tour to Rome to visit the pope, and the missionaries helped Kong translate the "beautiful letter" that he had written to him.[51] The missionary descriptions of Kong were a far cry from how the SVD had depicted Kong's father only thirty years before, when Georg Stenz had ridiculed him and Confucianism.

The aesthetic look of the SVD's journals also shifted radically. Pictures of Sinicized versions of the Virgin Mary proliferated within its pages. In one image, the Virgin Mary, dressed as a Chinese mother, holds the young Jesus, depicted as a Chinese child (fig. 1). In another painting as well, the Madonna and child are surrounded by bamboo (fig. 2). Nativity scenes, featuring Jesus, Mary, Joseph, and an angel as Chinese and the three Magi as Confucian scholars, also appeared in the journal (fig. 3).[52]

These Sinicized illustrations represented a striking transformation of the missionary journal's style. In the nineteenth century, the SVD's main journal depicted Jesus, the Virgin Mary, and Joseph in the style of Renaissance perspective paintings (fig. 4). The nativity scenes were clearly drawn in a Western style (fig. 5). Only thirty years earlier, the missionary Stenz had described his encounter with "crowds of slit-eyed Chinese," their eyes filled with "cunning, pride, and scorn," dressed in "ragged clothes that did not hide their filthy bodies."[53] The SVD's departure from Stenz's era was now complete: if once SVD missionaries had described Chinese as "slit-eyed," now they represented Jesus with those same characteristics.

EMBRACING CONFUCIANISM, REJECTING BUDDHISM

Although missionaries embraced Confucianism after the First World War, they continued to attack Buddhism, Daoism, and Chinese folk religions. Well into the 1930s, SVD and BMS missionaries published articles

FIGURE 1 A Chinese Madonna and child in the *Steyler Missionsbote,* 1935.
(From "Maria Jungfrau, hilf, das ich schau, dein Kind an meinem ende," *Steyler Missionsbote* 62, no. 8 [1935]: 211.)

FIGURE 2 A Chinese Madonna and child in the *Steyler Missionsbote*, 1938, painted by Luka Tscheng. (From "Mutter, gib mir nun dein Kind," *Steyler Missionsbote* 65, no. 8 [1938]: 211.)

FIGURE 3 A Chinese nativity scene in the *Steyler Missionsbote*, 1933. (From "Und sie opferten Gold, Weihbrauch, und Myrrhen [Mt. 2,44. Chinesische-japanischer Mischstil]," *Steyler Missionsbote* 59, no. 4 [1933]: 89.)

FIGURE 4 The dominant artistic style of the SVD missionary journal in 1896. (From "Die heilige Familie," *Kleiner Herz-Jesu-Bote* 23, no. 6 [1896]: 45.)

FIGURE 5 A Western-style nativity scene in the SVD's missionary journal in 1896. (From "Die Anbetung der hl. drei Könige (Nach Fra Fiesole.)" *Kleiner Herz-Jesu-Bote* 23, no. 4 [1896]: 29.)

that denounced the "religious inclinations" of the "heathenish country folk." Just as they did in the early twentieth century, they portrayed rural China as dotted with "heathen temples" and exotic pagodas. Rival religions continued to have a strong hold on Chinese spiritual life, and missionaries acknowledged that they had to compete within a dynamic and dangerous spiritual market.[54]

Among these religious rivals, missionaries were most preoccupied with and fascinated by Buddhism. The SVD in particular produced a flood of articles throughout the 1920s and 1930s about the religion. Spurred by the growth of the society's work in Japan, as well as on the Tibetan border in northwest China, missionaries produced frequent articles about encounters with Buddhist monks and ethnographic reports of Buddhist rituals. Regular readers of *Steyler Missionsbote* were introduced to the broad range of Buddhist practices, from burials in Japan to the process of choosing the next Panchen Lama.[55]

Missionaries could not hide their admiration for—and at times, jealousy of—the outpouring of devotion that Buddhism inspired. Witnessing a crowd of Chinese praying before a Buddhist statue, one SVD missionary wrote: "How much piety and faith, how much dedication and prayer, how much confidence and trust and mourning and tears have I seen pour forth from the faithful in front of this image. I finally understood the compelling power of Buddhism among the people." He wondered how Christianity could achieve a similar degree of popular devotion in China.[56]

German missionaries also expressed personal admiration for the Buddhists that they met. One SVD missionary in Japan reported in 1937 that a Shingon monk had invited him and his colleagues on numerous occasions to tour his monastery. They accepted the invitation. During the visit, they were overwhelmed by the "warm" and "lovely" demeanor of the monks in charge of the monastery. For a moment, the monk's hospitality had "blurred the fact that Buddhism remains an untrue teaching." Such ambivalence—of personal respect for Buddhist leaders while rejecting the theological beliefs they espoused—permeated the missionary reports of the 1920s and 1930s.[57]

SVD missionary reports about Buddhism revolved around the question of how Buddhism had become embedded in the fabric of everyday religious life in both China and Japan. Missionaries asked: How had Buddhism—a foreign religion like Christianity—become "adapted so finely to the Asian soul"? Why had the faithful in China and Japan accepted Buddhism so readily, while Christianity remained foreign?[58] SVD missionaries attributed the popularity of Buddhism to its ability to meld itself with indigenous religious traditions. One missionary in Japan noted, "In every household, Shintoism and Buddhism coexist side by side, even though the two religions share very little in common."[59] Such theological flexibility allowed Buddhists to adapt themselves to the daily needs of the Japanese.

Similarly, SVD missionaries in China remarked that Buddhism had permeated East Asian religious life because of an amalgamation between the "original Indian form of the religion with Daoism and other indigenous Chinese religions into a powerful religion of the people [*Volksreligion*]." Chinese Buddhism, the missionary noted, had appropriated the canon of Daoist gods. Like his colleague in Japan, the missionary credited Buddhism's popularity in East Asia with its protean ability to recast itself in the form of Chinese indigenous religious traditions.[60]

For the Protestant BMS, the potency of Buddhism—and East Asian religions more broadly—lay also in its malleability, its ability to draw from diverse religious traditions and ideas. Nor was the inspiration for Buddhists limited to Asian religions: missionaries credited Buddhism's success to its imitation of Western missionary methods. The BMS missionary Voskamp recounted how, strolling past a building with open windows on a Sunday morning, he was surprised to hear children laughing. He soon realized that it was a Buddhist Sunday school. The Buddhists, Voskamp marveled, had taken a page from the European missionary playbook. Curious, Voskamp stopped to observe. Voskamp noted how the Buddhist teachers deployed slogans that recalled the rhetoric of Christian evangelization. He reported that Buddhists claimed that "all that is Holy lies in Buddha, and Buddha is the name above all names." Voskamp admitted: "I was shaken to my core: old enemies with a new face! A clever Chinese student will say that Christianity has stolen from the older and more venerable Buddhist tradition."[61]

Voskamp saw the Buddhist model of theological adaptability as a danger to Christianity's future in East Asia. He warned of the possible development of a new "East Asian religion," consisting of a "mixture of Shinto, Buddhist, Confucian, Daoist, and Christian ideas." Theologically and ideologically flexible, a new syncretic religion would appeal to adherents throughout East Asia. Voskamp feared that a new religion could be manipulated by power-hungry states. In particular, he believed that the Japanese had the ambition to use religion to unite the "peoples of Asia under the leadership of Japan." The Japanese could draw upon extant regional Buddhist networks to consolidate their dominance in East Asia.[62]

Voskamp and other European missionaries had good reason to be concerned, as Japanese Buddhists did actively seek to expand their influence in East Asia. Ever since the 1890s, Japanese Buddhists attacked Christianity, seeing it as incompatible with Japanese, and more broadly, Asian culture. At the World Conference of Religions in 1893, Japanese Buddhists argued that Buddhism could offer a peaceful alternative to Western imperialist militarism. Buddhism would also serve the same historical function that Christianity had played in Europe: just as Christianity had provided a common cultural reference for Europe during the Middle Ages, so too could Buddhism unify all of Asia behind its ideas. Japanese Buddhists further believed that they had a unique world-historical part to play. "Our nation is the only true Buddhist nation of all the nations in the world," wrote the Japanese intellectual Anesaki Masaharu. Japan possessed a unique "spiritual burden" to advance "the unification of Eastern and Western thought and the continued advancement of the East." Compelled by this expansionist enthusiasm, lay Buddhist organizations, aided by the Japanese Empire, mobilized their resources to spread Buddhism in Japan's colonies. Buddhism witnessed a broad surge of interest throughout East Asia during the 1920s and 1930s.[63]

The revival touched China as well. Led by activists such as Yang Wenhui and Taixu, Buddhist lay associations sought to occupy more ground in the Chinese cultural sphere. Throughout the 1920s, cultural elites in Shanghai flocked to organizations such as the World Buddhist Householder Grove and the Pure Karma Society, which served as spaces for civic participation and mobilization. These societies printed vernacular Buddhist tracts, pressed gramophone records, and sponsored a radio station. Buddhist publications gained a wide circulation.[64] Armed with these plentiful resources, Buddhist civic associations engaged in active social work, aiming to relieve suffering. A young Chinese Christian working for the BMS reported that Buddhism had earned itself "a good name" because Buddhist organizations dedicated their energies to public charity. The BMS, he argued, needed to expand its public presence and offer more aid to the poor and needy.[65]

German missionaries took note of the surge in Buddhist activity, viewing it as a threat to their work. The SVD missionary Paul Konrad, for example, reported that Buddhists had built a temple close to the Catholic cathedral in Qingdao. The "impressive height" of the temple's steeple, Konrad wrote, "draws all eyes toward it."[66] The Buddhist intentions were clear: they wanted to eclipse the Catholic cathedral. Konrad also noted that the Buddhists attempted to attract followers with opulent displays of wealth. The space inside the temple was filled with gilded statues of the Buddha, as well as books, journals, and prayer chits. The Buddhists had succeeded in garnering a substantial crowd. Every week, Konrad reported, more than two hundred people gathered for services, and their seminary was filled with students.

Although he admired Buddhism's organizational structure and capability, Konrad criticized its theology and cosmology. He could not accept Buddhist ideas involving Nirvana and reincarnation, as they contradicted Christianity's fundamental notions of existence, being, and the soul. "The strict asceticism of Buddhism is a dark religion, because it focuses so narrowly on the sins of the sinner and the destruction of the self," Konrad wrote. Christianity, on the other hand, "fights against sin for the sake of achieving a higher self. [We Christians] believe in the possibility of communion with God Himself."[67]

Thus, unlike their attempt to forge an alliance with Confucianism, missionaries rejected a possible synthesis with Buddhism. For most missionaries, Buddhism and Christianity remained diametrically opposed; converts to Christianity had to abandon their former Buddhist faith. In their pamphlets, missionaries made it clear that their converts had to choose between the two faiths—one could not be both Christian and Buddhist. "Christ or Confucius?" read titles of missionary pamphlets in the late nineteenth century; now, in the 1930s, they were titled "Christ or Buddha?"[68]

German missionaries continued to write about Buddhism within a zero-sum framework, where Christianity and Buddhism competed for not only numbers of converts, but also recognition in a public space. One missionary in Japan wrote of his experience administering last rites in a secular hospital to a Christian convert. The missionary reported, with pride, that they had converted the normally Buddhist sanctuary into a Christian one. "In the place of the throned Buddha we put a cross," he boasted. "It was the first time in the history of this hospital that the Buddha had to yield to the cross." The missionary rejoiced when he saw the Buddhist statue hauled away and placed in a corner.[69]

Missionaries ascribed the Asian preference for Buddhism to certain defects of spiritual, moral, and political character. One SVD missionary argued that the Tibetan and Chinese worship of the Dalai Lama reflected the Chinese propensity to need a "superman" (*Übermensch*).[70] Asians, the missionary claimed, had been unable to break the "natural fetters" of fear, which in turn propelled them to worship Daoist priests and Buddhist spiritual leaders like the Dalai Lama. The Chinese had put their faith in the wrong place: no *Übermensch* could break the bondages and the misery of the earthly world, nor could future reincarnations lead to a better place. For missionaries, an *Übermensch* could only subject the world to further oppression and tyranny. Only Christ's humble and self-sacrificing love would save the world. One missionary wondered aloud: "Who will break apart the power of the Lamas? Only Christ's powerful grace can plead with the pagan world."[71]

CONCLUSIONS: NEW GLOBAL ENEMIES

Why did the missionaries embrace Confucianism when they continued to reject Buddhism? Partly, Confucianism no longer posed a serious political threat: Chinese secular nationalists—and missionaries a generation earlier—had defanged it. As Wilhelm Oehler, an influential Basel missionary, wrote in 1930, Confucianism "is now dethroned."[72] Buddhism, on the other hand, was a rival world religion, with deep financial resources that supported its international expansion. Witnessing Chinese cultural elites flock to Buddhism in the 1920s, the missionaries saw it as viable competition.

More importantly, missionaries now defined Confucianism not as a religion, but rather as a cultural force. As Voskamp argued in 1924, modern Chinese society viewed Confucius as an "educator, political philosopher, and a social reformer," not a religious prophet.[73] Sharing the view that Confucianism was a philosophy and not a religion, one SVD missionary wrote: "Confucianism offers no explanations of God, nor does it have anything to say or offer about the afterlife." In the nineteenth century, missionaries considered Confucianism a religion allied with other Chinese folk religions and Confucius as a deity. Now participation in Confucian rituals did not reflect religious devotion. Instead, it signaled a respect for China's ancient culture and intellectual tradition. Missionaries now understood Confucianism as a cultural heritage, compatible with the religious teachings of Christianity. In effect, German Protestants and Catholics had become Jesuits.[74]

Missionaries also began to see Confucianism as a positive political force, one that could insulate the Chinese political landscape from broader global threats. They recognized that they needed allies to combat the rise of other, more dangerous global enemies lurking on the horizon—Buddhists, secularists, and Communists. In Confucianism, the missionaries had a friend. Along with Christianity, Confucianism could serve to inculcate moral values during a period of tumultuous international instability.

The specter of global threats to Christianity was, of course, not new to the 1920s and 1930s. As we have seen, in the late nineteenth century German missionaries held a global hermeneutics of suspicion toward Europeans and Chinese in equal measure. Missionaries excoriated the rise of European secularism at the same time that they lambasted

Confucianism. Yet in the nineteenth century, the exact connections and links between Christianity's global opponents were murky. At most, the missionaries defined the threats to Christianity vaguely as "forces of impiety." Missionaries in the late nineteenth century conceived of Christianity as an undisputed global force, engaging in battles on multiple fronts against opponents that bore no relation to one another. European secularism and Chinese Confucianism were separate and local threats. But in the 1930s, global forces now had the capability to endanger Christianity's international supremacy. Buddhism, Communism, and secularism could mobilize transnational networks and resources to challenge Christianity.

Because of the global nature of the opponents that they faced, missionaries had to reformulate their political and cultural positions in order to stem the advance of these rival ideologies. In the nineteenth century, the solution to the anti-Christian threat in China had been to attack the local political system with the resources of global Christianity. If China could rid Confucianism of its bureaucratic reach, Christianity's future there could be secured. To rid themselves of their pesky opponents, missionaries sought to interfere in local politics and discredit Confucian ideology at large. By the 1930s, however, such tactics were no longer useful, as the character of the enemy had changed. The bigger challenge to Christian legitimacy was the expansion of global rivals. To confront their global enemies, missionaries realized that they needed to change their approach. They had to make local allies, so they reached out to their old enemy Confucianism. An alliance with Confucianism, missionaries believed, offered Christianity a way to forge a new bond with the Chinese people. Unlike Communism and secularism, which, they argued, violated fundamental tenets of Chinese culture, Christianity shared common ideas and aims with Confucianism. Together, they could transform China in the midst of global instability. No longer repelled by Confucianism's "Chinese" character, now missionaries were drawn to Confucianism precisely because of its "Chineseness."

And indeed, BMS and SVD missionaries began portraying Confucianism as a good bedfellow, a like-minded bastion of conservative values. Like Christianity, Confucianism stood for hierarchical order in a time of dramatic change. Missionaries in 1900 saw Confucian ancestor worship as a backward force, an impediment to China's modernization. Now they saw the Confucian veneration of the past as a source of stability, a protective force that helped prop up the old order. Confucianism stood for some semblance of morality, as opposed to what missionaries saw as the amoral ideologies of the new age.

But the softening stance of the SVD and BMS toward Confucianism was not driven solely by political calculation. Some missionaries were genuinely moved by the traditional cultural expressions they witnessed. One SVD missionary, new to China, commented on his first Chinese funeral. Included in the funeral procession was a long line of kowtows, where the family members of the deceased threw themselves on the ground to demonstrate their grief. The missionary was "totally struck" by the public display: "I was moved by the thought that I was standing among a people who had so long ago created these forms of mourning, and have preserved them for more than two thousand years."[75] On the surface, at least, many missionaries evinced respect for the ancient cultures that they encountered.

The BMS and the SVD were not the only missionary societies that reconsidered their ideas during the 1920s and 1930s. As Grant Wacker writes, by the 1930s, "thousands of Christians on both sides of the Pacific had come to view conversionary missions as culturally imperialistic at best and morally indefensible at worst."[76] The most famous case was that of the writer Pearl S. Buck, who caused a scandal in 1932 when she charged the missionary methods of her parents as arrogant and ignorant. Scholars such as Lian Xi have credited cultural liberalism, and especially the ascendancy of the Social Gospel within American mainline churches, as the main agent of change behind this "conversion of missionaries" from a chauvinistic, paternalistic worldview to an increasing emphasis on inclusion and tolerance.[77]

The Sinophilic turn of the BMS and SVD, on the other hand, was not an embrace of liberal theology, or of liberalism in general. Instead, SVD and BMS missionaries adopted a Sinophilic tone in order to combat the effects of the "liberal-modernist" nexus. Confucianism, or traditional Chinese culture, was an ally in a global battle against atheism, rationalism, and materialism. The missionaries hoped that Confucianism could be harnessed to more effectively convert China to Christianity. Continuities remained between missionaries writing before and after the war. They continued to depict China as an unruly, dangerous, wild place, full of bandits, robbers, and enemies of the gospel. But their enemy had shifted from xenophobic Confucian gentry to Communist insurrection, from a dominant Confucian ideological landscape to resurgent Buddhism. Moreover, the stakes had changed. Missionaries no longer saw their prize as the soul of China. The stage now was global. A failure in China meant triumph for the Communist and atheist insurgency worldwide. Likewise, Buddhism's rise portended a serious challenge to the fortunes of Christianity not only in China, but in the rest of East Asia. Abandoning an inchoate church to these pernicious global forces meant a betrayal of the decades and centuries of hard work from their predecessors.

Yet the Germans could not let go of their belief in the ultimate supremacy of Christianity. Even though German Catholic and Protestant missionaries embraced Confucianism to serve as a bulwark against rival ideologies, they feared syncretism. What if, they worried, Chinese converts were to believe that Christianity and Confucianism were equivalent in moral and spiritual authority? These fears signaled a divergence between liberal and conservative visions for an indigenous Chinese church. For liberal missionaries and liberal Chinese church leaders, an indigenous church meant more than a church staffed by Chinese or an institution free from Western intervention. Rather, an indigenous Chinese church stood for a total, pure synthesis between Confucian and Christian culture: two civilizations met each other as equals. Conservatives believed that even the suggestion of equality diluted the supremacy and purity of the Christian message.

Missionaries dismissed the liberal Chinese approach to the indigenous church as a minority view, limited to elite circles. In their congregations, German missionaries continued to preach the message of Christian superiority, hoping to insulate those congregations from beliefs about Christian and Confucian parity. But in the 1930s, the walls that the missionaries believed to have built for their Chinese congregants began to crack. Liberal Chinese views about the indigenous church—which the missionaries considered heterodox—began to infiltrate BMS and SVD congregations. The ever-porous borders became increasingly more permeable, and the missionary designs for an independent Chinese church separated farther from what the Chinese Christians in their congregations hoped to create. The divergence between German missionaries and their Chinese congregants soon became a chasm in the 1930s and 1940s, as the political situation in China became increasingly unstable.

CHAPTER SEVEN

Unfulfilled Promises

IN JULY 1931, SVD bishop Augustin Henninghaus received a letter from the Propaganda Fide that shocked him. It informed him that more than forty secular Chinese priests in his diocese had signed a petition, asking the Propaganda Fide to ordain a Chinese bishop in the SVD-controlled southern Shandong. Henninghaus was incensed: Chinese priests had bypassed his authority by convening secretly and contacting the Propaganda Fide.

The Vatican, on the other hand, viewed the petition as an opportunity, an occasion to pressure Henninghaus. Having long wanted a Chinese bishop in the region, the Propaganda exhorted him to ordain more Chinese leaders for the church. A power struggle, brewing for some time, was now out in the open.[1]

Henninghaus should not have been surprised by the petition. As we have seen, the initiative to ordain more Chinese clergy, actively promoted by the Propaganda, had gained steam after the First World War. The SVD itself had been preparing for a Chinese bishop and had set up institutions, such as its Chinese novitiate, to help facilitate the transfer of power. By the early 1930s, however, citing Chinese spiritual immaturity, Henninghaus and other SVD missionary leaders still refused to consecrate a Chinese bishop in the region. The Propaganda was anxious. Armed with an actual petition from Chinese priests, the Propaganda Fide finally had leverage that could embarrass the SVD leadership into action.

Like the SVD, the BMS adopted a more cautious approach to indigenous ordination as it was surrounded by calls for the creation of an independent church. Even though the BMS had written a 1922 church constitution mandating that its congregations move toward independence, by the early 1930s the society had turned over only one congregation to the hands of a Chinese pastor. Missionaries continued to complain about the unreadiness of their Chinese congregations for independence.[2]

Why did such reluctance toward indigenization persist in both missionary societies? In previous chapters, I examined intellectual and cultural movements that contributed to the obstinate German mistrust of relinquishing power to Chinese priests. In this chapter, I turn my attention to the political and social contexts in China that deepened missionary suspicion of Chinese spirituality. Intensifying tensions between Nationalist, Communist, and Japanese forces left the Germans fearful for the survival of Chinese congregations that had no patronage or support. Throughout the 1920s and 1930s, SVD and BMS missionaries faced an almost impossible situation: they were tasked with the goal of establishing independent Chinese congregations, yet political and economic instability threatened the survival of all congregations. A dependent Chinese congregation, they believed, was better than an independent congregation that ceased to exist.

SVD and BMS missionaries also pointed to the dire economic straits of the Chinese congregations to justify their reluctance to allow independent Chinese management. Missionary leaders believed that independence required financial stability. Persistent economic deprivation meant that few of the missionary congregations could muster both the financial and institutional resources to support their own clergy. Some Chinese clergy entreated the Germans to stay, arguing that they were still unprepared for independence.

Ironically, the political and economic instability that prompted the Germans to maintain their power also necessitated that they relinquish it. Two devastating geopolitical situations accelerated the indigenization process: the escalation of the Sino-Japanese conflict during the 1930s and the Nazi seizure of power in 1933. For both missionary societies, the global circumstances were crippling. For both, the timetable and decision to indigenize were ultimately things they could not control.

SOUTHERN INSTABILITY, NORTHERN UNREST

Since the beginning of their work in China, the SVD and BMS had focused their attention in rural areas. As latecomers to the country, their choice had partly been involuntary, as competing missionary groups had already occupied urban areas in Guangdong and Shandong. But they were motivated by theological reasons as well: they believed that they had a particular calling to serve the poor. In the late nineteenth century, with plentiful financial resources coming from Germany, both the BMS and the SVD had expanded their operations rapidly. Yet the infusion of missionary funds, and the establishment of infrastructure—mission schools and stations—was unable to fundamentally alter the structural poverty of the surrounding areas. The congregations that missionaries wanted to make financially independent remained destitute well into the 1920s. Their strategy of focusing on the rural poor, which had contributed to their success in the nineteenth century, proved to be their undoing in the twentieth.

Both the SVD and the BMS shared, in particular, one unchanging and unchangeable obstacle: geography. The BMS's missionary stations in the counties of Nanxiong and Shixing lay at the foot of a continuous line of mountains known as the Nanling that marked the boundary between Central and South China. The area historically served as a choke point: any inland traveler or merchant who crossed the Nanling had to enter one of these two counties.[3] Nanxiong served as one of the primary depots for the salt trade, connecting the salt merchants of Central China with coastal traders. Besides trade, Shixing and Nanxiong relied on agricultural production. Because of its moderate climate, high humidity, and clearly delineated seasons, the whole region was suited to agricultural production and forestry. Shixing was known in particular as the "rice basket of northern Guangdong." The area also produced tobacco leaf, vegetable oils, and jute fiber (for the production of textiles).[4]

But proximity to the mountains put any commercial activity in constant danger. Bandits, who hid in the mountains to evade the prying eyes of the state, constantly threatened the areas around Nanxiong and Shixing. They ransacked the goods of merchants and farmers and found effective refuge in the mountainous terrain.[5] State neglect further curbed economic development. Unlike Chinese Christians in Hong Kong, who became economic brokers, translators, and upwardly mobile local elites, converts in these areas remained poor.[6] These agrarian poor became the objects of attention for multiple groups—Christian missionaries starting in the nineteenth century and Communists in the 1920s and 1930s.

In 1926, the Berlin leadership agreed to begin its experiment with church independence in Shixing, whose main missionary station offered an opportunity for the BMS to test Chinese self-governance. The missionaries uniformly expressed optimism about the venture. For one, the risks were lower, since the society had invested less capital in Shixing than in urban missionary stations such as Guangzhou. Shixing had other advantages. With two hundred regular congregants at its central station, the county boasted one of the BMS's largest congregations. The missionaries were confident that Chinese leaders had a solid base to work with and hoped that they could soon expand the work even further. They assigned the Chinese pastor Ling Deyuan to spearhead the effort in the county, making him the BMS's first independent Chinese pastor.[7]

Yet after four years of arduous work, Ling admitted to his German supervisors that he had failed to execute their original vision. The coffers of his congregations were still empty. The amount of money the church collected, Ling reported, barely covered the wages of the staff, let alone the money needed for more costly expenses, such as making chapel repairs, replenishing church supplies, and printing Christian tracts. The congregations had failed, Ling continued, to meet any of the criteria for financial independence outlined in the 1922 church constitution.[8]

Ling blamed his Chinese congregants for the slow growth of the work. The Chinese were unwilling to tithe. Such reluctance, Ling and his German supervisors argued, reflected an "immature faith."[9] The parishioners, one missionary lamented, did not recognize the important spiritual discipline that tithing reflected. Instead, the Chinese viewed it as an onerous imposition: "The Chinese church members see the financial responsibility laid out in the Church constitution as a tax, similar to the ones levied by the state. All of the enlightened talk of indigenization has been thrown into the wind."[10]

Instead of blaming the congregants, some missionaries pointed to the Chinese clergy for the sluggish development of church independence. "It pains me to say," the missionary Heinrich Wahl wrote to Director Siegfried Knak, "but none of our Chinese pastors have demonstrated any interest in implementing the new Church constitution and taking steps toward church independence." He continued, "If Chinese leaders felt any urgency to become independent from us foreigners, they would have tried every possible method to strive for this goal." Instead, Wahl witnessed half-hearted and haphazard attempts among the BMS's Chinese clergy to encourage more financial giving from the congregations. Wahl also implied that their Chinese congregants refused to tithe because they distrusted Chinese church leaders: they suspected the Chinese clergy of embezzling church funds. The hermeneutics of suspicion ran both ways: just as the missionaries feared the insincere faith of "rice Christians," the Chinese congregants also worried about corruption within the church leadership.[11]

Further preventing Chinese congregational participation was a rising tide of anti-Christian and antiforeign activity during the mid-1920s. Communists and Nationalists, still incensed by the extraterritorial rights that missionaries enjoyed, agitated against missionary schools, hoping to wrest control from foreigners and place them in the hands of the Chinese. An already tense situation between Chinese and foreigners further exploded when on May 30, 1925, Shanghai police fired into a crowd of protestors who were demonstrating against injuries and deaths of Chinese workers in Japanese factories. Twelve people were killed. What followed was a surge throughout China of antiforeign and anti-imperialist activity. Churches were vandalized, Chinese Christians harassed, foreigners killed. The most prominent case involved the killing in 1927 of J. E. Williams, a Presbyterian missionary and vice president of Nanking University. Subsequently, many missionaries decided they could not continue their work in China. More than two thousand missionaries left the country; many never returned.[12]

The BMS's congregations were also affected by the vehement anti-Christian sentiment. In 1926, Ling Deyuan reported, "The anti-Christian movement has spread throughout the countryside in the form of newspaper reports and articles, as well as pamphlets and speeches." Chinese activists disrupted Christian activity across the country, particularly in rural areas. In public speeches, they called missionaries foreign imperialists who were intent on exploiting poor Chinese regions. They interrupted church services and vandalized church property. Ling worried about younger Christians, who were still "weak in the faith," wondering whether they had been swayed by the secular arguments.[13]

German Catholics were equally beleaguered by obstacles to their work in northern China. The SVD's missionary work was focused in southern Shandong, which was plagued by natural disasters, famines, and political unrest. Shandong had long been one of China's key agricultural regions, but it was also one of its poorest. As the historian Joseph Esherick notes, "flat land, cereal agriculture, dense population and impoverished villages" characterized the Shandong plains.[14] The flatness of the plains contributed to the region's impoverishment, as drainage was a recurring problem. The plains depended on yearly rainfall, rendering them more susceptible to natural disasters. A repeating cycle of flood and drought devastated the region. The center of the SVD's activity, southwest Shandong, was particularly vulnerable to flooding from the Yellow River. Such instability, coupled with low levels of commercialization and urbanization, led to seasonal recurrences of banditry. As Esherick notes, in the late nineteenth century, "Banditry had clearly become an integral part of southwest Shandong."[15]

Banditry was a problem that persisted well into the 1920s and 1930s when a series of famines devastated the entire region; they were so frequent that Western relief workers referred to China as "the Land of Famine."[16] The Yellow River—which came to be known internationally as "China's Sorrow"—flooded in 1925, 1933, and 1935. Compounding the effect of the natural disasters was the lack of governmental aid to the region. Throughout the 1920s, R. G. Tiedemann writes, "much of northern China was disrupted by frequent warlord struggles, civil war, soldier-banditry, and fierce resistance by local self-defense organizations against all outside predators."[17] In the late 1920s, in an attempt to unify the country, Chiang Kai-shek entered into a brief alliance with warlords Feng Yuxiang (dubbed the "Christian General" because of his conversion to Christianity) and Yan Xishan during the northern expedition of 1927. The tentative alliance soon disintegrated, and competing armies tried to conscript rural farmers.

To withstand the military requisitions of the Nationalist Party (Guomindang) and the rising tide of regional banditry, rural farmers and villagers established or revived local self-defense groups, generally referred to as Red Spear associations. Harkening back to the Boxers, members of the associations believed that their spells rendered them invulnerable to Western weapons. As Elizabeth Perry notes, the line between a "defensive" and predatory stance among Red Spear associations was often blurry.[18]

Other than organizing themselves to protest warlord attempts to collect taxes, they also vandalized missionary property and church buildings. To SVD missionaries, it became increasingly difficult to distinguish between Chinese allies and opponents.

ENEMIES EVERYWHERE: COMMUNISTS AND NATIONALISTS

Starting in the mid-1920s, Chinese Christians, in both the north and the south, witnessed the rise of yet another group antagonistic to Christianity—Communists. A surge of new members joined the CCP after the May Thirtieth Movement of 1925. The party soon expanded rapidly in both urban and rural areas in China. As Hans Van de Ven writes, by 1927 the CCP had transformed from a small circle of diverse radical intellectuals into a centralized "mass political party." The party was bolstered further by its cooperation with the Guomindang when they joined forces in a United Front with the intent of ridding the country of warlordism. The United Front gave the Communists an opportunity to concentrate their efforts in rural areas, and they fanned out into the countryside with the aim of organizing peasant associations. Their efforts proved successful, or so they thought. A CCP report from 1926 boasted that eight hundred thousand peasants had joined peasant associations. Chen Duxiu bragged at the Fifth Party Congress in 1927 that the CCP had organized ten million peasants. Guangdong was a particularly active hub of Communist activity: the party began many of its experiments with peasant organization there, in some of the same areas where the BMS worked.[19]

At first, Chinese Christians in the BMS expressed skepticism toward the Communist threat. At the BMS's 1927 synod, one Chinese pastor, Ma Dajing, gave a presentation on Chinese Communism. In it, he compared the CCP to the early Christian church, pointing out the common ideals the two groups shared. Both the Communists and the early Christians shared a concern for the poor and wanted to eradicate inequality. But unlike the early church fathers, "Communists spread their ideals through brute force and greed." The Communists, Ma claimed, "formed communities filled with irresponsibility, meanness, misdeeds, and laziness."[20] Ma remained unconvinced that the Chinese Communists would ever gain a strong foothold among Chinese communities because of these harmful characteristics.

Ma's comments sparked a vigorous debate. The pastor Ling Deyuan admired the Communist ideals of eradicating inequality, and he argued that it was still too early to make a judgment on the Communists' nature and character. Christians needed to be patient and monitor whether Communism could actually pose a threat to Christianity. Other missionaries argued that while the Communists had some good ideas, they were impractical and their proposals would never work in reality. The discussion concluded with one pastor commenting, "Communism can work only when sin is destroyed and no longer rules the world."[21]

Any ambivalence toward Communism soon disappeared. After 1927, descriptions of "Communist robbers" disrupting the mission society's work pervaded the reports to the German home board. The surge of these incidents of anti-Christian violence was not coincidental: after 1927, the Chinese Communists increased their presence in Guangdong due to Chiang Kai-shek's purge of Communists and the disintegration of the United Front. Many of the party cadres flooded into the Guangdong countryside and took up guerrilla activities.[22] In 1929, the CCP established an office in Shixing. Communists interrupted Ling's church services and destroyed chapels. Members of his congregation were so scared that they stopped going to church. Ling reported that he could barely conduct his daily pastoral work. Other Chinese Christian pastors bemoaned the fact that their congregations had come under daily attacks from Chinese Communists, who harassed Christians with slogans such as "Destroy imperialism, down with Christianity."[23]

The BMS missionaries recognized that Communists were a potent ideological attraction to the poor and dispossessed farmers—the same group that the missionaries sought to convert. In 1931, the BMS missionary Karl Zehnel reported: "There is a general consensus here that it is foolish to think that Communism poses no danger to China. Eighty percent of the Chinese live outside cities; they live in rural areas and work in agriculture. And Communism has made its inroads in China mainly among the poor and rural population." Comparing the situation to Germany, Zehnel wrote: "It is hard to understand the Chinese situation from a German perspective. Even though we have a large number of leftist farmers, they are in no way a decisive population. The majority of our farmers are content. In China, however, the relationship is somewhat different."[24]

Zehnel argued that it was imperative for the missionaries to engage the Communist threat and not shy away from it. Chinese preachers should be exposed to the basic ideas of Communism in the BMS's seminary and be prepared for dialogue with the Communists. Just as missionaries had helped Chinese converts dismantle the basic ideas of Confucianism in the nineteenth and early twentieth centuries, missionaries now needed to train the Chinese Christians to refute the basic claims of Communism.[25]

The Communists were not the only threat to the Chinese Christians; the Nationalist troops posed an equal challenge to their missionary work. Starting in 1927, as Rebecca Nedostup has shown, the Nationalist government engaged in an extensive campaign to rid the country of religious elements they labeled as "superstition."[26] Even though the government did not officially designate Christianity as a superstitious religion, many pro-Nationalist intellectuals espoused anti-Christian ideas. The historian Thoralf Klein has shown how the National Revolutionary Army, the military arm of the Guomindang, spread anti-Christian propaganda throughout Guangdong, disseminating satirical posters with caricatures of missionaries and teaching peasants songs that mocked Christianity. One Berlin missionary noted that the Communists and Nationalists, despite all their differences, were united in their anti-Christian stance: like the Communists, the Nationalists "reject and resist the public propagation of religion, in any form."[27]

Even more destructive to the missionary effort was the intensifying war between Nationalist and Communist troops in southern China. In July 1931, Chiang Kai-shek began the first of his various encirclement campaigns against the Jiangxi Soviet, in hopes of crushing the Communist Party.[28] The Jiangxi Soviet lay not far from Shixing and Nanxiong, and the encirclement campaign unsettled the BMS's operations. The Nationalists enlisted all men and women from the ages of eighteen to fifty-five to build public roads. They used BMS chapels to quarter their troops, forcing BMS preachers to move. Unable to travel freely, Chinese evangelists could no longer continue their pastoral work among more remote congregations. Chinese Christians were "afraid to show their faith openly," Ling Deyuan wrote, and many stopped going to church out of fear of governmental repression in the future.[29]

Ling reported in 1932 that battles between the Communists and Nationalists had rendered the situation in Shixing and Nanxiong dire. The

optimism of the early 1920s of financial independence and church indigenization was a distant memory. Ling lamented that the Chinese Christians
were "too spiritually weak" to counter the Communist threat. Communists
had swarmed into Nanxiong and Shixing and ruined BMS property: "All of
the chapels in the region are in a terrible condition. The walls and doors are
smeared with dirt, the inventory plundered. The Chinese Christians are
constantly hoping and waiting for funds that they can use to repair church
property." Political instability contributed to skyrocketing food prices. Ling
wrote that his Chinese congregants could scarcely find employment and
survive, let alone contribute and tithe to the church.[30]

Plummeting church attendance exacerbated the situation. The BMS
reported poor retention rates among its communities: people either left
for a governmental position or joined the CCP. Political violence had
further intimidated Chinese Christians. One Chinese pastor had been
shot and killed by Communists. Ling maintained that church independence was impossible; churches needed financial support from the
German missionaries.[31]

The BMS was not the only missionary society facing grave assaults
on its work in Guangdong. The Basel missionaries encountered similar
threats to their work in the northeastern part of the province. Anti-
Christian protestors stormed the missionary schools, and school enroll-
ments dropped. A missionary was kidnapped. Many Chinese Christians
abandoned the church. Some left because of fear; others joined the
Communist-led peasant associations, persuaded by the rhetoric of social
justice. Like their Berlin counterparts, Basel missionaries had to manage
serious financial difficulties because of the loss of personnel.[32]

Political instability also tormented the German Catholics in the north.
Similar to the Basel and Berlin missionary societies, the SVD clashed
with the rising Communist presence in Shandong. The Communist
leader Li Dazhao saw the emergence of Red Spear groups in Shandong as
signs of an impending class war between peasants and the landholding
elite. Sensing opportunity, the Communists reached out to these groups
as potential allies. In 1925, Communists dispatched their members to
arm and train for revolutionary action the Red Spear associations, which
then directly targeted SVD parishes.[33]

In January 1928, a group of bandits calling themselves the Band of
Ten-Thousand Knives (Wandaohui) occupied the SVD's residence in Poli,

holding one priest, two SVD lay brothers, and six sisters hostage. The troops seized the Catholic mission, hoping to use the ransom to pay for their costs.[34] A three-week-long standoff ensued, as Henninghaus and other SVD priests desperately tried to persuade provincial officials to send troops to resolve the occupation. Some priests wanted to pay the ransom. Anton Wewel, the rector of the residence, adopted an inflexible position, urging Henninghaus not to negotiate with the "devilish bandits, who fully deserve a bloody death. We will not be able to save the hostages unless we deliver swift punishment to these inhuman devils." Instead, he urged decisive military action. The whole region, Wewel wrote, "hates these bandits, as they have caused so much trouble in the area for so long. These evil-doers should be wiped off the face of the earth." Henninghaus sided with the hardliners and persuaded the provincial governor to dispatch troops. On February 5, 1928, provincial military troops entered Poli. After two days of skirmishes, the bandits retreated into neighboring villages. The freed hostages were scared, but unharmed.[35]

The SVD missionaries saw the raid as an act of betrayal, believing that the bandits could not have infiltrated the missionary compound without the help of an insider. Wewel surmised that the bandits received aid from a "traitor [named] Li, who led them to the church at eight o'clock, the exact time when the normally locked door was open." The occupation of the station was a "well-planned" act of revenge: Wewel suggested that the "traitor Li" was the husband of a woman who had grown up in the SVD orphanage in Poli and had been embittered by the experience. He lamented that even those who had grown up in SVD institutions could not be trusted. Enemies surrounded them; converts were prone to moments of weakness and betrayal.[36]

Still, the missionaries found several silver linings after the conclusion of the hostage crisis. The events were reported widely in Germany, including articles in the influential Catholic newspaper *Kölnische Volkszeitung*. Superior General Wilhelm Gier confided to Henninghaus, "These media reports have won us new benefactors for the mission." The media coverage, the missionary leaders in Europe hoped, could garner more support and broader sympathy for the work in China.[37]

Besides such social disorder gaining more donors in Germany, the missionaries believed that they could capitalize on the trouble in Shandong in a more classic way: conversion. In the crowds of refugees who sought shelter in their mission stations, the missionaries saw untapped reserves. In a report from Caozhou, the missionaries Karl Weber and Johannes Dahmen evoked scenes of mass suffering. "Villagers and farmers fled from the countryside to seek protection behind the solid walls of the city," they wrote. "As if rescued from a fire, the clumsy ox-wagons carried people, chickens, and pigs, as well as grain, cooking utensils, and fuel." Newly converted Christians brought their still unconverted families with them, and immediately the SVD saw the numbers in catechism classes grow from twenty students to fifty. Weber and Dahmen remarked: "Look at how Providence creates good out of evil! . . . We have really experienced a wonder of God's mercy, when after weeks of patient and insistent instruction, as well as fervent prayer, the light of faith is lit in the dark heart of the pagan, and the newly converted astounds you with their proclamation: 'I see, I believe.' "[38]

Yet the missionaries also cautioned against too much optimism. Experiences with social dislocation caused the SVD missionaries to become increasingly skeptical of the new Christians whom they had baptized. The Chinese who entered their congregations were primarily "young men and women who are new to the faith and have no elder Christian sponsors." Furthermore, many Christians had been influenced by the "anti-religious attitudes from the South," causing "many of the new Christians to waver in their faith." Faced with hordes of hungry and desperate refugees, missionaries were not sure whom they could trust. Many Chinese, the missionaries wrote, were unmoved by the message of the gospel. As Weber and Dahmen noted, "some remain deaf and their hardened pagan hearts have not melted completely." Missionary leaders decided that they should make more "strict selections" before admitting someone to catechism lessons.[39]

Other than placing higher demands on admissions, missionaries also paid closer attention to their spiritual curriculum and subjected students to strict instruction. Catechumens had to pray through the rosary twice a day and memorize lessons daily. The missionaries administered tests twice a week, and students had to pass tests before they were baptized.

Attrition rates were high. For various reasons—most of their converts came from transient populations—more than 30 percent of the converts left the faith. Missionaries also expelled students whom they felt uncomfortable baptizing. One missionary lamented, "It often hurts the priest's heart to let some of these diligent children go, but experience forces us to do so."[40]

Faced with such losses, the turbulent political environment, and the daily experience of teaching catechism classes, missionaries became further obsessed with judging the spiritual "maturity" and "immaturity" of the Chinese Christians whom they trained and baptized. The invest-ment that the SVD had put into the classes had increased rather than diminished over the years, yet the society still did not see the growth for which it had hoped. Frustrations in the field persuaded SVD missionary leaders that the region was too volatile for independent Chinese leader-ship. They delayed transferring authority to an incipient Chinese hier-archy and rejected the notion that the region was prepared for a Chinese bishop. The SVD's hermeneutics of suspicion toward the Chinese Christians grew during the late 1920s and early 1930s. In a landscape where loyalties and identities were constantly shifting, the SVD intensi-fied traditional methods of conversion and religious indoctrination, hoping to preserve a shred of predictability in a volatile political situation.

A PETITION, A BETRAYAL

Already feeling under siege, the SVD leaders cried betrayal when they learned that more than forty Chinese priests in their vicariate had peti-tioned the Propaganda Fide and circumvented the SVD's authority. The petition emerged from a slight: Henninghaus did not invite any Chinese priests to attend the regional synod in 1931, and worse, at the meeting he had reiterated that no Chinese priest was prepared to assume indepen-dent authority of prefectures in the vicariate. Infuriated, the Chinese priests organized and drafted a letter addressed to apostolic delegate Celso Costantini, who immediately forwarded it to the Vatican.[41]

With the Chinese petition in hand, the Propaganda pounced. "We beseech and pray that you begin to prepare a new indigenous mission," the prefect of the Propaganda Cardinal Willem van Rossum wrote to Henninghaus. The Vatican gave Henninghaus a new title, prefect of the papal household, and suggested that he demonstrate his gratitude toward the papacy by enacting the principles of *Maximum illud* and turning over power to one of the many Chinese priests he had helped to develop. The Propaganda further pressured Henninghaus by placing his ministry in the public limelight. In a savvy manipulation of the press, the Propaganda dedicated the front page of *L'Osservatore Romano,* the official Vatican newspaper, to celebrating the fiftieth anniversary of Henninghaus's ordination. Essentially a paean to Henninghaus, the article lauded his progressive reforms and in particular his efforts to elevate indigenous clergy to positions of influence.[42]

Henninghaus understood that the Vatican had outmaneuvered him. He publicly accepted the honor but privately was distraught. "Since Rome has now said A, we must say B," he lamented to Superior General Gier. "I cannot say that we are comfortable with how things are proceeding. This anniversary gift is very unwelcome." He conceded that he had no choice but to comply with the Vatican's request. He sent his approval to turn a region in the vicariate over to indigenous control. The Propaganda replied immediately, praising Henninghaus for instituting the plans "without delay."[43]

Having strong-armed Henninghaus, the Propaganda set its gears in motion. It began by designating the district Yanggu as the new apostolic prefecture. The choice of Yanggu was symbolic: it encompassed Poli, the SVD's first major mission area when Josef Freinademetz and Johann Baptist von Anzer had begun their work in Shandong 1882. The mission in the Yanggu area was also flourishing. One missionary boasted, "The crops have ripened." In 1932 alone, he had overseen the establishment of more than sixty-five new congregations and enrolled more than five hundred catechumens in classes.[44]

The Propaganda deferred to Henninghaus's authority by allowing him to choose the new prefect. Yet selection proved difficult. Henninghaus recognized that there were two camps among the Chinese priests: those who had signed the petition, and those who had demonstrated loyalty by not signing it. Henninghaus labeled the petitioners "revolutionaries," accusing them of being swayed by Nationalist, Communist, and "revolutionary" ideas. Henninghaus, in particular, believed that the priests had been emboldened by the political instability around them, and he was furious that they had adopted an antagonistic stance toward his authority: they had internalized the exact ideas that the missionaries were trying to eliminate.

Unwilling to negotiate with the revolutionaries, Henninghaus approached two of his oldest and most trusted Chinese priests, Dominicus Chao (Zhang Xiuwen) and Ambrosius Chen. Both rejected the offer, claiming they were unfit for the position.[45] Henninghaus then offered the post to Thomas Tian (Gengxin), one of the first entrants into the SVD Chinese novitiate who was still in temporary vows. Tian initially rejected the offer; he knew that he was an unpopular choice among the more progressive Chinese priests. To satisfy the non-SVD Chinese priests in the region, Tian suggested that Henninghaus "should appoint a bishop among the 'revolutionaries.' " However, after further pressure from several SVD missionaries, Tian accepted the nomination. But he made two demands. He wanted to appoint his own staff and bring priests whom he trusted to his own prefecture. And he asked the SVD to reassure him that it would continue to support him financially. The SVD agreed to his demands.[46]

The momentous day—the day on which the SVD appointed its first Chinese priest in a position of ecclesiastical leadership—was February 2, 1934. Yanggu was elevated to an apostolic prefecture, and Thomas Tian officially became the apostolic prefect of Yanggu. The SVD's Chinese novitiate had thus paid dividends. An SVD brother was on the path to becoming a bishop. Even though SVD missionaries had turned over control in the region to the Chinese, they had relinquished power to one of their own.[47]

The "revolutionary" priests were not assuaged by Tian's appointment. Henninghaus, they objected, had bypassed more experienced candidates: Tian had not yet professed his perpetual vows. The region had also received only an apostolic prefect, not a full bishop as the priests had hoped. This meant that Tian, and the rest of the Chinese, remained subordinate to Henninghaus. Henninghaus himself, they noted, had made it clear in a memorandum to the entire apostolic vicariate that Yanggu was still in a "preparatory stage," and Tian was responsible for reporting to him. The SVD also retained an overwhelming majority within leadership positions in the prefecture. Finally, they complained, Tian passed over the Chinese priests who had signed the petition, appointing those who were either SVD missionaries or trained by the SVD.[48]

The radicals had a point. Tian's ordination did not mean complete independence of the Yanggu region from SVD control. The SVD continued to influence personnel decisions in the region. In 1934, SVD superior general Josef Grendel dictated Tian's selection of Chinese priests, warning Tian not to choose from the "revolutionaries." Grendel made it clear to Tian that he was a member of the SVD and subject to the authority of the mission society.

Yet Tian was not just a pawn of the SVD. He also saw in the SVD a source of funds that he and his prefecture desperately needed. He did not want the SVD to withdraw financial support from the region—the congregations were still too poor to function on their own. Natural disasters also made a dire situation worse. In 1933 and 1934, the Yellow River flooded three districts in the prefecture. Tian reported, "Over 5,000 Christians are starving" and asked the SVD to send aid. The money that the SVD sent to the Chinese priests became their only source of income. Without the SVD's support, a grateful Tian wrote, "We would be in the gravest distress."[49]

Despite Tian's dependence on the SVD, his ordination as an apostolic prefect marked a significant milestone for the Chinese clergy in the region. It demonstrated to the Chinese priests that their voices were heard. Tian's selection signaled to the region that the Vatican was committed to pursuing the policy set out in *Maximum illud*. Although Tian was chosen as a compromise between the "radicals" and the SVD's overcautious policy, his ordination was nonetheless proof that the Chinese petition was not falling upon deaf ears.

BACK IN EUROPE: THE NAZI DEATHBLOW

Like the SVD, in the early 1930s the BMS was forced to turn over control to Chinese priests more rapidly than it expected. While the SVD was pushed by an alliance of Chinese and European pressures, in the BMS case, the demands came primarily from Europe. The rise of Hitler and the National Socialist Party, and the subsequent restrictions that the Nazis placed on foreign policy, forced the BMS to radically alter its work abroad.[50]

At first, Knak and the missionary leaders expressed cautious enthusiasm about Hitler and the National Socialists. In 1931, in his annual memorandum addressed to the entire society, Knak noted that the National Socialist Party had become a "real force" in German politics. Roused by Hitler's nationalism, Knak wrote, "I cannot feel anything but joy in my heart that such a nationalist movement has emerged in Germany. Without them, we would become nothing but passive tools in the hands of the French." Yet, Knak warned that a Nazi government could lead to a German civil war. Just as the Chinese countryside had been torn apart by the conflict between nationalists and socialists, Knak worried that a similar situation could happen in Germany.[51]

A year later, Knak once again mentioned Hitler in his annual report. This time, he sounded more alarmed. While he maintained that socialism remained the largest threat to Germany, he disapproved of the "radical anti-Semitism and racial hatred that underlie the agenda of the National Socialists." Despite these reservations, Knak rejoiced when Hitler became chancellor in 1933. In a letter circulated to the missionary society, Knak proclaimed Hitler's triumph a "gift from God" (*Gottesgeschenk*).[52]

Many others in the mission society also mounted a defense of Hitler. In China, BMS missionaries assuaged the fears of Chinese congregants who were concerned that Hitler's election portended a new geopolitical relationship between China and Germany. The Germans blamed the Anglo-American press for spreading "abominable propaganda" and "lies" about Hitler and the Germans. The attacks on Hitler, the missionaries claimed, belonged to the broader Anglo-American assault on Germany and the Germans.[53]

While Knak and the BMS celebrated the Nazi rise to power, they loathed the German Christians (Deutsche Christen), a movement led by pro-Nazi Protestant clergy calling for a synthesis between National Socialism and Christianity. The German Christians rose to political prominence along with the National Socialists. In July 1933, representatives of the German Christians won more than two-thirds of the votes cast in Protestant church elections, launching them into influential church positions throughout Germany. At its height, the movement had close to six hundred thousand members. Theologically, Doris Bergen writes, "German Christians appropriated the notion of the people's church but gave it a twist by using racial categories to define the *Volk*."[54] Arguing that the German churches should be enclosed racial entities, rather than open to a universal fellowship of all believers, German Christians called for the creation of a purely "Aryan" *Volkskirche*.

Knak immediately grasped the threat that the German Christians posed toward missionary work. In private correspondence, he denounced German Christian theology, arguing that German Christian errancy stemmed from their false views of the Bible: "The German Christians preach that Scripture is not the sole source of God's revelation. Instead, they teach that we can know God through nature and history. If that is the case, we do not need missionary work. We draw upon the Holy Scriptures to preach that Christ alone is the way to know God the father." The German Christians, Knak continued, committed a grave error by trying to graft the Nazi "leader principle" (*Führerprinzip*) onto the church. God had already delivered a leader to the church in the form of Jesus, and the German Christians had gone too far by comparing Hitler's appointment as chancellor to Christ's Second Coming. Employing the same language to warn against Wilhelm's conflation of Christ and Confucius, he cautioned that the German Christians promoted a "dangerous form of syncretism that we must resist."[55]

More galling to Knak was the German Christian stress on Aryan racial superiority and the desire to exclude non-Aryans and Jewish Christians from the German church community. "An Aryan clause in the Church," Knak wrote, "is a falsehood." He argued that if the church allowed for an Aryan clause to stand, "We would also have to debate if Negroes and Chinese can become members, elders, or pastors in Lutheran churches across the world. As the history of our missionary work has shown, these debates are ridiculous." While the German state, Knak contended, had every right to pass racially based laws, such as antimiscegenation, the church was a place where all peoples and races were welcome, as long as an individual accepted Christ. Defending missionary work within the Jewish community, Knak pointed out that scripture had shown that first converts to Christianity were Jews, and the church had welcomed them. The goal of Christian missions was to expand Christianity to include all races, rather than to create exclusive walls.[56]

Knak's and the BMS's promotion of racial inclusivity ruffled feathers. In 1935, the BMS exhibited posters throughout Berlin depicting its missionary work in Africa. The council of the St. Nikolai Church in the city sent a letter of protest, complaining about the "display of a strongly idealized Negro." The council leaders wrote: "We find your posters misguided, as it is likely to cause indignation among the majority of our people. During such a period that emphasizes racial thinking, we should focus our efforts on caring for our own race, and the care for our own countrymen should be placed at the forefront of the church's calling." They concluded, "The Council asks that you refrain from displaying all advertisements of these kinds."[57]

Knak was troubled. He defended the posters. In a pointed, but polite, response, he wrote, "For longer than the National Socialists have even existed, German Protestant missionaries have held that race [*Rasse*] and the people [*Volk*] are different categories." Missionaries, he pointed out, had worked to strengthen the German *Volk* while still allowing other races to flourish. The goal of making the German *Volk* powerful did not contradict the act of missionary welfare abroad; rather, the two acts were inseparably linked. Knak turned the tables on the church council, arguing that German missionaries had in fact fulfilled the vision of National Socialism abroad, as they had preached the uniqueness of German theology to other nations. "I cannot accept the criticism that our advertisements are not suitable for the current climate," Knak concluded.[58]

But the council's disapproval signaled the precarious political standing of the BMS under the Nazi regime. Supporters of foreign mission work retracted their donations, afraid of being on the wrong side of Nazi racial policy. The BMS leadership reported that ever since the Nazi rise to power, "the mission work is in greater financial need than we have ever experienced." The flourishing financial ecosystem that the missionary society drew upon in the nineteenth century had long disappeared.[59]

Even more devastatingly, the Nazi restriction on foreign export limited the amount of financial support that the mission society could send to China. Starting in 1934, the Nazi government intensified the Weimar restrictions on exporting foreign currency abroad. The BMS now could not transfer money from Germany to China without the risk of paying hefty fines.[60]

Missionaries in the field and missionary leaders alike talked about the ban in increasingly desperate terms. The BMS leadership warned its missionaries in the field that they should expect "deep and heavy cuts to European salaries, child support, pensions, and funding for the individual stations."[61] The budget cuts could not have come at a worse time. A missionary in China wrote that he and his colleagues faced "a severe shortage in raw materials, and the threat of a new round of inflation." In the midst of such a "desperate worldwide economic situation," he worried that they had to consider the real possibility of terminating the missionary work entirely.[62]

The Nazi restriction on foreign currency exchange applied equally to the Catholics. In October 1935, the apostolic vicar of Qingdao, Georg Weig, reported to the home board that because of the Nazi restrictions they "had reached the end of their financial capability."[63] When Tian asked the SVD superior general for financial aid in November 1935, Grendel rejected the request, citing the Nazi currency ban.

Unlike the BMS, the SVD had expressed reservations about the National Socialists from the beginning of their rise to power. In March 1933, the society had refused to send delegates to participate in a ceremony replacing the German black-white-red flag with the Nazi swastika flag at the German consulate in Qingdao. The SVD missionary Johann Weig, nephew of Johann Baptist von Anzer and of no direct relation to bishop Georg Weig, observed the ceremony. He reported: "The crowd enthusiastically chanted '*Heil Hitler*' and saluted Hindenburg. The word on the street, however, is that 'The Center Party missed the event.' "[64]

Weig later made his contempt for the Nazis even more explicit. Upon hearing the news that the Nazis signed the nonaggression pact with the Soviets in 1939, Weig commented: "Nazis and Bolsheviks are now brothers! Modern politics has no respect for itself anymore. It has no shame. The regime of the Third Reich is built on lies and hypocrisy. The struggle against Bolshevism was used as a slogan that justified the Nazi seizure of power, the destruction and deprivation of the Jews, the surveillance of all independent-minded men and women, the establishment of concentration camps, the murder of many noble people. Based on these premises, all was allowed—and now!" Weig lamented: "*Domine miserere!* How clearly Pius XI had foreseen everything."[65]

But just as it had helped the mission society immediately after the First World War, the SVD's international character buffered its work from financial catastrophe. From November to December, Bishop Georg Weig traveled throughout Europe and the United States, hoping to garner more financial support. The SVD leadership also circumvented the Nazi restrictions on currency by transferring money to Qingdao through their Dutch missionary holdings and being paid in Dutch guilders. Drawing on its international connections, the SVD was able to retain a modicum of stability despite the Nazi restrictions in Germany.[66]

Nonetheless, the Nazi policies accelerated the SVD's desires to cede more control of the region. Unable to procure funds from the SVD, Tian used his position as apostolic prefect to ask the Propaganda Fide for help. The SVD also saw an opportunity to cut its financial losses by transferring more responsibility to the Propaganda. In January 1938, Grendel sent a proposal to the prefect of the Propaganda, Cardinal Pietro

Fumasoni-Biondi, requesting that Yanggu be named apostolic vicariate and Tian a bishop. The Propaganda agreed, and in July 1939, Tian was appointed the vicar apostolic of Yanggu, the titular bishop of Ruspae. In October 1939, he traveled to Rome, where Pope Pius XII and Celso Costantini consecrated him as the new bishop. The Vatican finally got what it wanted: a Chinese bishop in southern Shandong. The SVD also got what it wanted: an SVD man in the position.[67]

Unlike the SVD, the BMS suffered the consequences of the Nazi currency restrictions without any country to which they could turn. The leaders were forced to reduce the number of missionaries they sent abroad. By the end of 1935, only ten men and five women remained in the field—the society's lowest number of foreign missionaries in China since 1898. Next came the stations. The BMS missionary leadership ceded Nan'an, on the Guangdong-Jiangxi border, to the China Inland Mission. It had to lay off fifty Chinese workers, including preachers, teachers, and Bible carriers. The Nazi restrictions on foreign exchange achieved the goals of the German Christians: it devastated the scope of foreign missionary work abroad. The *Volkskirche* that Knak had hoped to create had quickly become a mirage.[68]

In 1935, the mission inspector Johannes Müller circulated a memorandum asking missionaries to prepare for the eventual withdrawal of financial support for the Chinese congregations. Müller argued that the Berlin missionaries should follow the example set by the Presbyterian missionary in China John Nevius. Stressing Chinese independence and self-support, the "Nevius model" refused payment to indigenous workers and limited missionary presence. Presbyterian missionaries imported Nevius's ideas to Korea, where the model was credited with the success of numerous conversions and the rapid development of independent churches. Müller hoped that the BMS could draw upon this lead and transition to a less centralized—and less costly—model. The missionary society agreed and quickly decided to implement the Nevius model in its congregations. By 1936, the society no longer compensated indigenous clergy. Its congregations were now technically independent, no longer subject to control from the leadership in Berlin.[69]

Besides achieving the intended effect of limiting missionary work abroad, the Nazi restrictions resulted in a series of unexpected consequences: it accelerated the BMS's indigenization. Financial desperation ultimately pushed the BMS missionaries to make their congregations independent and turn over control to the Chinese Christians.

Yet the Chinese Christians of the BMS did not welcome independence; they emphatically protested the cuts. Persistent poverty shattered the trust between the Chinese and the missionary leadership. The Chinese accused the Germans of abandoning them out of political calculation, rather than financial necessity. The missionary inspector Alfred Oelke reported that the Chinese refused to believe that money had run out; they thought that the Germans were intentionally withholding it. "Even though we keep insisting that we are at the end of our financial capability, the Chinese no longer trust us. There is such bitter need here," Oelke wrote. He continued, "Our Chinese congregants say to us, you must have a little bit of money! At least use it to help the poorest among us."[70]

Like the missionaries themselves, the Chinese Christians argued that their churches were unprepared for independence and still in need of German help. Without German funds for food, clothing, and building materials, they asked, how could the Chinese congregations sustain themselves? Faced with so many challenges, they wondered how they could maintain their everyday responsibilities of pastoral care and evangelization.[71]

THE JAPANESE THREAT

Soon, yet another external threat appeared on the horizon: the escalation of the Second Sino-Japanese War. After the resumption of hostilities in July 1937, the Japanese advance through China was swift and brutal. By November, Beijing and Shanghai had fallen, and the Nationalist government had transferred its capital from Nanjing farther west, to Chongqing. By December, the Japanese had entered Nanjing, and six weeks of pillaging, raping, and killing in the streets of the former capital ensued. The next year was not much better for the Chinese war effort. To slow down the Japanese, Chiang Kai-shek ordered his troops to destroy the dikes that controlled the flow of the Yellow River. The ensuing flooding that devastated much of Central China resulted in around half a million Chinese deaths; between three and five million people were forced to abandon their homes. But it did slow down the Japanese troops. Unable to march on Chongqing directly, the Japanese sought to encircle the new capital and cut off international supply lines feeding it. In October 1938, they launched an operation on Guangdong and captured Guangzhou.[72]

The escalation of the war devastated the BMS's work in Guangdong. Church congregations fell into a state of chaos, halting any incipient progress that the BMS congregations had made toward independence. Japanese aerial bombings destroyed the area, and Chinese pastors and German missionaries reported rising numbers of casualties. The Guangzhou mission station became a refugee station. The region, missionary reports read, experienced "widespread deprivation and desperation."[73]

German missionaries and Chinese Christians alike appealed to the leadership in Berlin for financial assistance. But the board of directors in Germany, hampered by the Nazi currency restrictions as well as the onset of war in Germany, could not send any funds. Receiving no answers from Berlin, missionaries turned to the international missionary community for financial support. In 1940, missionaries asked the liberal NCC for financial aid, despite their theological reservations toward the group. The missionaries received a donation of four thousand U.S. dollars, which they used to pay the salaries that they owed the Chinese Christians. In his letter thanking the NCC for the donation, one missionary, Georg Kohls, wrote: "Although we German missionaries also suffer from insufficient income, I still think it proper first of all to provide our Chinese co-workers with the most necessary means to keep up their living and the evangelistic work. . . . They are in such a desperate condition."[74]

The war also devastated the SVD's work in North China, where the Japanese occupation was even more intense and sustained. After 1937, the SVD leadership received, with increasing frequency, reports describing how both Chinese and Japanese troops targeted SVD missionaries and Chinese Christians, killing or jailing them. Even though the SVD missionaries had criticized the Nazi regime, Chinese nationalists attacked them, citing Germany's formal alliance with Japan. The Japanese, on the other hand, suspected that Chinese troops used churches as sites for meetings and organizing resistance movements. Japanese soldiers targeted and attacked Chinese priests. In one particularly gruesome episode in 1938, Japanese troops killed one Chinese priest, two Chinese sisters, and eighteen other Chinese Catholics who were seeking protection in a military garrison. The following year, they arrested four missionary brothers in Qingdao, shutting down the SVD's elementary school. Almost five hundred students were displaced, no longer able to attend classes. On the ground, the SVD's internationalism worked against the society—to the Japanese, the SVD seemed to be conspiring with the Chinese, while to the Chinese, it appeared to be an ally of the Japanese.[75]

Compounding the war difficulties, in 1941, the bishop of Qingdao, Georg Weig, died from a sudden illness in Qingdao. His SVD colleagues surmised that his fund-raising travels in Europe and the United States had overworked him. Still, despite his efforts, resentment toward Weig had grown among his Chinese parishioners during his final years. They perceived him as cavorting abroad instead of staying to suffer with them during the war.[76]

Who would succeed Weig? The SVD leaders admitted that they had no suitable European candidates. In the worst-case scenario, they fretted, the Propaganda would transfer control of the Qingdao vicariate to another missionary society.[77] But their worry had little basis. For the Propaganda, ordaining a European missionary as bishop had become impossible. Not only would parishioners rebel against the choice, the Propaganda itself had expressed its commitment to more indigenous clergy. Weig's successor, it concluded, would have to be a local, indigenous priest. Costantini and the Propaganda suggested that they transfer Tian from his post in Yanggu to Qingdao, a much bigger vicariate. Tian had gained a good reputation for his prudence and hard work in Yanggu, as well as his diplomatic approach to resolving tensions between the Japanese and Chinese. The SVD agreed, applauding the suggestion as "a very appropriate solution." At the very least, Qingdao remained in the hands of an SVD bishop.[78]

Upon his transfer to Qingdao, Tian nominated the secular priest Thomas Niu (Huiqing) to replace him in Yanggu. Costantini accepted this nomination; Grendel also approved of Niu, describing him as "a very zealous priest and a good missionary." Even though he was not a member of the SVD, Niu had been educated in SVD seminaries. "After Monsignor Tian," Grendel remarked, "he has always been the most capable among the indigenous priests."[79]

The Propaganda had thus achieved its goal: the SVD had transferred power to indigenous clergy. The SVD originally had no plans to devolve power so quickly. But like the BMS, the war had forced the SVD to give up its control in the region. Increasingly isolated as Germans, and lacking an infusion of European talent, the SVD had few candidates to push and scarce leverage in discussions over new appointments. Deference to the Vatican was hardly a choice.

Despite being technically independent from the SVD, Tian did not cut off communication with his former supervisors. Even as the war intensified, and as correspondence between Europe and China became more difficult, Tian continued to send the SVD leadership updates about his work. He maintained the habit of reporting the statistics every quarter about the state of his vicariate. In 1943, Tian wrote that even though no new missionary stations had been created, he had some happy news: several Chinese youth had taken holy orders. Tian praised his benefactors, remarking that they had laid the foundations for the growth in the vicariate. He expressed a steady loyalty to the SVD missionary leadership.[80]

But it was toward the end of the war that the SVD missionaries suffered their most catastrophic destruction. In May 1945, Chinese Communist soldiers plundered the SVD headquarters in Daijiazhuang. The SVD estimated the material damage to be in the millions. Seven pastors, two lay brothers, and thirty missionary sisters were held hostage. As he rang a bell calling for help, the SVD missionary in charge of the novitiate was executed. The Communists shot him four times: once in the head and three times in the rest of his body. The soldiers escaped with the SVD's livestock before the Japanese arrived.[81]

BAPTISM BY FIRE

Despite the devastation that Shandong suffered during the war, Catholic life recovered relatively quickly following it. Tian's presence was crucial. He had never left Qingdao during the war, and Catholics looked to him as a symbol of religious continuity in the region. He had also maintained his pastoral work, traveling throughout the region even in the depths of wartime. The Vatican rewarded him for his constancy. In 1946, Pope Pius XII made Thomas Tian the first archbishop of Beijing and the first Chinese cardinal.[82] In 1948, an SVD man, Augustin Olbert, occupied Tian's former position, and Tian presided over the consecration. Aided by the Vatican and the Propaganda Fide, by 1948 the SVD had once more retained its position in the Shandong peninsula, and it seemed that the society was in a firm position to restore its prewar work in the area.

The Berliners were not so lucky; they never recovered from the war, which decimated the society's staff. Once with a staff numbering fifty, the BMS now employed five full-time ordained Chinese pastors and two part-time pastors. Only a quarter of the normal staff of evangelists and Bible women remained in their service; the rest had been dismissed. Church membership had collapsed, with some congregations numbering less than a quarter of their prewar populations. One of the healthier congregations in Shixing had boasted close to 376 congregants in 1927, but by 1946, it counted only 168 members. Many of the BMS's smaller churches and chapels had shut down. Some districts and areas of Guangdong were in better shape. A church in Nanxiong, for example, had retained most of its 170 members.[83]

The remaining Chinese Christians appealed to the Berliners for help. The pastor Ling Deyuan, for example, sent a letter in May 1947 to Knak, begging him to send more personnel and funds to China.[84] But the Germans were no longer able, or willing, to provide the funding that the Chinese needed. Knak decided to turn over the BMS's assets to the World Lutheran Federation. Instead of appointing a German, the federation chose a Norwegian, Thorvald Gogstad, who, as the new superintendent, would oversee all of the BMS's holdings. The choice stung. Previously in charge of a Lutheran Bible school in Hunan, Gogstad had never worked in Guangdong. The mission society had hoped that the BMS missionary inspector Georg Kohls, who had stayed in China through the hard years of war and served as assistant to the previous superintendent, would be appointed.[85]

The Chinese pastors, too, felt betrayed by Gogstad's appointment. "The pain," Pastor Lan Ti'en wrote in a latter to Knak, "is similar to the pain that a son feels when a mother abandons him." Still feeling indebted to the Germans, Lan expressed outrage on behalf of the BMS. The federation's decision signaled a decisive break with the German missionary society, ending an eighty-year relationship. Why did they not choose Kohls, someone who knew the congregations, Chinese pastors, and history of the region intimately? Lan also worried of Gogstad's status as an outsider: "He speaks a different language, he does not understand local conditions, nor the people of the church; it is inevitable that there will be some difficulties between him and the Chinese congregations." Before the war, Lan argued, the BMS had already put the Chinese congregations on a solid path toward self-reliance and self-support, and they needed only a brief period of financial assistance to get back on their feet. Was there no way that the Germans could stay?[86]

The BMS could not give the Chinese pastors an answer they wanted. The society was itself financially devastated in a partitioned Germany. It could no longer send the financial and personnel support that the Chinese requested. The Berlin missionaries acknowledged that their position in China was now forever altered. "The war has completely changed the relationship of the Europeans to the Chinese," Kohls remarked in 1947. "Some Chinese pastors rejoice," he reported, "saying 'the papacy of the European missionaries has ended and will never return.' " He continued: "All missionaries who come to China must be prepared for this new orientation. The positions of leadership in the missionary conferences and stations will be held by Chinese pastors."[87]

Kohls's predictions of increasing European irrelevance came true. No longer did Europeans dominate the leadership of the church congregations; the Chinese now took control of the appointments. In 1947, the Chinese pastors elected their candidate to become the pastor of a congregation, snubbing Knak's suggestions. Their candidate, Ling Deyuan explained, had much more experience; Knak's nominee, also Chinese, had fewer than five years of experience working for the Lutheran church. At the BMS's 1948 synodal meeting, Superintendent Gogstad chaired the meeting, but he mainly played the part of coordinating communication and efforts among the different congregations. The transfer of power from the missionaries to the Chinese was complete.[88]

Though declawed, the BMS leadership still dreamed of one day returning to China. In 1947, Knak promised Ling Deyuan, "In five years, we Berliners will return in full force and take back the missionary work from the Norwegians."[89] Little did he know that in fewer than five years all missionaries would be expelled from China.

CONCLUSIONS: A PERSISTENT SUSPICION

Even after the war, missionary fears of "inauthentic" Chinese spirituality remained. The BMS missionary Georg Kohls commented on "immature thinking" among the Chinese leaders and how Chinese pastors still had much to learn in a new political and spiritual landscape. In 1948, Knak continued to express the need to continue the battle against "syncretism" and the "strong influence of Americans."[90]

What can we make of such persistent suspicion? One could argue, as some scholars have, that Western distrust of Chinese spirituality stemmed from an enduring sense of missionary paternalism.[91] There is much evidence to back up this argument. As was the case with the BMS and

SVD, missionaries continued to hold attitudes of superiority even after the traumas of two catastrophic world wars. When missionaries talked about Chinese Christian spiritual "maturity," their rhetoric harkened back to nineteenth-century missionary rhetoric that required Chinese converts to demonstrate theological orthodoxy and loyalty to their particular denominational outlook.

By the 1940s, missionary demands for loyalty came in direct conflict with rising Chinese nationalist sentiment. And in truth, the Chinese nationalist critique of German recalcitrance did have its merits: German missionaries held unreasonable expectations for financial solvency within congregations. They had not abandoned their desire to foster a perfect form of faith in China, a perfection that would compensate for what they believed was no longer possible in Europe. A flourishing Chinese Christian church could realize the nostalgia for an age when European Christendom once dominated, before the onslaught of war, destruction, and secularism.

Yet cultural chauvinism and nostalgia do not completely explain the German suspicion of Chinese faith. After two decades of unrelenting political chaos—beleaguered by enemy after enemy, some perceived and others too real—the Germans felt a sense of responsibility to their Chinese converts. With paternalism came not only arrogance, but also duty, a desire to protect their "spiritual children." They wanted to see their congregations and parishes as financially self-sufficient and self-sustaining before they withdrew support. The deteriorating Chinese political scene rendered such a scenario impossible.

Chinese Christians recognized that they needed foreign help to survive. During the war, Chinese Christian leaders continued to ask the missionaries for financial assistance, and they felt abandoned when the missionaries withdrew support. Immediately after the war, Chinese Christian leaders of the BMS appealed to the Germans to return to China. They were the "spiritual children" of the German missionaries, they said, and the Germans had a responsibility to protect them. The critique advanced by left-leaning Chinese church activists since the 1920s, which portrays the missionaries as tightly controlling the finances of Chinese churches, is only partly true. Chinese church members themselves recognized the ramifications of the withdrawal of Western funds, and they fought bitterly to try to keep Western missionaries from leaving.

Despite continuing missionary practices from the nineteenth century, both missionary societies underwent dramatic changes from the 1920s to the 1940s. By the 1930s, both the SVD and the BMS had built a church hierarchy with Chinese leaders. The SVD admitted Chinese brothers as official members to its society, and it could boast its first Chinese bishop, Thomas Tian. Similarly, by the mid-1930s the BMS had several independent church congregations run solely by Chinese pastors. Formally, the missionary director addressed the Chinese Christian leaders as equals, rather than as a superior. Change, although slow, nonetheless came.

Internationally, the fates of the two missionary societies diverged. For the BMS, whose finances were linked intimately to the political situation in Germany, it was that domestic crisis—not the one in China—that ultimately dealt a devastating blow to the society's operations. Nazi restrictions on foreign exchange served as an unintended catalyst that stopped the flow of resources from Germany to China, forcing the missionaries to rely more on the Chinese Christians. On the other hand, the SVD, with its headquarters in Rome and missionary seminaries throughout the world, had become a truly international organization. Its fortunes were not linked to the fates of any single nation. Although it was curtailed by the Nazi ban on foreign exchange, the SVD ultimately could depend on the Vatican and other Catholic missionary societies for support.

The advantage of having a powerful international force like the Vatican as an ally cannot be understated. The Chinese priests in SVD regions had a higher authority to whom they could appeal, and they were unafraid to bypass their direct superiors by writing directly to the Vatican. In moments of desperation, Chinese priests could ask the Vatican for both political and economic aid. Chinese Protestant pastors, on the other hand, lacked an external authority to whom they could turn. The only way that unhappy Protestants could redress their grievances to individual church organizations was by leaving. And splinter denominations did emerge from Western missionary societies, such as the True Jesus Church, Watchman Nee and his Little Flock, and Wang Mingdao's Christian Church in Christ.[92]

But independence was risky. Without a charismatic individual at the helm, it was difficult to cultivate a fledgling church organization. Until 1949, for most Chinese Christians, the safest option was to keep silent, continue to serve in their congregations, and patiently hope for a better political and economic situation. But the success of the Communist Revolution forced Chinese Christians to renounce all ties to the West. Whatever the disagreements within individual congregations, few, if any, wanted to disclaim—to repudiate, to condemn publicly, to banish totally—the Western missionaries whom they had learned from, worked with, and suffered alongside for decades. After 1949, Chinese Christians had to choose: declare allegiance to the CCP, or go underground. Remaining silent was no longer an option.

CHAPTER EIGHT

Fruits of the Spirit

ON SEPTEMBER 23, 1950, the *Renmin Ribao (People's Daily)* published on its front page a "Christian Manifesto," signed by fifteen hundred Protestant church leaders throughout the country. To ensure the success of the Communist Revolution in 1949, the manifesto called upon all Chinese Christians to "cultivate a patriotic and democratic spirit" and to dispossess themselves of foreign and "imperialist" influences. The manifesto marked a major turning point for Protestant churches in China, which had until then refused to align themselves with any explicit political parties. For Christians sympathetic to progressive and Communist politics, the Christian Manifesto stood for the beginning of an independent Chinese Christianity unencumbered by foreign influence. Influential advocates of the manifesto, led by the prominent church leader Wu Yaozong, established the Three-Self Patriotic Church in 1951, the only Protestant organization sanctioned by the CCP. Its Catholic counterpart, the schismatic Chinese Patriotic Catholic Association, was established in 1957, driving the Roman Catholic Church underground and severing diplomatic ties between the Vatican and the People's Republic of China.[1]

Western missionaries felt crushed by the manifesto. The prominent British missionary Leslie Lyall called it a "betrayal," and religious conservatives branded its signers traitors.[2] Chinese Christians, Lyall and others believed, had collaborated with the Communists for politically expedient reasons, not spiritual ones: they joined the Patriotic Church for the sake of survival. This interpretation, which the historian Ryan Dunch calls the "control-and-resistance paradigm," continues to dominate popular understanding of the Three-Self Patriotic Church. Conservative evangelical church groups in the United States, for example, extol as the true heroes people such as Wang Mingdao and Watchman Nee, who refused to join the Patriotic Church and suffered persecution and imprisonment as a result. The scholarly literature has also focused on these resistance figures, seeing in them the precursors to the contemporary underground church movement in China that has revived in recent years.[3]

Defenders of the Three-Self Patriotic Church see its theology as a genuine attempt to grapple with the difficulties posed by the Sinicization of Christianity in China. These studies focus primarily on national-level religious leaders, such as Wu Yaozong, Ding Guangxun, and Zhao Zichen. Rather than seeing cooperation with the Communists as a betrayal of authentic Christian faith, these scholars argue that collaboration was an attempt by Christian theologians to work out the thorny theological question of how to be simultaneously Christian and Chinese, a persistent question that has existed since Christianity's entry into China. Furthermore, by engaging in dialogue with the CCP, Christians have been, as Dunch argues, "participants in a 'long conversation' with the state," which "has led to modifications on both sides about the place of Christianity in China's 'socialist modernity.'" In Dunch's frame, the Communist government of the People's Republic was only the latest in a long line of Chinese states that saw Christianity as a threat, and the Three-Self Patriotic Church is an attempt by Chinese Christians to carve out a religious space for themselves.[4]

This chapter examines the stories of two Chinese Christians who worked with German missionaries before 1949 and subsequently supported the Patriotic Church after 1949. One was Ling Deyuan, the BMS pastor who was thoroughly a product of the German society's educational institutions. He signed the Christian Manifesto in 1950. The other is Chen Yuan, a prominent scholar and president of the Catholic University of Beijing (Fu Ren University), run by the SVD after 1933. In a "self-criticism" published in the Guangming daily newspaper in 1952, Chen denounced his missionary colleagues and supported the Communist cause.[5]

The two figures are an unlikely pairing. They lived in different worlds. Chen spent most of his adult life in Beijing as a famous and celebrated academic. Ling toiled in obscurity in the rural mountains of Guangdong. I consider their stories together to illuminate the difficult decisions that Chinese Christians had to make throughout the first half of the twentieth century. Their lives demonstrate the range of options that Chinese Christians had and especially how that range narrowed during the 1940s and 1950s. Faced with new ideologies, political instability, and a series of catastrophic wars, Chinese Christians had to adapt and persevere in the face of hostile political, economic, and social conditions throughout the first half of the twentieth century.

By focusing on the stories of Ling and Chen, I hope to avoid "the control-and-resistance paradigm" that has dominated literature on the relationship between religion and the People's Republic of China. Indeed, as Ling's and Chen's lives show, Chinese Christians faced options more complex than merely choosing between "resistance" or "collaboration." I do not use the binary labels of loyalty and betrayal, collaborator and resistor, authentic and inauthentic. As David Lindenfeld and Miles Richardson have argued, scholarship about indigenous Christians must move beyond "dualistic terms" and instead emphasize "a sense of agency even under conditions of foreign domination, and inventiveness, and resiliency in shaping their religious responses."[6] In this chapter, I seek to heed Lindenfeld's and Richardson's call: I hope to represent the lives of Chinese Christians like Chen and Ling in all their complexities and contradictions.[7]

THE SEMINARIAN AND THE JOURNALIST

Chen Yuan and Ling Deyuan were born in the same decade and in the same province of Guangdong, but they belonged to very different Chinas. Chen was born in the southern county of Xinhui, situated in the western part of the Pearl River Delta. At the intersection of the Xi and Tan rivers, Xinhui developed a wealthy and bustling local economy. It also nurtured cultural elites: Xinhui traditionally produced a steady stream of imperial scholars. Ling, on the other hand, came from the mountainous regions in Guangdong's northwest corner, in the county of Shixing. As we have seen, even though Shixing lay at an important commercial juncture, the area suffered from the instability of constant banditry and poverty.

Born in 1883, Ling came from a humble farming family in Shishixiacun in Shixing County. According to a Communist hagiography, he loved to farm ever since he was a young child, tending after cows and harvesting crops at the age of six or seven. He had received his education from Chinese private learning institutes when he was young but dropped out because he could not afford the tuition.[8] Instead, he enrolled in the BMS's free elementary school, where he was soon recognized as talented and fervent in the faith. The missionaries recommended that he continue to study at the BMS's seminary in Guangzhou.

Chen, on the other hand, was born into a well-to-do family of traditional Chinese doctors in 1880. Until the age of seventeen, he attended private learning institutes, receiving a rigorous classical Chinese education. He then traveled to Beijing to take the civil service examination but was unable to procure a position. Like many of his reform-minded contemporaries, he came of age just as the traditional examination system was coming under attack and the number of positions in the government was shrinking. By 1905, the Qing dynasty had eliminated the system.

Frustrated by his inability to gain a foothold through the traditional path, Chen turned his attention to political activism. He started by organizing and spreading anti-Qing ideas in Guangzhou. Along with a group of local intellectuals, Chen launched a patriotic illustrated weekly newspaper, the *Shishi Huabao (Illustrated Times)*, in 1905. Chen later boasted, "At the time, the coastal cities leaned much more toward nationalist ideas, and freedom of speech was restricted in the inland areas. The *Shishi Huabao* was the only revolutionary paper that circulated inland." As an editor of the paper, Chen contributed regular opinion pieces.[9]

At the same time that Chen Yuan was penning revolutionary articles, Ling Deyuan was finishing his schooling, having ascended the BMS's educational ladder. Ling had entered seminary right after the BMS had revised its seminary curriculum, so he was exposed to a range of courses, both secular and theological. To graduate, Ling took a series of oral and written examinations, and on April 21, 1906, when he was twenty-three, he passed his final seminary exam.[10]

Passing the exam did not lead to immediate ordination: Ling had to gain some practical experience in the congregations first. From 1906 to 1914, he worked in Shixing Province. The BMS put him in charge of several chapels that the Western missionaries had abandoned because of frequent bandit raids. To the surprise of the BMS missionaries, Ling was successful in not only preserving, but also expanding the work. Ling's supervisor, Karl Zehnel, noted that Ling, "unlike other Chinese preachers, knew the names of every single member in his congregation, including their baptismal names. He enjoyed great esteem and garnered much respect, in spite of his youth."[11] Ling traveled throughout the province in hopes of expanding the ministry. He helped train street preachers, preached sermons in rural areas, and assisted with the educational program in the seminaries. A crucial voice in spearheading the movement to gain higher wages and pensions for the Chinese assistants, Ling also sought to organize the Chinese workers serving in the BMS.

Inspired by the Chinese Revolution of 1911, Ling believed that free education was crucial to the salvation of the nation, and he suggested that the BMS establish an elementary school in the more rural areas of the province. In 1913, the BMS missionaries agreed to his request, and they built an elementary school in Nanxiong County, the first educational institution in the province to accept both boys and girls. Ling was charged with selecting the Chinese staff, and he brought in a group of progressive-minded individuals—all of whom later became members of the CCP. Because of his steady contributions, Ling received his ordination papers in February 1914, earning him the title of *Vikar*, or assistant pastor. The process of becoming a *Vikar* had taken more than twenty years.[12]

Like Ling, Chen Yuan's political consciousness was decisively formed by the 1911 revolution. During the revolutionary period, he continued to write short editorial pieces and commentary on current affairs. Throughout, Chen evinced a tone of guarded optimism toward the changes in China. He "pitied the important bureaucrats and court officials of yesterday, who have become useless in a day, as well as the rich merchants and landowners, who have become peasants overnight," lamenting the "unpredictability of change in all current affairs."[13]

Chen wrote several prescient analyses about the challenges that the revolutionary parties faced. In a December 1911 article, he argued that three forces undermined the legitimacy of the Republic: rival political factions, "corrupt local gentry," and "deceptive Qing army officials" who wanted to retain their power. Chen's caution proved correct. Local gentry and military strongmen such as Yuan Shikai took on increasingly important roles in the government, fracturing the stability of the Republic.[14]

In October 1912, Chen campaigned as a "revolutionary journalist" in the Republic's first parliamentary elections. He entered politics during a moment of enthusiasm for the revolutionary Guomindang. The Guomindang became the largest party in the parliament, winning 269 of 596 seats in the House of Representatives and 123 of 274 seats in the Senate. Song Jiaoren, who along with Sun Yatsen had cofounded the Guomindang, became the new Republic's first prime minister. Yet Song was assassinated in March 1913, upon orders from Yuan Shikai. Soon, Yuan continued his assault on the Guomindang by dismissing all of the Nationalist provincial governors in May 1913. In the summer of 1913, Nationalist revolutionaries in the south tried to overthrow Yuan in a "second revolution," but Yuan easily quelled the revolt. It became clear that Yuan wanted to found a new dynasty. In 1914, he dissolved the parliament; the next year, he proclaimed himself the emperor of the Chinese Empire.[15]

These turbulent years witnessed the rise of rival intellectual and political voices, all presenting competing moral visions for China's future. Western missionaries believed that the 1911 revolution signaled new opportunities for Christianity to make inroads into the new Chinese state, while Confucians hoped to ground the new China in traditional teaching. All described the country as mired in intellectual and spiritual crisis, for which they had the antidote.

Yuan Shikai chose Confucianism, and he revitalized traditional Confucian rites to legitimize his rule. In June 1913, he issued orders to restore the national worship of Confucius. In August, members of the Confucian Religion Association (Kongjiao Hui), headed by the prominent reformer Kang Youwei, proposed writing clauses in the constitution that would make Confucianism the "national religion" of China. Yuan Shikai supported these proposals and started to rededicate old imperial temples with Confucian rituals. He planned to outlaw non-Confucian religions. Yuan understood Confucianism would help to legitimize his dynasty, linking his reign to that of ancient Chinese lineages.[16]

Yuan's attacks on religious freedom made a deep imprint on Chen. As a member of the Guomindang, Chen had opposed Yuan's coup, and he rejected Yuan's proposals to transform Confucianism into a state religion. Chen argued that the new China needed to establish protections for the freedom of religions. As a vocal proponent of religious freedom, Chen came in contact with Ma Xiangbo and Ying Lianzhi. Ma and Ying were prominent critics of Yuan's attempts to establish state Confucianism, and they welcomed Chen into a reading club that they had formed called the Fu Ren Society. The society formed the basis of the later Chinese Catholic University in Beijing. As he became more frustrated with politics, Chen turned toward academia, a space where he imagined he could be more free.

CHEN THE INTELLECTUAL
Stimulated by the political debates over the place of religion in public life, Chen Yuan produced his most important, imaginative, and influential work from 1917 to 1924. He joined in debates provoked by New Culture Movement intellectuals regarding the relationship between religious organizations and the new Chinese state. Chen's works were published in important periodicals and journals of the time, such as the *Eastern Miscellany (Dongfang Zazhi)*, and Christian youth publications, such as *Progress and Improvement of the Youth (Qingnian Jinbu)*. During this period as well, Chen became involved with the Protestant church in Beijing headed by the missionary, and later U.S. ambassador to China, John Leighton Stuart. Stuart's church was renowned for its progressive attitudes toward ordaining Chinese pastors, and Chen was baptized there.[17]

The work that established his academic reputation, *An Investigation of the Yelikewen Religion (Yuan Yelikewen Kao)*, was serialized in the *Eastern Miscellany* in 1917 and is often considered the foundational work of Chinese comparative religion. It begins with a puzzle posed by historians of the Yuan dynasty: scholars had long known about a religion called the Yelikewen, but no one knew what religion it was. Drawing on the methods of the new historicism and his training in traditional Chinese philology, Chen claimed that the Yuan Yelikewen represented a group of Roman Catholics, not a tribe or ethnicity.[18]

Chen argued that the Mongol conquests of Central Asia and Europe during the Yuan dynasty had brought Catholicism to China. The Mongol invasions led to the capture of "countless Catholic and Eastern Orthodox Christians." These prisoners of war were then resettled in "the tens of thousands of miles north and west of the Great Wall." But Chen noted that the Christians did not retain their status as prisoners for long: many enjoyed prestigious positions within the Yuan bureaucracy. They did not have to pay taxes and were exempt from compulsory military service. The Mongols, in short, respected Catholicism.[19]

Given how Christians enjoyed prominent positions under the Yuan dynasty, Chen asked, "How did the Yelikewen decline and disappear?" Chen's answer: after the end of the Yuan dynasty, the early Ming emperors persecuted Christianity and expelled Europeans from China. During the reign of Renzhong (1378–1425), the emperor ordered the destruction of Christian churches because of his Buddhist faith. Churches were ransacked and converted into Buddhist temples.[20]

Chen's scholarship was pathbreaking on many fronts. Traditional Chinese historians had long viewed the Yuan dynasty as a barbarian, outsider dynasty, unworthy of serious study. Highlighting the dynasty's vitality and dynamism, Chen argued that Han Chinese in fact had much to learn from the Mongols. He also forged a new approach to the study of Chinese history. Employed as a tool for dynastic legitimation, traditional Chinese histories focused on diplomacy, wars, and the biographies of emperors. They tended to denigrate popular religion or culture. Chen's work pointed to new ways that religion could shed light on state governance and power.[21]

By focusing on culture and religion, Chen belonged to a broader cohort of New Culture intellectuals who turned away from traditional political histories in an attempt to broaden the range of subjects considered worthy of serious historical inquiry. They considered dynastic histories too overtly political and wished to produce work that evaded such monikers. While claiming to be "apolitical," Chen's work engaged deeply with a political question: how should the state and religion interact? Read in light of the political battles in which Chen participated, his *Investigation* was a measured yet pointed argument for the virtues of religious freedom. Chen identified the tolerance of religious pluralism during the Yuan as crucial to the dynasty's vitality. The late Yuan rulers had reversed the religious freedom that Christians once enjoyed. For Chen, the crumbling apparatus for religious freedom contributed to the Yuan dynasty's demise: Chen argued that a strong state was founded on the acceptance and integration of foreign, disparate elements into the broader majority culture.

Chen's interest in Christianity reflected a larger interest: minority religions. From 1919 to 1923, he wrote prolifically on the various "marginalized" religions in China, publishing on the histories of Judaism,

Zoroastrianism, and Manicheanism. In all of these works, religious pluralism and the importance of religious freedom remained a consistent thread.[22]

One puzzle in particular drove Chen's studies: why did some religions successfully become "Chinese" while others continued to be labeled as foreign? Scarcely any scholarship, Chen observed, sought to compare the histories of two foreign religions in China: Christianity and Buddhism. In one piece, written in 1919, Chen noted that when Buddhism first entered China, the Chinese intelligentsia attacked it "much more aggressively than attacks on Christianity today." Buddhist sutras and sculptures were outlawed and burned. But the persecution did not diminish Buddhism's appeal; instead, it became even more popular and prosperous. Chen argued that Buddhists and Christians, as "friends in persecution," had much to learn from one another, and an increased dialogue between intellectuals of both religions "would lead to an ultimate revelation."[23]

Chen's greatest work synthesized his ideas on the relationship between foreign and "Chinese." In 1923, Chen published *Western and Central Asians in China Under the Mongols* (*Yuan Xiyuren Huahua Kao*). In it, he looked at the western regions (Xiyu) of the Yuan dynasty, which encompassed a large part of Central Asia with a diverse mix of tribes, including Uyghurs, Tibetans, and Tanguts, and religions, such as Zoroastrianism, Manicheanism, Islam, and Buddhism. How, he wondered, had these different peoples become "Chinese"? Did they themselves embrace this identity?

In *Western and Central Asians,* Chen offered an explicit clarification of his concept of "Sinification" (*Huahua*). For Chen, to be Chinese was not an ethnic or racial identity but rather a cultural and intellectual inheritance. The most important facet within this heritage, Chen argued, was Confucianism. Confucianism, Chen wrote, "is a cultural tradition specific to China," and "it is the most important facet to consider when talking about Sinification." A foreigner could become Chinese by embracing Confucian learning (*Ruxue*). One could read the Confucian classics and learn how to create Chinese art and poetry. And in *Western and Central Asians,* he found historical precedents: he profiled scholars, painters, and writers from the western regions who had either become experts in the Confucian canon or produced art and literature according to the Confucian tradition.[24]

These "foreigners" professed different religious beliefs—they were Christians, Muslims, Buddhists, Manicheans—yet they all accepted the primacy of Chinese culture. Chen writes, "A peculiar moment came to pass in the Yuan dynasty, when Turks, Persians, who all had their own languages, all adopted Chinese customs and Chinese culture when they entered Chinese lands." Chen argued that foreign cultures and minorities had historically adopted the values and ideas of Chinese civilization. Confucianism had invited, empowered, and placated multiple religions and ethnicities. The Chinese tradition, Chen concluded, was expansive and tolerant: minorities need not fear Sinification.[25]

Chen applied his framework of Sinification to the history of Christianity in China. He portrayed Matteo Ricci and the early Jesuit missionaries as heroes for treating traditional Chinese culture with respect. Ricci, Chen wrote, "was a devoted student of Confucianism. Ricci loved the Chinese language, and he truly understood Chinese culture."[26] Ricci admired Confucian scholars, and his enthusiasm for Chinese culture helped ingratiate him with powerful Chinese intellectuals. The Chinese, in turn, were attracted to Ricci's knowledge of European mathematics and science. After the reign of Kangxi, however, because of the Rites Controversy and the influx of religious orders that "attacked the Jesuit method of evangelization and did not understand or respect Chinese culture," the Qing imperial court banned Christianity. Chen argued that Western missionaries had themselves to blame for their expulsion from China.[27]

Chen had a yet more negative view of the history of Protestantism in China. Despite its rapid expansion in the nineteenth century, Chen argued, "I still believe that Protestantism has not yet been able to be assimilated into Chinese culture." Chinese poets, for example, did not compose odes to Protestant chapels and pastors. In contrast, within a hundred years of Buddhism's entry into China, Chinese scholars and poets incorporated Buddhist imagery and iconography into their art. A tradition of Chinese artists and poets painting Catholic cathedrals and writing about Catholicism also existed. Ultimately, Chen attributed the widespread Chinese rejection of Christianity to the hubris of Protestant missionaries and their refusal to respect the value of Chinese civilization. Chen linked the decline of Western interest in Chinese civilization to geopolitics: "because of China's weakening national position and power, it has become difficult to attract Westerners to study Chinese culture."[28]

How should we categorize Chen in the intellectual landscape of the 1920s? Like other Chinese Christians, he occupied a tenuous middle ground. While Chen took pride in Confucianism and the tolerant strands of Chinese civilization, he diverged from his more conservative Sinocentric counterparts, who hoped to elevate Confucianism to the status of a state religion. He saw in the conservatives of his time xeno-phobia that threatened a potentially vibrant and religiously diverse Chinese state. As a Chinese Christian, Chen believed that Christianity could help to strengthen the Chinese nation and could be subsumed, without conflict, under a tolerant and inclusive Chinese culture. Yet Chen's pro-Christian stance conflicted with secular intellectuals on the left, who hoped to eradicate religion from the Chinese intellectual land-scape. Neither conservative nor radical, Chen and other moderates yearned to facilitate dialogue between China and the West and forge a synthesis between the two cultures based on mutual respect and equal power relations.

CHEN AND FU REN UNIVERSITY

Fu Ren University, also known as the Catholic University of Beijing, gave Chen an opportunity and an institution to put his ideas of Sino-Western dialogue into practice. Established in 1924 under the initiative of Benedictines from Pennsylvania, the university from its inception was conceived as a Sino-Western joint venture. The U.S. missionary society provided the funding; it also controlled personnel and curricular deci-sions. An American served as dean, overseeing the dormitories and student behavior. Western missionaries were thus placed in charge of the "moral education" and discipline of the students. On the other hand, the president was Chinese; he was responsible for the university's academic life. The prominent Catholic intellectual Ying Lianzhi initially served as president, but health problems soon forced him to choose a successor. Even though Chen Yuan was not Catholic, Ying anointed Chen because of his rising academic stature, charging him with the duty of attracting other Chinese intellectuals to join the faculty.

In the eight years that the Benedictines directed the university, they developed both the curriculum and school infrastructure. They built new dormitories and facilities to accommodate more students. Chen's presence helped attract a strong faculty in classical Chinese literature and history.

The growth was astonishing. During its first year of operation, the university matriculated twenty-three students; by 1933, it had six hundred.[29] But such rapid expansion, coupled with the financial devastation wreaked by the Great Depression in the United States, pushed the Benedictines toward financial insolvency. They searched for an organization to take over. After a brief search, the Propaganda Fide turned to the SVD.

The Chinese professors immediately voiced skepticism of the SVD takeover. Primarily, they were afraid that the university would lose its "American" character and decrease its amount of English instruction. The new American dean, Father Joseph Murphy, who was trained at the SVD's seminary in Techny, Illinois, reported to the SVD leadership, "The Chinese are afraid of 'German discipline' and are anxiously hoping that there will be some Americans among those who arrive this summer." The Chinese faculty requested that the SVD send American priests and teach more English classes. They warily viewed the Nazi rise to power. Murphy noted that the faculty and administration "suspect that the situation in Germany is becoming darker all the time, for the reports that reach us from Swiss newspapers or from travellers are anything but encouraging."[30]

The SVD superior general Josef Grendel tried his best to quell these concerns. He asked Murphy to assure the Chinese faculty that the university would "remain a Catholic university, where Americans and Germans work and try to bring honor to their respective Fatherlands. If one or the other country wants to support our work, they are of course more than welcome. But if they also seek certain commitments or obligations from us, or if they make demands, we must refuse them with politeness and with complete determination."[31] Grendel had appointed Murphy as dean partly to mollify the Chinese faculty and students—at least they still had an American in charge, not a German.

The SVD continued to advance the American Benedictine agenda of fostering Sino-Western collaboration by promoting cross-cultural exchange. The university's journal, the *Monumenta Serica*, reflected such efforts. Franz Xaver Biallas, an SVD missionary and Paris-trained Sinologist, served as the editor-in-chief.[32] Four of the eight members on the editorial board were Chinese scholars. Chen made his mark on the journal as an editor, and several of his articles were translated into English and published for a wider audience in the journal's first year. Chen also gave the journal its Chinese name: *Huayi xuezhi* (*The Scholarly Journal on China and Neighboring Countries*). The title reflected his interest in the broader Sinophone world, not just China itself. The first issue of *Huayi xuezhi* showcased its international character, containing articles from French, German, Chinese, and English scholars. Its areas of study were wide-ranging, covering subjects from literature to ancient archaeology. *Huayi xuezhi* soon became one of the most influential academic journals of Sinology, introducing the work of significant Chinese scholars to Western audiences.[33]

Other than the journal, the SVD demonstrated a commitment to other avenues for Sino-Western cooperation and collaboration. In 1936, Biallas proposed the establishment of an "Institute of Oriental Studies of the Catholic University of Peking." The institute would offer training for Western missionaries in traditional Chinese learning, including courses in Chinese philosophy and readings in the Confucian classics. Prominent Chinese scholars would be invited to teach the classes. Chen himself was scheduled to teach a course on reading and interpreting Chinese historical documents. Even though the missionaries on the home front enthusiastically supported the idea, the institute never was established because of lack of funding.[34]

The spirit of Sino-Western cooperation infused other disciplines as well. Fu Ren's art department became a center for producing Chinese Christian artwork. Chinese artists created scenes from the Bible, such as the nativity, the assumption, and Pentecost, in a Chinese artistic style. The university showcased these pieces in annual exhibitions. It also published exhibition catalogues and distributed miniaturized versions of the best paintings as calendars. The missionaries included the paintings in Chinese Catholic catechisms as a way to make them more accessible to Chinese readers. They also republished the paintings in their missionary journals for their European readership (see figs. 1–3).[35]

While the number of converts to Christianity among Chinese students remained low, the students, for the most part, openly embraced Westernization. In 1939, for example, the university held its first homecoming event. Fu Ren students competed with Yenching University students in athletic events, including track and field and soccer. A string quartet and orchestra composed of Chinese students played at the opening ceremony. Chen Yuan opened the festivities, and the missionary Heinrich Kroes commented, "The President delivered a witty speech,

often interrupted by rounds of applause." At the end of the day, the orga-
nizers screened a film that celebrated major events from the university's
previous year. Kroes remarked that even though the film "was really
poorly done, it nonetheless induced a spirit of jocularity and cheer."[36]

THE CHINESE PASTOR LING

At the same time that Chen Yuan established himself as an academic
scholar in the 1920s, Ling Deyuan found his footing as a Chinese pastor.
The BMS missionaries increasingly saw him as indispensable. In 1922,
he was selected to accompany the Germans to the National Church
Conference in Shanghai. He had impressed his missionary supervisors,
as they marveled at his ease in translating between Mandarin and the
local dialects of Guangdong. In contrast, another Chinese Christian
pastor who had traveled with the group "could not understand Mandarin.
Furthermore, his slight build and his unconfident constitution did not
help us make a good impression on the educated Chinese at the conference." Ling's fluency, more to the point, enabled him to debate other
Chinese Christian intellectuals. He helped to advance the BMS's criticisms of the NCC. With a "clear eye," one missionary reported, Ling had
railed against what he saw as "unjust practices" that the NCC supported.
He had ably defended the BMS's evangelistic principles.[37]

While the 1920s and the early part of the 1930s was a period of optimism and growth for Chen and the Catholic University of Beijing, the
BMS's confidence in its work was more muted in southern China. As we
have seen, missionaries made an attempt to transfer their authority to
Chinese pastors such as Ling. In 1926, the Berlin leadership decided to
attempt church independence in Ling's province of Shixing.

But they all recognized that several obstacles stood in the way of
achieving congregational independence. For one, missionary recalcitrance persisted. In particular, one missionary, Heinrich Wahl, refused to
relinquish his authority to Chinese pastors. Wahl frequently chastised the
Chinese for their insubordination and presumption that they were equals
to the Germans. Another missionary observed, "Wahl believes that he
alone has the power of leadership in Shixing, and nobody else." His impe-
rious attitude engendered a backlash among the congregants. One
missionary, Karl Zehnel, reported that in a conversation with the
missionary inspector Friedrich Leuschner, Leuschner had warned that

234 FRUITS OF THE SPIRIT

Wahl's approach portended a future conflict: "The people of Shixing are a difficult bunch. If a missionary cannot earn the trust of the people in Shixing, then they will be unable to accomplish anything."[38]

In contrast, in his decade-long work in Shixing, Ling had established both trust and goodwill in the community. He was renowned for his hospitality. Zehnel reported that Ling had guests stay with him almost every day. He also paid for their meals. The missionary advised Ling to curtail his generosity, but Ling replied, "It is impossible!" Because of his generosity, Ling lived in a state of constant poverty. Of the thirty-five dollars that he was paid each month, he spent thirty of them on food and for company. The little money left he spent on education for his nine children.[39]

Impressed by Ling, the BMS leadership decided to entrust the main missionary station in Shixing to Ling's charge. This decision did not go unrewarded: he proved to be a faithful worker. In the following two decades, he traveled throughout the region, tirelessly spreading the message of church independence. But as we have seen, the rural congregations were still too poor to become completely independent. An already unstable financial situation worsened further during the 1930s after German restrictions on foreign exchange hampered the ability of the BMS missionaries to send funds to China.

In 1935 Ling wrote that the "financial desperation is so much greater than we expected." The old method of constructing big church buildings as a way to attract congregants was no longer possible. Instead, he suggested that they "start over" and rethink how to develop completely independent churches. Missionary leaders in Germany had to change their definitions of indigenous churches. Perhaps, Ling suggested, the Chinese should start with smaller church groups and communities and build bigger, more expensive church buildings later.[40]

Financial problems devastated Chinese morale, and the will to carry out the prerogatives of independence grew weaker. In 1936, Ling commented, "The preachers in the congregation have no desire for independence." The Chinese feared that independence would sever the link between themselves and the missionaries and the little financial support that they still received would disappear altogether. Some Chinese pastors, as Ling suggested to the leaders, perceived the rhetoric of independence with increasing suspicion: it was merely a way to justify the German withdrawal of support from China.[41]

Financial struggles were not the only concerns for Ling and the German missionaries. By the mid-1930s, Ling witnessed the steady growth of sympathy toward Communism within his congregations and most clearly among the Chinese faculty who taught in the BMS's middle and elementary schools. They openly professed sympathy with socialism. "Even some wise and judicious Chinese preachers and congregants," Ling lamented, "have been tempted by these ideas and follow this false ideology."[42] Ling warned the German missionary leaders that socialism's appeal had enervated the enthusiasm for Christianity in their congregations.

As the Sino-Japanese War intensified, Ling saw large numbers in his congregation join the CCP to contribute to the war effort. The spirit of radicalization hit close to home. Of his six sons, five joined the CCP. Three sons joined during wartime, while the last two joined in 1948. One of his daughters also joined the party.[43]

But as the war continued, Ling himself became more sympathetic to the Communists. He had converted his church buildings into sanctuaries for war refugees and displaced villagers. Among the people he sheltered were members of the CCP whom he met through his family. At the same time, he had become increasingly disillusioned with the Nationalist Army. Between 1940 and 1941, the United Front between the Guomindang and the CCP broke down, and the Nationalists intensified their hunt for Communist members.[44] In the ensuing skirmishes between Nationalist and Communist forces, Ling harbored several members of the CCP who were persecuted by the Nationalists. In 1942, several Shixing Communists, on the run from Nationalist forces, approached Ling, asking him to hide radio equipment. He agreed to do it. Ling expressed disgust that the Chinese were engaged in such infighting when the larger, more dangerous enemy still loomed on the horizon.[45]

A RADICALIZED CHINA

Meanwhile, at Fu Ren, the festive ceremonies that students enjoyed would not last. As in Shixing, the Sino-Japanese War radicalized the student body and ended the harmonious atmosphere that had briefly permeated the university during the early 1930s. The missionary leadership and the Chinese faculty had to contend with an erupting Chinese nationalism within its student body. It also faced restrictions from the Japanese. Within a month of the Marco Polo Bridge Incident in July 1937, the

Japanese had captured Beijing. They established a puppet government, the Chinese Provisional Government, by December of the same year.

Colleges were faced with the options of accepting Japanese rule, closing their doors, or moving away from Japanese-occupied zones concentrated in eastern China. For the most part, Chinese colleges refused to recognize the occupation and chose to migrate to the interior. But Christian colleges, equipped with European and American connections, had more political options. They used their foreign status to obtain immunity from Japanese rule, and the Japanese generally left them alone. Fu Ren and the American-run Yenching University became the only two universities in northeast China that remained free of Japanese control. As such, they became protective spaces. The university administrators offered positions to Chinese professors who did not move south. More women enrolled in Fu Ren than before the war.[46]

Maintaining daily operations came at a cost: the SVD had to appease the occupiers. On May 21, 1938, the Provisional Government organized a parade to celebrate its victory at Xuzhou, the site of a desperate battle between Chinese and Japanese forces that had resulted in more than 130,000 casualties on both sides.[47] The Fu Ren middle school had not sent any of its students to attend the parade. It is unclear why the students had failed to appear, but the Japanese interpreted their absence as an act of open defiance and threatened to close down the school. The SVD rector, Rudolf Rahmann, appealed to Germany's ambassador to China, Oskar Trautmann. Might he intervene on Fu Ren's behalf, Rahmann pled, and organize a meeting with the Japanese general Kita Seiichi to explain the "misunderstanding"? Trautmann agreed to broker a meeting between Rahmann and Kita. Trautmann described the university as a central site of "German interests," as it offered German classes and its faculty consisted of Germans. Crisis was averted. Afterwards, Rahmann invited Japanese government officials to dinner on multiple occasions, hoping to improve the university's standing with the Japanese.[48]

To further improve relations with the Japanese, Rahmann signed an agreement with the Japanese embassy in 1938. The agreement stipulated that the university accept Japanese students, hire Japanese faculty, and treat Japanese as equals to the Chinese and Germans in the universities. The missionaries allowed the Xinmin Hui (People's Renovation Society), a puppet group established by General Kita, to mobilize propaganda for

the Japanese and to establish a branch on campus. The university administration also agreed to expel any anti-Japanese student movements from
the university. Cooperation with the Japanese government, the missionaries rationalized to one another, was a necessary evil: they had no other
choice if they wanted the university to continue. Chen Yuan also defended
the decision to cooperate with the Japanese. Even after 1949, Chen
boasted that Fu Ren was one of the few universities in China that operated without interruption even during the depths of the war.[49]

The decision to cooperate with the Japanese became a fatal misstep.
After the war, Chinese nationalists accused Fu Ren, and its foreign
missionary administrators, of "collaboration." The Guomindang government launched the first attack. In 1946, the Ministry of Education and
other local courts accused members of the Fu Ren faculty and student
body of treason when they harbored "Japanese spies" during the war. In
response, Chen and the SVD missionary leadership issued joint statements attesting that Fu Ren had "valiantly resisted the Japanese during
the war." Along with other university administrators, Chen signed statements guaranteeing that the accused were not "traitors to the Han
[Hanjian]."[50]

Facing external political pressures, the missionaries were further
troubled by the rise of increasingly vocal and vehement student protests.
During the four years between the end of the Sino-Japanese War in 1945
and the subsequent Communist victory, student demonstrations spread
throughout the country. In Beijing and Shanghai especially, strikes were
commonplace, as students increasingly lost faith in the Nationalist
government's ability to govern effectively. Reflecting broader trends,
student protests paralyzed Fu Ren. Students criticized the university as a
"poisonous environment that mixes classical fascism and feudalism" and
called for the expulsion of Western missionary leadership.[51]

Amidst student unrest, the united front between Western missionaries and the Chinese administrators collapsed. Disputes over how to
discipline the students had long been a source of tension between the
Chinese faculty and Western missionaries. Often, the tension concerned
trivial issues, such as personal hygiene. In 1946, the new rector, Harold
Rigney, chastised the students for their dirtiness, noting: "Nowhere on
the five continents I had visited have I seen such a dirty dormitory, where
university students not only totally disregard cleanliness but spit on the

wall and in some instances urinate in the cuspidors and against the wall
in the corridors. I told the president that such offenses should not be
tolerated, but rather be punished by dismissal." For Rigney and the SVD
missionaries, such behavior pointed to the failure of the SVD to instill
moral discipline over an increasingly unruly and radical student body. It
reflected the loss of authority, the further loosening of their tenuous
control of a chaotic and unpredictable political environment. Rigney
lamented that "the SVD has lost a great deal of control over the university,
especially during the last years. As a result, much inefficiency has crept
in, and a lack of Catholic spirit prevails."[52]

Chen, along with other Chinese administrators, stood up for the
students. He refuted Rigney's characterization of the students and claimed
that the rector was "being too harsh and dictatorial." He felt that the
missionaries did not understand the rapidly changing Chinese political
and cultural landscapes, nor did they grasp the fact that the students had
just survived a brutal wartime experience. The students' juvenile behavior
was a trivial concern compared with what they had just withstood. In turn,
Chen's criticisms offended Rigney and the other missionaries.[53]

On August 19, 1948, the Guomindang turned its scrutiny away from
uncovering instances of collaboration and toward leftist student activity at
Fu Ren. Claiming that Communist agents were behind the "student troubles," the government set up special criminal tribunals that issued arrest
warrants for hundreds of students in Beijing and Shanghai. Fu Ren was
included in this crackdown. Nationalist police flanked the university and
raided student dormitories to arrest ten "professional Communist agitators" and fourteen other students who harbored them.[54]

The Chinese faculty and Western missionary responses to the
Guomindang's police action further exposed the widening rifts between
the two sides. Incensed by the police raid, Chen and other Chinese
members of the staff vehemently protested and issued statements
expressing sympathy toward Communist and leftist students.[55] Western
missionaries, on the other hand, welcomed the Nationalist clampdown.
Rector Rigney wrote that the university was "cursed" by leftist students,
and he argued that the university authorities needed to cooperate with the
external authorities to expel the Communists from their midst. He
further claimed that preventing the Guomindang authorities from
entering the dormitories would itself be a form of imperialism: the

Nationalists could accuse missionaries of exercising extraterritorial powers if the university prohibited the state from inspecting its property.[56]

The Guomindang's action severed the alliance between the Chinese faculty and the Western missionaries. For the SVD missionaries, Communism presented a grave political problem. Communist revolution had divided the European continent in two; Germany itself was now fractured. They warned that if China were to fall to Communism, the future of Christianity in the country would be bleak. Chen and the Chinese faculty had different immediate concerns. China had just emerged from a traumatic war with the Japanese. The breakdown of the United Front and the Nationalist purges of the Communists during the war remained a fresh wound: the Guomindang had placed its own political interests above the salvation of the nation. The Guomindang's actions against Fu Ren's left-leaning students only further exposed its moral bankruptcy. For Chen and the Chinese faculty, the construction of a stable nation—not stemming the advance of global Communist revolution—was the more pressing issue. For many Chinese intellectuals like Chen, the Guomindang's vindictive politics was more of a threat to China's fragile political situation than the CCP was.

MAKING CHOICES IN THE NEW CHINA

To the Western missionary establishment's relief and surprise, the Communist victory in 1949 did not result in an immediate crackdown. Some missionaries even began to feel hopeful about potential collaboration with the CCP. One German missionary commented that the Chinese Communists were at heart xenophobic, not antireligious. Unlike the Soviets, who wanted to uproot the influence of Orthodox Christianity from the country, he noted that Chinese Communists did not call for the total destruction of Christianity from its landscape. Instead, the Communists wanted the transfer of power from European missionaries to Chinese. "If the churches are in the hands of the Chinese alone," he predicted, "I believe our troubles will be fewer."[57]

And indeed, rather than cracking down on church attendance, the Communists saw in the churches talent that they could extract. Rowland Cross, the secretary of the China Committee of the Foreign Missions Conference of North America, circulated a confidential newsletter in 1950 reporting on how Chinese Christians were faring in the new China. Cross noted, "Rural Church members, instead of being deprived of religious freedom, as many expected, are actually being pulled into participation in local political set-ups." Rural Chinese Christians, he continued, "not only belong to the right class, but are also able to read and write, are recognized as honest and trustworthy in character, and even have the ability to chair a meeting; they are accordingly regarded as persons qualified to hold local political and social responsibilities." Chinese Christians, Cross hoped, could thus shape the direction of the regime from the inside.[58]

Cross felt much more pessimistic about the future of foreign missionaries in China. Zhou Enlai, he reported, had decreed that missionaries were permitted to stay until their visas expired. But the possibility of renewal was small, and he expected that the missionaries would have to leave China eventually. "In other words," Cross concluded, "the foreign missionary presence is at present tolerated in the belief and intention that time will before long remove their unwanted presence."[59] Cross proved prophetic. Using the pretense of escalating tensions during the Korean War, the CCP expelled the foreign missionaries in 1951.

National Chinese Christian leaders had prepared for the expulsion of foreign missionaries a year earlier. The Christian Manifesto of September 1950 advanced by major figures within the Chinese Protestant establishment paved the way for the CCP's control of mainstream Chinese Christianity. Zhou Enlai represented the CCP in the negotiations over the contents of the manifesto. Chinese Protestants could continue their worship as long as they joined a state-sanctioned church led by Chinese and stripped of foreign leadership. The individual Chinese Protestant thus had a clear choice to make: declare loyalty to the state-sanctioned church or be branded as a collaborator with the "foreign imperialists."

Abandoned by the German missions and with nowhere else to turn, the decision for the BMS Chinese Christians seemed self-evident. Ling Deyuan signed the manifesto. Because of his signature, Communist hagiographers claimed him as one of their own after 1949. They referred to him as a patriot who had, even during his time as an evangelist and pastor for the church, "always supported the work of the Chinese Communist revolution."[60] Cross proved correct about Chinese Christians under the Communist regime: the Communists incorporated Ling, as well as other Christians, into their local political organizations.

In an ironic turn, the foreign missionary society supplied the CCP with its first generation of local leadership in many rural areas. Ling was a typical example of the Christian turned cadre. An educated man with strong organizational skills, he offered the Chinese Communists what they needed to penetrate local society. Elected to a Guangdong provincial committee, he worked with the CCP's provincial secretary (Shuji), as well as the provincial governor (Xianzhang). Ling's decision to join the party bolstered his career, and his standing in the community remained undiminished. Local Communist accounts celebrated his family as "progressive revolutionaries" who had heroically fought in the Sino-Japanese War and had resisted the Nationalists. The accounts conveniently underplayed his past as a Christian pastor; his background as a Chinese Christian leader did not come back to haunt him, as it did later for many others during the Cultural Revolution.[61]

The CCP also used patriotic Christians like Ling to reinforce its credentials among the Chinese Christian community. The Communists could claim that they had accomplished what the foreign missionaries had failed to deliver: they had created an indigenous Chinese church, devoid of foreign influence. With the help of progressive liberal Christians, the CCP co-opted the rhetoric of indigenization that had prevailed within Christian circles during the 1920s. "Indigenization" proved to be a malleable claim. Various parties—Chinese Christians, foreign missionaries, and ultimately, the CCP—used the term to pursue their particular political agendas.

Unlike Ling, Chen Yuan had other options in 1949. After the Communist victory, Chen's friend Hu Shi tried to persuade him to board a plane headed to Nanjing with other Nationalist intellectuals. Chen refused the offer. Instead, he sided with the student protestors and welcomed the soldiers of the People's Liberation Army when they entered Beijing in February 1949.[62] Three years later, in his public "self-criticism," published in the Guangming daily newspaper (*Guangming Ribao*), Chen called the SVD missionaries in charge of Fu Ren "foreign imperialists" who "told me nothing; I was only a president in name." He wrote, "As president of Fu Ren University, I was a puppet of the imperialists for thirty years." As for his hefty body of scholarly work—more than eighty-six articles and books—he repudiated them with a simple statement: "my previous historical research, in its biases, interpretation, and methodology, was all wrong." They had been written by a "selfish and careerist man." His former views, he said, had all been a mistake.[63]

CONCLUSIONS: THE CENTER CANNOT HOLD

In a way, the Communist victory in 1949 continued a familiar pattern for Ling Deyuan and Chen Yuan, who had become accustomed to charges of collaboration. From the 1920s to the 1940s, both men had to repeatedly withstand accusations of aiding the foreign imperialists. Ling's congregations in rural Guangdong were attacked by bandits and soldiers who wanted to expel the foreign missionaries from China's borders. Ever since the 1920s, students had accused Chen and Fu Ren University of being agents of cultural imperialism because of foreign missionary support.

From the 1920s until the 1940s, both Ling and Chen lived under a state of incessant beleaguerment. Both faced pressures from three formidable entities: a radicalized and politically active constituency (for Ling, his congregants, and for Chen, his students); a foreign missionary establishment that tried to assert its influence through financial means; and a Nationalist government suspicious of their activities. The two men had to navigate these conflicting agendas and accommodate all parties. The documents show them as masterful mediators, attentive to the needs and desires of each faction. They knew what each party wanted to hear, and they tried to negotiate with the needs of each. And they tried to pacify the new Communist leaders after 1949: Ling's signature on the Christian Manifesto and Chen's "self-criticism" can be seen as continuing this policy of accommodation and appeasement.

Yet, of course, the Communist victory did radically rupture both of their lives. After 1949, Chen and Ling had to engage in acts of historical revisionism. They had to denounce publicly their former colleagues. They disowned their previous work. And these acts of historical erasure swept aside many of their accomplishments. Ling was one of the most active and tireless workers for the indigenous church movement, and he helped to keep afloat a nascent church community in moments of true desperation during the war. During his tenure as Fu Ren president, Chen sponsored various Sino-Western ventures that sought to engage in and enhance cross-cultural dialogue. After 1949, the establishments that Ling and Chen had helped to create were political anachronisms.

For Ling and his congregants, the end of these institutions was a true loss. For them, Christianity was not an abstraction, but a lived encounter with people, physical spaces, and sources of funding that they could rely in times of crisis. Despite the slow decline of German support after 1936, for many Chinese congregants the BMS's churches operated as places of shelter, sources of community, and providers of material goods. The German missionaries of the BMS supplied Chinese evangelists with food, money for books to be printed, and transportation and fuel costs. Ever since the nineteenth century, Christianity had represented for Chinese Christians not only the hope of life beyond their mortal coils, but a bulwark against the vagaries and brutalities of rural life in China. Chinese Christians saw the foreign missionaries as their protectors, and it is unsurprising that they were reluctant to part ways. Even on the eve of the Communist victory, Chinese Christians continued to write letters beseeching BMS missionaries to return to China.

Similarly, for Chen, the Catholic University of Beijing offered refuge for Chinese students. From the 1920s until the 1940s, the university protected students from external enemies: Japanese, Nationalists, and Communists. Chen sought to create an active and open environment for the university so that it could operate as a functioning, normal institution in times of intense abnormality. He negotiated with the students in order to quell the strike; he tried to appease external authorities so that the ministry of education would not exert authority over university matters; and he mollified the foreign missionaries, who controlled the university finances.

Chen saw that he needed to negotiate among multiple warring parties in order to keep the university open for business. He co-opted much of the language that had been used to criticize him in the late 1920s, when leftist students accused him of being a "puppet of imperialism." During the 1950s, he employed that exact same language to absolve himself of further critique. He knew exactly what the template for a Communist conversion narrative required and conformed his self-criticism to that model.

Chen Yuan's career illustrates the challenges of being a Christian intellectual in a rapidly changing China. In many ways, Chen held a consistent position: he remained a staunch Chinese nationalist from the beginning of his career to the very end. Ever since his earliest anti-Manchu writings, Chen argued for the primacy of Han culture and the necessity for foreign cultures, religions, and ideas to adapt to the more tolerant, enlightened, and benevolent structure of Chinese civilization. Throughout four regime changes, his primary loyalty remained to a Han-led version of the Chinese nation. When the Communists presented the most plausible option to advance this vision, Chen followed their lead.

Ling, on the other hand, was responsible for the care of church buildings and individual congregants whom the missionaries left behind. What occupied Ling were not larger questions of orthodoxy and correct Christian practice, but how to sustain church congregations troubled by economic and political instability. For the Chinese Christians in Ling's congregations, the establishment of an indigenous Christian church and the withdrawal of foreign funding meant the loss of financial and political protections that they had previously enjoyed.

What emerges from Ling's decades-long correspondence with the BMS leadership is a portrait of resilience. Chinese Christians like Ling endured more than three decades of constant war, devastation, and destruction. It is astonishing to consider how Christianity survived at all during these turbulent decades. How did it survive? It required the resourcefulness and adaptability of individual Chinese Christians who confronted each political and economic challenge to the best of their abilities.

Thus, while the narratives of Christianity in China after the Communist Revolution have focused on the important relationship between religion and politics, theology and ideology, Ling's story points us to another dimension. The early twentieth century in China saw a rise in economic thinking, or what Wen-hsin Yeh calls "economic sentiments." As Yeh argues, the Chinese "rearranged their ethics and rationality in accordance with the production of wealth."[64] After the end of more than a decade of disastrous war with the Japanese, middle-class and petty bourgeois urbanites turned to Communism in the hopes of economic protection. The Nationalists had set up expectations of an economically paternalistic state during the war. When those expectations no longer could be met, urbanites turned to the Communist Party, which claimed it could fulfill the failed promises of the Nationalists.

And so it went for Chinese Christians: their lives were also dominated by economic thinking. As opposed to Shanghai urbanites, who obsessed over the production and retention of material wealth, Ling's rural poor were simply concerned with survival. In the late nineteenth and early twentieth centuries, Western missionary societies, both Protestant and Catholic, had offered poor Chinese Christians a way to survive. The missionary society had acted as a state-within-a-state, establishing alternative educational programs, welfare institutions, and opportunities for stable work. The societies ran smoothly when they had solid financial support from Europe. Once they lost funding, the edifice crumbled. Chinese Christians turned to a new protector—the CCP, which they hoped could tolerate a modicum of religious freedom while also delivering the promises of economic justice.

Christianity offered poor Chinese something else: an opportunity to participate in a larger world. Chinese Christians increasingly saw themselves as full participants in the global Christian community.[65] These trends can be seen in the careers of Ling and Chen. In 1947, Ling appealed to the World Lutheran Federation for more funds, asking for help from this broader world brotherhood. Chen received a major award from the Vatican and participated in a series of international exchanges. But after 1949, they were forced to deny this global communion. Chen had to repudiate the flourishing Sino-Western cooperation and collaboration that Fu Ren helped to promote; Ling denounced the connection with his missionary friends and the World Lutheran Federation that he had joined. Instead, they joined a different global community: the Communist international.

Many Chinese Christians joined this new world willingly. They believed that the CCP could put an end to the decades of strife and turmoil that racked China during the first half of the twentieth century. They hoped that the party's adoption of the language of "indigenous church" could usher in a new era of religious freedom. Perhaps a Chinese church could finally flourish. Ling Deyuan was among those hopefuls. He died in 1951 of a heart attack, spared of having to witness the decimation of the religious security that he had worked to bring to his congregations.

Chen Yuan was one of the unlucky. In 1958, after severe public criticism of his work, he joined the CCP at the age of seventy-eight. In an article that made ripples throughout Chinese academia, "The Party Has Given Me New Life," Chen wrote: "I am eighty this year, and I really have joined the Communist party in my twilight years. It is a pity that I did not join earlier." He concluded the piece with a commitment to defending Communist goals, writing: "I think people of different ages cannot stop the forces of progress. I will use all of my powers to keep working for the aims and goals of the party."[66]

Chen's public support for Communism helped save his life. During the Cultural Revolution, Mao Zedong and Zhou Enlai both personally ordered that Chen not be troubled. But the political unrest prevented him from continuing to engage in what he wanted to do: research. Unhappy and depressed, he complained to his daughter-in-law, "What am I to do now? Just wait for death?"[67] For the rest of his life, he lived essentially in a state of house arrest. Upon his death at the age of ninety-one in 1971, the religiously pluralistic China that Chen hoped to help construct was nowhere to be found. His dreams of reviving the dynamic religious tolerance of the Yuan dynasty had long since withered away.

Failure and Success

IN 1952, DAVID PATON, an Anglican missionary, published a sensa-
tional article calling Christian missions in China a "debacle." The expulsion of Christian missionaries from China had compelled Paton to reflect
on the previous hundred years of missionary work. "Considering the vast
amount of money, personnel, thought, and devotion that has gone into the
Christian schools and colleges in China," Paton wrote, "our intellectual
failure is remarkable." Paton blamed himself, and other Western missionaries, for Christianity's failures. Driven apart by national and confessional
differences, missionaries never presented a "united front" to the Chinese.
Protestants were further divided into two categories, either "a somewhat
extreme liberal Protestant or a somewhat extreme conservative Protestant
version." The liberal Protestant abandoned Christian theology altogether,
urging an adoption of "Confucianism in Christian dress." Conservatives,
Paton charged, encouraged in their congregations a "crude drive for pros-
perity," which he equated with Chinese popular superstition. They taught
Chinese Christians how to memorize confessional doctrines, without
inculcating solid faith. Most unforgivable, Paton lamented, was the way
missionaries, both liberal and conservative, displayed an "unconscious
arrogance" to the Chinese.[1]

In certain ways, Paton's diagnosis of missionary "failure" in China
was astute. He was right to attribute much of the mission field's

fragmentation to confessional disagreements. Since the middle of the nineteenth century, missionaries were preoccupied by the denominational and national rivalries that existed in China. Despite the international conferences that missionaries organized throughout the nineteenth and twentieth centuries to foster ecumenical cooperation, disagreement continued to divide the mission field. Pietist missionaries from Berlin criticized the liberal theology of Anglo-American Protestants, who in turn despised the Baptists. Similarly, the Catholic SVD found Jesuits elitist, their missionary methods unsuited to the majority of the Chinese population. In many instances, such as the case of the BMS and Chinese Christian intellectuals, theological disagreements prevented missionaries from building bridges with potential allies.

Yet Paton may have been too harsh in his criticism of missionary attitudes toward the Chinese. It is perhaps true that many missionaries continued to hold an "unconscious arrogance" toward their Chinese Christian converts, but they, like Paton himself, were self-reflective and critical of their work and humbled by their sense of failure. Throughout the nineteenth and twentieth centuries, missionaries subjected their work to constant evaluation, and they altered their tactics, their views of traditional China, and, in some instances, their theology. Even the BMS and the SVD, two of the most vehemently anti-Confucian missionary societies of the nineteenth century, evinced a broad acceptance of Confucian and traditional Chinese ideas by the mid-1930s.

While their embrace of former enemies was certainly motivated by a political response to the rise of global Communism and secularism, it was also a genuine attempt to find common ground between China and Europe, between Christianity and Confucianism. Throughout the 1920s and 1930s, Chinese Christians and European missionaries worked together to synthesize Christianity and Confucianism. They established universities, wrote treatises, reformed their church congregations, and sought to train a native clergy. What ultimately doomed these joint ventures was an increasingly unstable political scene. In 1952, when Paton was writing, it seemed that the institutions that the missionaries and Chinese Christians had built in the 1920s and 1930s would not withstand the Sino-Japanese War and the civil war between the Nationalists and Communists. But they proved to have a longer afterlife than Paton predicted. Ever since the post-Deng reforms of the late 1970s, and especially after religious toleration was officially inscribed in 1982, China has witnessed a revival in all of the major religions—Buddhism, Daoism, Islam, and Christianity.

In the West, popular reports of the explosion of China's Christian growth have often focused on the underground church. Some missionary groups in the West claim that more than one hundred million Chinese are Christians—an enormous discrepancy from the official number reported by the Chinese government of thirty million. Western church groups also tend to overemphasize the theological and political distinctions between underground and the government-sponsored Patriotic churches. Conservative evangelical groups, in particular, produce regular reports that portray the Chinese government as intent on eradicating nongovernmental forms of Christianity.[2]

But often the line between state churches and underground churches is more porous than evangelical Christians would like to think. House churches are not necessarily breeding grounds for antistate activity, but rather spaces for inculcating patriotic sentiment.[3] Chinese Christianity has evolved beyond the "domination-resistance" model that has long preoccupied the portrayal of church-state relations in Communist China. In Wenzhou, as Nanlai Cao has shown, evangelical Christianity has a publicly active profile—state officials openly celebrate Christmas, and "boss Christians" fund churches and serve as crucial middlemen between local entrepreneurs and the state.[4] Even the Patriotic churches are adapting their message: the theology found in many Protestant state churches, for example, is now indistinguishable from what one finds in a Western evangelical church. Recent Chinese converts also at times tend not to see attendance in the state churches as a form of allegiance to the Chinese government. When the journalist Liao Yiwu asked a recent Christian convert why he joined a Patriotic church, he replied: "The holy figure on the cross above the pulpit is my Lord, whether it was above the pulpit at a government church or inside a living room. It's not President Hu Jintao or Chairman Mao."[5]

Despite the major steps that have been made to reconcile the Communist state with Christianity, tensions remain. In April 2014, the Chinese government demolished the Sanjiang Church in Wenzhou as part of a broader campaign, Ian Johnson reports, "to reduce Christianity's public profile."[6] The Chinese government continues to consider the underground churches as a threat to their political legitimacy. The majority of Chinese Christians remain underground. Richard Madsen approximates that three out of four Chinese Catholics belong to the underground Catholic Church, and for Protestants, Yang Fenggang estimates that four out of five Chinese Protestants belong to an underground church.[7]

Among these underground churches, the same issues endure that German missionaries faced in the nineteenth and early twentieth centuries—the blurred lines between heterodox and orthodox faith, the problem of establishing stable church institutions in rural China. As Daniel Bays argues, "The great majority of Chinese Protestants live in rural areas, and many have only minimal knowledge of the Christian doctrines and ritual behavior that would be familiar to most urban Christians."[8] Sectarian groups dominate the religious landscape. They often advance a millenarian and eschatological Christian vision and promote a religious culture of hybridity between Chinese popular religion and Christianity. The BMS of the 1920s would have approved of the focus that contemporary Protestant religious groups place on personal piety and literal interpretations of the Bible. But it also would have been worried about the "syncretism" between Christianity and popular Chinese religious culture. The Catholic revival, similarly, has been mostly rural in nature, and as Richard Madsen has argued, it is dominated by a pre–Vatican II "counterreformation" vision of Catholicism.[9] Despite the SVD's own reforms to adopt more of a liberal Jesuit approach to missionary work after the First World War, the society retained this vision of Catholic missionary conversion. Both the SVD and the BMS of the 1920s would not have found the Christian landscape that we witness in China today to be fundamentally alien.

While BMS and SVD missionaries of the 1920s would be pleasantly surprised by the current state of Christianity in China, they would be mortified by how dramatically Christianity has weakened in Europe. The Second World War dealt a mortal blow to European visions of missionary work. After the Second World War, Protestant and Catholic missionaries returned home and brought what they learned abroad with them. For one, they abandoned their allegiance to the idea of individual conversion. In 1965, both the World Council of Churches and the Roman Catholic Church renounced proselytization as a "corruption of Christian witness" and an impediment to religious freedom across the world, effectively repudiating the missionary directives that had dominated the Christian landscape of the nineteenth and early twentieth centuries.[10]

Moved by these broad changes, individual missionary societies followed suit. After the Second World War, German Pietists abandoned their allegiance to Gustav Warneck's idea of individual conversion. Germany's Protestant Missionary Council dissolved in 1976 and became the Evangelisches Missionswerk, an organization that is dedicated to promoting ecumenism, cross-cultural engagement, and social work beyond the borders of Germany. Similarly, the BMS changed its name to the Berliner Missionswerk. Its current mission statement contains no mention of the hope for individual conversion. Instead of sending missionaries to establish congregations throughout rural areas, it now partners with local churches. Resembling a secular nongovernmental organization, the Berliner Missionswerk provides social services, rather than promises of eternal salvation.[11]

Changes in fundamental doctrines accompanied these strategic changes: Protestants and Catholics alike decided to set aside their previous confessional animosities. After the Second World War, missionaries participated in the European ecumenical movement, which sought to bridge the differences between Protestants and Catholics. The impulse toward "reconciliation" also extended beyond Christianity to other religions. During the Second Vatican Council, Catholics revised their claims that there is no salvation outside the church. The Dogmatic Constitution of the Church (*Lumen Gentium*) accepted the radical possibility that non-Christians, such as Muslims, and even atheists could find salvation beyond "the visible boundaries of the Catholic Church."[12]

The details of how missionaries facilitated both interconfessional and interreligious dialogue after they returned to Europe—as well as ecumenism's broader effect on Europe's religious landscape—belong to a different story, a different book. Nonetheless, I suggest here that the seeds of Europe's ecumenism and engagement with other religions and cultures can be found within the Christian missionary experience of the late nineteenth and early twentieth centuries. The attempt to find common ground with other religions certainly accelerated after the Second World War, but many of these ideas were in place decades before then. In the German case, interreligious dialogues were sparked by reflections on missionary failure. Spurred by their anxieties, German missionaries and theologians began to rethink and, in some cases, renounce the religious convictions that they once held. They no longer preached the unchallenged supremacy of Christianity. The insights that missionaries gleaned from their work strengthened Christianity's presence worldwide, but it simultaneously weakened the theological and religious authority of Christianity in Europe.[13]

The weakening sense of Christian superiority helped to usher in a new secular age in Europe. I invoke the term "secularization" with a certain amount of trepidation, as the question of Europe's secularization has sparked long-lasting and vigorous debate. While "many historians," the historian Hugh McLeod writes, "have agreed in identifying secularization as the central theme of Western Europe's modern religious history," few agree upon the terms or the parameters of the discussion.[14] Some define secularization as the decline of church attendance, others pinpoint its meaning in the differentiation between church and state, and still others argue that it is the decline of subjective, personal faith. Here I use the term following Jeffrey Cox: "secularization is best understood less as an empirical theory subject to confirmation or refutation than as a master narrative, a large organizing story, rooted in centuries of rhetorical engagement about the direction of modern history." For Cox, the "master narrative" that secularization encapsulates is one of religious change.[15]

The narrative of religious change that I have examined in this book is twofold. The first is a story of the Christian acceptance of religious pluralism: Christian missionaries altered their beliefs when they encountered other religions and civilizations. In the nineteenth century, they preached the superiority of Christianity to other religions. By the 1930s and 1940s, however, they renounced their former triumphalist tones. By then, even the European missionary—the most fervent of Christians—accepted the possibility that Christianity needed to be tempered by different religions to ensure its future survival. Even when conservative Christian missionaries continued to excoriate other global religions, such as Buddhism, they also exposed their European audience to religious alternatives to Christianity. European missionaries thus contributed to, in Charles Taylor's words, a change that "takes us from a society in which it was virtually impossible not to believe in God, to one in which faith, even for the staunchest believer, is one human possibility among others."[16]

Such self-reflection led to a second broad change: the decline of religious authority. As the sociologist Mark Chaves has argued, "Secularization is best understood not as the decline of religion, but as the declining scope of religious authority."[17] Faced with challenges from diverse religions, cultures, and social norms, European missionaries relinquished the hierarchical control over their own congregations. The story of the German missionary enterprise from the nineteenth to the twentieth century is one of devolving institutional power. Once-hierarchical, patriarchal institutions unwilling to accommodate other religious institutions began to give up their own sense of mission and elevated sense of rhetoric.

Missionaries relinquished power, at times willingly, at other times unwillingly. But in all cases, they unintentionally contributed to their own secularization. In this book, I have tried to tell a narrative of unintended consequences: Christian missionaries laid the foundation for the decline of their own religious authority. Starting in the 1920s, they began to loosen control over their own congregations, transferring power to Chinese pastors. Challenged by a surging Chinese nationalism, they sought to merge Christian theology with Confucianism. While certainly responding to broad cultural and political changes, missionaries were equally agents who pushed forward these dramatic transformations. Secularization was fueled not only by nonreligious challenges to Christianity, but by the rethinking internal to Christianity, advanced by Christians.[18]

The career of Father Arnold Sprenger of the SVD illuminates how the institutional and theological changes of the 1920s left their imprint on the SVD's post–World War II landscape. Born in the Rhine region of Germany in 1929, Sprenger, after ordination in 1958, originally thought to move to Indonesia to evangelize and engage in parish work. But the superior general had different plans for him. The SVD had decided to reestablish Fu Ren University in Taiwan in 1960, with the hope of one day returning to reclaim their university in China. The university needed language instructors, and Sprenger had earned a doctorate in linguistics at Georgetown University. He moved to Taiwan after his training and joined the faculty of one of the first foreign language programs in the country at Fu Ren University. He served as the departmental chair from 1967 to 1983 and helped to found the department's Graduate School of German Language and Literature. Fu Ren is now one of the premier institutions in Taiwan for the study of German, and many Taiwanese students who have studied abroad in Germany in the past thirty years have personal connections to Sprenger. Since 1987, Sprenger has worked in both

Taiwan and the People's Republic. Even though technically retired, he still serves as a bridge between Catholic communities in China, Taiwan, and Europe.

Sprenger understands missionary work as work that is lived through action rather than preaching. For him, the missionary must live in community with nonbelievers. Beyond academic research, the missionary scholar also must provide moral direction and guidance for students. But Sprenger does not see these moral values as lying solely within the Christian tradition. He writes, "It is of the utmost importance that Confucian and Christian philosophical and religious values be investigated on a level of reflection and experience where they challenge and support each other at the same time."[19] He believes in intercultural and interfaith dialogue, arguing that Christianity needs to incorporate insights from various religions. Sprenger's beliefs do not appear out of a vacuum: they reflect the Catholic Church's global attempt to engage with diverse religions and culture, as well as a century-long dialogue between Christianity and Confucianism internal to the SVD.

Compare Sprenger's career with that of missionaries in the late nineteenth century. In many ways, Sprenger's openness to Christianity is a continuation of the example of Josef Freinademetz, who happily wore Chinese clothes and professed his love for the Chinese people. He was venerated for his progressive attitudes toward traditional Chinese culture. But Freinademetz's career points us to the differences between the contemporary missionary and the missionary of the late nineteenth century. During his time in China, Freinademetz spent much of his energy engaging in street evangelism, administering the sacraments, and educating Chinese to enter the priesthood. He rejected the Jesuit approach to missionary work, such as the focus on elite education and the establishment of secular schools. He would have considered Sprenger's work today as much too "secular," as not focused enough on evangelization.

Freinademetz's openness toward traditional Chinese culture was also an exception. His provincial superior, Bishop Johann Baptist von Anzer, was an outspoken critic of Confucianism and called Yanzhou district in Shandong the "bulwark of the devil."[20] Sprenger's rejection of overt missionary work, along with his assertion of the need for further dialogue with the Confucian tradition, would have been unthinkable to the SVD of the late nineteenth century.

Sprenger's experience and outlook have become the norm for most contemporary SVD missionaries. As a requirement for ordination, missionaries have to obtain a master's of divinity in world mission. Most of the SVD missionaries in the United States study at the Catholic Theological Union in Chicago. The largest seminary in Southeast Asia that prepares SVD priests is the Divine Word Seminary in Tagaytay City in the Philippines. Before professing final vows, all SVD missionaries are required to spend between one and three years in a "cross-cultural training program," where they are sent to a different continent to learn another language and live in a different culture. Most, if not all, of the priests who pursue postformation studies travel to European or North American institutions of higher education.

Even though the ethnic backgrounds of instructors at the Divine Word Seminaries have diversified, their theological training and education are still rooted within a European tradition. The SVD has therefore retained its European identity; its devotional practice remains Eurocentric. The missionary society's institutional hierarchy and structure have also continued unchanged since the early twentieth century. Many of the training facilities and theological seminaries established in the early 1900s still remain. Its largest seminary, founded in Sankt Augustin, Germany, in 1913, continues to train priests. The seminary in Techny, Illinois, is also more than a century old. It has used the same global headquarters in Rome, the Collegio del Verbo Divini, since 1928. When compared to its Protestant counterpart, the SVD has maintained a remarkable amount of institutional and theological continuity. The Berliner Missionswerk has now essentially become a secular organization—it no longer has its own seminaries, trains its own missionaries, or engages in evangelism. Instead, it partners with local churches and provides funding and assistance to them.

But in one crucial way, the SVD has changed dramatically since the 1950s: it has undergone a complete demographic shift. More than 60 percent of the priests in the order now come from Southeast Asia. Father Antonio Pernia of the Philippines served as the first non-European superior general from 2000 to 2012. The generalate itself is a multicultural group, consisting of members from Poland, Brazil, Argentina, the United States, Angola, and India. Even though the official language in the SVD missionary headquarters is Italian, a smattering of Tagalog, Indonesian, Chinese, Vietnamese, English, German, French, and Spanish can be heard throughout the halls. It is common to meet missionaries comfortable conversing in five languages.

The surge in members from outside of Europe has come at the same time as numbers of priestly vocations from Europe decline. In 1990, recognizing the shrinking numbers, the society declared Western Europe as a secular zone. For the first time, the SVD designated Europe as a field that needed to receive missionaries rather than as a base for training and sending missionaries. Now missionaries from Africa, East Asia, and Latin America regularly serve in European parishes to fill the declining numbers of vocations for the priesthood.

Many studies that focus on the recent globalization of Christianity have drawn attention to the widening gulf that now exists between an increasingly liberal secular northern Europe and a conservative evangelical Global South.[21] The most spectacular instance of such a rift has occurred in the Anglican Communion, which, with about eight million congregants, is the third-largest Christian church group in the world. Lamin Sanneh recounts a central conflict at the 1998 Lambeth Conference, where all Anglican bishops gather every ten years. At the meeting, Western church leaders accused Third World Christianity as being "bankrolled by conservative groups in the United States" that sought to stem progressive advances in the rest of the world. Armed with these funds and a reactionary agenda, Third World Christianity, liberal church leaders claimed, posed "a threat to the West's hard-earned liberal achievements." Sanneh, writing in 2003, concluded, "All of that seems like a prescription for a major cultural schism." And Sanneh was prescient. The fractures have only widened in the Anglican Communion. More than 230 conservative Anglican bishops, mostly from the Global South, boycotted the 2008 Lambeth Conference, citing fundamental disagreement with North American churches over the ordination of homosexual bishops and the blessing of same-sex marriages.[22]

Yet the gulf between a liberal West and a conservative Global South was not, as some liberal church leaders would like to believe, a recent phenomenon, nor merely the consequence of funding by American conservatives. As I have shown in this book, the fundamental divergences between liberal and conservative strands of Christianity are rooted within the missionary movements of the nineteenth century. A battle between different visions of Christianity in different geographic regions has long been afoot.

In the case of the German missionary enterprise in China, it is certainly true that the turn toward a more liberal, inclusive view of Christian missions was a "hard-earned" achievement that included surviving two catastrophic world wars. Yet many of the liberal clergy in the West who are eager to excoriate "Third World Christianity" today tend to forget the genealogy of their own liberalism. It was precisely the encounter with other global religions and cultures—as well as the challenge from indigenous Christians—that pushed Western missionary leaders to embrace the liberalism that they now espouse.

The German case reveals that it was not the Europeans themselves who first embraced liberalism. Rather, Chinese Christians in the 1920s were pushing German missionaries to *become* more liberal. The Germans, on the other hand, had bristled at the apparent liberalism of the Chinese Christian leadership, who had been trained, for the most part, in an American-inflected liberal Social Gospel theology. The ultimate shift in both the BMS and the SVD to adopt more liberal positions was provoked by external stimuli. These "hard-earned" liberal achievements cannot be attributed to the efforts of the West, or to liberalism, alone. Rather, the modern global Christian landscape was produced through the cooperation and interactions among a multitude of transnational forces and actors.

Furthermore, the gulf between Europe and the Global South may not be as big as scholars and theologians claim. An examination of the SVD in its current incarnation shows that it is difficult to pinpoint its place on any theological spectrum. As in any large international organization, the theological outlooks and perspectives of its members are diverse. The SVD has produced vocal exponents of both conservative and liberal theological positions. The late American SVD missionary Father Anthony Zimmerman, for example, was an outspoken member of the antiabortion movement in the United States and took conservative, orthodox positions on most issues related to the church. On the other end of the theological spectrum, Fernando Lugo, who was president of Paraguay from 2008 to 2012, was also a member of the SVD and a committed adherent to liberation theology. Here, the tables are turned—members of the Global South being much more liberal than the northern Europeans and Americans. Immediate local contexts matter more in determining theological orientation, rather than broader generalizations of a "Global South" juxtaposed against a "liberal North."

As Christianity gains more adherents in the Global South, organizations like the SVD will become increasingly important as intermediaries between the North and South. If the current SVD is any indication, a certain section of the church is already working to bridge that divide. Priests like those of the SVD, along with the Jesuits, the Franciscans, and other major missionary organizations, are administering the institutions of education and social work in the Global South; they are educating the next generation of Catholic believers. These missionaries are willing to open dialogues about how to interpret the gospel in an increasingly multicultural fashion. If there is a divergence between the "liberal North" and the "Global South," perhaps organizations like the SVD can help to bridge those gaps and prevent the gulf from widening.

Yet the calling of the historian is not prognostication. An examination of the German missionary enterprise from 1860 to 1950 reminds us how radically different the world of those missionaries was from ours, how brief and fleeting it was: little remains from that previous world but a "shadow-filled edifice."[23] This history is made of intellectual and theological shifts in the midst of intense political change: within the span of a generation, German missionaries dramatically changed their views about China. It is a story of institutional about-faces as well, with new members incorporated into the missionary society. These stories demonstrate the malleability and flexibility of Christianity, with constantly shifting individuals, institutions, and ideas. This book shows how seemingly conservative, immovable institutions are not immune to the forces of global social, political, and cultural change.

Finally, how does the story of the missionaries intersect with the broader narratives of German history? As I have shown, the German missionary embrace of Confucianism and other cultures in the 1920s and 1930s occurred at the same time that Germany itself was experiencing an upswing of racism and xenophobia and the National Socialists were rising to power. An examination of the German missionary enterprise provides one corrective to the hegemony of that overarching narrative. It offers us stories of German individuals, institutions, and ideas that lived out alternatives to the racial hatred of interwar Germany. A study of the German missionary enterprise in its global context shows the uneasy relationship that German Christians had with the Nazi Party.

Perhaps a final story can illustrate what I mean. The BMS's Georg Kohls, one of the last of the Berliners to leave China, was born in 1885 in the Prussian city of Graudenz (now the Polish city of Grudziądz). He had the typical profile of the late-nineteenth-century missionary. Like so many of his predecessors in the BMS, Kohls came from a lower-class background: his father was a barely literate shoemaker with nine children. Kohls apprenticed as a tailor until the age of nineteen. Just when he finished his apprenticeship, he had a deeply spiritual experience, whereby he "was confronted by his own sin for the first time." Kohls joined a youth group, and his pastor found him to be an impressive, enterprising young man. The pastor recommended that he go to Berlin. There, Kohls joined another youth group, the Ostdeutschen Jünglingsbund. It was during these classes that Kohls found the liberation that he sought: "Especially in the youth group I recognized myself as a poor miserable sinner, but that the Lord Jesus could free me." This encounter with Christ inspired him to want to become a missionary, and he sought entrance into the BMS.[24]

In 1905, he was admitted to the BMS's seminary, and by 1911, he was on a boat to China. His early years there were difficult. His wife, Anna Braune, traveled to China in 1920 but died from typhus within a year of her arrival, fourteen days after she delivered a daughter. Kohls remarried in 1923 and spent the next thirty-eight years in China. Like so many missionaries before him, Kohls's career as a missionary provided him with the opportunity to live a cosmopolitan life that he would not have been able to imagine as a tailor. After the First World War, he traveled with his second wife, Lotti Kohls, to the United States, stopping in Philadelphia, New York, San Francisco, and Honolulu.[25]

As I was paging through Kohls's papers in the archives, nothing seemed out of the ordinary—his career mapped perfectly onto the typical trajectory of a young missionary in China. Yet what brought Kohls to my attention was a series of letters detailing a conflict between him and his supervisor in China, Alfred Oelke, that he wrote in 1938 to Johannes Müller, then superintendent over the entire mission. Müller was a close confidant, and he and Kohls were also related by marriage (Lotti Kohls was Müller's niece). Kohls complained that Oelke's wife was spreading rumors about him, whispering to other Germans that Kohls was "envious of Oelke's position as supervisor" and warning other members of the congregation to "keep their distance from Kohls."[26]

The conflict stemmed from Oelke's support of the Nazis. In 1936, Oelke had written: "There are only two paths for the future of Germany. We stand or we fall with National Socialism."[27] At a service in Guangzhou in May 1938, Kohls had led an offering prayer without mentioning Hitler or the political strength of Germany. After the service, Oelke's wife criticized Kohls, saying that it was "people like Herr Kohls, who not even once mentioned the *Führer,* and surely never prayed for him," who helped contribute to the fragmented political situation in Germany. Kohls's omission led to further bickering among factions within the missionary society that supported and opposed the National Socialists.[28]

After the Berlin missionaries were expelled from China in 1951, Kohls never returned to Germany. Despite pleas by Siegfried Knak asking him to retire in Germany, Kohls refused. Instead, he and his wife were reunited with his two sons in California. They settled in Berkeley, and Lotti worked for the university ministry, becoming the first minister to Chinese students in Berkeley. Kohls became an assistant pastor at St. Michael's Lutheran Church in Oakland. He relocated to San Diego in 1958, becoming a pastor for the Lutheran church there and establishing a German service. His wife continued to perform outreach to the Chinese in the United States. He lived until 1986, just past his one-hundredth birthday.

Compare the life of Georg Kohls with that of Johann Baptist von Anzer, the SVD's first bishop. Both had provincial backgrounds. Both were thrust into a cosmopolitan world—a world previously inaccessible to them—through their missionary work. But consider the differences. Like many other nineteenth-century missionaries, Anzer, to the end of his life, continued to be ethnocentric, convinced of Europe's historical world mission, committed to discrediting and undermining the Confucian legacy. He remained, despite his cosmopolitan experiences, a European chauvinist. Kohls, on the other hand, confronted his disappointment with his native Germany and created a new home in the United States. Lotti and Georg yearned to return to China; they later wrote that they had once expected to die there and how they hoped to see China again one day. If Anzer's life offers an example of the limits of personal transformation as a result of cosmopolitan encounters, then Kohls's life suggests its possibilities. Traveling to China forced Kohls to question his assumptions of cultural superiority. But the act of crossing borders does not guarantee a more expansive worldview. For Anzer, the encounter with others reinforced his hierarchical notion of civilization. The divergent paths of these two individuals point us to the unpredictable, fractured nature of the transnational encounter.

These individual stories also illuminate the broader historical shifts that incubated moments of cultural exchange. What a difference a generation makes: Kohls changed his mind about traditional Chinese culture as he witnessed Germany's destructive power and its subsequent ruin, while Anzer died in 1903 with the optimism of nineteenth-century Europe—and Germany's power and prestige—at its zenith. In German missionaries like Kohls and Anzer, as well as Chinese Christians like Ling Deyuan and Chen Yuan, we see how individuals adapted to the chaos of nineteenth- and twentieth-century world history, and how they tried to make sense of the political, economic, and social conditions that surrounded them. Their struggles alert us to a history of transnational encounters filled with stories of both missed opportunities and fruitful cross-cultural engagement. Theirs is a history, like so many others, of tragedy and hope, of failure and success.

NOTES

INTRODUCTION

1. Stenz, *In der Heimat des Konfuzius*, 103.
2. Ibid., 104.
3. Stenz, "Chinesische Christ," 54. Stenz did express admiration for the Confucian temple in Qufu and its environs, writing that "a conscious sense of awe" fell over him in the "deep stillness and silence that reigned over the majestic old trees" surrounding the Confucian temple.
4. Mühlhahn, *Herrschaft und Widerstand*, 331; Steinmetz, *Devil's Handwriting*, 417.
5. Hermanns, "Wie ich Konfuzius' Stammhalter sah," 48, 50.
6. Voskamp, *Confucius und das heutige China*, 1–2.
7. Carl Johannes Voskamp, "Chinesischen Klassiker und das Evangelium," unpublished manuscript, July 1924, BMW 1/4326, sec. 19.
8. Slezkine, *Jewish Century*, 1.
9. The Antioch debate is recounted in Acts 15 and Galatians 3.
10. See Walls, *Missionary Movement*, 7–9.
11. Dunch, "Beyond Cultural Imperialism," 317.
12. For more on the Western impact on Chinese ideas, see Levenson, *Confucian China*. For a discussion about whether "Western impact" actually mattered, see Cohen, *Discovering History*. For more on missionary attempts to import Western law to China, see Liu, *Clash of Empires*. For missionary translations of texts in the realm of geology, see Wu, *Empires of Coal*.
13. The death toll during the Boxer unrest has been notoriously difficult to ascertain, ranging from lows of 32,000 to highs of 250,000. See Rummel, *China's Bloody Century*, 39. For anti-Christian movements throughout the

nineteenth century, the classic work is Cohen, *China and Christianity*. Its twentieth-century manifestations find discussion in Lutz, *Chinese Politics and Christian Missions*.

14. For more on the historiographical shift toward investigating Chinese Christians, see Standaert, "New Trends."

15. See, e.g., Fairbank, ed., *Missionary Enterprise*; Levenson, *Confucian China*; Cohen, "Christian Missions and Their Impact."

16. Bays, ed., *Christianity in China*, ix. For the statistics gathered by the Pew Research Center, see Pew Forum, "Global Christianity," 97.

17. See, e.g., Dunch, *Fuzhou Protestants*.

18. For exact statistics, see the appendix in Tiedemann, ed., *Handbook*, 977–1004. For the common view of German insignificance after the First World War, see Latourette, *History of Christian Missions*, 743.

19. Fairbank, "Assignment for the '70's," 877.

20. Horst Gründer articulated this position in his influential *Christliche Mission*. Even in recent works that focus on the global dimensions of German history, missionaries are described solely as agents of the "civilizing mission." See, e.g., Conrad, *Globalisation and the Nation*, 93–100.

21. For a good overview of the scholarship on missions and imperialism, see Etherington, ed., *Missions and Empire*.

22. For a discussion of the "transnational" turn in German history, see the useful "Forum."

23. Latourette, *Emergence*, 61.

24. Ibid.

25. Sanneh and Carpenter, eds., *Changing Face*, vii. For other works that encapsulate an optimistic view of Christianity's globalization, see Walls, *Cross-Cultural Process*; Sanneh, *Whose Religion Is Christianity?*; Sanneh, *Disciples of All Nations*. A good example of scholarship that shows the malleability of Christianity from its foundation is MacCulloch, *History of Christianity*.

26. For work on contemporary Chinese Catholicism, see Madsen, *China's Catholics*.

27. See Latourette, *Christianity in a Revolutionary Age*, 521–23.

28. See Pew Forum, "Global Christianity," 13. See also Jenkins, *Next Christendom*, 3.

29. Benedict XVI, "To Brazilian Bishops," par. 6.

30. For more on European secularization after the 1960s, see Hölscher, "Europe in the Age of Secularisation"; Brown, *Death of Christian Britain*; McLeod, *Religious Crisis of the 1960s*. For the American context, see Hollinger, *After Cloven Tongues*.

31. Benedict XVI, *What It Means to Be a Christian*, 45.

32. See Lian, *Conversion of Missionaries*; Bays and Wacker, eds., *Foreign Missionary Enterprise at Home*.

CHAPTER ONE THE MISSIONARY IMPULSE

1. Gützlaff, *Journal*, 19. For more on the *Lord Amherst*, see Hsü, "Secret Mission of the Lord Amherst." For Gützlaff's publication successes, see Lutz, *Opening China*.

2. Gützlaff, *Journal*, 334.

3. Ibid., 338–40.

4. Ibid., 393.

5. O'Malley, "Mission and the Early Jesuits." The literature on the early modern Jesuit missions is vast, but there is no better place to start than O'Malley, *First Jesuits*. For a global history of the Jesuits, see Clossey, *Salvation and Globalization*.

6. Ricci's fascinating career has inspired much good scholarship. See, e.g., Hsia, *Jesuit in the Forbidden City*; Spence, *Memory Palace*. For more on the first generation of Chinese Catholic converts in the late Ming and early Qing dynasties, see Huang, *Liang toushe*.

7. Daughton, *Empire Divided*, 29.

8. Walls, "Eighteenth-Century Protestant Missionary Awakening," 28.

9. Guilday, "Sacred Congregation de Propaganda Fide," 480.

10. See Menegon, *Ancestors, Virgins, and Friars*, 284–85. See also Brockey, *Journey to the East*, 12.

11. Cited in D'Costa, "Catholicism and the World Religions," 23.

12. Bays, *New History*, 32. For more on the Chinese Rites Controversy, see Minamiki, *Chinese Rites Controversy*; Mungello, *Chinese Rites Controversy*.

13. Tiedemann, "Indigenous Agency," 214.

14. On Shanxi, see Harrison, *Missionary's Curse*, 28; for more on the Collegio de' Cinesi, see Menegon, *Ancestors, Virgins, and Friars*, 127.

15. Menegon, *Ancestors, Virgins, and Friars*, 3.

16. Young, *Ecclesiastical Colony*, 13.

17. Ward, *Protestant Evangelical Awakening*, 16.

18. Pietism is a difficult concept to define, and scholars have debated the similarities and continuities between seventeenth- and nineteenth-century Pietism. The best overview of Pietism is the four-volume *Geschichte des Pietismus*. For the nineteenth and twentieth centuries, see volumes 3 and 4: Brecht et al., eds., *Geschichte des Pietismus. Bd. 3*; Lehmann, ed., *Geschichte des Pietismus. Bd. 4*.

19. Ward, *Protestant Evangelical Awakening*, 57. See also Strom, "Pietism and Community," 1.

20. Ward, *Protestant Evangelical Awakening*, 60.

21. Walls, "Eighteenth-Century Protestant Missionary Awakening," 31. For more on the Tranquebar Mission, see Jeyaraj and Young, eds., *Hindu-Christian Epistolary Self-Disclosures*, 24. For a further articulation of Lüthy's "Protestant International," see Bosher, "Huguenot Merchants and the Protestant International," 77.

22. Jensz, *German Moravian Missionaries*, 18–21.

23. For an overview of the Moravians, see Hutton, *History of Moravian Missions*.

24. Walls, *Cross-Cultural Process*, 202.

25. The best overview of Protestant missions during this period is Ward, *Protestant Evangelical Awakening*.

26. Sheehan, *Enlightenment Bible*, 57–62.

27. MacCulloch, *History of Christianity*, 806; Aubert, "Catholic Church," 6. For more on the recent move to reconsider religion's relationship to the Enlightenment, see Sheehan, "Enlightenment, Religion, and the Enigma of Secularization."

28. MacCulloch, *History of Christianity*, 805. For more on anti-Jesuit rhetoric throughout the seventeenth and eighteenth centuries, see Cubitt, *Jesuit Myth.*

29. The definitive work on the relationship between the French Revolution and Catholicism is McManners, *French Revolution and the Church*. On Napoleon shutting down the Propaganda Fide, see Daughton, *Empire Divided*, 34.

30. Lehmann, "Pietism in the World of Transatlantic Religious Revivals," 18. For a good comparative overview, see Blumhofer and Balmer, *Modern Christian Revivals.*

31. Clark, "New Catholicism," 11. See also Blackbourn, "Catholic Church in Europe."

32. MacCulloch, *History of Christianity*, 873–74. For more on the British missionary enterprise, see Cox, *Imperial Fault Lines*. For more on the complicated relationship between British missionaries and imperialism, see Porter, *Religion Versus Empire?*

33. Porter, *Religion Versus Empire?*, 40.

34. Hobsbawm, *Age of Revolution*, 223.

35. Hogg, *Ecumenical Foundations*, 13.

36. For more on the German Christendom Society, see Wiegelt, "Deutsche Christentumsgesellschaft," 125–50.

37. See von Rohden, "Excerpts," 1.

38. Richter, *Geschichte*, 1.

39. Ibid.

40. Von Rohden, "Excerpts," 1.

41. Moch, *Moving Europeans*, 4.

42. Köllman, "Population of Barmen," 589, 593.

43. See Holborn, *History of Modern Germany*, 595–98; Clark, "Religion and Confessional Conflict," 91–92.

44. Axmann, "Lebensabriss des E. Faber," 397. For more on Faber's life, see Wu, "Ernst Faber."

45. Carl Johannes Voskamp, "Lebenslauf," n.d., BMW 1/4326, 8. For more on the typical profile of BMS missionaries, see Pakendorf, "Brief History," 108.

46. Walls, *Missionary Movement*, 171; Miller, *Social Control*, 50–51.

47. Miller, *Social Control*, 31–32. For more on the influence of Jänicke on Prussian noblemen, see Bigler, *Politics of German Protestantism*, 129–30.

48. Pakendorf, "Brief History," 107; Richter, *Geschichte*, 21. From 1833 to 1838, the Gerlach brothers, Pietist Lutherans who helped establish the conservative newspaper *Kreuzzeitung* and became part of the camarilla surrounding Friedrich Wilhelm IV, sat on the BMS board. For more on the Gerlach brothers and the "Pietist Aristocrats," see Bigler, *Politics of German Protestantism*, 125–58.

49. On mission festivals, see Rennstich, "Mission," 315–16. See Köllman, *Sozialgeschichte der Stadt Barmen*, 200–201, for more on the Wuppertal Festival Week. On the BMS's funding structure, see Pakendorf, "Brief History," 108.

50. Jensz, "Function of Inaugural Editions," 374; Jensz and Acke, "Form and Function," 368.

51. "Germany," *Missionary Register*, 427. On German Catholic reading culture, see Zalar, " 'Knowledge Is Power.' "

52. See also Wu, "Converting Individuals."

53. On auxiliary organizations, see Gerber, *Voskamps*, 32; Pakendorf, "Brief History," 108. For a detailed history of auxiliary organizations in Brandenburg, see Richter, *Geschichte*, 72–87. Lists of these organizations were publicized, along with the amount of money that each auxiliary organization donated, in the appendices of the yearly reports. See, e.g., *Bericht des Missions-Verein für China in Berlin*, 5.

54. Lutz, *Opening China*, 31–33.

55. For more on the multiple roles that missionaries had in the field, see ibid., 66–69.

56. Clark, "New Catholicism," 14; Jonas, *France and the Cult of the Sacred Heart*, 215–20. On the Trier pilgrimage, see Schieder, "Kirche und Revolution." For more on popular Catholicism in the Rhineland, see Sperber, *Popular Catholicism*. On Marian apparitions, see Harris, *Lourdes*, and Blackbourn, *Marpingen*.

57. Jonas, *France and the Cult of the Sacred Heart*, 125.

58. Daughton, *Empire Divided*, 36; Gründer, *Christliche Mission*, 47.

59. Jonas, *France and the Cult of the Sacred Heart*, 126–28; Gründer, *Christliche Mission*, 47–48.

60. Daughton, *Empire Divided*, 35.

61. Young, *Ecclesiastical Colony*, 23. For more on the Oeuvre's success, see Curtis, *Civilizing Habits*, 15.

62. Clark, "New Catholicism," 18–24.

63. Jonas, *France and the Cult of the Sacred Heart*, 5.

64. Bornemann, *Remembering Arnold Janssen*, 19; Bornemann, *Arnold Janssen*, 23.

65. The literature on the *Kulturkampf* is vast, but two good places to start are Ross, *Failure of Bismarck's Kulturkampf*, and Bennette, *Fighting for the Soul of Germany*.

66. Bornemann, *Arnold Janssen*, 39–40.

67. See, e.g., "Auferstehen," 27–28; "China das große Land."

68. On the journal's early years, see Bornemann, *Arnold Janssen*, 43.

69. For more on the anti-Jesuit law, see Gross, "Kulturkampf and Unification."

70. Bornemann, *Arnold Janssen*, 60.

71. Bornemann, *Remembering Arnold Janssen*, 70.

72. The definitive biography on Anzer is Rivinius, *Im Spannungsfeld von Mission und Politik*. Freinademetz's biography is exhaustively covered in Bornemann, ed., *Selige P. J. Freinademetz*.

73. "Avant-propos," 5–6.

74. "China das große Land," 29.
75. "Avant-propos," 5.
76. Warneck, *Warum ist das 19. Jahrhundert ein Missionsjahrhundert?* The text that Warneck derided is Mott, *Evangelization of the World.*

CHAPTER TWO   RESPONDING TO FAILURE

1. Naquin, *Millenarian Rebellion,* 111.
2. Ibid., 11.
3. Ibid., 264.
4. Wakeman, "Rebellion and Revolution," 213. On the Tiandihui, see Murray and Qin, *Origins of the Tiandihui.*
5. Ownby and Heidhues, eds., *"Secret Societies,"* 16.
6. Goossaert, *Taoists of Peking,* 30.
7. On messianism and Chinese popular religion, see ter Haar, "Messianism and the Heaven and Earth Society," 162; Naquin, *Millenarian Rebellion,* 9.
8. Murray and Qin, *Origins of the Tiandihui,* 63.
9. For an extensive exploration of the Chinese Triad's blood covenant, see ter Haar, *Ritual and Mythology,* 151–79.
10. On the similarities between Christian and popular Chinese religious rituals and how Chinese outsiders confused Christianity with other Chinese religions, see Harrison, *Missionary's Curse,* 25–29.
11. An account of Gabriel Taurin Dufresse's beheading can be found in Clark, *China's Saints,* 165–67. On Shanxi Catholics accused of aiding the White Lotus Rebellion, see Harrison, *Missionary's Curse,* 25–26.
12. Tiedemann, ed., *Handbook,* 127.
13. For more on Protestant expansion in the early nineteenth century, see Bays, *New History,* 41–47; Cohen, "Christian Missions and Their Impact," 548.
14. D'Elia, *Catholic Missions,* 56–57. For a succinct and excellent overview of Catholic geopolitical rivalries, see Young, *Ecclesiastical Colony,* 15–23. The Spanish Dominicans worked in the southeastern province of Fujian. For an excellent history of the Dominican mission in Fujian, see Menegon, *Ancestors, Virgins, and Friars.* The Paris Foreign Mission Society had the largest geographical range in China but largely cornered the southwest, working in Sichuan, Guizhou, Yunnan, Guanxi, Guangdong, and later Manchuria and Tibet. For a history of the Paris Foreign Mission Society, in a different geographical context, see Daughton, *Empire Divided.* The Franciscans worked in Shandong, Shanxi, Shenxi, Hubei, and Hunan. For a history of the Franciscan missionaries in Shandong, see Mungello, *Spirit and the Flesh.* The Lazarists, formally known as the Congregation of the Mission, entered China in 1784 after the suppression of the Jesuits and worked in Hebei, Jiangxi, Henan, and Zhejiang. They are also known as the Vincentians. For a history of the Lazarists, see van den Brandt, *Lazaristes en Chine.* The Jesuits, the oldest mission in China, also have the largest amount of literature dedicated to them. They were centered primarily around Jiangsu, Anhui, and Hebei. In 1847 they reestablished their missions

in Shanghai. For the history of early Jesuit missions, see Brockey, *Journey to the East;* Hsia, *Jesuit in the Forbidden City.*

15. Quoted in Lovell, *Opium War,* 5.

16. Cohen, "Christian Missions and Their Impact," 550. The classic work on the Treaty Ports is Fairbank, *Trade and Diplomacy.*

17. For Gützlaff's role in the Treaty of Nanjing, see Lutz, *Opening China,* 103–10. For his European tour, see ibid., 229–36.

18. Lutz and Lutz, "Karl Gützlaff's Approach to Indigenization," 272; Lutz, *Opening China,* 295–96. See also Kriele, *Geschichte,* 95. For the best history of the Basel mission in southern China, see Klein, *Basler Mission.*

19. Lutz and Lutz, "Karl Gützlaff's Approach to Indigenization," 270–74.

20. Lutz, *Opening China,* 263.

21. Cohen, "Christian Missions and Their Impact," 551.

22. Platt, *Autumn in the Heavenly Kingdom,* xxiii. Classic works on the Taipings include Wakeman, *Strangers at the Gate;* Kuhn, *Rebellion and Its Enemies;* Spence, *God's Chinese Son.*

23. On the fascinating Roberts, see Teng, "Reverend Issachar Jacox Roberts." On the religious beliefs of the Taipings, see Shi, *Taiping Ideology;* Wagner, *Reenacting the Heavenly Vision;* Weller, *Resistance, Chaos, and Control in China;* Reilly, *Taiping Heavenly Kingdom.*

24. On the *Arrow* war, see Wong, *Deadly Dreams.*

25. Young, *Ecclesiastical Colony,* 29.

26. Ibid., 45.

27. Cohen, "Anti-Christian Tradition in China," 169–70. For a detailed account of both official and gentry anti-Christianity, see Cohen, *China and Christianity,* especially chapters 3 and 4.

28. Cited in Young, *Ecclesiastical Colony,* 45. For more on the Tianjin Massacre, see Fairbank, "Patterns Behind the Tientsin Massacre."

29. The idea of global anti-Christian resistance comes from MacCulloch, *History of Christianity,* 897. For more on the Xhosa, see Peires, *Dead Will Arise.* On Japanese millenarian sects right before the Meiji Restoration, see Wilson, *Patriots and Redeemers.*

30. A Google Ngram search of "missionary martyrs" within English books shows little interest before 1840 and a spike after the 1850s, especially after missionaries were killed in the Sepoy Rebellion. For examples of nineteenth-century compendia of missionary martyrs, see Smith, *Heroes and Martyrs;* Croil, *Noble Army of Martyrs.*

31. Hogg, *Ecumenical Foundations,* 42.

32. Ibid., 61. The Scandinavians also held their own missionary conference. For more on German missionary conferences, see Döhler, "Deutschen Missionskonferenzen."

33. Cox, *British Missionary Enterprise,* 174.

34. For a list of Protestant meetings at both the regional and national levels, see Tiedemann, ed., *Handbook,* 52–53.

35. On the Catholic synods, see Metzler, *Synoden*, 100–104. The five church regions were (1) Zhili (North, Southeast, East) and Liaodong, which covered Manchuria and Mongolia; (2) Shandong, Shanxi, Henan, Shaanxi, and Gansu; (3) Hunan, Hubei, Zhejiang, Jiangxi, and Jiangnan; (4) Sichuan, Yunnan, Guizhou, and Tibet; and (5) Guangdong, Guangxi, Hong Kong, and Fujian.
36. Johnson, ed., *Report*, xviii.
37. Walsh, *Memorial of the Futtehgurh Mission*, 331.
38. Gough, "Best Means," 269.
39. Metzler, *Synoden*, 51.
40. Lutz, "Attrition," 24.
41. Wolferstan, *Catholic Church*, 284.
42. Lutz, "Attrition," 25.
43. For more on medical missions, see Gulick, *Peter Parker*.
44. Metzler, *Synoden*, 53.
45. Bogner, "Zur Entwicklung der Berliner Mission," 327–29.
46. Pakendorf, "Brief History," 110. Wangemann's son wrote a hagiographical biography of his father; see Wangemann, *D. Dr. Wangemann.*
47. Wangemann, *Missions-Ordnung*, 54. For a recounting of Wangemann's voyages, see Wangemann, *Reise-Jahr in Süd-Afrika* and *Zweites Reisejahr.*
48. Wangemann, *Mission-Ordnung*, 55.
49. Bogner, "Zur Entwicklung der Berliner Mission," 334. For a clear definition of the missionary's responsibilities, see Wangemann, *Missions-Ordnung*, 66–70.
50. Wangemann, *Missions-Ordnung*, 22.
51. For a more comprehensive account of the missionary schooling system, see Kim, *Deutscher Kulturimperialismus.*
52. Gerber, *Voskamps*, 33. For an example of a final examination, see "Worter des Abschluss von John. Voskamp," October 7, 1884, BMW 1/4326.
53. Franke, *Sinologie*, 8.
54. *Conference on Missions Held in 1860*, 31–32.
55. Voskamp recounts his travails learning Chinese in Voskamp, *Tagebuch*, 24. On Freinademetz's journey, see Bornemann, ed., *Selige P. J. Freinademetz*, 45–53.
56. For the 1803 synod, see Metzler, *Synoden*, 54–55. For more on the 1851 conference in Shanghai, see Metzler, *Synoden*, 79–80. For more on the 1880 regional synods, see Tiedemann, ed., *Handbook*, 573.
57. For a quick overview of the different sessions related to indigenous clergy, see the Table of Contents of Yates, Nelson, and Barrett, eds., *Records*, and Lewis, Barber, and Hykes, eds., *Records*.
58. Huonder, *Einheimische Klerus*, 6.
59. For more on Venn, Anderson, and the Three-Self formula, see Shenk, "Rufus Anderson and Henry Venn," 170–71.
60. Metzler, *Synoden*, 79–80.
61. Yates, Nelson, and Barrett, eds., *Records*, 284.
62. Baldwin, "Self-Support," 284–85.
63. Yates, Nelson, and Barrett, eds., *Records*, 268.

64. For more on Legge's fascinating career, see Girardot, *Victorian Translation*. For more on Young J. Allen, see Bennett, *Missionary Journalist*.

65. Metzler, *Synoden*, 92.

66. *Conference on Missions Held in 1860 at Liverpool*, 25.

67. Hogg, *Ecumenical Foundations*, 49; Shenk, "Rufus Anderson and Henry Venn," 171.

68. Liu, *Translingual Practice*, 46.

69. Tiedemann, ed., *Handbook*, 573.

70. Reinders, "Blessed Are the Meat Eaters," 524–25. See also Stewart, "Hermeneutics of Suspicion."

71. Tiedemann, "Indigenous Agency," 219. For a translation of the *Guidelines*, see Bornemann, ed., *Selige P. J. Freinademetz*, 1077–93.

72. Bornemann, ed., *Selige P. J. Freinademetz*, 1084, 1099.

73. Ibid., 1100. For more on the Chinese Virgins, see Entenmann, "Christian Virgins." For an overview of women in modern Chinese society, see Hershatter, *Women in China's Long Twentieth Century*; Hershatter, *Gender of Memory*.

74. Young, *Ecclesiastical Colony*, 23.

75. Metzler, *Synoden*, 78; Young, *Ecclesiastical Colony*, 38.

76. Young, *Ecclesiastical Colony*, 34.

77. Hogg, *Ecumenical Foundations*, 49.

78. Hutchison, "Innocence Abroad," 79.

79. Hutchison, *Errand to the World*, 134–35.

80. Ibid., 135.

81. For more on the Missionsausschuß, see Mirbt, "Ausschuß"; Ustorf, *Sailing on the Next Tide*, 141–42.

82. On Fabri's relationship to imperialism, see Bade, *Friedrich Fabri*. For Fabri's famous pamphlet on imperialism, see Fabri, *Bedarf Deutschland der Colonien?*

83. Warneck, *Modern Missions*, 286–90.

84. Best, "Godly, International, and Independent," 588.

85. Hogg, *Ecumenical Foundations*, 72.

86. Lodwick, *Crusaders Against Opium*, 8–9.

87. Gründer, *Christliche Mission*, 50.

88. For more details on the attempts to establish direct Sino-Vatican relations, see Young, *Ecclesiastical Colony*, 54–62.

89. Rivinius, *Im Spannungsfeld von Mission und Politik*, 151–62. For more detail on the SVD's relationship to the German Empire, see Rivinius, *Weltlicher Schutz*. For more on the Italian precedent of issuing passports, see Young, *Ecclesiastical Colony*, 62–63.

90. Hartwich, ed., *Steyler Missionare I*, 25.

91. Cited in Rivinius, *Im Spannungsfeld von Mission und Politik*, 193.

92. Ibid., 247–50. See also Young, *Ecclesiastical Colony*, 64.

93. Cited in Rivinius, *Im Spannungsfeld von Mission und Politik*, 259.

94. Ibid., 273.

95. On Anzer's tour in Germany, see ibid., 262–70.

96. Young, *Ecclesiastical Colony*, 65.
97. Warneck, *Modern Missions*, 377.
98. Ibid., 375.
99. Ibid., 378.
100. Ibid., 373.
101. The classic articulation of the close connection between missions and imperialism is Gründer, *Christliche Mission*. For an overview of scholars who assume the close connection between missions and imperialism, see Best, "Godly, International, and Independent," 589.
102. Cox, *British Missionary Enterprise*, 177.

CHAPTER THREE MISSIONARY OPTIMISM

1. Steinmetz, *Devil's Handwriting*, 436. As Steinmetz notes, British Hong Kong and Macao were both islands unconnected to the mainland. The treaty was signed on March 6, 1898. Its text is printed in Leutner and Mühlhahn, eds., *Kolonialkrieg in China*, 164–68.
2. Zarrow, "Reform Movement," 20. On the 1898 reforms, see Karl and Zarrow, eds., *Rethinking the 1898 Reform Period*. On the relationship between the reforms of 1898 and Chinese religions, see Goossaert, "1898."
3. See Cohen, *History in Three Keys*, 84. See also Esherick, *Origins of the Boxer Uprising*, 136.
4. Esherick, *Origins of the Boxer Uprising*, 126.
5. Gustav Knak to Carl Johannes Voskamp, February 4, 1898, BMW 1/6547.
6. Kuo, " 'Christian Civilization,' " 235.
7. Esherick, *Origins of the Boxer Uprising*, xiii.
8. Ibid., 177–78. See also Cohen, *History in Three Keys*, 78, 113–18.
9. Huang, *China*, 249.
10. Hartwich, ed., *Steyler Missionare I*, 24.
11. Ibid., 45, 63, 71–74. See also Kuepers, *China und die katholische Mission*, 34–35; Lü, *Zhongguo guansheng fanjiao*.
12. Richter, *Geschichte*, 531–33. For more on the Triads, as well as organized crime in China in general, see Murray and Qin Baoqi, *Origins of the Tiandihui*. For a comparative perspective, see Liu, "Kuo-lu."
13. See Sweeten, *Christianity in Rural China*.
14. A dramatic retelling of the interrogation can be found in Freinademetz, "Eine Verfolgungsscene," 194. For a more even-handed account, see Bornemann, ed., *Selige P. J. Freinademetz*, 137–44.
15. Freinademetz, "Eine Verfolgungsscene," 195.
16. Ibid., 199; Bornemann, ed., *Selige P. J. Freinademetz*, 141.
17. See, e.g., Freinademetz, "Wer trägt die Hauptschuld," 39; Volpert, "Ein Mandarin," 46.
18. "Verfolgung in unserer mission," 140.
19. Leuschner, *Allerlei aus China*, 2; Voskamp, *Unter dem Banner des Drachens*, 82–83.

20. For more on the rise of Sinophobia in the late nineteenth century, see Steinmetz, *Devil's Handwriting*, 384–431. Stenz's quotation on "an earlier stage of civilization" is cited in ibid., 394. Leuschner's comments are from *Allerlei aus China*, 2.

21. See Stenz, *In der Heimat des Konfuzius*, 19–26; Voskamp, *Unter dem Banner des Drachen*, 118. Typical examples of BMS depictions of Chinese degeneracy can be found in Hubrig, *Li-tshyung-yin*; Leuschner, *Das Wichtigste aus den Tagen meines Lebens*; Leuschner, *Bilder des Todes*; Voskamp, *Mitteilungen*. I analyze these accounts in more detail in Wu, "Converting Individuals" and "Catholic and Protestant Individuals."

22. Voskamp, *Unter dem Banner des Drachen*, 117–18. For more on the distinction between superstition and religion, see Goossaert and Palmer, *Religious Question*, 50.

23. See Mühlhahn, *Herrschaft und Widerstand*, 326–27.

24. Richter, *Geschichte*, 525–26.

25. Hartwich, ed., *Steyler Missionare I*, 87.

26. Esherick, *Origins of the Boxer Uprising*, 80.

27. For more detail on the BMS's development in terms of missionary holdings, see Richter, *Geschichte*, 528–43. For more on the work of the Basel Missionary Society in Guangdong, see Klein, *Basler Mission*.

28. See Steinmetz, *Devil's Handwriting*, 455; Esherick, *Origins of the Boxer Uprising*, 184.

29. *Jahresbericht 1908*, 256–57. See also Richter, *Geschichte*, 537. For more on the education of Chinese girls, see Lutz, ed., *Pioneer Chinese Christian Women*, especially Lutz, "Women's Education," 393–420. For statistics on the SVD missions in 1908, see Hartwich, ed., *Steyler Missionare II*, 396.

30. Wangemann, *Missions-Ordnung*, 41.

31. Richter, *Geschichte*, 514–15.

32. Wangemann, *Missions-Ordnung*, 42–43.

33. For a brief description of the seminary in Guangzhou, see Richter, *Geschichte*, 539–42. For descriptions of the seminary in Jimo, see ibid., 622–26.

34. Copies of exams can be found in BMW 1/882, BMW 1/885, and BMW 1/888.

35. For more on the debate over whether to take control of secular schools, see Hartwich, ed., *Steyler Missionare I*, 454–58. For more on education at the preparatory level, see Breitkopf, "Priesterseminar," 118.

36. Breitkopf, "Priesterseminar," 119.

37. See *Moxiang baojian*.

38. Hartwich, ed., *Steyler Missionare I*, 403.

39. Breitkopf, "Priesterseminar," 119.

40. For more on the Taiyuan Massacre, see Thompson, "Reporting the Taiyuan Massacre."

41. Hevia, *English Lessons*, 258–70. See also Klein, "Media Events."

42. Dabringhaus, "Army on Vacation?," 464. For more on the Boxer funds, see Hunt, "American Remission of the Boxer Indemnity."

43. Hevia, "Leaving a Brand on China," 323.

44. Stenz, *Twenty-Five Years in China*, 121.

45. Goossaert and Palmer, *Religious Question*, 50–51.

46. See the statistics in Wolferstan, *Catholic Church*, 453; D'Elia, *Catholic Missions in China*, 62. For more on the "Golden Age," see Bays, *New History*, 92–97.

47. See Bays, *New History*, 115.

48. For BMS statistics in 1905, see Richter, *Geschichte*, 541–43. For SVD statistics in the same year, see Hartwich, ed., *Steyler Missionare II*, 155.

49. For a comparison of statistics in Africa and China, see *Jahresbericht 1908*, 244–47, 256–57.

50. Kwok, *Chinese Women and Christianity*, 11. See also Lutz, ed., *Pioneer Chinese Christian Women*.

51. Lutz and Lutz, "Karl Gützlaff's Approach to Indigenization," 288.

52. For more on the Berlin Women's Missionary Society, see Boetzinger, *"Chinesen ein Chinese werden."*

53. Hartwich, ed., *Steyler Missionare II*, 204.

54. Ibid., 97.

55. Hartwich, ed., *Steyler Missionare I*, 400–401; Hartwich, ed., *Steyler Missionare II*, 155.

56. Richter, *Geschichte*, 542.

57. Hartwich, ed., *Steyler Missionare II*, 171–73.

58. Ibid., 7, 75.

59. Mühlhahn, *Herrschaft und Widerstand*, 347; Hartwich, ed., *P. Arnold Janssen und P. Josef Freinademetz*, 43–44, 70–71.

60. Hartwich, ed., *Steyler Missionare I*, 498; Bettray, "Arnold Janssen," 99.

61. See Bornemann, ed., *Selige P. J. Freinademetz*, 727, n. 79; 438.

62. Young, *Ecclesiastical Colony*, 123.

63. The best book in English on Ma Xiangbo is Hayhoe and Lu, eds., *Ma Xiangbo*. There is no monograph on Ying. For more on his criticisms of missionary chauvinism, see Young, *Ecclesiastical Colony*, 174–80.

64. For more on Tianjin after the Boxer Uprising, see Rogaski, *Hygienic Modernity*.

65. Ying, *Yeshi ji*, 1, 9.

66. Ng, ed., *Jidujiao daxue*, 109–13.

67. Fang Hao, ed., *Ma Xiangbo xiansheng wenji*, 14.

68. "Auszüge aus dem Visitationsbericht von Arthur Brown," 1909, BMW 1/6602. See also Richter, *Geschichte*, 545–51.

69. For descriptions of the North China conference, see Schlunk, ed., *Durch Deutsch-Kiautschou*, 73–85. For a detailed rundown of the southern China conference, see Schlunk, ed., *Durch Chinas Südprovinz*, 95–101.

70. Schlunk, ed., *Durch Deutsch-Kiautschou*, 73–74. Out of twenty-six presentations, ten received the mark of "good," seven received "satisfactory," three received "mediocre," three received "insufficient," and three received "completely inadequate."

71. Ibid., 103; Richter, *Geschichte*, 549–52.

72. Schlunk, ed., *Durch Chinas Südprovinz*, 103–5.

73. Records of the *Gehilfen* conferences can be found in BMW 1/884, BMW 1/885, and BMW 1/890.

74. Friedrich Wilhelm Leuschner, "Gehilfenkonferenz 1909," November 29, 1909, BMW 1/890, 30.

75. The Committee to Friedrich Wilhelm Leuschner, February 9, 1910, BMW 1/890, 34.

76. Karl Zehnel, "Ausserordentlicher nach Antrag betreffend: Wiederaufnahme des Christen Ma min than in die christl. Kirche," August 1, 1905, BMW 1/6277, 17–18.

77. For the entire case, see, "Klage gegen Vikar Tschin Yin Yui," June 18, 1921, BMW 1/884, 1–3.

78. "Abschrift der Akten Fall Vikar Tschin jin jiu," June 18, 1921, BMW 1/884, 30.

79. "Protokoll der Synode Canton-Unterland von 9. bis 12. August 1910," August 12, 1910, BMW 1/6530.

80. Leuschner, "Gehilfenkonferenz 1909," 29.

81. "An das Comitee," September 30, 1910, BMW 1/6603.

82. "Abschrift aus Protokoll der Gehilfenkonferenz vom 17.–19. März 1911 in Schaugwan," March 19, 1911, BMW 1/884. For the discussion in Germany, see Wilhelm Glüer, "Anlage. Statut für eine Gehilfen-Pensionskasse der Berliner Mission," November 4, 1911, BMW 1/884. Chinese Christians contributed 2 percent of their income to the fund. Assistants who retired with fewer than ten years of service earned 25 percent of their previous income in retirement, while those who devoted between ten and twenty-five years of service earned 40 percent of their previous income. Workers with more than twenty-five years of service earned 50 percent of their income.

83. For the entire exchange, see August Kollecker, "Uebersetzung," February 23, 1912, BMW 1/884; the Committee to August Kollecker, May 4, 1912, BMW 1/884.

84. See Zarrow, *China in War and Revolution*.

85. August Kollecker to the Committee, September 3, 1912, BMW 1/884.

86. Gerber, *Voskamps*, 449.

87. Oswald Töpper, "Bericht des Missionars Osw. Toepper ueber das erste Halbjahr 1913," August 1, 1913, BMW 1/6282, 192.

88. Gerber, *Voskamps*, 138.

89. Ibid., 431.

90. Ibid., 432. There is a large literature in German on the career of Richard Wilhelm. See, e.g., Walravens and Zimmer, eds., *Richard Wilhelm*. For the best overview of Wilhelm's career in English, see Marchand, *German Orientalism*, 463–73. See also Richter, "Richard Wilhelm."

91. Hartwich, ed., *Steyler Missionare III*, 111.

92. For more on the Confucian Religion Association, see Chen, "Confucianism Encounters Religion."

93. Gerber, *Voskamps*, 448; Töpper, "Bericht," 190; Hartwich, ed., *Steyler Missionare III*, 414.

94. Hartwich, ed., *Steyler Missionare II*, 36–37.
95. Cited in Tiedemann, ed., *Handbook*, 576.

CHAPTER FOUR   A FRACTURED LANDSCAPE

1. Burdick, *Japanese Siege of Tsingtau*, 56.
2. The siege of Qingdao was also one of the first instances of air bombardments in military history. For a detailed account of the siege, see ibid.
3. Voskamp, *Aus dem belagerten Tsingtau*, 117.
4. Ibid., 122.
5. Burdick, *Japanese Siege of Tsingtau*, 194.
6. Voskamp, *Aus dem belagerten Tsingtau*, 125. The Voskamp family met further tragedy in the war. Another son, Herbert, had traveled back to Germany in 1913 on a trip and was conscripted into the army. He died on the Eastern Front.
7. Ibid., 16–17.
8. Carl J. Voskamp, "Bericht des Missionars C. J. Voskamp in Tsingtau, Nord-China ueber die Missionsarbeit im Jahre 1920," January 26, 1921, BMW 1/6288, 318–19.
9. Mohr's quotation is cited in Kirby, *Germany and Republican China*, 17. For more on the process of missionary repatriation, see Miotk, *Missionsverständnis*, 50–51.
10. Lehmann, *Zur Zeit*, 13.
11. Knak came from a family with a long missionary pedigree. His grandfather, Gustav Knak, a famous Pomeranian pastor, was intimately involved with the Jewish mission in Berlin. Siegfried's father, Johannes Knak, was a trustee of the BMS and oversaw the China field. Since childhood, Siegfried had close ties to the BMS. After studying theology with the renowned theologian Martin Kähler in Halle, he became director of the BMS.
12. Siegfried Knak to Carl Johannes Voskamp, February 12, 1925, BMW 1/4326. For the negotiation between the Berliners and the American Lutherans about the transfer of Voskamp's salary, see ULCA 19/5/1/2, Reel 1, Negative Number 104.
13. Clements, *Faith on the Frontier*, 147.
14. Schmidlin, "Todesstoß," 191.
15. Clements, *Faith on the Frontier*, 167.
16. "Abschrift eines Teils aus dem Brief von Mr. J. H. Oldham, London, an Missionsinspektor F. Würz," July 18, 1921, BMW 1/8234.
17. Cited in Elphick, *Equality of Believers*, 224–25.
18. "Abschrift eines Teils aus dem Brief von Mr. J. H. Oldham."
19. For more on the 1910 Edinburgh conference, see Stanley, *World Missionary Conference*.
20. Cited in Tiedemann, "Shandong Missions and the Dutch Connection," 288.
21. Hartwich, ed., *Steyler Missionare III*, 538. For details on the SVD and repatriation, see ibid., 526–47.
22. For more on the SVD in the United States, see Brandewie, *In the Light of the Word*. On the SVD in Mississippi, see Namorato, *Catholic Church in Mississippi*, 165–67.

23. Hartwich, ed., *Steyler Missionare III*, 534.
24. Ibid., 536–37.
25. Sibre, *Saint-Siège*, 555–56.
26. Ibid.
27. Ibid.
28. Traditional historiography places the blame on Woodrow Wilson for "betraying" China. For a revision to this story that places more of the blame on Chinese diplomatic blunders, see Elleman, *Wilson and China*.
29. Cited in Manela, *Wilsonian Moment*, 195.
30. The literature on the New Culture Movement and the May Fourth Movement is vast. For an overview of the historiography, see Chow et al., eds., *Beyond the May Fourth Paradigm*. For classic accounts, see Chow, *May Fourth Movement;* Schwarcz, *Chinese Enlightenment;* Schwartz, *Reflections on the May Fourth Movement*. A good recent account of echoes of the May Fourth Movement in contemporary China is Mitter, *Bitter Revolution*.
31. Bays, *New History*, 107.
32. On Yenching University, see West, *Yenching University*.
33. Xing, *Baptized in the Fire of Revolution*, 23–26.
34. See Bays, *New History*, 104–6.
35. Ibid., 106–7. For more on the fundamentalist-modernist controversy, see Lian Xi, *Conversion*. For a good overview of the controversy in the United States, see Longfield, *Presbyterian Controversy*.
36. For an overview of the Chinese delegation at the Paris Peace Conferences, see MacMillan, *Paris 1919*, 323–24. For more on the fascinating life of Lu, see Keegan, "From Chancery to Cloister." For an account of Koo's time at St. John's, see Craft, *Wellington Koo*, 8–13.
37. Levenson, *Confucian China*, 23.
38. Cited in Yamamoto and Yamamoto, "II. Anti-Christian Movement," 138. See also Bays, *New History*, 107–8.
39. For Wang's quotation, see Yang, *Jidujiao wenhua*, 202. On the *True Light* magazine and its critique of the anti-Christian movement, see ibid., 153–78.
40. Ibid., 180.
41. Rawlinson, Thorburn, and MacGillvray, eds., *Chinese Church*, 32–36.
42. Latourette, *History of Christian Missions*, 801.
43. Rawlinson, Thorburn, and MacGillvray, eds. *Chinese Church*, 76.
44. Ibid., vii–viii. See also Latourette, *History of Christian Missions*, 797; Bays, *New History*, 110.
45. Latourette, *History of Christian Missions*, 797.
46. Knak, "Christliche Nationalkonferenz," 151.
47. Ibid., 150.
48. Bericht des Jahres 1922 von Miss. Sup. C. J. Voskamp. Tsingtau, Nordchina, February 13, 1923, BMW 1/6288, 356.
49. Ibid.

50. Ibid., 151. For more on Cheng's 1923 visit, see "Persönliche Einladung zu einer Zusammenkunft im Berliner Missionshaus zu Ehren des Herrn Dr. Cheng Ching Yi," June 2, 1923, BMW 1/6604, 4.
51. Siegfried Knak to Henry Hodgkin, April 7, 1924, BMW 1/6195.
52. "Missionary Opinion," October 9, 1925, BMW 1/6195.
53. Knak to Hodgkin, April 7, 1924. See also Henry Hodgkin to Siegfried Knak, May 5, 1924, BMW 1/6195. By 1938, the Xinyi Hui counted more than 40,000 congregants. See Tiedemann, ed., Handbook, 997–1004. The Lutheran alliance was the sixth largest church organization, after the Church of Christ in China (125,498), the Methodists (104,582), the China Inland Mission (89,665), the Anglicans (Holy Catholic Church of China, 73,535), and the Southern Baptist Convention (40,784).
54. For discussion about the future of a German school in Qingdao, see, e.g., Wilhelm Seufert to Johannes Witte, February 24, 1923, Zentralarchiv des Evangelische Kirche der Pfalz, Abt. 180. 1., Nr. 230. Personal enmity between Voskamp and Richard Wilhelm continued and can be seen in numerous letters in the archive.
55. Knak to Hodgkin, April 7, 1924.
56. Knak, "Christliche Nationalkonferenz," 153.
57. See Chamedes, "Vatican and the Reshaping of the European International Order," 956. Benedict's quotation of the "suicide of Europe" is cited in Young, Ecclesiastical Colony, 185.
58. See Young, Ecclesiastical Colony, 192–94. See also Chen and Jiang, Zhongfan waijiao guanxi shi, 93–106.
59. Tiedemann, ed., Handbook, 577–78. Ernest Young also devotes a significant amount of attention to Cotta and Lebbé in Ecclesiastical Colony; see in particular chapters 7–10. Claude Soetens has collected Lebbé's writings in the three-volume Recueil des archives Vincent Lebbé.
60. Other than Henninghaus the German, there were French, Dutch, and Italian bishops, representing the Paris Foreign Mission Society, the Lazarists, the Jesuits, and the Franciscans. See Young, Ecclesiastical Colony, 197.
61. Ibid.
62. Ibid., 197–98.
63. Ibid., 198.
64. Response of Augustinus Henninghaus, Yanzhoufu, November 10, 1918, Propaganda Fide, new series, Vol. 633, 190–94.
65. Pollard, Papacy, 116.
66. Benedict XV, Maximum illud, sec. 16. For more on Maximum illud, see Miotk, Missionsverständnis, as well as Young's excellent discussions of it in chapters 9 and 10 of Ecclesiastical Colony.
67. Young, Ecclesiastical Colony, 212.
68. Cited in ibid., 203.
69. Maximum illud, sec. 14, sec. 16, sec. 18.
70. Ibid., sec. 26.

71. Tiedemann, ed., *Handbook,* 584.

72. Augustin Henninghaus to Wilhelm Gier, February 25, 1931, AG 606/1931–1939. For Henninghaus's public praise of Lebbé, see Young, *Ecclesiastical Colony,* 198.

73. Hartwich, ed., *Steyler Missionare VI,* 14.

74. Tiedemann, ed., *Handbook,* 581.

75. Soetens, *Pour l'Église chinoise,* 106. See also Liu, *Ganghengyi,* 104.

76. Hartwich, ed., *Steyler Missionare V,* 285–86. For more on Costantini's interest in Chinese art, see Lawton, "Unique Style." For Costantini's own writing on art, see Costantini, *L'art chrétien.* For more on the Discipuli Domini, see Metzler, ed., *Sacrae Congregationis,* 471.

77. For more on the synods, see Metzler, *Synoden.*

78. Weig, "Erste chinesische Plenarkonzil," 3.

79. D'Elia, *Catholic Native Episcopacy,* 72. For the entire synodal proceedings, see Concilium Sinense, ed., *Primum Concilium Sinense.* See also Metzler's account in *Synoden,* 181–222.

80. Cited in Liu, *Ganghengyi,* 157. See also Metzler, *Synoden,* 205.

81. Metzler, *Synoden,* 216.

82. Ibid., 216–17.

83. For more on the Donglu image, see Clarke, *Virgin Mary,* 84–111.

84. Metzler, ed., *Sacrae Congregationis,* 467.

85. For reports and pictures of the ordinations, see "Sacre des Evêques chinois." See also Metzler, ed., *Sacrae Congregationis,* 470.

86. See, e.g., Keith, "Annam Uplifted."

87. D'Elia, *Catholic Native Episcopacy,* iii.

88. Hartwich, ed., *Steyler Missionare VI,* 439.

89. Hartwich, ed., *Steyler Missionare V,* 343.

90. Ibid. See also Weig, "Zum Konzil."

91. Hartwich, ed., *Steyler Missionare VI,* 24.

92. Bornemann, ed., *History,* 126.

CHAPTER FIVE ORDER OUT OF CHAOS

1. Weitz, *Weimar Germany,* 23.

2. Knak, *Kirche als völkerverbindende Macht,* 13–14.

3. Rade, "Present Situation," 354–56. For more on Hoffmann's milieu and the circle of free-thinking secularists to which he belonged, see Weir, *Secularism and Religion.*

4. Rade, "Present Situation," 354, 356.

5. Borg, "Volkskirche," 187.

6. Knak and Beyer, "Heimat," 4–5.

7. Out of 221 synods, about 145 belonged to the conservative alliance. The alliance consisted of "Positive Unionists," the Confessional Lutherans, and the Pietists. For more on the Old-Prussian Union and its constitution, see Borg, *Old Prussian Church;* Lessing, *Zwischen Bekenntnis und Volkskirche;* Oxenius, *Entstehung.*

8. Lehmann, *Zur Zeit*, vol. 3, 607–8.
9. On the importance of the *Volkskirche* in German missionary thought, see Yates, *Christian Missions*, 34–56.
10. Hoekendijk, *Kirche und Volk*, 119–21.
11. Ibid., 169.
12. Knak, *Zwischen Nil und Tafelbai*, 133, 142.
13. Knak, *Mission und nationale Bewegung*, 8.
14. Frick, *Nationalität und Internationalität*, 73. For a discussion of the instability of the concepts of "cultured" and "natural" peoples, see Zimmerman, *Anthropology and Antihumanism*, 169–71.
15. Frick, *Nationalität und Internationalität*, 75, 79.
16. Ibid., 149–50.
17. Connelly, *From Enemy to Brother*, 68.
18. Schmidlin, "Katholische Missionswissenschaft," 12–13.
19. See, for example, Schmidlin, "Missionsfrage."
20. Knak, *Mission und nationale Bewegung*, 8.
21. Siegfried Knak, "An alle Missionare und Missionsschwestern der Berliner Mission in Kwangtung," August 4, 1923, BMW 1/6604.
22. Translation, with slight amendments, taken from Barth, *Word of God*, 176. For the full text of the Old-Prussian church constitution, see Kraus, *Evangelische Kirchenverfassungen*, 935–84. For the entire text of the constitution in China, see "Kirchenordnung von 1922," January 12, 1929, BMW 1/6621.
23. Borg, *Old Prussian Church*, 112–13.
24. "Kirchenordnung von 1922," 18.
25. Borg, *Old Prussian Church*, 113.
26. "Kirchenordnung von 1922," 20.
27. Ibid., 20–26.
28. Heinrich Wahl, "Arbeitsbericht der Station Tschichin III. Quartal 1924," September 30, 1924, BMW 1/6254, 267.
29. Borg, *Old Prussian Church*, 111.
30. "Kirchenordnung von 1922," 20–21.
31. Ibid., 25.
32. Ibid., 19.
33. For the entire proceedings, see "Die Generalsynode," July 20, 1924, BMW 1/6620.
34. "Generalsynode," 114. See also Heinrich Wahl, "Protokoll der 1. Ordentlichen Generalsynode," July 20, 1924, BMW 1/6620, 136.
35. "Generalsynode," 114.
36. Ibid.
37. Ibid.
38. Wilhelm Spiecker to All Missionaries in China, October 25, 1924, BMW 1/6620, 152.
39. "Generalsynode 1926. Missionarskonferenz," November 5, 1926, BMW 1/6620, 160.

40. Ling Deyuan to Siegfried Knak, February 1, 1924, BMW 1/6254.
41. See Heinrich Wahl, "Bemerkungen zur Frage der Besetzung Tschichins," June 21, 1926, BMW 1/6277; "Generalsynode 1926. Missionarskonferenz," November 5, 1926, BMW 1/6620, 163.
42. "Generalsynode 1926. Missionarskonferenz," 160.
43. Siegfried Knak, "Rundbrief an sämtliche Missionare und Schwestern der Berliner Mission in China," April 20, 1926, BMW 1/6604, 50.
44. Ibid., 51–52.
45. Siegfried Knak to Ling Deyuan, October 16, 1936, BMW 1/ 6610.
46. Cited in Lian, *Redeemed by Fire*, 49.
47. Bays, *New History*, 130.
48. "Engeldienst," 81. For the quotation on "cataclysmic times," see " 'Gehet zu Joseph!,' " 35.
49. For a short biography of Gier, see Steffen, "Gier, Wilhelm, SVD."
50. Bornemann, ed., *History*, 23–24.
51. For excerpts of Gier's reports, see Hartwich, ed., *Steyler Missionare V*, 176–218. For some pictures and detailed descriptions of Gier's trip, see Hagspiel, *Along the Mission Trail*.
52. Hartwich, ed., *Steyler Missionare V*, 197.
53. Ibid., 208.
54. Ibid., 212.
55. See Namorato, *Catholic Church in Mississippi*, 42.
56. Hartwich, ed., *Steyler Missionare VI*, 219; Hartwich, ed., *Steyler Missionare V*, 211.
57. "Zwei neue Noviziat," 139.
58. Hartwich, ed., *Steyler Missionare V*, 212.
59. Hartwich, ed., *Steyler Missionare VI*, 42–43.
60. Ibid., 218–19.
61. Ibid., 220–21.
62. Ibid., 472.
63. For Henninghaus's recounting of the process of ordaining George Weig bishop, see Augustin Henninghaus to Wilhelm Gier, February 25, 1931, AG 606/1931–1939. See also Hartwich, ed., *Steyler Missionare VI*, 287–90.
64. Friedrich's letter to the SVD leadership is relayed in Henninghaus to Gier, February 25, 1931, 2820.
65. Hartwich, ed., *Steyler Missionare VI*, 289.
66. Ibid., 292–94.

CHAPTER SIX FALLING IN LOVE WITH CONFUCIUS

1. Voskamp, "Die Chinesischen Klassiker und das Evangelium," unpublished manuscript, July 1924, BMW 1/4326, sec. 21.
2. Voskamp, *Confucius und das heutige China*, 10, 6, 14, 15.
3. Ibid., 15.
4. Pieper, *Unkraut, Knospen und Blüten*, 572.
5. Ibid., 570.

6. Ibid., 577.
7. Jensen, *Manufacturing Confucianism*, 33.
8. Pieper, *Unkraut, Knospen, und Blüten*, 570.
9. Steinmetz, *Devil's Handwriting*, 389.
10. Stenz, *In der Heimat des Konfuzius*, 19.
11. Ibid., 25.
12. Steinmetz, *Devil's Handwriting*, 494.
13. For the text of the "Hun Speech," see German History in Documents and Images (GHDI), "Wilhelm II: 'Hun Speech' (1900)," http://germanhistorydocs.ghi-dc.org/sub_document.cfm?document_id=755.
14. Hamer, *Mission und Politik*, 249.
15. Steinmetz, *Devil's Handwriting*, 479–80.
16. Cited in ibid., 489.
17. Quoted in Hon, "Constancy in Change," 327.
18. Wilhelm, *Seele Chinas*, 149.
19. Marchand, "Eastern Wisdom," 348.
20. Siegfried Knak to Carl Johannes Voskamp, May 15, 1926, BMW 1/4326.
21. Voskamp, *Chinesische Prediger*, 37.
22. Voskamp, "Chinesischen Klassiker," sec. 20.
23. Ibid., sec. 11. For more on Bertrand Russell in China, see Ogden, "Sage in the Inkpot." Russell published his reflections on China in Russell, *Problem of China*.
24. Knak, "Unzeit?," 31–32.
25. Knak, "Unsere Mission in China," 25.
26. Knak, "Unzeit?," 31.
27. Hartenstein, *Kampf um Christus*.
28. Voskamp, "Chinesischen Klassiker," sec. 21.
29. Knak, *Chinesischen Christen*, 49.
30. Knak, *Säkularismus und Mission*, 25.
31. Knak, *Chinesischen Christen*, 50.
32. For exact numbers, see Tiedemann, ed., *Handbook*, 998–99.
33. For an overview of liberal Protestant publications in the 1920s, see Li Yiya, *Shengtan*. On the National Christian Literature Association of China, see Wang, "Contextualizing Protestant Publishing."
34. Wu et al., eds., "Zhenli Zhoukan," 1.
35. Zhi Xin, "Bense jiaohui," 3.
36. See, e.g., Mi, "Diyiqi," 61; Zia, *Jidujiao yu Zhongguo sixiang*, 3.
37. Knak, *Chinesischen Christen*, 22.
38. Ibid., 51.
39. For an example, see Henninghaus, "Neujahrsgruss (1932)," 73–74.
40. Mayer, "Kampf um China," 49–50.
41. Mayer, "Bunte Missionspost," 21–22.
42. Zmarzly, "Bolschewisten stürmen eine Missionsschule," 49.
43. Zmarzly, "Was wollen die Missionare?," 83.
44. Schote, "Weise Rose," 86.

45. Stenz, *In der Heimat des Konfuzius*, 183.
46. Henninghaus, "Neujahrgruss (1914)," 56.
47. The SVD got its wish in 2003, when Freinademetz was canonized alongside the founder of the society, Arnold Janssen.
48. Henninghaus, *P. Jos. Freinademetz*, 153–54.
49. Ibid., 154–55.
50. Ibid., 154–58.
51. Pötter, "Hochzeit," 246. Kong Decheng died in 2008 and was the last descendent of Confucius who earned a courtly title of "duke."
52. "Maria Jungfrau"; "Mutter, gib mir nun dein Kind"; "Und sie opferten Gold, Weihbrauch, und Myrrhen."
53. Stenz, *Twenty-Five Years in China*, 7.
54. Hermanns, "Konfuzius' Stammhalter"; Konrad, "Mein Besuch."
55. See, for example, " 'Pantschen Lama' " and Pazuke, "Wie der Buddhist in Japan seine Toten begräbt."
56. Könige, "Zu den Buddhistenmönchen," 60.
57. Sauerborn, "Besuch beim Bonzen," 240.
58. Konrad, "Mein Besuch (Schluss)," 208. See Horlemann, "Divine Word Missionaries," for an overview of the SVD's work in northwest China. For more on the SVD's work in Japan, see Bornemann, ed., *History*, 321–27. Even though the SVD had established a missionary presence in Japan as early as 1907, its work accelerated in the late 1920s: it founded a seminary in Taijimi in 1929, which served as a base for its work. The SVD's work in northwest China was established after 1922.
59. Pazuke, "Wie der Buddhist in Japan seine Toten begräbt," 273.
60. Könige, "Zu den Buddhistenmönchen," 60.
61. Carl Johannes Voskamp to Siegfried Knak, March 3, 1921, BMW 1/6553.
62. Ibid. For more on Protestant missionary views of Buddhism, see Scott, "Dharma Through a Glass Darkly."
63. Anesaki's quotation is cited in Victoria, *Zen at War*, 15. For more on the transformation of Buddhism in Japan, see Snodgrass, "Engaged Buddhism," 171. See also Ketelaar, *Of Heretics and Martyrs*. For the Buddhist critique of Christianity's compatibility with Japanese culture, see Anderson, *Christianity and Imperialism*, 41–46.
64. See Welch, *Buddhist Revival*. For the use of the term "activism," rather than "revival," see Jessup, "Householder Elite," 1–2. For more on Buddhist print culture, see also Scott, "Conversion by the Book."
65. "Schreiben junger chinesen Xen Fu Faithan–Zukunft der Kirche," n.d., BMW 1/6610.
66. Konrad, "Mein Besuch," 177.
67. Konrad, "Mein Besuch (Schluss)," 208.
68. Hermanns, "Christus oder Buddha?," 130–32.
69. Mühlbauer, "Ich will nicht Sterben," 299.
70. Hermanns, "Asiatische Übermenschen," 146–47.

71. Götsch, "Beim lebenden Buddha," 71.
72. Oehler, "Alte Missionsbefehl," 50.
73. Voskamp, "Chinesischen Klassiker," sec. 20.
74. Könige, "Zu den Buddhistenmönchen," 60.
75. Bellingröhr, "Mein erstes Begräbnis," 272.
76. Cited in Wacker, "Pearl S. Buck," 854.
77. See Lian, *Conversion of Missionaries*, 13.

CHAPTER SEVEN UNFULFILLED PROMISES

1. Cardinal Willem van Rossum to Augustin Henninghaus, December 23, 1931, AG SVD 612/1931–1958.
2. Knak, "Rundbrief an sämtliche Missionare und Schwestern der Berliner Mission in China," April 20, 1926, BMW 1/6604, 51–52; Heinrich Wahl, "Jahresbericht der Station Tschichin (Chihing für 1925)," January 1, 1926, BMW 1/6255.
3. Lin Lifang, *Nanxiong Zhuji fangyan zhi*, 2.
4. Shixing xian difangzhi bianzuan weiyuanhui, ed., *Shixing xianzhi*, 1.
5. James Scott writes about these mountain people in the "Zomia" region, which runs throughout southern China. See Scott, *Art of Not Being Governed*.
6. For more on the upwardly mobile elites in Hong Kong, see Smith, *Chinese Christians*.
7. Ling Deyuan, "Tagebuch Tschichin pro Quartal 1923," March 30, 1923, BMW 1/6255, 240; see also Wahl, "Jahresbericht (1925)."
8. Karl Zehnel, "Bericht Namyung für das Vierteljahr Juli–Okt. 1927," November 12, 1927, BMW 1/6238.
9. Ibid.
10. Heinrich Wahl, "Arbeitsbericht der Station Tsichin," June 30, 1925, BMW 1/6255.
11. Heinrich Wahl to Siegfried Knak, February 1, 1924, BMW 1/6254, 261.
12. Bays, *New History*, 111–12. For more on the May Thirtieth Movement, as well as labor protests in Shanghai, see Perry, *Shanghai on Strike*.
13. Ling Deyuan, "Bericht des Pastor Lin Det En," July 8, 1926, BMW 1/6238.
14. Esherick, *Origins of the Boxer Uprising*, 2.
15. Ibid., 22.
16. Li, *Fighting Famine*, 283.
17. Tiedemann, "Communist Revolution," 138.
18. For more on the Red Spear associations, see Perry, *Rebels and Revolutionaries*. See also Tiedemann, "Communist Revolution," 137–38.
19. Van de Ven, *From Friend to Comrade*, 241; Saich and Yang, eds., *Rise to Power*, li. For more on Communist activities in Guangdong, see Chan, "Communists in Rural Guangdong."
20. Karl Zehnel, "Bericht Namjung," July 4, 1927, BMW 1/6238.
21. Ibid.
22. Chan, "Communists in Rural Guangdong," 78.

23. Ling Deyuan, "Bericht Tschichin vom 3. Vierteljahr 1927," January 14, 1928, BMW 1/6255; Ling Deyuan, "Bericht-Tschichin vom 2. Vierteljahr 1929," July 29, 1929, BMW 1/6255.

24. Karl Zehnel, "Vortrag: Kommunismus und Mission in China," February 1931, BMW 1/6608.

25. Ibid.

26. See Nedostup, *Superstitious Regimes*.

27. Zehnel, "Vortrag." For more on the National Revolutionary Army's activities, see Klein, "Anti-Imperialism at Grassroots," 294.

28. Litten, "Myth of the 'Turning-Point,' " 7. On the Nationalist campaigns in Guangdong, see also Fitzgerald, "Warlords, Bullies, and State Building."

29. Ling Deyuan, "Jahresbericht 1931," January 28, 1932, BMW 1/6255.

30. Ibid.

31. Ling Deyuan, "Bericht Tschichin des. P. Lin det en über die 3. u. 4. Quartal," January 15, 1929, BMW 1/6255. See also Friedrich Richter, "Bericht über das IV. Quartal 1932," January 7, 1933, BMW 1/6255; Karl Zehnel, "Bericht—Namyung. über das dritte Vierteljahr 1929," October 4, 1929, BMW 1/6238.

32. See Klein, "Anti-Imperialism at Grassroots," 297–99.

33. Perry, *Rebels and Revolutionaries*, 213–24.

34. Joseph Weiss to Joseph Kretschmer, January 20, 1928, AG 606/1925–1930, 3049–50. The collection of SVD correspondence about the incident begins in AG 606/1925–1930, 3046 and ends around p. 3080. Who constituted the Wandaohui? Later Communist historiography has claimed that the incident was the earliest revolutionary insurrection in Shandong Province and that the Communists had been organizing peasant associations as well as establishing contact with local Red Spear associations in Yanggu. But by all accounts, the connection between the Communists and the bandit leaders was tenuous. Contemporary accounts denied any links between the Communists and the Red Spears. One of the SVD priests who had been held captive described the bandits as "outsiders" who came from neighboring villages. He felt pity for them: the group had been forcibly recruited into the army of the warlord Zhang Zuolin, who had refused to pay them. According to the priest, the bandits were motivated by desperation, not ideology. Also see Tiedemann, "Communist Revolution," 143.

35. Anton Wewel to Augustin Henninghaus, January 23, 1928, AG 606/1925–1930, 3052–53.

36. Ibid., 3052.

37. Wilhelm Gier to Augustin Henninghaus, March 2, 1928, AG 606/1925–1930, 3078.

38. Karl Weber and Johannes Dahmen, "Kriegsschrecken vor den Toren Tsaochowfu's," May 1928, AG 606/1925–1930, 3081–82.

39. Ibid., 3086.

40. Ibid.

41. The entire episode is also recounted in Leopold Kade to Josef Grendel, September 2, 1938a, AG 612/1931–1958.

42. Cardinal Willem van Rossum to Augustin Henninghaus, December 23, 1931, AG 612/1931–1958, 4451.

43. Krins, "Wie Kardinal Tien," 350.

44. Fleckner, *Thomas Kardinal Tien*, 39.

45. Krins, "Wie Kardinal Tien," 351. Chao was a child from the congregation in which Richard Henle and Franz Nies were murdered in 1897. He was ordained in 1909 and served for many years as a deacon in Jining. See Hartwich, ed., *Steyler Missionare II*, 370, and for reports of his ordination, 401–2.

46. Leopold Kade to Josef Grendel, September 2, 1938, AG 612/1931–1958, 4569; Krins, "Wie Kardinal Tien," 351.

47. Kade to Grendel, September 2, 1938, 4570. For the complete chronology of the ordination, see the series of correspondence in AG 612/1931–1958, 4469–4477.

48. Krins, "Wie Kardinal Tien," 351–52.

49. Thomas Tien to Josef Grendel, August 9, 1934, AG 612/1931–1958.

50. Karl Gramatte to Siegfried Knak, February 8, 1932, BMW 1/6608.

51. Siegfried Knak, "An Alle unsere Mitarbeiter in Afrika und China," Advent 1931, BMW 1/15, 14.

52. Siegfried Knak, "Rundbrief an alle Mitarbeiter auf den Missionsfeldern," October 1932, BMW 1/15, 46; Schmitt to Siegfried Knak, October 23, 1933, BMW 1/6538.

53. Siegfried Knak to Missionar Killus, Waichow, August 23, 1934, BMW 1/6609.

54. Bergen, *Twisted Cross*, 10.

55. Siegfried Knak to Lotti Kohls, March 16, 1935, BMW 1/3509.

56. Ibid.

57. Ev. Gemeindekirchenrat von St. Nikolai to Siegfried Knak, August 8, 1935, BMW 1/6609.

58. Siegfried Knak to Ev. Gemeindekirchenrat, August 12, 1935, BMW 1/6609.

59. The Committee to the German General Consulate in Canton, October 19, 1934, BMW 1/6609.

60. For more on the *Devisenstellen*, see Ellis, "German Exchange Control."

61. The Committee to the Gesamt Wirtschafts-Rat, Südafrika, z. Hd. Herrn Superintendenten Wedepohl, Superintendenten bezw. Missionarskonferenz d. Ostafrika-Synoden, Herrn Superintenden Oelke, Canton, October 9, 1934, BMW 1/6609.

62. "Niederschrift der G. S. A. Sitzung von 15.–16. Oktober 1934," October 16, 1934, BMW 1/6609.

63. Georg Weig to Josef Grendel, October 3, 1935, AG 616, 4182.

64. Hartwich, ed., *Johann Weig*, 130.

65. Ibid., 205.

66. Josef Grendel to Heinrich Meyer, February 29, 1936, AG 616.

67. Cardinal Pietro Fumasoni-Biondi to Josef Grendel, January 11, 1938, AG 612/1931–1958.

68. Lehmann, *Zur Zeit*, 146.

69. Missionar Killus to Siegfried Knak, March 19, 1936, BMW 1/6610.

70. Alfred Oelke to Siegfried Knak, December 12, 1935b, BMW 1/6609.

71. Lehmann, *Zur Zeit*, 150–51; Alfred Oelke to Siegfried Knak, December 12, 1935a, BMW 1/6609.

72. For good overviews of the Second Sino-Japanese War, see Hsiung and Levine, *China's Bitter Victory*, and Mitter, *Forgotten Ally*. A good account of the Rape of Nanjing can be found in Mitter, *Forgotten Ally*, 124–44. For more on the Japanese operations in Guangdong, see Lee, *Britain and the Sino-Japanese War*, 149–50. The estimate of half a million dead from the flooding comes from Mitter, *Forgotten Ally*, 163.

73. For an example of this type of report, see Ma Dajing, "Bericht ueber das 1. Quartal 1938," July 27, 1938, BMW 1/6239.

74. Georg Kohls to Charles Luther Boynton, May 22, 1940, BMW 1/6611.

75. Hartwich, ed., *Johann Weig*, 194, 204.

76. Augustin Olbert to Josef Grendel, November 10, 1941, AG 616, 4308.

77. Josef Grendel to Augustin Olbert, June 25, 1942, AG 616, 4309–10.

78. Josef Grendel to Celso Costantini, October 16, 1942, AG 616, 4317. See also Sibre, *Le Saint-Siege*, 495.

79. Grendel to Costantini, November 19, 1942, AG 616.

80. Thomas Tian to Josef Grendel, November 15, 1943, AG 616, 4329–31.

81. Hartwich, ed., *Johann Weig*, 251.

82. For more on the decision to make Tian the first Chinese Cardinal, see Sibre, *Saint-Siège*, 187–89. Sibre argues that Tian was a compromise candidate, as the Propaganda was reluctant to consecrate the much more outspoken and politically controversial Yu Bin. Instead, in the relatively obscure Tian, it found a more "neutral candidate."

83. See Daniel Nelson, "A Detailed Survey of the Berlin Mission in South China," 1946, BMW 1/6612.

84. Ling Deyuan to Siegfried Knak, May 23, 1947, BMW 1/6612.

85. For details of the conflict, see letters such as Lan Ti'en to Siegfried Knak, June 1, 1947, BMW 1/6612. Correspondence continues in BMW 1/6612.

86. Ibid.

87. Georg Kohls, "Auszug aus einem Brief von Miss. Kohls," January 21, 1947, BMW 1/6612.

88. See Ling Deyuan to Siegfried Knak, August 14, 1947, BMW 1/6612.

89. Siegfried Knak to Ling Deyuan, August 17, 1947, BMW 1/6612, 68–69.

90. Georg Kohls, "Auszug aus einem Brief von Miss. Kohls"; Siegfried Knak to Georg Kohls, November 3, 1948, BMW 1/6612, 181.

91. See, e.g., Tiedemann, ed., *Handbook*, 571. See also Paton, "First Thoughts."

92. For more on these indigenous church groups, see Lian, *Redeemed by Fire*.

CHAPTER EIGHT   FRUITS OF THE SPIRIT

1. Ling, *Changing Role*, 150. For the complete text of the manifesto, see Merwin and Jones, eds., *Documents of the Three-Self Movement*, 19–20.

2. Quoted in Gao, "Y. T. Wu," 344.

3. For an overview of this literature, see chapter 7 in Bays, *New History*. For more on Wang Mingdao and Watchman Nee, see Lian Xi, *Redeemed by Fire*. See also Liao, *God Is Red*, for examples of contemporary criticism of the Patriotic Church in China. For more on the "control-and-resistance paradigm," see Dunch, "Christianity and 'Adaptation,' " 155–56.

4. See Dunch, "Christianity and 'Adaptation,' " 156. For a defense of the Patriotic Church, see Wickeri, *Seeking the Common Ground*. For more on Wu, see Gao, "Y. T. Wu." For a biography of Ding, see Wickeri, *Reconstructing Christianity*. On Zhao, see Glüer, *Christliche Theologie*.

5. Chen Yuan, "Ziwo jiantao," 613.

6. Lindenfeld and Richardson, eds., *Beyond Conversion and Syncretism*, 7–8.

7. The sections on Chen Yuan in this chapter appeared in an earlier form in Wu, "Catholic Universities."

8. Shaoguan shi zhengxie xuexi he wenshi ziliao weiyuanhui, ed., *Shaoguan wenshi ziliao*, 115.

9. Chen Zhichao, ed., *Chen Yuan laiwang shuxinji*, 806.

10. Ling's final examination can be found in August Kollecker, "Protokoll über das Examen von 3 Seminaristen am 21. April 1906," April 21, 1906, BMW 1/886.

11. Karl Zehnel to Siegfried Knak, July 6, 1926, BMW 1/4458.

12. Ling's ordination papers can be found in BMW 1/882, BMW 1/885, and BMW 1/888.

13. Chen Yuan, "Xin zhengfu," 434.

14. Chen Yuan, "Shijü zhi kelü," 437. For the best work on political factions immediately after the 1911 revolution, see Young, *Politics*.

15. Zarrow, *China in War and Revolution*, 78.

16. For more on the Confucian Religion Association, see Chen Hsi-yuan, "Confucianism Encounters Religion."

17. There is significant academic debate over Chen Yuan's personal faith. In his later life, Chen claimed that he had never been a serious Christian and had attended church only for social reasons. Most research has concluded, however, that Chen was baptized. See Liu Xian, "On Chen Yuan's Study of Religions."

18. Chen Yuan, "Yuan yelikewen kao," 8.

19. Ibid., 57.

20. Ibid., 37–39.

21. See Hsiao Chi-Ching, "Tui chen chuxin de shixuejia Chen Yuan," 113.

22. For an overview of Chen Yuan's complete publication history, see the appendix in Liu Naihe, ed., *Chen Yuan nianpu*, 861–919.

23. Chen Yuan, "Yesu jidu renzi shiyi xu," 406–7.

24. Chen Yuan, "Yuan xiyu ren huahua kao," 212. For the English translation, see Chen Yuan, *Western and Central Asians in China*.

25. Chen, "Yuan xiyu ren huahua kao," 221.

26. Chen Yuan, "Jidujiao ruhua shi," 477.

27. Chen Yuan, "Jidujiao ruhua shilue," 462.

28. Ibid., 463–65.

29. Chen, *Rise and Fall of Fu Ren University*, 113. By 1947, the university had more than twenty-three hundred students and was the second-largest university in Beijing, after Beijing University.
30. Joseph Murphy to Josef Grendel, February 15, 1935, AG 641/1934–1935; Murphy to Grendel, March 17, 1935, AG 641/1934–1935.
31. Josef Grendel to Joseph Murphy, April 8, 1935, AG 641/1934–1935.
32. For a history and biography of Biallas, see Kollár, *Leben im Konflikt*.
33. The journal is still one of the most influential journals in Sinology today. For a translation of Chen's pioneering work on the Chinese Jesuit painter Wu Yushan, see Chen Yuan, "Wu Yü-shan."
34. For more on the attempt to establish the institute, see Kollár, *Leben im Konflikt*, 128–33. An institute of oriental studies was eventually created in 1961, when Fu Ren was reopened in Taiwan.
35. Flyers for these exhibitions were distributed widely and mailed to invite various eminent professors to attend. See "The Fourth Exhibition of Chinese Christian Art at the Catholic University of Peking. May 27th to 29th. 1939," May 19, 1939, AG 641/1938–1939. For a collection of paintings of the Madonna and child, see Pettus, ed., *Christian Sacred Pictures*.
36. Heinrich Kroes, "Der erste Heimkehrtag der Katholischen Universität in Peking," n.d., AG 641/1938–1939, 7852.
37. Zehnel to Knak, July 6, 1926.
38. Ibid.
39. Ibid.
40. "Niederschrift über die G. S. A. Sitzung am 19. Juni 1935," June 19, 1935, BMW 1/6609.
41. Ling Deyuan, "Bericht des Pastor Lin Tet En," July 30, 1936, BMW 1/6543, 63–64.
42. Ibid., 59.
43. Shaoguan shi zhengxie xuexi he wenshi ziliao weiyuanhui, ed., *Shaoguan wenshi ziliao*, 117.
44. For more on the Second United Front, see Shum, *The Chinese Communists' Road to Power*.
45. Shaoguan shi zhengxie xuexi he wenshi ziliao weiyuanhui, ed., *Shaoguan wenshi ziliao*, 117.
46. Lutz, *China and the Christian Colleges*, 363–66. For more on Fu Ren as a neutral space during the war, see Liu Naihe, ed., *Liyun chengxuelu*, 64.
47. See Hsu and Zhang, *History of the Sino-Japanese War*, 221–30. For eyewitness accounts of the battle, see Zhongguo renmin zhengzhi xieshang huiyi quanguo weiyuanhui wenshi ziliao yanjiu weiyuanhui, ed., *Xuzhou huizhan*.
48. "Anlage zum Bericht Nr. 439 der Botschaft in Hankow vom 17. June d. J.," June 13, 1938, Peking II. R 3499, Politisches Archiv des Auswärtigen Amts (PA AA). For the entire incident, see Oskar Trautmann, "Schließung der Mittelschule der Katholischen Universität in Peping," June 17, 1938, Peking II. R 3499, PA AA. For Rahmann's description of the diplomatic crises, see Rudolf Rahmann

to Josef Grendel, July 23, 1938, AG 641/1938–1939. For a complete list of the events to which the missionary leaders invited the Japanese, see "Chronik der Katholischen Universität Peking," n.d., AG 641/1938–1939.

49. "Understanding between Dr. Rudolph Rahmann of the Catholic University and Rokuzo Yaguchi of the Japanese Embassy," July 12, 1938, AG 641/1938–1939. The same document was also forwarded to the German Embassy in China. The document can be found in "Understanding between Dr. Rudolph Rahmann of the Catholic University and Rokuzo Yaguchi of the Japanese Embassy," July 12, 1938, Peking II. R 9208/3499: Deutsche Botschaft China. Katholische Universität in Peking. Politisches Archiv des Auswärtigen Amtes. For Chen's defense of Fu Ren's wartime experience, see Chen, "Ziwo jiantao," 616. To compare the SVD's wartime behavior to how John Leighton Stuart and Yenching University handled similar dilemmas, see Shaw, *American Missionary in China*, 109–42. For more on the Xinmin Hui, see Boyle, *China and Japan at War*, 92–95.

50. A number of such cases are collected in Juanmin: Zhengzhilei [Political Files] 657 in Beiping Furen Daxue dangan ziliao (1925–1952) [Beijing Fu Ren University Archives, 1925–1952], Fu Jen Catholic University History Office (FJCUHO). See, e.g., "Fuda Zhang Xinpei, Gao Tiehou dengren youguan hanjian tewu wenti gei fayuan de zhengming [Letter to the Higher Court of Hebei Stating that Gao Tiehou is suspected to be a spy of the Japanese yet no witness could be found]," July 20, 1946, FJCUHO: Political Files 657. For Chen's defense of himself, see Yuan to the Higher Court of Hebei, August 8, 1946, FJCUHO: Political Files 657. For more context on Chinese "collaboration" with Japanese authorities, see Brook, *Collaboration*.

51. Liu, *Chen Yuan nianpu*, 517. For more on student protests across China, see Lutz, *China and the Christian Colleges*, especially chapter 11, "Civil Conflict and the Politicizing of College Youth."

52. Harold Rigney, "Monthly Report for August 1946: Diary," October 1, 1946, AG 641/1943–1947, 8141, 8138.

53. Ibid., 8141.

54. For more on the tribunals in Shanghai and Beijing, see Pepper, *Civil War in China*, 76–77.

55. Harold Rigney to Aloysius Kappenberg, August 30, 1948, AG 641/1948; Liu, ed., *Liyun chengxuelu*, 64.

56. Rigney to Kappenberg, August 30, 1948.

57. Pastor Wedel to Alfred Oelke, March 1, 1950, BMW 1/6613.

58. Rowland M. Cross, "Overseas Newsletter V.," June 13, 1950, BMW 1/6613, 243.

59. Ibid., 249.

60. Shaoguan shi zhengxie xuexi he wenshi ziliao weiyuanhui, ed., *Shaoguan wenshi ziliao*, 117.

61. Shixing xian difangzhi bianzuan weiyuanhui, ed., *Shixing xianzhi*, 964.

62. Liu, *Chen Yuan nianpu*, 534–35.

63. Chen Yuan, "Ziwo jiantao," 613, 614, 626.

64. Yeh, *Shanghai Splendor,* 9.
65. See Henrietta Harrison's powerful argument in *Missionary's Curse,* 8–10.
66. Cited in Chen Tushou, "Chen Yuan xiaozhang rudang."
67. Cited in Liu Xiaosheng, "Shou ze duoru."

CONCLUSION
1. Paton, "First Thoughts," 33, 34, 38.
2. See Lambert, "Counting Christians," for a discussion of the discrepancies between official statistics and evangelical estimates. Most scholars accept the numbers cited by the Pew Forum of sixty-seven million Christians, or 5 percent of the total population. See Pew Forum, *Global Christianity,* 97–99. See also Wenzel-Teuber, "2012 Statistical Update." One of the most vocal evangelical groups that produces constant reports of Chinese state persecution is the China Aid Association, which funds underground house churches and offers legal aid to Chinese Christians.
3. On how underground churches serve to reinforce patriotism, see Koesel, "China's Patriotic Pentecostals."
4. See Cao, *Constructing China's Jerusalem,* 4–8.
5. Liao Yiwu, *God Is Red,* 222. For more on the contemporary religious revival in China, see Yang, *Religion in China;* Goossaert and Palmer, *Religious Question.*
6. See Johnson, "Church-State Clash."
7. Madsen, "Catholic Revival," 472; Yang, "Red, Black, and Gray Markets," 105.
8. Bays, "Chinese Protestant Christianity Today," 495.
9. Madsen, "Catholic Revival," 476.
10. The World Council of Churches issued its statement first, in 1961. See Uzzell, "Don't Call It Proselytism."
11. For the mission statement of the Berliner Missionswerk, see Berliner Missionswerk, "Berliner Missionswerk—in weltweiter Partnerschaft verbunden," http://www.berliner-missionswerk.de/ueber-uns.html. For a somewhat cheery view of the history of the Evangelisches Missionswerk, see Dutz, "Mission verpflichtet."
12. Gaillardetz, *Church in the Making,* 72.
13. Elmer Miller argued in 1970 that missionaries were agents of secularization in the lands that they encountered; I am arguing that missionary work secularized Europe. See Miller, "Christian Missionary."
14. McLeod, *Secularisation in Western Europe,* 4. The literature on secularization is its own cottage industry. For a good, balanced overview, see Swatos and Christiano, "Introduction—Secularization Theory." For a more sustained exploration of the literature, see Martin, *On Secularization.* For comparisons between America and Europe, see Berger, Davie, and Fokas, eds., *Religious America, Secular Europe?;* Brown, Snape, and McLeod, eds., *Secularisation in the Christian World.* For an attack on secularization theory, see Stark, "Secularization, R.I.P." For a defense of the utility of the concept, see Bruce, *God Is Dead,* and Bruce, *Secularization.*

15. Cox, "Towards Eliminating the Concept of Secularisation," 17.

16. Taylor, *Secular Age*, 3.

17. Chaves, "Secularization as Declining Religious Authority," 750.

18. This position has been shown in Gauchet, *Disenchantment of the World, and* Berger, *Sacred Canopy.*

19. Sprenger, "Moral Education in Taiwan," 172.

20. Cited in Steinmetz, *Devil's Handwriting*, 417.

21. This widening gulf is most clearly discussed in Jenkins, *Next Christendom.*

22. Sanneh and Carpenter, eds., *Changing Face,* 220. For a good report on the 2008 Lambeth Conference, see Butt, "Lambeth Conference."

23. See Sebald, *Rings of Saturn,* 19.

24. Georg Kohls, "Lebenslauf," June 24, 1905, BMW 1/3506, 7.

25. Lotti Kohls produced a travelogue detailing their trip; see Kohls, *Erlebnisse.*

26. Georg Kohls to Johannes Müller, August 29, 1938, BMW 1/3509.

27. Alfred Oelke to Siegfried Knak, April 24, 1936, BMW 1/6610.

28. Kohls to Müller, August 29, 1938.

GLOSSARY

Anesaki Masaharu　姉崎　正治
Bagua jiao　八卦教
Bense jiaohui　本色教會
Cai Yuanpei　蔡元培
Chen Duxiu　陳獨秀
Cheng Jingyi　誠靜怡
Chen Yuan　陳垣
Chuanjiao yaogui　傳教要規
Dadaohui　大刀會
Dagongbao　大公報
Daijiazhuang　戴家莊
Dai Jitao　戴季陶
Ding Guangxun　丁光訓
Dongfang Zazhi　東方雜誌
Donglu　東閭
Feng Yuxiang　馮玉祥
Fudan　復旦
Fumushi　副牧師
Fu Ren　輔仁
Guangming Ribao　光明日報
Guomindang　國民黨
Hanjian　漢奸
Huahua　華化
Huayi xuezhi　華裔學志
Huizhou　惠州

Hu Jintao　胡錦濤
Hu Shi　胡適
Jiangxue She　講學社
Jiao'an　教案
Jiaozhou Bay　膠州灣
Jining　濟寧
Juye　巨野
Kang Youwei　康有為
Kita Seiichi　喜多　誠一
Kong Decheng　孔德成
Kongjiao Hui　孔教會
Kong Lingyi　孔令貽
Lan Ti'en　藍體恩
Liang Qichao　梁啟超
Liao Yiwu　廖亦武
Li Dazhao　李大釗
Ling Deyuan　凌德淵
Liu Tingfang　劉廷芳
Lukeng　鹿坑
Lu Zhengxiang　陸徵祥
Ma Dajing　馬達經
Mao Zedong　毛澤東
Ma Xiangbo　馬相伯
Moxiang Baojian　默想寶鑑
Nanling　南嶺

Nanxiong   南雄
Niu Huiqing   牛會卿
Qingdao   青島
Qingnian Jinbu   青年進步
Qufu   曲阜
Renmin Ribao   人民日報
Ruxue   儒學
Sanzijing   三字經
Shengjiao Zazhi   聖教雜誌
Shengming she   生命社
Shengming yuekan   生命月刊
Shijing   詩經
Shishi Huabao   時事畫報
Shishixiacun   獅石下村
Shixing   始興
Shuji   書記
Song Jiaoren   宋教仁
Taixu   太虛
Taiyuan   太原
Tan River   潭江
Tiandihui   天地會
Tian Gengxin   田耕莘
Wandaohui   萬刀會
Wang Jingwei   汪精衛
Wei Enbo   魏恩波
Wenshe   文社
Wu Leichuan   吳雷川
Wu Yaozong   吳耀宗
Xianzhang   縣長
Xinhui County   新會縣

Xinmin Hui   新民會
Xi River   西江
Xu Guangqi   徐光啟
Yanggu   陽穀
Yang Wenhui   楊文會
Yan Xishan   閻錫山
Yanzhou   兗州
Yenching University   燕京大學
Yihe quan   義和拳
Yijing   易經
Ying Lianzhi   英斂之
Yu Rizhang   余日章
Yuan Shikai   袁世凱
Yuan Xiyuren Huahua Kao   元西域人
    華化考
Yuan Yelikewen Kao   元也里可溫考
Zhangjiazhuang   張家莊
Zhang Xiuwen   張秀文
Zhang Zhiyi   張志一
Zhao Zichen   趙紫宸
Zhendan Daxue   震旦大學
Zhenli Zhoukan   真理周刊
Zhiguo   治國
Zhongguo Tongmenghui   中國同盟會
Zhonghua Jidujiao Wenshe   中華基督
    教文社
Zhonghua Shengmu   中華聖母
Zhonghua Xinyi Hui   中華信義會
Zhou Enlai   周恩來

BIBLIOGRAPHY

ARCHIVES CONSULTED

Germany

BERLIN

Evangelisches Landeskirchliches Archiv in Berlin
   Archiv des Berliner Missionswerks
      BMW 1/15: Rundschreiben an alle Superintendenten und Missionare, 1931–1936.
      BMW 1/882: Missionsgehilfen in China. Miscellanea.
      BMW 1/884: Gehilfen in China.
      BMW 1/885: Gehilfen in China/Oberland.
      BMW 1/886: Missionsgehilfen, Examen.
      BMW 1/888: Examen und Ordination der Gehilfen.
      BMW 1/890: Gehilfenkonferenzen in China/Oberland.
      BMW 1/3506–1/3509: Kohls, Georg. Bd. 1–Bd. 4.
      BMW 1/4326: Voskamps, Personalia.
      BMW 1 / 4458: Zehnel, Karl. Missionar.
      BMW 1/6195: National Christian Council, Bd. 1.
      BMW 1/6237–1/6239: Berichte der Missionsstation Namchiung, Bd. 1–Bd. 3.
      BMW 1/6253–1/6255: Berichte der Missionsstation Tschichin, Bd. 1–Bd. 3.
      BMW 1/6277: Tschichin.
      BMW 1/6288: Tsingtau West, Bd. 2.
      BMW 1/6530: Synode China.
      BMW 1/6537–1/6538: Synode Süd China, Bd. 15–Bd. 16.
      BMW 1/6547: Acta betreffend: Konferenz Kreis Nord-China Kiautschou 1898–1903.

BMW 1/6602–1/6613: China Allgemeines, Bd. 1–Bd. 8.

BMW 1/6620–1/6621: Generalsynode in China, Bd. 1–Bd. 2.

BMW 1/8234: Deutscher Evangelischer Missionsausschuss Krieg, Bd. 6.

Politisches Archiv des Auswärtigen Amtes

    Peking II. Akten der Botschaft in China.

    R 3499 Katholische Universität in Peking, Bd. 1 (1934–1938).

    R 3503 Katholische Universität in Peking, Bd. 2 (1944–1945).

SPEYER

Zentralarchiv der Evangelischen Kirche der Pfalz

    Abt. 180. 01. Deutsche Ostasienmission.

    Nr. 230. Korrespondenz mit Missionar Wilhelm Seufert.

    Korrespondenz mit der Mission in Tsingtau (1923–1926).

Italy

ROME

Archivium Generalatus Societatis Verbi Divini

    AG 605. Regione di Shantung Meridonalis.

    AG 606. Vicariato di Shantung Meridonalis.

    AG 612. Vicariato Apostolico di Tsaochowfu.

    AG 616. Vicariato Apostolico di Tsingtao.

    AG 640. Casa SVD a Peking.

    AG 641. Univerità di Peking.

    AG 642. Procura di Shanghai.

Taiwan

TAIPEI

Fu Jen Catholic University History Office

    Political Files 649, 1929–1936.

    Political Files 652, 1944–1948.

    Political Files 657, 1946–1947.

United States

ELK GROVE VILLAGE, ILLINOIS

Evangelical Lutheran Church in America Archives

    ULCA 19/5/1/2: United Lutheran Church of America. Board of Missions.
        Secretary of Asia-China. Minutes, Correspondence, Subject Files 1922–1959,
        Reel 1.

Vatican City

Archivio Storico, Congregazione per l'Evangelizzazione dei Popoli o "de Propaganda
    Fide" (Propaganda Fide)

    New Series, Volume 633.

NEWSPAPERS AND MAGAZINES

Allgemeine Missionszeitschrift
Berliner Missionsberichte
Chinese Recorder
Christliche Welt, Die
Da Gongbao 大公報
Jiaohui Xinbao 教會新報
Katholischen Missionen, Die
Missions Catholiques, Les
Shengjiao Zazhi 聖教雜誌
Steyler Missionsbote
Wenshe Yuekan 文社月刊
Yishibao 益世報
Zeitschrift für Missionswissenschaft
Zhenli Zhoukan 真理周刊

PRINTED PRIMARY SOURCES AND SECONDARY SOURCES

Anderson, Emily. *Christianity and Imperialism: Empire for God.* London: Bloomsbury, 2014.

Aubert, Roger. "The Catholic Church at the End of the Eighteenth Century." In *The Church Between Revolution and Restoration,* edited by Roger Aubert, Johannes Beckmann, Patrick J. Corish, and Rudolf Lill, 3–10. New York: Crossroad, 1981.

"Auferstehen, aber zuvor leiden." *Kleiner Herz-Jesu-Bote* 1, no. 4 (1874): 27–28.

"Avant-propos." *Annales de l'Association de la propagation de la foi* 1, no. 1 (1827): 3–6.

Axmann, Rainer. "Lebensabriss des E. Faber." *Jahrbuch der Coburger Landesstiftung* 34 (1989): 393–422.

Bade, Klaus J. *Friedrich Fabri und der Imperialismus in der Bismarckzeit: Revolution, Depression, Expansion.* Freiburg im Breisgau: Atlantis-Verlag, 1975.

Baldwin, S. L. "Self-Support of the Native Church." In Yates, Nelson, and Barrett, eds., *Records of the General Conference of the Protestant Missionaries of China,* 283–94.

Barth, Karl. *The Word of God and Theology.* Translated by Amy Marga. London: T & T Clark, 2011.

Bays, Daniel H. "Chinese Protestant Christianity Today." *China Quarterly* 174, no. 2 (2003): 488–504.

———, ed. *Christianity in China: From the Eighteenth Century to the Present.* Stanford, CA: Stanford University Press, 1996.

———. *A New History of Christianity in China.* Malden, MA: Wiley-Blackwell, 2012.

Bays, Daniel H., and Grant Wacker, eds. *The Foreign Missionary Enterprise at Home: Explorations in North American Cultural History.* Tuscaloosa: University of Alabama Press, 2003.

Bellingröhr, Heinrich. "Mein erstes Begräbnis in China." *Steyler Missionsbote* 67, no. 10 (July 1940): 270–72.

Benedict XV. *Maximum illud: Apostolic Letter on the Propagation of the Faith Throughout the World.* November 30, 1919. Translated by Thomas J. M. Burke. Divine Word Missionaries, Mission Encyclicals. http://www.svdcuria.org/public/mission/docs/encycl/mi-en.htm.

Benedict XVI. "To Brazilian Bishops: Society Thirsts for Spirituality." CatholicCulture.org http://www.catholicculture.org/culture/library/view.cfm?recnum=9108.

———. *What It Means to Be a Christian: Three Sermons.* Translated by Henry Taylor. San Francisco: Ignatius Press, 2006.

Bennett, Adrian A. *Missionary Journalist in China: Young J. Allen and His Magazines, 1860–1883.* Athens: University of Georgia Press, 1983.

Bennette, Rebecca Ayako. *Fighting for the Soul of Germany: The Catholic Struggle for Inclusion After Unification.* Cambridge, MA: Harvard University Press, 2012.

Bergen, Doris L. *Twisted Cross: The German Christian Movement in the Third Reich.* Chapel Hill: University of North Carolina Press, 1996.

Berger, Peter L. *The Sacred Canopy: Elements of a Sociological Theory of Religion.* Garden City, NY: Doubleday, 1967.

Berger, Peter L., Grace Davie, and Effie Fokas, eds. *Religious America, Secular Europe?: A Theme and Variation.* Burlington, VT: Ashgate, 2008.

Bericht des Missions-Verein für China in Berlin. Umfassend die Jahre 1850–1854. Berlin: Wiegandt und Grieben, 1854.

Best, Jeremy. "Godly, International, and Independent: German Protestant Missionary Loyalties Before World War I." *Central European History* 47 (2014): 585–611.

Bettray, Johannes. "Arnold Janssen und der chinesische Klerus." *Verbum* 2 (1960): 98–100.

Bigler, Robert M. *The Politics of German Protestantism: The Rise of the Protestant Church Elite in Prussia, 1815–1848.* Berkeley: University of California Press, 1972.

Blackbourn, David. "The Catholic Church in Europe Since the French Revolution. A Review Article." *Comparative Studies in Society and History* 33, no. 4 (1991): 778–90.

———. *Marpingen: Apparitions of the Virgin Mary in Bismarckian Germany.* Oxford: Oxford University Press, 1993.

Blumhofer, Edith Waldvogel, and Randall Herbert Balmer. *Modern Christian Revivals.* Urbana: University of Illinois Press, 1993.

Boetzinger, Vera. *"Den Chinesen ein Chinese werden": Die deutsche protestantische Frauenmission in China 1842–1952.* Stuttgart: Steiner, 2004.

Bogner, Artur. "Zur Entwicklung der Berliner Mission als Bürokratisierungsprozess." In *Weltmission und religiöse Organisationen. Protestantische Missionsgesellschaften im 19. und 20. Jahrhundert,* edited by Artur Bogner, Bernd Holtwick, and Hartmann Tyrell, 313–53. Würzburg: Ergon, 2004.

Borg, Daniel R. *The Old Prussian Church and the Weimar Republic: A Study in Political Adjustment, 1917–1927.* Hanover, NH: University Press of New England, 1984.

———. "Volkskirche, 'Christian State' and the Weimar Republic." *Church History* 35, no. 2 (July 1966): 186–206.

Bornemann, Fritz. *Arnold Janssen der Gründer des Steyler Missionswerkes, 1837–1909: Ein Lebensbild nach zeitgenössischen Quellen.* Steyl: Sekretariat Arnold Janssen, 1970.

———, ed. *A History of Our Society.* Rome: Apud Collegium Verbi Divini, 1981.

———, ed. *Remembering Arnold Janssen: A Book of Reminiscences.* Rome: Collegium Verbi Divini, 1978.

———, ed. *Der selige P. J. Freinademetz 1852–1908. Ein Steyler China-Missionar. Ein Lebensbild nach zeitgenössischen Quellen.* Bozen: Freinademetz Haus, 1977.

Bosher, J. F. "Huguenot Merchants and the Protestant International." *William and Mary Quarterly* 52, no. 1 (1995): 77–102.

Boyle, John H. *China and Japan at War, 1937–1945: The Politics of Collaboration.* Stanford, CA: Stanford University Press, 1972.

Brandewie, Ernest. *In the Light of the Word: Divine Word Missionaries of North America.* Maryknoll, NY: Orbis, 2000.

Brandt, Joseph van den. *Les Lazaristes en Chine, 1697–1935: notes biographiques, recueillies et mises à jour.* Beijing: Imprimerie des Lazaristes, 1936.

Brecht, Martin, Martin Sallmann, Gustav Adolf Benrath, and Ulrich Gäbler, eds. *Geschichte des Pietismus. Bd. 3: Der Pietismus im neunzehnten und zwanzigsten Jahrhundert.* Göttingen: Vandenhoeck & Ruprecht, 2000.

Breitkopf, Eduard. "Ein Priesterseminar im Heidenland." *Steyler Missionsbote* 55, no. 8 (May 1927): 118–22.

Brockey, Liam M. *Journey to the East: The Jesuit Mission to China, 1579–1724.* Cambridge, MA: Harvard University Press, 2007.

Brook, Timothy. *Collaboration: Japanese Agents and Local Elites in Wartime China.* Cambridge, MA: Harvard University Press, 2005.

Brown, Callum G. *The Death of Christian Britain: Understanding Secularisation, 1800–2000.* London: Routledge, 2009.

Brown, Callum G., M. F. Snape, and Hugh McLeod, eds. *Secularisation in the Christian World: Essays in Honour of Hugh McLeod.* Burlington, VT: Ashgate, 2010.

Bruce, Steve. *God Is Dead: Secularization in the West.* Malden, MA: Blackwell, 2002.

———. *Secularization: In Defense of an Unfashionable Theory.* Oxford: Oxford University Press, 2011.

Burdick, Charles B. *The Japanese Siege of Tsingtau.* Hamden, CT: Archon, 1976.

Butt, Riazat. "Lambeth Conference: Archbishop Blames Liberals for Church Rift." *Guardian,* August 3, 2008. http://www.theguardian.com/world/2008/aug/04/anglicanism.religion.

Cao, Nanlai. *Constructing China's Jerusalem: Christians, Power, and Place in Contemporary Wenzhou.* Stanford: Stanford University Press, 2010.

Chamedes, Giuliana. "The Vatican and the Reshaping of the European International Order After the First World War." *Historical Journal* 56, no. 4 (2013): 955–76.

Chan, Gordon Y. M. "The Communists in Rural Guangdong, 1928–1936." *Journal of the Royal Asiatic Society* 13, no. 1 (2003): 77–97.

Chaves, Mark. "Secularization as Declining Religious Authority." *Social Forces* 72, no. 3 (1994): 749–74.

Chen, John Shujie. *The Rise and Fall of Fu Ren University, Beijing: Catholic Higher Education in China*. New York: Routledge Falmer, 2004.

Chen Fangzhong 陳方中 and Jiang Guoxiong 江國雄, eds. *Zhongfan waijiao guanxi shi* 中梵外交關史 [The History of Sino-Vatican Relations]. Taipei: Shangwu yinshuguan, 2004.

Chen Hsi-yuan. "Confucianism Encounters Religion: The Formation of Religious Discourse and the Confucian Movement in Modern China." PhD diss., Harvard University, 1999.

Chen Tushou 陳徒手. "Chen Yuan xiaozhang rudang qianhou bolan 陳垣校長入黨前后波瀾 [The Tumult Before and After the President Chen Yuan Joined the Communist Party]." June 29, 2013, http://chentushou.blog.21ccom.net/?p=15.

Chen Yuan 陳垣. "Jidujiao ruhua shi 基督教入華史 [The History of Christianity's Entrance into China] (1927)." In *Chen Yuan Quanji: Di er ce* 陳垣全集: 第二冊, edited by Chen Zhichao 陳智超, 466–79. Hefei: Anhui University Press, 2009.

———. "Jidujiao ruhua shilue 基督教入華史略 [A Chronicle of Christianity's Entrance into China] (1924)." In *Chen Yuan Quanji: Di er ce* 陳垣全集: 第二冊, edited by Chen Zhichao 陳智超, 456–65. Hefei: Anhui University Press, 2009.

———. "Shijü zhi kelü 時局之可慮 [Concerns About our Current Situation] (1911)." In *Chen Yuan Quanji: Zaonian wen* 陳垣全集: 早年文, edited by Chen Zhichao 陳智超, 437. Hefei: Anhui University Press, 2009.

———. *Western and Central Asians in China Under the Mongols. Their Transformation into Chinese*. Translated by L. Carrington Goodrich and Ch'ien Hsing-hai. Los Angeles: Monumenta Serica, 1966.

———. "Wu Yü-shan 吳漁山: In Commemoration of the 250th Anniversary of His Ordination to the Priesthood in the Society of Jesus." *Monumenta Serica* 3 (1938): 130–70b.

———. "Xin zhengfu heduo jiuzheng ye 新政府何多舊政也 [The Similarities Between the Old and New Governments] (1911)." In *Chen Yuan Quanji: Zaonian wen* 陳垣全集: 早年文, edited by Chen Zhichao 陳智超, 434. Hefei: Anhui University Press, 2009.

———. "Yesu jidu renzi shiyi xu 耶穌基督人子釋義序 [Preface to the Life of Jesus] (1919)." In *Chen Yuan Quanji: Di er ce* 陳垣全集: 第二冊, edited by Chen Zhichao 陳智超, 406–7. Hefei: Anhui University Press, 2009.

———. "Yuan xiyu ren huahua kao 元西域人華化考 [A Study of the Sinification of the Western Regions] (1934)." In *Chen Yuan Quanji: Di er ce* 陳垣全集: 第二冊, edited by Chen Zhichao 陳智超, 209–389. Hefei: Anhui University Press, 2009.

———. "Yuan yelikewen kao 元也里可溫教考 [An Investigation of the Yelikewen Religion] (1917)." In *Chen Yuan Quanji: Di er ce* 陳垣全集: 第二冊, edited by Chen Zhichao 陳智超, 1–60. Hefei: Anhui University Press, 2009.

———. "Ziwo jiantao 自我檢討 [A Self-Reflection] (1952)." In *Chen Yuan Quanji: Di ershi er ce* 陳垣全集: 第二十二冊, edited by Chen Zhichao 陳智超, 612–26. Hefei: Anhui University Press, 2009.

Chen Zhichao 陳智超, ed. *Chen Yuan laiwang shuxinji* 陳垣來往書信集 [Collected Correspondence of Chen Yuan]. Shanghai: Shanghai guji chubanshe, 1990.

"China das große Land der Hoffnungen und Schmerzen Jesu." *Kleiner Herz-Jesu-Bote* 1, no. 4 (1874): 29–30.

Chow, Kai-Wing, Tze-Ki Hon, Hung-Yok Ip, and Don C. Price, eds. *Beyond the May Fourth Paradigm: In Search of Chinese Modernity.* Lanham, MD: Rowman and Littlefield, 2008.

Chow, Tse-tsung. *The May Fourth Movement: Intellectual Revolution in China.* Cambridge, MA: Harvard University Press, 1960.

Clark, Anthony E. *China's Saints: Catholic Martyrdom During the Qing (1644–1911).* Bethlehem, PA: Lehigh University Press, 2011.

Clark, Christopher M. "The New Catholicism and the European Culture Wars." In Clark and Kaiser, eds., *Culture Wars,* 11–46.

———. "Religion and Confessional Conflict." In *Imperial Germany 1871–1918,* edited by James Retallack, 83–105. Oxford: Oxford University Press, 2008.

Clark, Christopher M., and Wolfram Kaiser, eds. *Culture Wars: Secular-Catholic Conflict in Nineteenth-Century Europe.* Cambridge: Cambridge University Press, 2003.

Clarke, Jeremy. *The Virgin Mary and Catholic Identities in Chinese History.* Hong Kong: Hong Kong University Press, 2013.

Clements, Keith. *Faith on the Frontier: A Life of J. H. Oldham.* Edinburgh: T & T Clark, 1999.

Clossey, Luke. *Salvation and Globalization in the Early Jesuit Missions.* Cambridge: Cambridge University Press, 2008.

Cohen, Paul. "The Anti-Christian Tradition in China." *Journal of Asian Studies* 20, no. 2 (1961): 169–80.

———. *China and Christianity: The Missionary Movement and the Growth of Chinese Antiforeignism, 1860–1870.* Cambridge, MA: Harvard University Press, 1963.

———. "Christian Missions and Their Impact to 1900." In *The Cambridge History of China, Vol. 10: Late Ch'ing 1800–1911, Part 1,* edited by John King Fairbank, 543–90. Cambridge: Cambridge University Press, 1978.

———. *Discovering History in China: American Historical Writing on the Recent Chinese Past.* New York: Columbia University Press, 2010.

———. *History in Three Keys: The Boxers as Event, Experience, and Myth.* New York: Columbia University Press, 1997.

Concilium Sinense, ed. *Primum Concilium Sinense anno 1924 a die 14 maii ad diem 12 iunii in ecclesia S. Ignatii de Zi-Ka-Wei celebratum: acta, decreta et normaa, vota, etc.* Shanghai: Typographia Missionis Catholicae, 1929.

Conference on Missions Held in 1860 at Liverpool. London: John Nisbet, 1860.

Connelly, John. *From Enemy to Brother: The Revolution in Catholic Teaching on the Jews, 1933–1965.* Cambridge, MA: Harvard University Press, 2012.

Conrad, Sebastian. *Globalisation and the Nation in Imperial Germany.* Cambridge: Cambridge University Press, 2010.

Costantini, Celso. *L'art chrétien dans les missions: manuel d'art pour les missionnaires.* Paris: Descleé, de Brouwer, 1949.

Cox, Jeffrey. *The British Missionary Enterprise Since 1700.* New York: Routledge, 2008.

———. *Imperial Fault Lines: Christianity and Colonial Power in India, 1818–1940.* Stanford, CA: Stanford University Press, 2002.

———. "Towards Eliminating the Concept of Secularisation: A Progress Report." In Brown, Snape, and McLeod, eds., *Secularisation in the Christian World,* 13–26.

Craft, Stephen G. V. K. *Wellington Koo and the Emergence of Modern China.* Lexington: University Press of Kentucky, 2003.

Croil, James. *The Noble Army of Martyrs and Roll of Protestant Missionary Martyrs from A.D. 1661 to 1891.* Philadelphia: Presbyterian Board of Publication, 1894.

Cubitt, Geoffrey. *The Jesuit Myth: Conspiracy Theory and Politics in Nineteenth-Century France.* Oxford: Oxford University Press, 1993.

Curtis, Sarah Ann. *Civilizing Habits: Women Missionaries and the Revival of French Empire.* Oxford: Oxford University Press, 2010.

Dabringhaus, Sabine. "An Army on Vacation? The German War in China (1900/1901)." In *Anticipating Total War: The German and American Experiences, 1871–1914,* edited by Manfred F. Boemke, Roger Chickering, and Stig Förster, 459–76. Cambridge: Cambridge University Press, 1999.

Daughton, J. P. *An Empire Divided: Religion, Republicanism, and the Making of French Colonialism, 1880–1914.* Oxford: Oxford University Press, 2006.

D'Costa, Gavin. "Catholicism and the World Religions." In *The Catholic Church and the World Religions: A Theological and Phenomenological Account,* edited by Gavin D'Costa, 1–33. London: T & T Clark, 2011.

D'Elia, Pasquale M. *The Catholic Missions in China: A Short Sketch of the History of the Catholic Church in China from the Earliest Records to Our Own Days.* Shanghai: Commercial Press, 1934.

———. *Catholic Native Episcopacy in China: Being an Outline of the Formation and Growth of the Chinese Catholic Clergy, 1300–1926.* Shanghai: T'usewei Print Press, 1927.

Döhler. "Die deutschen Missionskonferenzen." *Allgemeine Missionszeitschrift* 26 (1899): 493–511, 549–66.

Dunch, Ryan. "Beyond Cultural Imperialism: Cultural Theory, Christian Missions, and Global Modernity." *History and Theory* 41, no. 3 (2002): 301–25.

———. "Christianity and 'Adaptation to Socialism.'" In *Chinese Religiosities: Afflictions of Modernity and State Formation,* edited by Mayfair Mei-hui Yang, 155–78. Berkeley: University of California Press, 2008.

———. *Fuzhou Protestants and the Making of a Modern China, 1857–1927.* New Haven, CT: Yale University Press, 2001.

Dutz, Freddy. *Der Mission verpflichtet: 25 Jahre Evangelisches Missionswerk in Deutschland.* Breklum: Manfred Siegel, 2002.

Elleman, Bruce A. *Wilson and China: A Revised History of the Shandong Question.* London: M. E. Sharpe, 2002.

Ellis, Howard S. "German Exchange Control, 1931–1939: From an Emergency Measure to a Totalitarian Institution." *Quarterly Journal of Economics* 54, no. 4 (August 1940): 1–158.

Elphick, Richard. *The Equality of Believers: Protestant Missionaries and the Racial Politics of South Africa.* Charlottesville: University of Virginia Press, 2012.

"Engeldienst. Ein Wort an unsere Freunde." *Steyler Missionsbote* 48 no. 11/12 (August/September 1921): 81–82.

Entenmann, Robert. "Christian Virgins in Eighteenth-Century Sichuan." In Bays, ed., *Christianity in China*, 180–93.

Esherick, Joseph. *The Origins of the Boxer Uprising.* Berkeley: University of California Press, 1987.

Etherington, Norman, ed. *Missions and Empire.* Oxford University Press, 2005.

Fabri, Friedrich. *Bedarf Deutschland der Colonien?* Lewiston, NY: Edwin Mellen Press, 1998.

Fairbank, John King. "Assignment for the '70's." *American Historical Review* 74, no. 3 (February 1969): 861–79.

———, ed. *The Missionary Enterprise in China and America.* Cambridge, MA: Harvard University Press, 1974.

———. "Patterns Behind the Tientsin Massacre." *Harvard Journal of Asiatic Studies* 20, no. 3/4 (December 1957): 480–511.

———. *Trade and Diplomacy on the China Coast: The Opening of the Treaty Ports, 1842–1854.* Cambridge, MA: Harvard University Press, 1953.

Fang Hao 方豪, ed. *Ma Xiangbo xiansheng wenji* 馬相伯先生文集 [Collected Works of Ma Xiangbo]. Shanghai: Shanghai shudian, 1990.

Fitzgerald, John. "Warlords, Bullies, and State Building in Nationalist China: The Guangdong Cooperative Movement, 1932–1936." *Modern China* (1997): 420–58.

Fleckner, Johannes. *Thomas Kardinal Tien.* St. Augustin: Steyler Verlag, 1975.

"Forum: Asia, Germany and the Transnational Turn." *German History* 28, no. 4 (November 18, 2010): 515–36.

Franke, Herbert. *Sinologie an deutschen Universitäten.* Wiesbaden: Franz Steiner, 1968.

Freinademetz, Josef. "Eine Verfolgungsscene aus China." *St. Michaels-Kalender* 12 (1891): 193–200.

———. "Wer trägt die Hauptschuld an der Bluttat von Tschantjatschuang?" *Kleiner Herz-Jesu-Bote* 25, no. 5 (1898): 38–39.

Frick, Heinrich. *Nationalität und Internationalität der christlichen Mission.* Gütersloh: C. Bertelsmann, 1917.

Gaillardetz, Richard R. *The Church in the Making: Lumen Gentium, Christus Dominus, Orientalium Ecclesiarum.* New York: Paulist Press, 2006.

Gao Wangzhi. "Y. T. Wu: A Christian Leader Under Communism." In Bays, ed., *Christianity in China*, 338–52.

Gauchet, Marcel. *The Disenchantment of the World: A Political History of Religion.* Princeton, NJ: Princeton University Press, 1997.

" 'Gehet zu Joseph!' " *Steyler Missionsbote* 48, no. 5/6 (February/March 1921): 33–36.

Gerber, Lydia. *Von Voskamps 'heidnischem Treiben' und Wilhelms 'höherem China.'* Hamburg: Hamburger Sinologische Gesellschaft, 2002.

"Germany." *Missionary Register of the Church Missionary Society* 20 (1832): 427.

Girardot, Norman. *The Victorian Translation of China: James Legge's Oriental Pilgrimage*. Berkeley: University of California Press, 2002.

Glüer, Winfried. *Christliche Theologie in China: T. C. Chao, 1918–1956*. Gütersloh: Gütersloher Verlagshaus Mohn, 1979.

Goossaert, Vincent. "1898: The Beginning of the End for Chinese Religion?" *Journal of Asian Studies* 65, no. 2 (2006): 307–35.

———. *The Taoists of Peking, 1800–1949: A Social History of Urban Clerics*. Cambridge, MA: Harvard University Press, 2007.

Goossaert, Vincent, and David A. Palmer. *The Religious Question in Modern China*. Chicago: University of Chicago Press, 2011.

Götsch, P. "Beim lebenden Buddha." *Steyler Missionsbote* 55, no. 5 (February 1927): 69–71.

Gough, F. F. "The Best Means of Elevating the Moral and Spiritual Tone of the Native Church." In *Records of the General Conference of the Protestant Missionaries of China*, 255–67. Shanghai: Presbyterian Mission Press, 1877.

Gross, Michael B. "Kulturkampf and Unification: German Liberalism and the War Against the Jesuits." *Central European History* 30, no. 4 (1997): 545–66.

Gründer, Horst. *Christliche Mission und deutscher Imperialismus: Eine politische Geschichte ihrer Beziehungen während der deutschen Kolonialzeit (1884–1914) unter besonderer Berücksichtigung Afrikas und Chinas*. Paderborn: Schöningh, 1982.

Guilday, Peter. "The Sacred Congregation de Propaganda Fide (1622–1922)." *Catholic Historical Review* (1921): 478–94.

Gulick, Edward V. *Peter Parker and the Opening of China*. Cambridge, MA: Harvard University Press, 1973.

Gützlaff, Karl Friedrich August. *Journal of Three Voyages Along the Coast of China, in 1831, 1832 & 1833, with Notices of Siam, Corea, and the Loo-Choo Islands*. London: F. Westley and A. H. Davis, 1834.

Hagspiel, Bruno. *Along the Mission Trail. Vol. IV: In China*. Techny, IL: Mission Press, S.V.D., 1927.

Hamer, Heyo E. *Mission und Politik*. Aachen: Verlag an der Lottbek, 2002.

Harris, Ruth. *Lourdes: Body and Spirit in the Secular Age*. New York: Viking, 1999.

Harrison, Henrietta. *The Missionary's Curse and Other Tales from a Chinese Catholic Village*. Berkeley, CA: University of California Press, 2013.

Hartenstein, Karl. *Der Kampf um Christus im Fernen Osten*. Stuttgart: Evang. Missionsverlag, 1937.

Hartwich, Richard, ed. *Johann Weig: Chronik der Steyler Mission in Tsingtao 1923–1947*. St. Augustin: Steyler, 1980.

———, ed. *P. Arnold Janssen und P. Josef Freinademetz, Briefwechsel 1904–1907: Korrespondenz zwischen zwei Seligen*. St. Augustin: Steyler, 1978.

———, ed. *Steyler Missionare in China. I. Missionarische Erschliessung Südshantungs 1879–1903*. Nettetal: Steyler, 1983.

———, ed. *Steyler Missionare in China. II. Bischof A. Henninghaus ruft Steyler Schwestern, 1904–1910*. Nettetal: Steyler, 1985.

————, ed. *Steyler Missionare in China. III. Republik China und Erster Weltkrieg, 1911–1919.* Nettetal: Steyler, 1987.

————, ed. *Steyler Missionare in China. V. Aus Kriegsruinen zu neuen Grenzen, 1920–1923.* Nettetal: Steyler, 1989.

————, ed. *Steyler Missionare in China. VI. Auf den Wogen des Chinesischen Bürgerkrieges, 1924–1926.* Nettetal: Steyler, 1991.

Hayhoe, Ruth, and Yungling Lu, eds. *Ma Xiangbo and the Mind of Modern China, 1840–1939.* Armonk, NY: M. E. Sharpe, 1996.

Henninghaus, Augustin. "Neujahrgruss an die Wohltäter der Mission Süd-Schantung." *Steyler Missionsbote* 41, no. 4 (January 1914): 55–61.

————. "Neujahrsgruss aus Yenschowfu, Südschantung, China." *Steyler Missionsbote* 59, no. 4 (January 1932): 73–81.

————. *P. Jos. Freinademetz S.V.D. Sein Leben und Wirken.* Yanzhou: Katholische Mission, 1926.

Hermanns, P. M. "Asiatische Übermenschen." *Steyler Missionsbote* 66, no. 6 (March 1939): 146–50.

————. "Christus oder Buddha?" *Steyler Missionsbote* 61, no. 5 (February 1934): 130–32.

————. "Wie ich Konfuzius' Stammhalter sah." *Steyler Missionsbote* 63, no. 2 (November 1935): 46–50.

Hershatter, Gail. *The Gender of Memory: Rural Women and China's Collective Past.* Berkeley: University of California Press, 2011.

————. *Women in China's Long Twentieth Century.* Berkeley: University of California Press, 2007.

Hevia, James L. *English Lessons: The Pedagogy of Imperialism in Nineteenth-Century China.* Durham, NC: Duke University Press, 2003.

————. "Leaving a Brand on China: Missionary Discourse in the Wake of the Boxer Movement." *Modern China* 18, no. 3 (1992): 304–32.

Hobsbawm, Eric J. *The Age of Revolution: 1789–1848.* New York: Vintage, 1996.

Hoekendijk, Johannes C. *Kirche und Volk in der deutschen Missionswissenschaft.* Translated by Erich-Walter Pollman. München: Chr. Kaiser, 1967.

Hogg, William R. *Ecumenical Foundations: A History of the International Missionary Council and Its Nineteenth Century Background.* New York: Harper, 1952.

Holborn, Hajo. *A History of Modern Germany.* New York: A. A. Knopf, 1959.

Hollinger, David A. *After Cloven Tongues of Fire: Protestant Liberalism in Modern American History.* Princeton, NJ: Princeton University Press, 2015.

Hölscher, Lucian. "Europe in the Age of Secularisation." In Brown, Snape, and McLeod, eds., *Secularisation in the Christian World,* 205–18.

Hon, Tze-ki. "Constancy in Change: A Comparison of James Legge's and Richard Wilhelm's Interpretations of the Yijing." *Monumenta Serica* 53 (2005): 315–36.

Horlemann, Bianca. "The Divine Word Missionaries in Gansu, Qinghai, and Xinjiang, 1922–1953: A Bibliographic Note." *Journal of the Royal Asiatic Society of Great Britain and Ireland* 19, no. 1 (January 2009): 59–82.

Hsia, Ronnie Po-chia. *A Jesuit in the Forbidden City: Matteo Ricci, 1552–1610*. Oxford: Oxford University Press, 2010.

Hsiao Chi-Ching 蕭啟慶. "Tui chen chuxin de shixuejia Chen Yuan 推陳出新的史學家陳垣 [The Innovative Historian Chen Yuan]." *Xin Shixue* 新史學 16 (3), no. 3 (September 2005): 101–36.

Hsiung, James C., and Steven I. Levine. *China's Bitter Victory: The War with Japan, 1937–1945*. Armonk, NY: M. E. Sharpe, 1992.

Hsü, Immanuel C. Y. "The Secret Mission of the Lord Amherst on the China Coast, 1832." *Harvard Journal of Asiatic Studies* 17, no. 1/2 (June 1954): 231–52.

Hsu, Long-hsuen, and Mingkai Zhang. *History of the Sino-Japanese War (1937–1945)*. Taipei: Chung Wu, 1971.

Huang, Ray. *China: A Macro History*. Armonk, NY: M. E. Sharpe, 1997.

Huang Yinong 黃一農. *Liang toushe: Ming mo Qing chu de di yi dai Tian zhu jiao tu* 兩頭蛇：明末清初的第一代天主教徒 [The Two-Headed Snake: The First Generation of Catholic Converts in the Late Ming and Early Qing Dynasties]. Xinzhu: Qinghua University Press, 2005.

Hubrig, Friedrich. *Li-tshyung-yin, ein treuer Zeuge in der chinesischen Mission*. Berlin: Buchhandlung der Berliner evangelischen Missionsgesellschaft, 1899.

Hunt, Michael H. "The American Remission of the Boxer Indemnity: A Reappraisal." *Journal of Asian Studies* 31, no. 3 (1972): 539–559.

Huonder, Anton. *Der einheimische Klerus in den Heidenländern*. Freiburg im Breisgau: Herdersche Verlagshandlung, 1909.

Hutchison, William R. *Errand to the World: American Protestant Thought and Foreign Missions*. Chicago: University of Chicago Press, 1987.

———. "Innocence Abroad: The 'American Religion' in Europe." *Church History* 51, no. 1 (1982): 71–84.

Hutton, J. E. *A History of Moravian Missions*. London: Moravian Publication Office, 1922.

Jahresbericht der Berliner Missionsgesellschaft, 1908. Berlin: Berliner Missionsgesellschaft, 1908.

Jenkins, Philip. *The Next Christendom: The Coming of Global Christianity*. Oxford: Oxford University Press, 2002.

Jensen, Lionel. *Manufacturing Confucianism: Chinese Traditions and Universal Civilization*. Durham, NC: Duke University Press, 1997.

Jensz, Felicity. "The Function of Inaugural Editions in Missionary Periodicals." *Church History* 82, no. 2 (June 2013): 374–80.

———. *German Moravian Missionaries in the British Colony of Victoria, Australia, 1848–1908: Influential Strangers*. Leiden: Brill, 2010.

Jensz, Felicity, and Hanna Acke. "The Form and Function of Nineteenth-Century Missionary Periodicals: Introduction." *Church History* 82, no. 2 (June 2013): 368–73.

Jessup, James Brooks. "The Householder Elite: Buddhist Activism in Shanghai, 1920–1956." PhD diss., University of California, Berkeley, 2010.

Jeyaraj, Daniel, and Richard Fox Young, eds. *Hindu-Christian Epistolary Self-Disclosures: "Malabarian Correspondence" Between German Pietist Missionaries and South Indian Hindus (1712–1714)*. Wiesbaden: Harrassowitz, 2013.

Johnson, Ian. "Church-State Clash in China Coalesces Around a Toppled Spire." *New York Times*, May 29, 2014. http://www.nytimes.com/2014/05/30/world/asia/church-state-clash-in-china-coalesces-around-a-toppled-spire.html.

Johnson, James, ed. *Report of the Centenary Conference on Protestant Missions of the World*. London: James Nisbit, 1888.

Jonas, Raymond A. *France and the Cult of the Sacred Heart: An Epic Tale for Modern Times*. Berkeley: University of California Press, 2000.

Karl, Rebecca, and Peter Zarrow, eds. *Rethinking the 1898 Reform Period: Political and Cultural Change in Late Qing China*. Cambridge, MA: Harvard University Press, 2002.

Keegan, Nicholas M. "From Chancery to Cloister: The Chinese Diplomat Who Became a Benedictine Monk." *Diplomacy and Statecraft* 10, no. 1 (1999): 172–85.

Keith, Charles. "Annam Uplifted: The First Vietnamese Catholic Bishops and the Birth of a National Church, 1919–1945." *Journal of Vietnamese Studies* 3, no. 2 (2008): 128–71.

Ketelaar, James Edward. *Of Heretics and Martyrs in Meiji Japan: Buddhism and Its Persecution*. Princeton, NJ: Princeton University Press, 1990.

Kim, Chun-Shik. *Deutscher Kulturimperialismus in China*. Stuttgart: Steiner, 2004.

Kirby, William C. *Germany and Republican China*. Stanford, CA: Stanford University Press, 1984.

Klein, Thoralf. "Anti-Imperialism at Grassroots: Christianity and the Anti-Christian Movement in Northeast Guangdong." In *The Chinese Revolution in the 1920s: Between Triumph and Disaster*, edited by Mechthild Leutner, Roland Felber, M. L. Titarenko, and A. M. Grigoriev. 289–306. London: Routledge, 2002.

———. *Die Basler Mission in Guangdong (Südchina) 1859–1931: Akkulturationsprozesse und kulturelle Grenzziehungen zwischen Missionaren, chinesischen Christen und lokaler Gesellschaft*. München: Iudicium, 2002.

———. "Media Events and Missionary Periodicals: The Case of the Boxer War, 1900–1901." *Church History* 82, no. 2 (2013): 399–404.

Knak, Siegfried. *Die chinesischen Christen unter den gegenwärtigen Wandlungen in China*. Berlin: Furche-Verlag, 1928.

———. "Die christliche Nationalkonferenz in Shanghai." *Berliner Missionsberichte* (1922): 150–55.

———. *Die Kirche als völkerverbindende Macht. Ein Vortrag gehalten am 12. Januar 1919*. Magdeburg: Verlag der Evangelischen Buchhandlung Ernst Holtermann, 1919.

———. *Mission und nationale Bewegung*. Leipzig: Verlag und Bücherstube der Mädchen-Bibel-Kreise, 1933.

———. *Säkularismus und Mission*. Gütersloh: C. Bertelsmann, 1929.

———. "Unsere Mission in China unter den antichristlichen Strömungen." *Berliner Missionsberichte* (1926): 23–28.

————. "Unzeit?" *Berliner Missionsberichte* 3 (March 1926): 31–35.

————. *Zwischen Nil und Tafelbai.* Berlin: Heimatdienst-Verlag, 1931.

Knak, Siegfried, and Georg Beyer. "Heimat. (Juni 1918 bis Juni 1919.)" *Jahresbericht der Berliner Missionsgesellschaft,* 1918: 2–7.

Koesel, Karrie. "China's Patriotic Pentecostals." *Review of Religion and Chinese Society* 1, no. 2 (2014): 131–55.

Kohls, Lotti. *Erlebnisse auf eine Reise nach China.* Berlin: Berliner Evangelische Missionsgesellschaft, 1926.

Kollár, Miroslav. *Ein Leben im Konflikt: P. Franz Xaver Biallas SVD (1878–1936) Chinamissionar und Sinologe im Licht seiner Korrespondenz.* St. Augustin: Institut Monumenta Serica, 2011.

Köllman, Wolfgang. "The Population of Barmen Before and During the Period of Industrialization." In *Population in History,* edited by D. V. Glass and D. E. C. Eversley, 588–607. London: Edward Arnold, 1965.

————. *Sozialgeschichte der Stadt Barmen im 19. Jahrhundert.* Tübingen: J. C. B. Mohr (Paul Siebeck), 1960.

Könige, Theodor. "Zu den Buddhistenmönchen auf den Loa-schän." *Steyler Missionsbote* 57, no. 3 (December 1929): 58–60.

Konrad, Paul. "Mein Besuch in heidnischen Tempeln von Tsingtau." *Steyler Missionsbote* 64, no. 7 (April 1936): 177–80.

————. "Mein Besuch in heidnischen Tempeln von Tsingtau (Schluss)." *Steyler Missionsbote* 64, no. 8 (May 1936): 208–9.

Kraus, Dieter, ed. *Evangelische Kirchenverfassungen in Deutschland. Textsammlung mit einer Einführung.* Berlin: Duncker & Humblot, 2001.

Kriele, Eduard. *Geschichte der Rheinischen Missionsgesellschaft: Die Rheinische Mission in der Heimat.* Barmen: Missionshaus, 1928.

Krins, Hubert. "Wie Kardinal Tien Bischof Wurde." *Verbum* 9 (1967): 344–53.

Kuepers, J. J. A. M. *China und die katholische Mission in Süd-Shantung: Die Geschichte einer Konfrontation.* Steyl: Drukkerij van het Missiehuis, 1974.

Kuhn, Philip A. *Rebellion and Its Enemies in Late Imperial China: Militarization and Social Structure, 1796–1864.* Cambridge, MA: Harvard University Press, 1970.

Kuo, Ya-pei. " 'Christian Civilization' and the Confucian Church: The Origin of Secularist Politics in Modern China." *Past & Present* 218, no. 1 (2013): 235–64.

Kwok, Pui-lan. *Chinese Women and Christianity, 1860–1927.* Atlanta: Scholars, 1992.

Lambert, Tony. "Counting Christians in China: A Cautionary Report." *International Bulletin of Missionary Research* 27, no. 1 (2003): 6–10.

Latourette, Kenneth Scott. *Christianity in a Revolutionary Age: A History of Christianity in the 19th and 20th Centuries. Vol. 5: 20th Century Outside Europe.* New York: Harper, 1962.

————. *The Emergence of a World Christian Community.* New Haven, CT: Yale University Press, 1949.

————. *A History of Christian Missions in China.* London: Society for Promoting Christian Knowledge, 1929.

Lawton, Mary S. "A Unique Style in China: Chinese Christian Painting in Beijing." *Monumenta Serica* 43 (1995): 469–89.

Lee, Bradford. *Britain and the Sino-Japanese War: A Study in the Dilemma of British Decline.* Stanford, CA: Stanford University Press, 1967.

Lehmann, Hartmut, ed. *Geschichte des Pietismus. Bd. 4: Glaubenswelt und Lebenswelten.* Göttingen: Vandenhoeck & Ruprecht, 2004.

———. "Pietism in the World of Transatlantic Religious Revivals." In *Pietism in Germany and North America, 1680–1820,* edited by Jonathan Strom, Hartmut Lehmann, and James Van Horn Melton, 13–22. Burlington, VT: Ashgate, 2009.

Lehmann, Hellmut. *Zur Zeit und zur Unzeit: Geschichte der Berliner Mission 1918–1972 in Drei Bänden.* 3 Volumes. Berlin: Berliner Missionswerk, 1989.

Lessing, Eckhard. *Zwischen Bekenntnis und Volkskirche: Der theologische Weg der Evangelischen Kirche der altpreußischen Union (1922–1953) unter besonderer Berücksichtigung ihrer Synoden, ihrer Gruppen und der theologischen Begründungen.* Bielefeld: Luther-Verlag, 1992.

Leuschner, Friedrich Wilhelm. *Allerlei aus China.* Berlin: Buchhandlung der Berliner evangelischen Missionsgesellschaft, 1901.

———. *Bilder des Todes und Bilder des Lebens aus China.* Berlin: Buchhandlung der Berliner evangelischen Missionsgesellschaft, 1914.

———. *Das Wichtigste aus den Tagen meines Lebens.* Berlin: Buchhandlung der Berliner evangelischen Missionsgesellschaft, 1901.

Leutner, Mechthild, and Klaus Mühlhahn, eds. *Kolonialkrieg in China. Die Niederschlagung der Boxerbewegung 1900–1901.* Berlin: Links, 2007.

Levenson, Joseph R. *Confucian China and Its Modern Fate: A Trilogy.* Berkeley: University of California Press, 1968.

Lewis, W. J., W. T. A. Barber, and J. R. Hykes, eds. *Records of the General Conference of the Protestant Missionaries of China, held at Shanghai, May 7–20.* Shanghai: American Presbyterian Mission Press, 1890.

Li, Lillian M. *Fighting Famine in North China: State, Market, and Environmental Decline, 1690s–1990s.* Stanford, CA: Stanford University Press, 2007.

Lian Xi. *The Conversion of Missionaries: Liberalism in American Protestant Missions in China, 1907–1932.* University Park, PA: Penn State University Press, 1997.

———. *Redeemed by Fire: The Rise of Popular Christianity in Modern China.* New Haven, CT: Yale University Press, 2010.

Liao Yiwu. *God Is Red: The Secret Story of How Christianity Survived and Flourished in Communist China.* New York: HarperOne, 2011.

Lindenfeld, David F., and Miles Richardson, eds. *Beyond Conversion and Syncretism: Indigenous Encounters with Missionary Christianity, 1800–2000.* New York: Berghahn Books, 2012.

Ling, Oi Ki. *The Changing Role of the British Protestant Missionaries in China, 1945–1952.* Madison, NJ: Fairleigh Dickinson University Press, 1999.

Lin Lifang. *Nanxiong Zhuji fangyan zhi* 南雄珠璣方言志 [Dialects of the Nanxiong Zhuji Region]. Guangzhou: Jinan University Press, 1995.

Litten, Frederick. "The Myth of the 'Turning-Point'—Towards a New Understanding of the Long March." *Bochumer Jahrbuch zur Ostasienforschung* 25 (2001): 3–44.

Liu, Lydia He. *The Clash of Empires: The Invention of China in Modern World Making.* Cambridge, MA: Harvard University Press, 2004.

———. *Translingual Practice: Literature, National Culture, and Translated Modernity—China, 1900–1937.* Stanford, CA: Stanford University Press, 1995.

Liu Cheng-yun. "Kuo-lu: A Sworn Brotherhood Organization in Szechwan." *Late Imperial China* 6, no. 1 (1985): 56–82.

Liu Guopeng 劉國鵬. *Ganghengyi yu Zhongguo tianzhujiao de ben di hua* 剛恆毅與中國天主教的本地化 [Celso Costantini and the Indigenization of the Catholic Church in China]. Beijing: Shehui kexue wenxian chubanshe, 2011.

Liu Naihe 劉乃和, ed. *Chen Yuan nianpu peitu changbian* 陳垣年譜配圖長編 [Chronology of Chen Yuan's Life with Pictures]. Shenyang: Liaohai chubanshe, 2000.

———, ed. *Liyun chengxuelu* 勵耘承學錄 [Records of Learning and Meditation]. Beijing: Beijing Normal University Press, 1992.

Liu Xian. "On Chen Yuan's Study of Religions." PhD diss., Chinese University of Hong Kong, 2005.

Liu Xiaosheng 劉小生. "Shou ze duoru: 'Guobao' Chen Yuan de beijü" 壽則多辱："國寶"陳垣的悲劇 [A Long Life Brings Many Moments of Disgrace: The Tragedy of Chen Yuan]. *Gongshi Wang* 共識網 [21ccom.net], January 25, 2014. http://www.21ccom.net/articles/rwcq/shzh/2014/0125_99644.html.

Li Yiya 李宜涯. *Shengtan qian de chuangzuo* 聖壇前的創作 [Creations Before the Altar]. Taipei: Xiuwei, 2010.

Lodwick, Kathleen. *Crusaders Against Opium: Protestant Missionaries in China, 1874–1917.* Lexington: University of Kentucky Press, 1996.

Longfield, Bradley J. *The Presbyterian Controversy: Fundamentalists, Modernists, and Moderates.* Oxford: Oxford University Press, 1991.

Lovell, Julia. *The Opium War: Drugs, Dreams and the Making of China.* London: Picador, 2011.

Lü Shiqiang 呂實強. *Zhongguo guansheng fanjiao de yuan ying (1860–1874)* 中國官紳反教的原因 (一八六〇~一八七四) [The Chinese Literati and Anti-Christianity, 1860–1874]. Taipei: Institute of Modern History, Academia Sinica, 1973.

Lutz, Jessie G. "Attrition Among Protestant Missionaries in China, 1807–1890." *International Bulletin of Missionary Research* 36, no. 1 (January 2012): 22–27.

———. *China and the Christian Colleges, 1850–1950.* Ithaca, NY: Cornell University Press, 1971.

———. *Chinese Politics and Christian Missions: The Anti-Christian Movements of 1920–28.* Notre Dame, IN: Cross Cultural Publications, 1988.

———. *Opening China: Karl F. A. Gützlaff and Sino-Western Relations, 1827–1852.* Grand Rapids, MI: William B. Eerdmans, 2008.

———, ed. *Pioneer Chinese Christian Women: Gender, Christianity, and Social Mobility.* Bethlehem, PA: Lehigh University Press, 2010.

————. "Women's Education and Social Mobility." In Lutz, ed., *Pioneer Chinese Christian Women*, 393–420.

Lutz, Jessie G., and Rolland Ray Lutz. "Karl Gützlaff's Approach to Indigenization: The Chinese Union." In Bays, ed. *Christianity in China*, 269–91.

MacCulloch, Diarmaid. *A History of Christianity: The First Three Thousand Years*. London: Allen Lane, 2009.

MacMillan, Margaret. *Paris 1919: Six Months That Changed the World*. New York: Random House, 2001.

Madsen, Richard. "Catholic Revival During the Reform Era." *China Quarterly* 174, no. 2 (June 2003): 468–87.

————. *China's Catholics: Tragedy and Hope in an Emerging Civil Society*. Berkeley: University of California Press, 1998.

Manela, Erez. *The Wilsonian Moment: Self Determination and the International Origins of Anticolonial Nationalism*. Oxford: Oxford University Press, 2007.

Marchand, Suzanne L. "Eastern Wisdom in an Era of Western Despair: Orientalism in 1920s Central Europe." In *Weimar Thought: A Contested Legacy*, edited by Peter E. Gordon and John P. McCormick, 341–60. Princeton, NJ: Princeton University Press, 2013.

————. *German Orientalism in the Age of Empire: Religion, Race, and Scholarship*. Cambridge: Cambridge University Press, 2009.

"Maria Jungfrau, hilf, das ich schau, dein Kind an meinem ende." *Steyler Missionsbote* 62, no. 8 (1935): 211.

Martin, David. *On Secularization: Towards a Revised General Theory*. Burlington, VT: Ashgate, 2005.

Mayer, Adam. "Bunte Missionspost." *Steyler Missionsbote* 59, no. 1 (1931): 19–22.

————. "Der Kampf um China." *Steyler Missionsbote* 58, no. 3 (December 1930): 49–55.

McLeod, Hugh. *The Religious Crisis of the 1960s*. Oxford: Oxford University Press, 2007.

————. *Secularisation in Western Europe, 1848–1914*. New York: St. Martin's, 2000.

McManners, John. *The French Revolution and the Church*. London: S.P.C.K. for the Church Historical Society, 1969.

Menegon, Eugenio. *Ancestors, Virgins, and Friars: Christianity as a Local Religion in Late Imperial China*. Cambridge, MA: Harvard University Press, 2009.

Merwin, Wallace, and Francis P. Jones, eds. *Documents of the Three-Self Movement*. New York: National Council of Churches, 1963

Metzler, Josef, ed. *Sacrae Congregationis de Propaganda Fide memoria rerum: 350 anni a servizio delle missioni, 1622–1972* [350 Years in the Service of the Missions]. Vol. 3: 1815–1972. Rome: Herder, 1971.

————. *Die Synoden in China, Japan und Korea, 1570–1931*. Paderborn: F. Schöningh, 1980.

Miller, Elmer S. "The Christian Missionary, Agent of Secularization." *Anthropological Quarterly* (1970): 14–22.

Miller, Jon. *The Social Control of Religious Zeal: A Study of Organizational Contradictions.* New Brunswick, NJ: Rutgers University Press, 1994.

Minamiki, George. *The Chinese Rites Controversy: From Its Beginning to Modern Times.* Chicago: Loyola University Press, 1985.

Miotk, Andrzej. *Das Missionsverständnis im historischen Wandel am Beispiel der Enzyklika "Maximum illud."* Nettetal: Steyler, 1999.

Mirbt, Carl. "Ausschuß der deutschen evangelischen Missionsgesellschaften." In *Deutsches Kolonial-Lexicon, Bd. 1,* edited by Heinrich Schnee, 103. Leipzig: Quelle & Meyer, 1920.

Mitter, Rana. *A Bitter Revolution: China's Struggle with the Modern World.* Oxford: Oxford University Press, 2004.

———. *Forgotten Ally: China's World War II, 1937–1945.* New York: Houghton Mifflin Harcourt, 2013.

Mi Xingru 米星如. "Diyiqi benkan chuban yihou 第一期本刊出版以後 [In Response to the First Issue]." *Wenshe Yuekan* 文社月刊 1, no. 1 (October 1925): 55–62.

Moch, Leslie P. *Moving Europeans: Migration in Western Europe Since 1650.* Bloomington: Indiana University Press, 2003.

Mott, John Raleigh. *The Evangelization of the World in This Generation.* New York: Student Volunteer Movement for Foreign Missions, 1900.

Moxiang baojian 默想寶鑑 [Treasures of Silent Prayer]. Beijing: Jiaoshitang, 1894.

Mühlbauer, Ferdinand. "Ich will nicht Sterben." *Steyler Missionsbote* 62, no. 11 (August 1935): 299.

Mühlhahn, Klaus. *Herrschaft und Widerstand in der "Musterkolonie" Kiautschou: Interaktionen zwischen China und Deutschland 1897–1914.* München: Oldenbourg, 2000.

Mungello, David E. *The Chinese Rites Controversy: Its History and Meaning.* Nettetal: Steyler, 1994.

———. *The Spirit and the Flesh in Shandong, 1650–1785.* Lanham, MD: Rowman and Littlefield, 2001.

Murray, Dian H., and Qin Baoqi. *The Origins of the Tiandihui: The Chinese Triads in Legend and History.* Stanford, CA: Stanford University Press, 1994.

"Mutter, gib mir nun dein Kind." *Steyler Missionsbote* 65, no. 8 (1938): 211.

Namorato, Michael V. *The Catholic Church in Mississippi, 1911–1984: A History.* Westport, CT: Greenwood, 1998.

Naquin, Susan. *Millenarian Rebellion in China: The Eight Trigrams Uprising of 1813.* New Haven, CT: Yale University Press, 1976.

Nedostup, Rebecca. *Superstitious Regimes: Religion and the Politics of Chinese Modernity.* Cambridge, MA: Harvard University Press, 2009.

Ng, Peter Tze-Ming 吳梓明, ed. *Jidujiao daxue Huaren xiaozhang yanjiu* 基督教大學華人校長研究 [Research on Chinese Christian University Presidents]. Fuzhou: Fujian jiaoyu chubanshe, 2001.

Oehler, Wilhelm. "Der alte Missionsbefehl im neuen China." *Jahrbuch der vereinigten deutschen Missionskonferenzen* (1930): 48–59.

Ogden, Suzanne P. "The Sage in the Inkpot: Bertrand Russell and China's Social Reconstruction in the 1920s." *Modern Asian Studies* 16, no. 4 (1982): 529–600.

O'Malley, John. "Mission and the Early Jesuits." *The Way Supplement* 79 (Spring 1994): 3–10.

O'Malley, John W. *The First Jesuits.* Cambridge, MA: Harvard University Press, 1993.

Ownby, David, and Mary Somers Heidhues, eds. *"Secret Societies" Reconsidered: Perspectives on the Social History of Modern South China and Southeast Asia.* Armonk, NY: M. E. Sharpe, 1993.

Oxenius, Hans Goetz. *Die Entstehung der Verfassung der evangelischen Kirche der altpreussischen Union von 1922.* Berlin: Ernst-Reuter-Gesellschaft, 1959.

Pakendorf, Gunther. "A Brief History of the Berlin Mission Society in South Africa." *History Compass* 9, no. 2 (2011): 106–18.

"Der 'Pantschen Lama,' der 'lebende Buddha.' " *Steyler Missionsbote* 54, no. 9 (June 1926): 143.

Paton, David. "First Thoughts on the Debacle of Christian Missions in China." *African Affairs* 51, no. 202 (1952): 33–41.

Pazuke, Joseph. "Wie der Buddhist in Japan seine Toten begräbt." *Steyler Missionsbote* 56, no. 12 (September 1929): 273–74.

Peires, J. B. *The Dead Will Arise: Nongqawuse and the Great Xhosa Cattle-Killing Movement of 1856–1857.* Bloomington: Indiana University Press, 1989.

Pepper, Suzanne. *Civil War in China: The Political Struggle, 1945–1949.* Lanham, MD: Rowman and Littlefield, 1999.

Perry, Elizabeth J. *Rebels and Revolutionaries in North China, 1845–1945.* Stanford, CA: Stanford University Press, 1980.

———. *Shanghai on Strike: The Politics of Chinese Labor.* Stanford, CA: Stanford University Press, 1993.

Pettus, W. B., ed. *Christian Sacred Pictures.* Beijing: California College in China, 1937.

Pew Forum on Religion and Public Life. *Global Christianity: A Report on the Size and Distribution of the World's Christian Population.* December 19, 2011. http://www .pewforum.org/2011/12/19/global-christianity-exec/.

Pieper, Rudolf. *Unkraut, Knospen und Blüten aus dem "blümigen Reiche der Mitte."* Steyl: Verlag der Missionsdrückerei, 1900.

Platt, Stephen R. *Autumn in the Heavenly Kingdom: China, the West, and the Epic Story of the Taiping Civil War.* New York: A. A. Knopf, 2012.

Pollard, John. *The Papacy in the Age of Totalitarianism, 1914–1958.* Oxford: Oxford University Press, 2014.

Porter, Andrew N. *Religion Versus Empire?: British Protestant Missionaries and Overseas Expansion, 1700–1914.* Manchester: Manchester University Press, 2004.

Pötter, Rudolf. "Hochzeit im Hause Konfuzius." *Steyler Missionsbote* 64, no. 9 (1937): 246.

Rade, Martin. "The Present Situation of Christianity in Germany." *American Journal of Theology* 24, no. 3 (July 1920): 339–67.

Rawlinson, Frank Joseph, Helen Thorburn, and Donald MacGillvray, eds. *The Chinese Church: As Revealed in the National Christian Conference Held in Shanghai.* Shanghai: Oriental Press, 1922.

Reilly, Thomas H. *The Taiping Heavenly Kingdom: Rebellion and the Blasphemy of Empire.* Seattle: University of Washington Press, 2004.

Reinders, Eric R. "Blessed Are the Meat Eaters: Christian Antivegetarianism and the Missionary Encounter with Chinese Buddhism." *Positions: East Asia Cultures Critique* 12, no. 2 (2004): 509–37.

Rennstich, Karl. "Mission—Geschichte der protestantischen Mission in Deutschland." In Brecht et al., eds., *Geschichte des Pietismus, Bd. 3,* 308–20.

Richter, Julius. *Geschichte der Berliner Missionsgesellschaft.* Berlin: Verlag der Buchhandlung der Berliner evangelischen Missionsgesellschaft, 1924.

Richter, Ursula. "Richard Wilhelm—Founder of a Friendly China Image in Twentieth Century Germany." *Bulletin of the Institute of Modern History, Academia Sinica* 20 (1991): 153–81.

Rivinius, Karl Josef. *Im Spannungsfeld von Mission und Politik: Johann Baptist Anzer (1851–1903), Bischof von Süd-Shandong.* Nettetal: Steyler, 2010.

———. *Weltlicher Schutz und Mission: Das Deutsche Protektorat über die Katholische Mission von Süd-Shantung.* Köln: Böhlau, 1987.

Rogaski, Ruth. *Hygienic Modernity: Meanings of Health and Disease in Treaty-Port China.* Berkeley: University of California Press, 2004.

Ross, Ronald J. *The Failure of Bismarck's Kulturkampf: Catholicism and State Power in Imperial Germany, 1871–1887.* Washington, DC: Catholic University of America Press, 1998.

Rummel, R. J. *China's Bloody Century: Genocide and Mass Murder Since 1900.* New Brunswick, NJ: Transaction, 1991.

Russell, Bertrand. *The Problem of China.* London: Allen and Unwin, 1966.

"Sacre des Evêques chinois." *Les Missions Catholiques* 58 (November 26, 1926): 565–72; (September 3, 1926): 425–27; (September 3, 1926): 577–79; (September 24, 1926): 460–61.

Saich, Tony, and Benjamin Yang, eds., *The Rise to Power of the Chinese Communist Party.* Armonk, NY: M. E. Sharpe, 1996.

Sanneh, Lamin O. *Disciples of All Nations: Pillars of World Christianity.* Oxford: Oxford University Press, 2008.

———. *Whose Religion Is Christianity?: The Gospel Beyond the West.* Grand Rapids, MI: W. B. Eerdmans, 2003.

Sanneh, Lamin O., and Joel A. Carpenter, eds. *The Changing Face of Christianity: Africa, the West, and the World.* Oxford: Oxford University Press, 2005.

Sauerborn, L. "Besuch beim Bonzen." *Steyler Missionsbote* 64, no. 10 (July 1937): 240–41.

Schieder, Wolfgang. "Kirche und Revolution: Sozialgeschichtliche Aspekte der Trierer Wallfahrt von 1844." *Archiv für Sozialgeschichte* 14 (1974): 419–54.

Schlunk, Martin, ed. *Durch Chinas Südprovinz. Bericht über die Visitation des Missionsinspektors Sauberzweig Schmidt in Südchina 1904–1906. 2. Heft seines literarischen Nachlasses*. Berlin: Buchhandlung der Berliner evangelischen Missionsgesellschaft, 1908.

———, ed. *Durch Deutsch-Kiautschou. Aus den Aufzeichnungen des Missionsinspektors Sauberzweig-Schmidt über seine Visitation in Nordchina im Jahre 1905. 3. Heft seines literarischen Nachlasses*. Berlin: Buchhandlung der Berliner evangelischen Missionsgesellschaft, 1909.

Schmidlin, Josef. "Die katholische Missionswissenschaft." *Zeitschrift für Missionswissenschaft* 1 (1911): 10–21.

———. "Die Missionsfrage vor dem Völkerbund." *Zeitschrift für Missionswissenschaft* 16 (1926): 316–18.

———. "Der Todesstoß gegen die deutschen Missionen?" *Zeitschrift für Missionswissenschaft* 9 (1919): 191–94.

Schote, Albert. "Eine weise Rose aus dem blumigen Reiche der Mitte." *Steyler Missionsbote* 59, no. 4 (1932): 85–87.

Schwarcz, Vera. *The Chinese Enlightenment: Intellectuals and the Legacy of the May Fourth Movement of 1919*. Berkeley: University of California Press, 1986.

Schwartz, Benjamin I., ed. *Reflections on the May Fourth Movement: A Symposium*. Cambridge, MA: Harvard University Press, 1972.

Scott, Gregory Adam. "Conversion by the Book: Buddhist Print Culture in Early Republican China." PhD diss., Columbia University, 2013.

———. "The Dharma Through a Glass Darkly: On the Study of Modern Chinese Buddhism Through Protestant Missionary Sources." *Shengyan yanjiu* 2 (July 2011): 47–73.

Scott, James C. *The Art of Not Being Governed: An Anarchist History of Upland Southeast Asia*. New Haven, CT: Yale University Press, 2009.

Sebald, W. G. *The Rings of Saturn*. Translated by Michael Hulse. New York: New Directions, 1998.

Shaoguan shi zhengxie xuexi he wenshi ziliao weiyuanhui 韶關市政協學習和文史資料委員會, ed. *Shaoguan wenshi ziliao. Di sanshierji. Shaoguan lishi mingren zhuan lüe* 韶關文史資料. 第三十二集. 韶關歷史名人傳略. Shaoguan: Shaoguan shi wenshi weiyuanhui, 2006.

Shaw, Yu-ming. *An American Missionary in China: John Leighton Stuart and Chinese-American Relations*. Cambridge, MA: Harvard University Press, 1992.

Sheehan, Jonathan. "Enlightenment, Religion, and the Enigma of Secularization: A Review Essay." *American Historical Review* 108, no. 4 (October 2003): 1061–80.

———. *The Enlightenment Bible: Translation, Scholarship, Culture*. Princeton, NJ: Princeton University Press, 2005.

Shenk, Wilbert R. "Rufus Anderson and Henry Venn: A Special Relationship?" *International Bulletin of Missionary Research* 5, no. 4 (October 1981): 168–72.

Shixing xian difangzhi bianzuan weiyuanhui 始興縣地方誌編纂委員會, ed. *Shixing xianzhi* 始興縣誌 [Gazetteer of Shixing County]. Guangzhou: Guangdong renmin chubanshe, 1997.

Shi Youzhong. *The Taiping Ideology: Its Sources, Interpretations, and Influences*. Seattle: University of Washington Press, 1967.

Shum, Kui-Kwong. *The Chinese Communists' Road to Power: The Anti-Japanese National United Front, 1935–1945.* Oxford: Oxford University Press, 1988.

Sibre, Olivier. *Le Saint-Siège et l'Extrême-Orient (Chine, Corée, Japon): De Léon XII à Pie XII (1880–1952).* Rome: École Française de Rome, 2012.

Slezkine, Yuri. *The Jewish Century.* Princeton, NJ: Princeton University Press, 2006.

Smith, Carl T. *Chinese Christians: Elites, Middlemen, and the Church in Hong Kong.* Oxford: Oxford University Press, 1985.

Smith, Lucius E. *Heroes and Martyrs of the Modern Missionary Enterprise: A Record of Their Lives and Labors.* Chicago: D. B. Cooke, 1853.

Snodgrass, Judith. "Engaged Buddhism in 1920s Japan: The *Young East* Mission for Social Reform, Global Buddhism, and World Peace." In *Routledge Handbook of Religions in Asia,* edited by Bryan Turner and Oscar Salemink, 158–73. New York: Routledge, 2015.

Soetens, Claude. *Pour l'Église chinoise. 1919–20.* Louvain-la-Neuve: Publications de la Faculté de théologie, 1982.

———. *Recueil des archives Vincent Lebbé.* 3 volumes. Louvain-la-Neuve: Publications de la Faculté de théologie, 1982–1986.

Spence, Jonathan. *God's Chinese Son: The Taiping Heavenly Kingdom of Hong Xiuquan.* London: HarperCollins, 1996.

———. *The Memory Palace of Matteo Ricci.* New York: Penguin, 1985.

Sperber, Jonathan. *Popular Catholicism in Nineteenth-Century Germany.* Princeton, NJ: Princeton University Press, 1984.

Sprenger, Arnold. "Higher Moral Education in Taiwan." In *Chinese Foundations for Moral Education and Character Development,* edited by Tran van Doan, Vincent Shen, and George F. McLean, 155–84. Washington, DC: Council for Research in Values and Philosophy, 1991.

Standaert, Nicolas. "New Trends in the Historiography of Christianity in China." *Catholic Historical Review* 83, no. 4 (1997): 573–613.

Stanley, Brian. *The World Missionary Conference, Edinburgh 1910.* Grand Rapids, MI: Wm. B. Eerdmans, 2009.

Stark, Rodney. "Secularization, R.I.P." *Sociology of Religion* 60, no. 3 (1999): 249–73.

Steffen, Paul B. "Gier, Wilhelm, SVD." In *Biographisch-Bibliographisches Kirchenlexicon* XXXII (2011): 509–13.

Steinmetz, George. *The Devil's Handwriting: Precoloniality and the German Colonial State in Qingdao, Samoa, and Southwest Africa.* Chicago: University of Chicago Press, 2007.

Stenz, Georg M. "Der chinesische Christ." *Steyler Herz-Jesu-Bote* 28, no. 4 (January 1901): 54–57.

———. *In der Heimat des Konfuzius: Skizzen, Bilder und Erlebnisse aus Schantung.* Steyl: Druck und Verlag der Missionsdruckerei, 1902.

———. *Twenty-Five Years in China, 1893–1918.* Techny, IL: Mission Press, 1924.

Stewart, David. "The Hermeneutics of Suspicion." *Journal of Literature and Theology* 3, no. 3 (November 1989): 1–12.

Strom, Jonathan. "Pietism and Community in Europe and North America." In *Pietism and Community in Europe and North America: 1650–1850*, edited by Jonathan Strom, 1–14. Leiden: Brill, 2010.

Swatos, W. H., and K. J. Christiano. "Introduction—Secularization Theory: The Course of a Concept." *Sociology of Religion* 60, no. 3 (1999): 209–28.

Sweeten, Alan R. *Christianity in Rural China: Conflict and Accommodation in Jiangxi Province, 1860–1900.* Ann Arbor: University of Michigan Press, 2001.

Taylor, Charles. *A Secular Age.* Cambridge, MA: Harvard University Press, 2007.

Teng, Yuan Chung. "Reverend Issachar Jacox Roberts and the Taiping Rebellion." *Journal of Asian Studies* 23, no. 1 (1963): 55–67.

ter Haar, Barend J. "Messianism and the Heaven and Earth Society: Approaches to Heaven and Earth Society Texts." In Ownby and Heidhues, eds., *"Secret Societies" Reconsidered,* 153–76.

———. *Ritual and Mythology of the Chinese Triads: Creating an Identity.* Leiden: Brill, 1998.

Thompson, Roger R. "Reporting the Taiyuan Massacre: Culture and Politics in the China War of 1900." In *The Boxers, China, and the World,* edited by Robert A. Bickers and R. G. Tiedemann, 65–92. Lanham, MD: Rowman and Littlefield, 2007.

Tiedemann, R. G. "Communist Revolution and Peasant Mobilisation in the Hinterland of North China: The Early Years." *Journal of Peasant Studies* 24 (1996): 132–52.

———, ed. *Handbook of Christianity in China: Vol. 2, 1800 to the Present.* Leiden: Brill, 2009.

———. "Indigenous Agency, Religious Protectorates, and Chinese Interests: The Expansion of Christianity in Nineteenth-Century China." In *Converting Colonialism: Visions and Realities in Mission History, 1706–1914,* edited by Dana L. Robert, 206–41. Grand Rapids, MI: William B. Eerdmans, 2008.

———. "Shandong Missions and the Dutch Connection: 1860–1919." In *The History of the Relations Between the Low Countries and China in the Qing Era (1644–1911),* edited by W. F. Wande Walle and Noël Golvers, 271–98. Leuven: Leuven University Press, 2003.

"Und sie opferten Gold, Weihbrauch, und Myrrhen (Mt. 2, 44. Chinesische-japanischer Mischstil)." *Steyler Missionsbote* 59, no. 4 (1933): 89.

Ustorf, Werner. *Sailing on the Next Tide: Missions, Missiology and the Third Reich.* Frankfurt am Main: Peter Lang, 2000.

Uzzell, Lawrence A. "Don't Call It Proselytism." *First Things,* no. 146 (October 2004): 14–16.

Van de Ven, Hans. *From Friend to Comrade: The Founding of the Chinese Communist Party, 1920–1927.* Berkeley: University of California Press, 1991.

Victoria, Brian Daizen. *Zen at War.* New York: Weatherhill, 1997.

Volpert, Anton. "Ein Mandarin, wie er sein soll." *Kleiner Herz-Jesu-Bote* 23, no. 6 (1896): 44–46.

Von Rohden, Ludwig. "Excerpts from *The History of the Rhenish Missionary Society* (1857)." German History in Documents and Images of the German Historical Institute (GHDI). http://germanhistorydocs.ghi-dc.org/sub_document .cfm?document_id=455.

Voskamp, Carl J. *Aus dem belagerten Tsingtau. Tagebuchblätter.* Berlin: Buchhandlung der Berliner evangelischen Missionsgesellschaft, 1915.

———. *Der chinesische Prediger.* Berlin: Buchhandlung der Berliner evangelischen Missionsgesellschaft, 1919.

———. *Confucius und das heutige China: Ein Vortrag, gehalten vor dem Ausbruch der Boxerbewegung.* Berlin: Buchhandlung der Berliner evangelischen Missionsgesellschaft, 1902.

———. *Mitteilungen aus dem Leben des chinesischen Gelehrten Li-syn-tshoi.* Berlin: Buchhandlung der Berliner evangelischen Missionsgesellschaft, 1885.

———. *Tagebuch über die Reise von Berlin bis Kanton.* Berlin: Verlage des Berliner Missionshauses, 1886.

———. *Unter dem Banner des Drachens und im Reichen des Kreuzes.* Berlin: Buchhandlung der Berliner evangelischen Missionsgesellschaft, 1902.

Wacker, Grant. "Pearl S. Buck and the Waning of the Missionary Impulse." *Church History* 72, no. 4 (December 2003): 852–74.

Wagner, Rudolf G. *Reenacting the Heavenly Vision: The Role of Religion in the Taiping Rebellion.* Berkeley: Institute of East Asian Studies, University of California, Berkeley, 1982.

Wakeman, Frederic E. "Rebellion and Revolution: The Study of Popular Movements in Chinese History." *Journal of Asian Studies* 36, no. 2 (February 1977): 201–37.

———. *Strangers at the Gate: Social Disorder in South China, 1839–1861.* Berkeley: University of California Press, 1966.

Walls, Andrew. "The Eighteenth-Century Protestant Missionary Awakening in Its European Context." In *Christian Missions and the Enlightenment,* edited by Brian Stanley, 22–44. Grand Rapids, MI: W. B. Eerdmans, 2001.

Walls, Andrew F. *The Cross-Cultural Process in Christian History: Studies in the Transmission and Appropriation of Faith.* Maryknoll, NY: Orbis, 2002.

———. *The Missionary Movement in Christian History: Studies in the Transmission of Faith.* Maryknoll, NY: Orbis, 1996.

Walravens, Hartmut, and Thomas Zimmer, eds. *Richard Wilhelm (1873–1930) Missionar in China und Vermittler chinesischen Geistesguts.* St. Augustin: Institut Monumenta Serica Steyler Verlag, 2008.

Walsh, J. Johnston. *A Memorial of the Futtehgurh Mission and Her Martyred Missionaries: With Some Remarks on the Mutiny in India.* Philadelphia: J. M. Wilson, 1858.

Wang, Peter Chen-Main. "Contextualizing Protestant Publishing in China: The Wenshe, 1924–1928." In Bays, ed., *Christianity in China,* 292–306.

Wangemann, Hans. *D. Dr. Wangemann, Missionsdirektor: Ein Lebensbild dargeboten in dankbarer Erinnerung.* Berlin: Wiegandt & Grieben, 1899.

Wangemann, Hermann Theodor. *Missions-Ordnung der Gesellschaft zur Beförderung der evangelischen Missionen unter den Heiden zu Berlin.* Berlin: Missionshaus, 1882.

——. *Ein Reise-Jahr in Süd-Afrika: Ausführliches Tagebuch über eine i.d. Jahren 1866 und 1867 ausgeführte Inspectionsreise durch die Missions-Stationen der Berliner Missions-Gesellschaft.* Berlin: Missionshaus, 1868.

——. *Ein zweites Reisejahr in Süd-Afrika.* Berlin: Missionshaus, 1886.

Ward, W. R. *The Protestant Evangelical Awakening.* Cambridge: Cambridge University Press, 1992.

Warneck, Gustav. *Modern Missions and Culture: Their Mutual Relations.* Translated by Thomas Smith. Edinburgh: J. Gemmell, 1883.

——. *Warum ist das 19. Jahrhundert ein Missionsjahrhundert?* Halle: Fricke, 1880.

Weig, Georg. "Das erste chinesische Plenarkonzil in Schanghai 15. Mai bis 12. Juni 1924." *Katholischen Missionen* 53 (1924): 3–10.

——. "Zum Konzil nach Schanghai (China)." *Steyler Missionsbote* 52, no. 2 (1924): 24–28.

Weir, Todd. *Secularism and Religion in Nineteenth-Century Germany: The Rise of the Fourth Confession.* Cambridge: Cambridge University Press, 2014.

Weitz, Eric D. *Weimar Germany: Promise and Tragedy.* Princeton, NJ: Princeton University Press, 2007.

Welch, Holmes. *The Buddhist Revival in China.* Cambridge, MA: Harvard University Press, 1968.

Weller, Robert P. *Resistance, Chaos, and Control in China: Taiping Rebels, Taiwanese Ghosts, and Tiananmen.* Seattle: University of Washington Press, 1994.

Wenzel-Teuber, Katharina. "2012 Statistical Update on Religion and Churches in the People's Republic of China and in Taiwan." *Religions and Christianity in Today's China* 3, no. 3 (2013): 18–43.

West, Philip. *Yenching University and Sino-Western Relations, 1916–1952.* Cambridge, MA: Harvard University Press, 1976.

Wickeri, Philip L. *Reconstructing Christianity in China: K. H. Ting and the Chinese Church.* Maryknoll, NY: Orbis, 2007.

——. *Seeking the Common Ground: Protestant Christianity, the Three-Self Movement, and China's United Front.* Maryknoll, NY: Orbis, 1988.

Wiegelt, Horst. "Die Deutsche Christentumsgesellschaft." In Brecht et al., eds., *Geschichte des Pietismus. Bd. 3,* 125–50.

Wilhelm, Richard. *Die Seele Chinas.* Berlin: Verlag von Reimar Hobbing, 1926.

Wilson, George M. *Patriots and Redeemers in Japan: Motives in the Meiji Restoration.* Chicago: University of Chicago Press, 1992.

Wolferstan, Bertram. *The Catholic Church in China from 1860 to 1907.* London: Sands, 1909.

Wong, J. Y. *Deadly Dreams: Opium, Imperialism, and the Arrow War (1856–1860) in China.* Cambridge: Cambridge University Press, 1998.

Wu, Albert. "Catholic and Protestant Individuals in Nineteenth-Century German Missionary Periodicals." *Church History* 82, no. 2 (June 2013): 394–98.

———. "Catholic Universities as Missionary Spaces: Wilhelm Schmidt, Chen Yuan, and the Catholic University in Beijing." *Österreichische Zeitschrift für Geschichtswissenschaften* 24, no. 2, special edition on "Missionsräume/Missionary Spaces," edited by Christine Egger and Martina Gugglberger (June 2013): 92–112.

———. "Converting Individuals, Saving the State: Narratives of Conversion in Nineteenth-Century German Missionary Periodicals." In *Missions and Media: The Politics of Missionary Periodicals in the Long Nineteenth Century,* edited by Felicity Jensz and Hanna Acke, 79–96. Stuttgart: Franz Steiner, 2013.

———. "Ernst Faber and the Consequences of Failure: A Study of a Nineteenth-Century German Missionary in China." *Central European History* 47, no. 1 (2014): 1–29.

Wu, Shellen Xiao. *Empires of Coal: Fueling China's Entry into the Modern World Order, 1860–1920.* Stanford, CA: Stanford University Press, 2015.

Wu Zhenchun, Bao Guanglin, Zhang Qinshi, Peng Jinzhang, Wu Yaozong, Chen Guoliang, and Hu Xuecheng, eds. "Zhenli Zhoukan fakan ci." *Zhenli Zhoukan* 1, no. 1 (April 1923): 1–2.

Xing, Jun. *Baptized in the Fire of Revolution: The American Social Gospel and the YMCA in China: 1919–1937.* Bethlehem, PA: Lehigh University Press, 1996.

Yamamoto, Tatsuro, and Sumiko Yamamoto. "II. The Anti-Christian Movement in China, 1922–1927." *Far Eastern Quarterly* 12, no. 2 (1953): 133–47.

Yang Fenggang. "The Red, Black, and Gray Markets of Religion in China." *Sociological Quarterly* 47 (2006): 93–122.

———. *Religion in China: Survival and Revival Under Communist Rule.* Oxford: Oxford University Press, 2012.

Yang Jianlong 楊劍龍. *Jidujiao wenhua dui Wusi xinwenxue de yingxiang* 基督教文化對五四新文學的影響 [Christianity's Influence on the New Literature of the May Fourth Movement]. Taipei: Xiuwei Publishing, 2012.

Yates, M. T., R. Nelson, and E. R. Barrett, eds. *Records of the General Conference of the Protestant Missionaries of China.* Shanghai: Presbyterian Mission Press, 1877.

Yates, Timothy. *Christian Missions in the Twentieth Century.* Cambridge: Cambridge University Press, 1994.

Yeh, Wen-hsin. *Shanghai Splendor: A Cultural History, 1843–1945.* Berkeley: University of California Press, 2008.

Ying Lianzhi 英斂之. *Yeshi ji* 也是集. Tianjin: Da Gongbao guankan, 1933.

Young, Ernest P. *Ecclesiastical Colony: China's Catholic Church and the French Religious Protectorate.* Oxford: Oxford University Press, 2013.

———. *Politics in the Aftermath of Revolution: Liberalism and Dictatorship in Early Republican China.* Ann Arbor: University of Michigan Press, 1977.

Zalar, Jeffrey. "'Knowledge Is Power': The Borromaeusverein and Catholic Reading Habits in Imperial Germany." *Catholic Historical Review* 86, no. 1 (2000): 20–46.

Zarrow, Peter G. *China in War and Revolution, 1895–1949.* London: Routledge, 2005.

———. "The Reform Movement, the Monarchy, and Political Modernity." In Karl and Zarrow, eds., *Rethinking the 1898 Reform Period,* 17–47.

Zhi Xin 治心. "Bense jiaohui yu bense zhuzuo 本色教會與本色著作 [The Indigenous Church and Indigenous Writing]." *Wense Yuekan* 文社月刊 1, no. 6 (May 1926): 1–17.

Zhongguo renmin zhengzhi xieshang huiyi quanguo weiyuanhui wenshi ziliao yanjiu weiyuanhui 中國人民政治協商會議全國委員會文史資料研究委員會, ed. *Xuzhou huizhan* 徐州會戰 [The Battle of Xuzhou]. Beijing: Zhongguo wenshi chubanshe, 1985.

Zia, N. Z. 謝扶雅. *Jidujiao yu Zhongguo sixiang* 基督教與中國思想 [Christianity and Chinese Thought]. Jiulong: Jidujiao wenyi chubanshe, 1971.

Zimmerman, Andrew. *Anthropology and Antihumanism in Imperial Germany.* Chicago: University of Chicago Press, 2001.

Zmarzly, August. "Bolschewisten stürmen eine Missionsschule." *Steyler Missionsbote* 60, no. 2 (1932): 49.

———. "Was wollen die Missionare in China?" *Steyler Missionsbote* 59, no. 4 (January 1932): 82.

"Zwei neue Noviziat unserer Gesellschaft." *Steyler Missionsbote* 53, no. 9 (1925): 139.

ACKNOWLEDGMENTS

A first book requires the acknowledgment of many debts, and it gives me great pleasure to thank the many people who have shaped my work and life. I am forever indebted to my doctoral advisor, Margaret Lavinia Anderson, who believed in the idea from the beginning, tirelessly suffered through many drafts, and pushed my analysis of the sources further. Her intellectual imprint can be found throughout the book. The influence of Peggy and her husband Jim Sheehan on my life has been incalculable. They welcomed me into their house, filled me with mirth and food; they made Berkeley a home away from home.

Many other Berkeley teachers have shaped and formed my approach to the project. Wen-hsin Yeh transformed a European project into a Chinese one: she never stopped pushing me to think of how my stories could be situated within the frame of Chinese history. John Connelly helped me see the broader stakes of the project within the history of global Christianity. Andrew Jones inspired me with his kindness, humility, and erudition—as well as by introducing me to ackee and saltfish. Thomas Brady, Andrew Barshay, and Mary Elizabeth Berry encouraged me to think comparatively, across both time and space. The untimely death of Susanna Barrows in 2010 was a devastating blow; I wish I could have presented her with this book.

In Taiwan, Liu Cheng-yun and Wang Fansen introduced me to modern Chinese history. Kevin Chang and Chen Hsi-yuan were early champions of my work. Hoyt Tillman alerted me to the importance of Confucian-Christian comparisons. In New York, Elizabeth Blackmar and Samuel Moyn were scholarly models and sparked my interest in studying history.

I am grateful to the institutions that have given me the time and opportunity to travel, research, and write. The UC Berkeley History Department and Graduate Division provided me with scholarships to teach and travel. The German Academic Exchange Service (DAAD), the Fulbright IIE, and the Institute of History and Philology at the Academia Sinica, Taipei, allowed me to conduct research in Europe and in Taiwan. A Mellon/ACLS fellowship gave me precious time to write. A faculty development grant from the American University of Paris supported the final stages of revision.

Archivists were essential to the project. Many thanks to staff at the Evangelisches Landeskirchliches Archiv in Berlin, the Zentralarchiv der Evangelischen Kirche der Pfalz in Speyer, and the Fu Jen Catholic University History Office. I am grateful to Fathers Paulino Belamide, Franz Bosold, Augustine Li, Andrzej Miotk, and Herbert Scholz, who offered me a warm welcome, lodging, and complete access to the archives at the Collegio del Verbo Divino, Rome.

Since I arrived in Paris, Steve Sawyer and Miranda Spieler have been wonderful colleagues and mentors; their examples have made me strive to produce better work. Peter Hägel and Scott Sprenger have made the American University of Paris a wonderful, supportive place to work. I also thank my students, especially Michelle Tessmann, for valuable research assistance, and a stellar group of seniors—Abbie, Maren, Josh, Mary, Sandra, Shane, and Sven—who helped to clarify ideas and thoughts. Many thanks also to AUP's library staff, who helped to procure important documents.

Yale University Press has been a perfect press to work with, and I thank Jennifer Banks for her initial interest in the book proposal. I am grateful to Heather Gold for her patience in answering many queries and her enthusiasm for the project. My utmost gratitude goes to Jessie Dolch, who meticulously edited and improved the manuscript. My thanks also go to those at the Press who helped magically transform the manuscript into a book: Mary Pasti, Karen Stickler, Aldo Cupo, and, for the cover, Nancy Ovedovitz. I am grateful to Cynthia Col, who helped produce the index. I thank the two anonymous readers, who corrected my numerous errors and gave helpful suggestions. Many thanks also to Reinhard Sieder, the editor of the *Österreichische Zeitschrift für Geschichtswissenschaften*, who allowed me to reuse a previously published article as part of chapter 8, and to the Evangelisches Landeskirchliches Archiv in Berlin, the Zentralarchiv der Evangelischen Kirche der Pfalz in Speyer, the Fu Jen Catholic University, and the Auswärtiges Amt, Politisches Archiv und Historischer Dienst, in Berlin, all of which gave me permission to cite materials. I thank Frau A. Striegel and Martina Ludwig at the Steyler Missionswissenschaftliches Institut in Sankt Augustin, Germany, for reproducing the figures for the book. The maps were drawn by William L. Nelson.

I could not have written the book without the generosity of friends and colleagues at Berkeley. Ti Ngo, my dearest comrade and brother, supported me without fail. Julia Chuang was a source of encouragement and asked all the right questions. Roy Chan was a generous mentor. Ryan Acton and Alvin Henry made sure that I got my fix of opera and good meals. David Anixter, Shaun Halper, Mark Keck-Szajbel, Jacob Mikanowski, Hannah Murphy, and Radhika Natarajan taught me how to think about Europe. Radhika and Hannah also offered warm counsel and delicious meals during crucial moments. Amanda Buster, Cyrus Chen, Peiting Li, Jonathan Tang, Philip Thai, and Margaret Tillman made me feel welcome in the realm of Chinese history even though I was the stranger at the gate. Sarah Raff, Chris Lim, and Aphra buoyed me with their good cheer, wisdom, and generosity. Evelyn Shih's intellectual curiosity is an inspiration. Chuck Witschorik and Adolfo Ponce have been sources of wisdom, warmth, and care.

Away from Berkeley, many valuable friends enriched my life. In New York, Victor Lin cheered me with jazz and talk. In Germany, Benedikt Brünner gave valuable feedback. Jeremy Best helped alleviate the dullness of archives. Kira Thurman made everything about Germany better. Kevin Vander Schel clarified my confusions about theology. In Taiwan, Veli Hsu, Wenyi Huang, Ren-yuan Li, Andy Liu, Seiji Shirane, Gregory Scott, Jon Schlesinger, Wayne Soon, and Shirley Ye made the Academia Sinica a vibrant place to work. Shellen Wu taught me how to pursue Sino-German connections. In Paris Hannah Callaway was an uplifting and wonderful presence. My "NEHS family" has supported me through thick and thin. They have been more generous to me than I deserve. Gene Tsai, in particular, has been a dear friend for over two decades and counting.

I owe everything to my family. My uncle Huey Tang and aunt Rose Tang housed me and fed me in California. My brother-in-law Alex Kuo, his wife María Jiménez Buedo, and son Félix gave me thoughtful advice, many laughs, and merriment. My parents-in-law, Ming-Shang Kuo and Hwa-Mei Kuo, supported me with good cheer, generosity of spirit, and warmth. My brother, Phillip Wu, and my sister-in-law, Debby Chang, have been constant sources of encouragement and have suffered my presence throughout the years with patience, love, and goodness. I dedicate this book to my parents, Maw-Kuen Wu and Huichin Tang Wu, who never wavered in their faith, support, and belief in me. As the project neared completion, I realized more fully how every page of the book is indebted to them. And finally, my wife, Michelle Kuo, combed through every word of this book and toiled alongside me. Without her, I could have never finished it—life with her made the daily struggle of writing a joy. Through her loving heart and infectious spirit, she has shown me a life more expansive than I could have imagined. She teaches me how to open myself to the world with honesty and bravery. Her love sustains my life and work.

INDEX

Allen, Young J., 58

Anglican Society for Promoting Christian Knowledge: Holy Catholic Church of China congregants, 278n53; Lambeth Conference (2008), 256; pan-European character of, 24

Anglo-American missionary work, methods and presuppositions of, criticized by Germans, 63

anti-Christian movements: Anti-Christian Student Federation, 117; Big Sword Society (Dadaohui) raid, 73–74, 77, 83; and the Eight Trigrams (*Bagua jiao*), 41–42, 43; global anti-Christian resistance, 3–4, 48, 269n29. *See also* Boxer Uprising; Eight Trigrams; Heaven and Earth Society; Red Spear associations

anti-Christian positions: in China linked to persecutions in Germany, 36; of Communists, 197–99; hostility toward early SVD and BMS missionaries, 76–77; and nationalism, 3–4, 116; native clergy as a response to, 56, 119; Yongzheng's expulsion of Christian missionaries, 22

Anzer, Johann Baptist: European chauvinistic views of, 260–61; and the French Protectorate, 66–68; and SVD's mission in Shandong, 76, 203; Yanzhou dubbed "bulwark of the devil," 2

art. *See* Christian art

Awakened. *See* Pietism

Axenfeld, Karl: on Article 438 of the Versailles Treaty, 109; invocation of *Volkskirche*, 139–40, 141

Baptist Missionary Society, 27; Southern Baptists, 115, 278n53

Bays, Daniel H., 9, 114, 115–16, 250

Benedictines, 230–31

Berlin Missionary Society (BMS): expulsion from China, 260; financial instability, 212, 234; *Kirchenordnung* (church constitution) developed for Chinese congregations, 145–51; Ma Dajing's skepticism toward the Communist threat, 196; missionary revival of the nineteenth century, 19; missionary stations in northern China, 83–84, 84 (map 5); missionary stations in southern China, 80–81, 81 (map 3), 83; and the Nazis, 205–8, 210–11, 218; and the Prussian elite, 31, 366n48; purity of national interests and theology

Voskamp, Carl Johannes: calling as a missionary, 30; Chinese language instruction, 55; *Confucius and China Today*, 2; Confucius viewed with respect, 2, 161; and the Japanese siege of Qingdao, 106–7; liberal-modernistic theology resisted by, 122–23, 168–71, 278n54; support of the Chinese Revolution (1911), 100; voyage to China, 37, 38 (map 2), 74

Wacker, Grant, 188
Wahl, Heinrich, 147, 148
Wakeman, Frederic E., 42
Walls, Andrew F., 4, 20, 30
Wang Mingdao, 218, 221, 288n3
Wangemann, Hermann: *Missionsordnung* established by, 53–54
Ward, W.R., 23
Warneck, Gustav: Anglo-American missionary leaders criticized by, 63; on "Christian overculture" in Europe, 69; evangelical optimism of, 39; and the German Protestant Missionary Committee, 64
Watchman Nee, 218, 221, 288n3
Weber, Karl, 201
Wei Enbo, 151
Weig, Georg, 127, 131, 208–9, 213
Wilhelm, Richard: on Confucianism as a moral, political, and spiritual force, 100–101, 166; liberal views of, 11, 167–68, 170–71, 278n54
Wolferstan, Bertram, 51

women: attrition rates of Protestant missionaries in China, 52; Chinese Virgins, 61; footbinding, 6–7, 58, 80; obstacles to conversion to Christianity, 90–91; regulations for female evangelists, 61; right to vote in the BMS General Synod, 146; sent to China by the BMS, 90–91; sent to China by the SVD, 91. *See also* gender; sexuality
Wu Yaozong, 114, 220, 221

Xing, Jun, 115

Yanzhou, 2, 82, 82 (map 4), 156, 254
Yeh, Wen-hsin, 244
Yenching University, 232, 236, 290n49
Ying Lianzhi, 93–94, 101, 103, 225–26, 230; *Dagongbao* created by, 93–94; vision for Chinese Christianity, 93–94, 101
YMCA, 115, 171
Young, Ernest P., 23, 47, 62, 93, 124, 125, 278n59
Yuan Shikai: assault on the Guomindang, 224–25; Chen Yuan's opposition, 224–26; and German missionaries, 102; restoration of national worship of Confucius, 101–2, 225

Zarrow, Peter G., 72–73
Zehnel, Karl, 197–98, 233–34
Zhao Zichen, 114, 172, 221
Zhou Enlai, 240, 246